Critical Essays on Herman Melville's Typee

Critical Essays on
Herman Melville's
Typee

Milton R. Stern

G.K. Hall & Co. • Boston, Massachusetts

Library of Congress Cataloging in Publication Data
Main entry under title:

Critical essays on Herman Melville's Typee.
   (Critical essays on American literature)
   Bibliography: p.
   Includes index.
   1. Melville, Herman, 1819–1891.   Typee—Addresses,
essays, lectures.   I. Stern, Milton R.   II. Series.
PS2384.T83C7   813'.3   82-6070
ISBN 0-8161-8445-3   AACR2

This publication is printed on permanant/durable acid-free paper
MANUFACTURED IN THE UNITED STATES OF AMERICA

CRITICAL ESSAYS ON AMERICAN LITERATURE

This series seeks to publish the most important reprinted criticism on writers and topics in American literature along with, in various volumes, original essays, interviews, bibliographies, letters, manuscript sections, and other materials brought to public attention for the first time. We are delighted to add to our list this important volume on Herman Melville's *Typee* by Milton R. Stern, Distinguished Alumni Professor of English at the University of Connecticut. It contains an extensive introduction by Professor Stern as well as his essay on the publication history of the novel, an essay by John Wenke, and Joseph Wenke's "An Annotated Bibliography of *Typee* Studies," the most complete listing of scholarship on the novel ever published. In addition, there are reprinted essays and comments by Nathaniel Hawthorne, D. H. Lawrence, Richard Chase, Newton Arvin, Lawrance Thompson, James E. Miller, Jr., H. Bruce Franklin, Edgar A. Dryden, and John Seelye, among others. We are confident that this collection will make a permanent and significant contribution to American literary study.

James Nagel, GENERAL EDITOR

Northeastern University

CONTENTS

INTRODUCTION

I THE CORE OF *TYPEE* CRITICISM

The *Typee* criticism written in English during the past one hundred and thirty-five years lends itself rather clearly to two summary conclusions. First, the early evaluations addressed four simple and defined issues (missionaries, primitivism, verity-and-verisimilitude, and storytelling); when they had argued those issues back and forth for a while, they stopped. Second, evaluations since the 1940s have addressed one complex and amorphous issue (symbolic structures, subsuming myth, psychology, politics, and linguistics); they show no sign of abating. Less clear, but very much present, is another conclusion: the sophisticated examinations of *Typee* in the twentieth century are transmogrifications and developments of the issues raised in the nineteenth—by now, the corpus of *Typee* criticism has become depressingly repetitive.

In a volume such as this one, the causes for depression are not apparent: the criticism looks better than it is because it is culled and selected to reveal development. One sees repetition, but only as it manifests both continuity and the introduction of new points of departure. In fact, there are many additional nineteenth- and twentieth-century pieces that should be included in the table of contents and that are absent only because there are not world enough and space. But the total, unselected body of criticism cries out for moratorium: anyone contemplating committing *Typee*-ery should read the entire corpus to be sure that editors and journals will not continue to produce what oft was thought and twice as well expressed.

The early evaluators had a distinct advantage: they were literary people writing for a public, popular, literary marketplace, ranging from low-middlebrow to highbrow. They benefited from the advantages that accrue from whatever can be said in favor of the marketing necessities that for a season turn authors and books into lions and ephemera. Whatever can be said against the public literary marketplace—and there is much—one of its values is easy readability. Despite the mild boredom that arises from the brawling by Melville's contemporary reviewers about

1

the same few issues again and again, when one engages in the glum chore of reading the full body of *Typee* commentary from beginning to end, the early years of Melville criticism, confined as they are to reviews for the public, generally are fun. But when the reviewer must flit from book to book, even the greatest work cannot be examined deeply or repeatedly. *Sic transit gloria librorum* in the popular press.

The evaluators since the mid-twentieth century also had a distinct advantage: almost exclusively they were academics writing for each other, and they did not have to worry about public, much less popular, readability. They benefited from the advantages that accrue from whatever can be said in favor of the academic necessities that turn authors and books into heart-sinkingly heavy monuments. Whatever can be said against the academic literary marketplace—and there is much—one of its values is the freedom to theorize broadly and examine minutely. Such theorizing and examination, most of it not much fun, has been multiplied exponentially by academic publication pressures and by the apparent difficulty that editors and publishers have in defining and adhering to standards of excellence, and, therefore, exclusion. The multiplication currently is being diminished not by the strong and exclusionary eye of reason within the academic profession, but by the economics of the academic and publishing moment. However, so much print already has been produced by the academy that it is no longer feasible to observe what used to be an honored criterion in the old days, we are told, when there were giants in the earth: one reviews all previous secondary material to see if what one says is new. If it is not, one shuts up and tries something else.

What a review of *Typee* scholarship makes clear is what a review of any body of academic commentary on a major literary figure will reveal: since mid-century (1945—the end of World War II, the enactment of the G. I. Bill, and the sudden, pulsing growth of graduate programs—marks the transitional date in social history),[1] literary criticism has been caught in a vicious circle in which the quantity of secondary material to be examined results in a failure to examine the material sufficiently, which results in a spew of repetition, which results in an increased quantity of material to be examined. It is not that commentators in the academy of the earlier twentieth century were truer scholars or greater minds—giants are giants in all times and are relatively rare in all times—but that they had workable amounts of secondary material to contend with. In fact, critical questions in the later twentieth century are more sophisticated than they were when *Typee* and Melville came into full notice in the 1920s. But when the latter-day commentator must publish or perish and much of the secondary writing has to be ignored, even the least work can be deeply examined in the same way repeatedly. *Sic transit gloria librorum* in the scholarly and critical periodicals.

A comment by John Wenke, whose essay on *Typee* is included in this volume, is appropriate here: "The difference between and developmental relation of 'review' to 'scholarship' in *Typee* criticism is a revelation of topical concerns. Because of its intricate linkage between travel narrative, psychological novel, autobiography, and fabulation, the book lends itself to many literary markets. What contemporary reviewers loved in *Typee* explains what appalled them in *Pierre*. The sophistication of moderns— the critical dog chasing the disappearing tale—is often a narcissistic reflection of a critic's modish moment. *Typee* offers an especially clear example of generations remaking their own books."

But, like actual life, actual criticism is not appropriately subject to one-dimensional judgments. If it is truth to assert that popular reviews of *Typee* tended to result in readability and that academic criticism of *Typee* tends to be grimly dull and repetitive, it is cheap, foolish, and incorrect to offer that assertion as the whole truth. Though the early criticism of *Typee* is for the most part moderate fun to read, it is also, in its innocence, generally superficial and shallow. For all its glut and foolishness, the commentary that has developed in the twentieth-century academy contains criticism that is extraordinarily intricate, often elegant, sometimes profound, occasionally brilliant, and almost never, ever innocent. The reawakening of interest in Melville occasioned by his obituary notices in 1891, like the attention Melville enjoyed between 1846 and 1852 (from *Typee* to *Pierre*), created a body of commentary that produced neither literary theory nor minute examination of any of his books. It was commentary that did two things consistently: it established an outline of biographical fact and it developed a reappraising overview of Melville's oeuvre. This critical tendency was quickened in 1919 by the centennial observation of Melville's birth; it continued through the attendant reexamination and the accelerating production of notice in the 1920s, when Melville commentary began to be commandeered by the academy; and it intensified in the 1930s, when it was concentrated in fact-finding and was centered on authenticating the facts of Melville's life and literary reputation. In this sense, the *Typee* scholarship of the 1930s returned to the arguments about verity and verisimilitude that were bantered about in the 1840s; it also reflected the concerns raised by the rediscovery of Melville (especially among the English) in the 1880s and 1890s and on both sides of the Atlantic in the early 1900s.

It was not until the 1940s, when the New Criticism made itself felt in the graduate schools, that detailed examinations of individual works and theorizing about the thematic and symbolic dimensions of his language began to become the major mode and purpose of Melville criticism. This mode and purpose reached full stride in the 1950s and have steadily increased in quantity up to the time of this writing.[2]

Although critical movements generally were fully developed before they became widely established in the idioms and perspectives of American academic criticism, their temblors were felt before they were very old, and can be seismographed. The New Criticism fully arrived in the

American academy in the late 1940s, phenomenology in the 1950s, structuralism in the 1960s, and whatever comes under the headings of post-structuralism or deconstruction in the 1970s. These ideologies combined with Marxist, Freudian, and Jungian thought (which had begun to become effectually noticeable in American literary criticism in the 1920s) in no clear chronology of methodology. Similarly and consequently, the effects of critical schools were not evident in Melville criticism in a neat order of decades. Furthermore, commentary on *Typee* was not in exact correlation with Melville criticism generally, for discussions of Melville's "autobiographical" first two books continued to recall the critical questions of the 1840s long after the rest of Melville criticism had gone on to other things.

Nevertheless, good examples of methodological arrivals are chronologically visible. In the 1940s, close textual analysis influenced by the New Criticism was announced by Richard Chase's "An Approach to Melville." (See item P438 in Wenke's bibliography. Item numbers there are not prefixed with P or B, but in these references the prefix refers to the periodical or the book listings in the bibliography.) See also R. E. Watters's excellent essays (items P446 and P447)[3] and William Ellery Sedgwick's admirable *Herman Melville: The Tragedy of Mind* (item B203; the *Typee* chapter is reprinted in this volume); and "Herman Melville and the Problems of Moral Navigation," by Yvor Winters (items B192, B207). One of the best examples of phenomenological Melvilleana arrived not in the 1950s but in the 1960s: Paul Brodtkorb's *Ishmael's White World*.[4] Conversely, one of the best examples of the influence of structuralism (and Jungianism) appeared not in the 1960s but in the 1950s: James Baird's *Ishmael* (item B211). And a good example of the influence of deconstructionism in the 1970s is found in Thomas P. Joswick's essay, " 'Typee': The Quest for Origin" (item P505). As is apparent, the clearest examples for a methodological chronology in Melville criticism are not necessarily concerned with *Typee*, although most of them do pay attention to the book.

As noted above, samplings of Freudian, Marxist, and Jungian approaches to *Typee* do not follow a clear chronology, but they tend to increase from the 1950s to the present. A clear example of Marxist approaches is H. Bruce Franklin's 1976 essay, "Herman Melville: Artist of the Worker's World" (item B304). An excellent sample of Freudianism is provided in Newton Arvin's *Herman Melville* (1950, item B209; the *Typee* chapter is reprinted in this volume), and a dense sampling of Jungianism is provided by Martin Pops in 1970: *The Melville Archetype* (item B318).

The increased quantity of Melville criticism as a whole by far outdistanced in relative ratio the increased quantity of *Typee* criticism. Therefore, one can obtain a better overview of the nature and chronology of attention paid to Melville from a source such as the annual *MLA International Bibliography* than from a bibliography exclusively devoted to *Typee*. But *Typee* criticism serves perfectly well to illustrate the observa-

tion that the enlarged sophistication of methodology and idea, in the context of the history of academe since World War II, is reflected by the
enlargement and complication—and consequent repetitiousness—of both
the mode and quantity of Melville criticism.

As the examples indicate, actualities doggedly and ineluctably resist
tidy charts, and consequently the chronology of neither *Typee* criticism
specifically nor Melville criticism generally is an exact representation of
the advent of critical schools. The purposes of this volume include not
only the presentation of representative or influential statements about
Typee but also the chronological framework that suggests the general,
though not precise, development of Melville criticism. Because not all
critical schools have produced good and easily extricated extended
statements specifically about *Typee,* it would be highly artificial to try to
include all critical schools or to attempt to organize the selections around
principles of critical dogma. Similarly, not all highly respected books
about Melville contain sustained, connected, and therefore easily extricated discussions of *Typee*: one looks in vain in this volume for selections, for instance, from F. O. Matthiessen's marvelous *American Renaissance* (item B199), or Merlin Bowen's *The Long Encounter* (item B243),
or Edward Rosenberry's *Melville and the Comic Spirit* (item B232), or
Warner Berthoff's *The Example of Melville* (item B242), to name but a
few very different kinds of books. Conversely, works which center almost
entirely on *Typee* and therefore are too long are not included because of
space limitations. For instance, James Baird's *Ishmael* (item B211) is, in
effect, entirely about *Typee* and Melville's pagan archetypes. A coherent
extract of specifically pertinent sections would amount to almost fifty
pages, which fact, alas, dictates exclusion. The same is even more true of
Charles Anderson's groundbreaking study, *Melville in the South Seas*
(item B175).

Because of the great quantity of *Typee* criticism, there are many interesting and several excellent pieces that could not be included here, and
they should be brought to the attention of readers interested in a larger
selection of useful criticism. Several of the nineteenth-century reviews in
this category are discussed in part 2 of this introduction, but at least some
of the twentieth-century pieces should be mentioned here. Frank Jewett
Mather's "Herman Melville" (1919, items P377 and P378) and the thirteen
pages on *Typee* in Lewis Mumford's *Herman Melville* (1929, item B158)
provide excellent examples of early attempts to redefine Melville. Charles
R. Anderson's "Contemporary American Opinions of *Typee* and *Omoo*"
(1937, item P419) and his "Melville's English Debut" (1939, item P420),
together with "Some Notes and Reviews of Melville's Novels," by Mentor
Williams (item P462) are pioneering attempts to determine the literary
reputation of *Typee*. Ronald Mason's ten-page discussion of *Typee* in *The
Spirit Above the Dust* (1951, item B227) and Joseph Firebaugh's "Humorist as Rebel: The Melville of *Typee*" (1954, item P452) remain items of the

1950s not to be forgotten. The discussion of the publication of *Typee* in Merrell R. Davis's *Melville's Mardi* (1952, item B215) has been supplanted by Leon Howard's full and informative "Historical Note" in the "standard" edition of *Typee* (1968, item B265).

James E. Miller's pertinent section in *The Reader's Guide to Herman Melville* (1962, item B277), "*Typee* and *Omoo: The Quest for the Garden,*" provides a good overview of the novel in the criticism of the 1960s, as does Philip Young's introduction to *Typee* (1967, item B290). Some interesting specialized studies of the same decade are Winston Weathers's "Melville and the Comedy of Communications" (1963, item P489); John Bernstein's eleven-page discussion of *Typee* in *Pacifism and Rebellion in the Writings of Herman Melville* (1964, item B241); and Nicholas Canaday's six-page discussion of *Typee* in *Melville and Authority* (1968, item B244).

Paul Witherington's "The Art of Melville's *Typee*" (1970, item P540) is a companion piece to John Seelye's discussion of *Typee* in *Melville: The Ironic Diagram* (1970, reprinted in this volume). A. Carl Brehdal's nine-page section on *Typee* in *Melville's Angle of Vision* (1972, item B296) is a useful summary, and William B. Dillingham's twenty-two-page essay in *An Artist in the Rigging* (1972, item B300) offers an interesting thesis about two Tommos. Edward S. Grejda, in his sixteen-page discussion of *Typee* in *The Common Continent of Men* (1974, item B306) discusses Melville and racism. G. T. Tanselle's essay, "Bibliographical Problems in Melville" (1974, item P535), provides very useful information about editions of Melville. Among the discussions of innocence and history in *Typee* in the 1970s, one of the best essays is Faith Pullin's "Melville's *Typee*: The Failure of Eden," in *New Perspectives on Melville* (1978, item B319).

There are several more items worthy of mention, but finally every reader who becomes familiar with the scholarship and criticism will make other additions. Those, in each reader's individual case, together with the items mentioned here and reprinted in this volume, constitute the heart of the commentary on the intriguing first book of the writer who probably was the greatest imaginative genius of the American literary nineteenth century.

II THE DEVELOPMENT OF *TYPEE* CRITICISM

From the moment of publication,[5] Melville's exposé of Protestant missionary work in the South Seas became an issue for reviewers. Radicals like Margaret Fuller warned that people should pay attention to what Melville was saying about South Seas missions,[6] and Christian parlor-table periodicals responded with ill-concealed venom. Often defenders of Melville wrote solemn pieces of altruism, communitarianism, and cultural pluralism, as typified by the John Sullivan Dwight essay reprinted in this volume from the Brook Farm *Harbinger*. More often, like the "Four Months' Residence in the Marquesas" reprinted from the London *Times,* the notices supporting *Typee* against the missionaries were good humored and relatively gentle pieces.[7] But without exception, those who attacked Melville as unchristian and wicked were grim, humorless, and righteous, as William Oland Bourne's representative essay will attest.

Although the reception of *Typee* was extremely favorable, the single-issue fervor of the pro-missionary journals produced the erroneous impression that *Typee* was widely attacked. What the maligning journals lacked in representative quality they bitterly made up for in unanimously bilious and splenetic energy. Melville's American publishers, Wiley and Putnam, became nervous enough to insist upon a bowdlerized second edition. Melville acquiesced. Whatever ingenious arguments one might wish to construct to exonerate Melville,[8] the fact remains that Melville was only too quick, as a young and new author delighted with his success, to appease enemies of his book. Although he was embarrassed by the idea of an expurgated version ("Expurgated—Odious word," he winced as he completed the revision),[9] Melville complied readily enough. (The British publisher, John Murray, was of stronger stuff and refused to publish a bowdlerized edition.) The responses to the revised American edition were predictable. The reviewers for the *United States Catholic Magazine and Monthly Review* in 1847 and 1848[10] mourned for the first edition because they were perfectly willing to accept testimony that Protestant missions were indeed bad. But the *Biblical Repository and Classical Review* in 1849 offered Mr. Melville warm Protestant congratulations for finally mending his ways and deleting anti-Christian lies.[11] The skirmishes between Catholic and Protestant reviewers flared fitfully for a bit, and resentment from champions of the Protestant missionaries continued to flicker and erupt during the 1840s; but though missionary activity was the most spectacular and intense of the early contentions among reviewers, it was also the most parochial and the most temporal. Generally, the issue sighed out after the second American edition. Missionaries notwithstanding, *Typee* was greeted on the whole with pleasure and goodwill.

The far more durable issue of primitivism at first was connected inextricably with the missionary controversy—for a while it was the same issue. But the question of primitivism touches more deeply on ideological perspectives and remains central in *Typee* criticism to the present day. Many of Melville's contemporary reviews, like the anonymous unsigned review reprinted here from *Douglas Jerrold's Shilling Magazine,* extolled Melville's book as a pleasant, if somewhat sly, sojourn among the lotus eaters, an escape from the harsh realities of urbanized, industrialized, commercialized modern life. But most of those who addressed the issue saw it, like John Sullivan Dwight, as an ideological matter in which money, missionaries, and the modern represented a brutalizing capitalist civilization, and the primitive represented peace, love, communitarianism, nature, serenity, goodness, and sane humanity. On the other hand, those who defended the missionaries saw the primitive as raw, animalistic, depraved, and unenlightened, and civilization as good and redeeming. Furthermore, *civilization* repeatedly meant, both explicitly and implicitly, propriety, gentility, antisepsis, technological advance, and convention. As one would expect, therefore, sexuality, although not always centrally mentioned, was a constant undercurrent in the controversy. In a righteous show of ire, for instance, George Washington Peck sniffily dismissed *Typee* as a depository of "unchaste desire" (1847, item P147). Tradition and restriction were ranged against change and "naturalness"; it is not surprising that the question of primitivism lined up reactionaries against radicals, provincials against cosmopolitans, traditionalists against romantics, and that *Typee* became a minor *cause* in an ideological opposition of conservatives and progressives, between traditionally recognizable amalgams of allegiance and orientation in "right" and "left." This tendency toward an oversimplifying dichotomy creates either-or readings and oppositions that usually evade the complications Melville perceived. An interesting continuation of oppositions in the more intricate and subtle dimensions of twentieth-century criticism can be glimpsed in a juxtaposition of James Baird's *Ishmael* and the *Typee* chapter in D. H. Lawrence's *Studies in Classic American Literature* (reprinted in this volume). Baird, asserting a cultural exhaustion of traditional symbology, especially Christian symbology, in the Western world, sees *Typee* as an example of the Western white man's necessity to return to a primitive past for archetypal signs, new symbologic clothing, that will provide revivifying energies for his life. Lawrence, also seeing the same cultural exhaustion of traditional values and signs, finds a return to the past impossible. In the 1940s and 1950s, Sedgwick and Stern (both reprinted here) pointed out the distortion created by either-or positions on primitivism: Melville admired and loved much about the primitive, feared and hated much about the capitalist present, but concluded nevertheless that the primitive, in several of its most profound connotations, finally becomes both undesirable and impossible for the person who recognizes that identity is action within history. The essays by Richard Ruland, John Seelye, Thomas Scorza, and John Wenke in this volume, considering this central problem from several points of view, indicate that a recognition of richly mixed yearning for and final repudiation of the primitive emerges as the major continuum of critical thought concerning this aspect of *Typee*. However, although by now the choice of the major continuum or the clear division is no longer necessarily an identification of the "leftness" or "rightness" of any given critic, the perception of—in effect—the primitive as all good and the present as all bad, of the "native" population as all good and the Westerner as all bad (in *Typee* Melville refers to "white civilized man" as "the most ferocious animal on the face of the earth") continues for some readers to be a staple and an ideological position in *Typee* criticism to the present moment.[12] One of the most compact and compelling of the arguments proposing a complete moral division between the civilized and the primitive is provided by the discussion (reprinted in this volume) in Joyce Sparer Adler's *War in Melville's Imagination* (1981, item B331).

For Melville's contemporaries, the problem of verity was an inevitable corollary to their concern for the implications of primitivism. The omnipresent "v"-cries (verity, verisimilitude, and *vraisemblance*), heard most frequently between 1846 and 1849, centered on two repeated questions: was there such a person as Herman Melville and was his presentation of the South Seas "true"? The *Literary Gazette and Journal of Belles Lettres* (1846, item P102) explains its earlier neglect of *Typee* in this way:

> *The Marquesas,*[13] by Hermann [*sic*] Melville, call for our first mention, as the mob of our contemporary periodical brethren have dwelt at much length upon the wonderful adventures and extraordinary revelations of that narrative. Its geography, natural history, and other scientific branches of discovery, as well as the marvelous doings of its author (Master Hermann Melville of **** *****!), they have been pleased to consider to be real and authentic, and have consequently communicated all the information they could glean from them to their gaping readers, who have swallowed it as the Dutch burgomaster did the map illustrative of the voyages of Robinson Crusoe. But as we happened to fancy the name of Melville to be equivalent to that of Sinbad the Sailor, we certainly abstained from noticing this clever and entertaining production; as an apology for which, we beg Mr. Melville to accept this explanation, and do us the honour to dine with us on the 1st of April next: we intend to ask only a small party,—Messrs. Crusoe, Sinbad, Gulliver, Munchausen. . . .

Some of Melville's own countrymen were as skeptical as the English: the longest review dedicated to the argument that *Typee* is all fiction appeared in the Washington, D.C. *National Intelligencer* (1847, item P133). On both sides of the water doubt was occasioned by the literacy of a work claimed by a common sailor. In one of the very earliest reviews of *Typee,* the London *Spectator* (1846, item P3) identified an interesting cultural distinction between England and America, one which placed democracy on the side of credence. It was a distinction that was pointed out a few more times by others during the three years after the book's first publication: "Had this work been put forward as the production of an English common sailor, we should have had some doubts of its authenticity, in the absence of distinct proof. But in the United States it is different. There social opinion does not invest any employment with caste discredit; and it seems customary with young men of respectability to serve as common seamen, either as a probationership to the navy or as a mode of seeing life."

If there were doubts even before the book was published,[14] by 1850 they were dispelled even in the minds of hostile readers. In an editorial footnote in the third series of *Southey's Common-Place Book* (1850, item B8), Southey's son-in-law, John Wood Warter, wrote the following observation about Southey's response to some passages he had been reading on Hawaiian volcanoes: "Quite corroborated in those objectionable, but very graphic publications, *Typee* and *Omoo*, of the authenticity of which, I suppose, there can be no reasonable doubt" (p. 585). This Tory sigh gave place to more admiring certitude by 1892. In his introduction to a new edition of *Typee* (item B52), Arthur Stedman asserted that it "does seem difficult in 'Redburn' to separate the author's actual experience from those invented by him, this being the case in some of his writings" (p. xvii). For, "of Melville's four most important books, three, 'Typee,' 'Omoo,' and 'White-Jacket,' are directly autobiographical, and 'Moby-Dick' is partly so; while the less important 'Redburn' is between the two classes in this respect. Melville's other prose works . . . were, with some exceptions, unsuccessful efforts at creative romance" (p. xx).

By the time that Melville's death (September 28, 1891) had completed its reawakening of critical interest, the nineteenth century had drawn to a close. By 1913, when Sir James George Frazer published his epochal *The Belief in Immortality and the Worship of the Dead* (item B116), he quoted *Typee* and referred to it throughout volume 2 as a reliable source for ethnographic studies. And by 1936, whatever the literary judgment might be, the acceptance of *Typee* as fact was complete. In his *American Fiction*, (item B184) Arthur Hobson Quinn concluded that "*Typee* and *Omoo*, when read in comparison with the latest descriptions of the South Seas, illustrate the slight hold that any travel books except the greatest have upon posterity. The interest which carried *Typee* and *Omoo* was partly novelty. . . . But novelty alone was not sufficient—the books were believed to be records of fact, and even today their chief interest lies in the fidelity of Melville to the actual situation in the Marquesas and in Tahiti. In other words, their value is ethnological rather than literary" (p. 150). By the time the 1930s came to a close, the scholarship, detailed earlier in this essay, which concentrated on Melville's life and reputation had gone a long way toward a final sifting of fact from fiction. By now almost all commentators know that neither Stedman's judgment of *Typee* as "directly autobiographical" nor Quinn's dictum that it has "ethnological rather than literary" value is an accurate summation of the novel. In the more sophisticated current moment, Melville's first book is recognized as a work of considerable reality, both ethnographic and literary, a *fiction* whose verisimilitude and vraisemblance generate verities that remain vigorous and vexatious.

As for storytelling, Bronson Alcott's journal entry for December 9, 1846 (item B174), with the evocation of Defoe that occurred to so many contemporary readers, summed up reader reaction: "Read *Typee* by Melville—a charming volume, as attractive even as *Robinson Crusoe*. I almost found myself embarked to spend the rest of my days with those simple islanders of the South Seas" (p. 185). Alcott's languid condescension and delight was the mark of many contemporary reviews that focused upon how compellingly and entertainingly this man Melville could spin a yarn. Readers thought of the novel as an adventure story *cum* travelogue, a picturesque rendition of exotic innocents in the geography of paradise. At the very beginning of *Typee*, Tommo, a novice in the South Seas, imagines all the romantic stock and trappings of the coconut isles. "The Marquesas! What strange visions of outlandish things does the very name spirit up! Naked houris—cannibal banquets—groves of cocoa-nut—coral reefs—tatooed chiefs—and bamboo temples; sunny valleys planted with breadfruit trees—carved canoes dancing on flashing blue waters—savage woodlands guarded by horrible idols—*heathenish rites and human sacrifices.*" The invocation is a table of contents, a preview of all the materials of romance and adventure. Before the book is finished, Melville manages to complicate those materials into nuances of serious meanings, but for the most part his contemporary readers never got past the materials of the book. They were delighted enough with the romance and adventure when they were not arguing the issues that raised ideologies and politics. By 1853, Fitz-James O'Brien, one of Melville's most appreciative commentators, identified *Typee* as generically fresh and new in a literary world jaded with the stale sea-tale conventions of Maryatt and Cooper (see item P242), and because of this high narrative quality, by 1857 he hailed the book as the standard by which Herman Melville's work should be measured (see item P262).

Appreciation of the liveliness of the storytelling and its transmission of a sense of firsthand experience deepened at the end of the nineteenth century into a recognition that in effect the long-neglected Melville had been the major creator of the genre of the South Seas adventure-romance. In the year of Melville's death, Robert Louis Stevenson wrote (item P289), "There are but two writers who have touched the South Seas with any genius, both Americans: Melville and Charles Warren Stoddard; and at the christening of the first and greatest some influential fairy must have been neglected" (p. 114). Early in the new century Jack London explained one of the major motivations for his voyage of the *Snark* (item B111): "How often had we pored over the chart and centred always on that midmost bight and on the valley it opened—the Valley of Typee. 'Taipi' the chart spelled it, and spelled it correctly, but I prefer 'Typee,' and I shall always spell it 'Typee.' When I was a little boy, I read a book spelled in that manner—Herman Melville's 'Typee'; and many long hours I dreamed over its pages. Nor was it all dreaming. I resolved there and then, mightily, come what would, that when I had gained strength and years, I, too, would voyage to Typee. . . . The years passed, but Typee was not forgotten" (pp. 154–55). Very shortly thereafter, in an eleven page tribute to *Typee* titled "Southward Ho!" (items B110, 114), Holbrook Jackson summed up his own urge to travel and also the spate of recognitions of Melville as founder of a genre. "Doubtless," he wrote, "there are people who, having read 'Typee,' are not moved with an urgent desire to take ship for the Marquesas, but I have yet to hear of them. But there can be none in the early twenties who are so tame. Anyhow, I was not of their number. I had barely got half through the book when the South Seas filled my imagination with an overpowering longing. I seemed to have known them all my life; Herman Melville, most delightful and discursive of chroniclers, simply relit my memory. He made it all quite clear and revealed my destiny. My longing was no vague desire for novelty, it was simply homesickness" (p. 30). Henry Seidel Canby's summation of *Typee* and *Omoo* as "perfect of their kind, but still only superlative travel books" (item B139, pp. 262–63), was typical of the diminishing continuation into the twentieth century of *Typee*'s critical reputation as merely a romantic travelogue—diminishing even though the aroma of the coconut groves will always linger on the winds of fiction. In 1936 Percy Boynton (item B177) could still respond to the book the way the romance-seeking readers among Melville's contemporaries delightedly did. *Typee* and *Omoo*, he said, "offer a picture of life to allure any victim of a driving northern civilization: soft climes and balmy airs . . . a whole male population who loafed and invited their souls, and women who had little to do but exercise their graces" (p. 463). But long before 1936 the lotus-land that readers found in Melville had ceased to be.

Visits to Melville's Marquesas in the late nineteenth and early twentieth centuries disclosed the extent to which the bright isles and living culture Melville had chronicled had been destroyed by the civilization that had discovered them. World War I concluded (among other things) the celebration of Melville as a new story teller of the South Seas, and by 1922 an article called "The Men Who Found the South Seas" (item P382) was able to sum up Melville's contributions to the genre as a completed chapter in literary history. In the 1920s the serious reevaluation of Melville began, and after the fact-finding of the 1930s and the considerable recognition of several levels of critical and thematic issues in *Typee* in the 1940s and 1950s, the dismissal of the book as only an exercise in romantic adventure storytelling became an exercise in naiveté. Nevertheless, as late as 1963 it was still possible for a commentator to write that "one looks vainly in *Typee* . . . for . . . the philosophical speculation so characteristic of Melville. . . . *Typee* must be regarded as overwhelmingly romantic," as of only "straightforward and factual style" (item B261, pp. 41, 69). The real critical issue is "both . . . and," not "either . . . or." *Typee* is a book of romantic adventure, of travel, of ethnographic detail, of lively story-telling; *and* it is also, like everything Melville wrote, hardly devoid of "philosophical speculation" and of layered, intricate serious questioning of the relationship of humankind to perfection and to history.

As the essays in this volume amply demonstrate, the critical issues have gone far beyond the contexts that Melville's times sent into the first third of the twentieth century. Within the contexts of his own time, Melville himself was wryly aware of what his critical reputation (if any) was likely to be as the author of his early books. In his diary and his letters, he deprecatingly and humorously referred to himself as the author of "Peedee, Hullabaloo and Pog-Dog" and as the daddy of "Typee, Piddle-dee, &c." In one of his stunningly pyrotechnic letters to Hawthorne he made his assessment: "What 'reputation' H. M. has is horrible. Think of it! To go down to posterity is bad enough, any way; but to go down as a 'man who lived among the cannibals'! When I speak of posterity, in reference to myself, I only mean the babies who will probably be born in the moment immediately ensuing upon my giving up the ghost. I shall go down to some of them, in all likelihood. 'Typee' will be given to them, perhaps, with their gingerbread" (item B248, p. 130).

Typee and gingerbread complemented each other in the 1840s with clear success. But in the 1850s Melville's reputation went into a decline despite the efforts of stalwarts like Fitz-James O'Brien; and except for the researches of a few champions like Titus Coan, Melville's name was scarcely mentioned in literary reviews in the 1860s. Coached by Philarète Chasles, the French tried to summarize Melville in the late 1840s and early 1850s; Chasles did so with the usual Gallic combination of intelligent penetration, absurdities of certainty, and certainties of absurdity that have deconstructively applied to French approaches to American culture long before Derrida initiated current critical amusements. In the 1870s Melville all but disappeared, and he remained forgotten throughout the next three decades. Almost forgotten: led by the British, a Melville cult formed in the 1880s and swelled with Melville's death in the beginning of the following decade. On both sides of the Atlantic, the cognoscenti, encouraged by the efforts of Arthur Stedman, Robert Buchanan, Henry S. Salt, J. E. A. Smith, and W. Clark Russell, struggled for renewed attention to Melville's works. By the 1890s, then, Melville's reputation was in a state of general oblivion punctuated by intense bursts of revivalist admiration. It was not untypical that on the one hand the headline for an obituary in the New York Times, October 6, 1891, read "The Late Hiram Melville: A Tribute to his Memory from One Who Knew Him"; but that in the same decade the American Publishers Corporation issued new editions of Melville's work, Typee and Omoo drawing consistent praise from the critics. Even as late as 1930, there was still the doubleness of stature: in that one year Melville was considered for the Hall of Fame, and a critic writing a sympathetic overview of Melville's work could refer to Melville's fourth novel as Redfern twice on the first page of her essay.[15]

Since the 1940s, because the attention given to Moby-Dick, Billy Budd, The Piazza Tales, Pierre, and The Confidence Man has overshadowed Melville's other works, it has been a sometimes critical commonplace, and a mistaken one, to assume that Typee has been one of Melville's badly neglected works.[16] In fact, the reputation of *Typee*, up until the middle third of the twentieth century, fared better than did most of Melville's other books and remained a choice of readers even during the nineteenth-century decades when Melville himself was all but forgotten.[17] All through the nineteenth century *Typee* received notice when Melville's other books generally did not, and although devoted followers of Melville early recognized that *Moby-Dick* would emerge as his masterwork, *Typee* was one of the books always mentioned with pleasure along with it. "The book about cannibals" received very wide contemporary readership, as Van Wyck Brooks noted in *The Times of Melville and Whitman* (item B194): "Melville was read in the remotest corners of the country—in the high Sierras, in 1851, for instance, by 'Dame Shirley,' who spoke in her letters of his 'beautiful romance' and his 'palmgirdled isles of the Pacific' " (p. 145). The Melville revivalists in the 1880s consistently invoked *Typee* when reminiscing about the fame Melville once enjoyed, when referring to whatever recognition his name still commanded, and when predicting the revival of fame sure to come. When Melville's death occasioned the first resurrection of his name and new attention to his fame, *Typee*, along with *Moby-Dick*, immediately jumped into the lead in mentions of Melville's work.

From the mid 1890s until the 1920s, the critical consensus was that *Typee, Omoo, White-Jacket*, and *Moby-Dick* are Melville's greatest works and the basis for whatever lasting fame he might have. These four were repeatedly singled out in the reappraisals of the first two decades of the twentieth century. About 1919, *Israel Potter* and *The Piazza Tales* were added, *White-Jacket* beginning to drop in and out of the favored list. As late as 1966 the Syracuse Library *Gold Star List of American Fiction* still ranked *Typee* with *Omoo, Moby-Dick, The Complete Stories of Herman Melville*, and *Billy Budd* as the works of Melville to be listed. Lists, of course, may be quirky. But whatever the publication or the source, *Typee* tends to remain a fairly constant reference in the continuing appraisal of Melville's works.

During the 1940s and 1950s, and part of the 1960s, *Typee* commanded less attention than it used to, partly because it appeared to be an old fashioned kind of narrative not as inviting to new critical canons as Melville's later and weirder works. But it was never neglected altogether, and in the 1960s and 1970s it has begun to regain its former place as a work receiving constant and serious attention. The essays in this volume serve to indicate the depth and strength of that attention. They also serve to put readers on notice that although *Typee* is in fact a romantic tale of adventurous travel, a work of old-fashioned prose, and a quondam source of ethnographic information, it bears enough imaginative genius, enough marks of the hand of its maker, to invite and support probing and profound considerations in the various areas of human thought that lasting literature attracts. And that returns us to the beginning of this introduction, which is both caveat against and invitation to the body of *Typee* criticism.

Milton R. Stern

University of Connecticut

Notes

1. For just this reason, Joseph Wenke wisely and usefully uses 1945 to mark a change in the method of listing items in the superb bibliography he compiled for this volume.

2. The specifications for this general overview are developed in part 2 of this introduction.

3. See also Watters' "Melville's 'Isolatoes,' " *PMLA*, 40 (1945), 1138–48.

4. New Haven: Yale University Press, 1965. Unfortunately Brodtkorb does not discuss *Typee*, and his book therefore is not listed in Wenke's bibliography.

5. The history of the publication of *Typee* is given its fullest treatment in Leon Howard's "Historical Note." Also helpful are the materials in volume 1 of Jay Leyda's *The Melville Log* (1951, item B225) and the biographical account, based on the *Log*, in the standard Melville biography, Leon Howard's *Herman Melville* (1951, item B221). Especially useful and revealing is the correspondence relating to the publication and bowdlerization of *Typee*: see letters 1–13, 18–27, 47–52, 84, 147, and 252–56 in *The Letters of Herman Melville*, edited by Merrell R. Davis and William H. Gilman (1960, item B248).

6. Unsigned review of *Typee* in the *New York Tribune* (April 4, 1846). Accounts of Melville's bouts with the missionaries are inextricable from the growing search for the facts about his stay in the South Pacific. Reviewers and critics in the 1840s, 1890s, and 1920s, the three periods in which Melville received most of the attention given him prior to his full rehabilitation in the forefront of American literature, tended to see *Typee* as specifically and fully autobiographical. Research in the 1930s began to uncover the actual facts of Melville's reputation and his visit to the South Seas, thereby providing information about Melville and the missionaries. Representative samples are O. W. Riegel, "The Anatomy of Melville's Fame" (1930, item P431); John H. Birss, "Melville's Marquesas" (1932, item P422); William Braswell, "A Note on 'The Anatomy of Melville's Fame' " (1934, item P424); two articles by Daniel Aaron, "An English Enemy of Melville" (1935, item P416) and "Melville and the Missionaries" (1935, item P417); Russell Thomas, "Yarn for Melville's *Typee*" (1936, item P434); Robert Forsythe, "Herman Melville in the Marquesas" (1936, item P425); and, most especially, the work of Charles Roberts Anderson: "Contemporary American Opinions of *Typee* and *Omoo*" (1937, item P419); "The Romance of Scholarship: Tracking Melville in the South Seas" (1938, item P421); "Melville's English Debut" (1939, item P420); and *Melville in the South Seas* (1939, item B175), which became the basic source for all further researches in the subject. A good essay among the more recent examinations of Melville and the missionaries is "Some Notes and Reviews of Melville's Novels in American Religious Periodicals, 1846–1849," by Mentor Williams (1950, item P462).

7. Because there were so many friendly reviews it is inappropriate to try to list them here. A couple of good examples of friendly journals are *Graham's Magazine* and the *United States Magazine and Democratic Review* (see items P61 and P59). The *Eclectic Review*, the *Universalist Review*, the *New Englander*, the *Evangelist*, and the *Christian Observatory* summed up in their views the notices of the much smaller number of journals hostile to *Typee*. See items P30, P71, P73, P44, and P114.

8. For instance, David Williams, in "Peeping Tommo" (1975, item P539), argues that Melville's complicity in the bowdlerized edition is an aesthetic attempt by Melville to write himself out of the book in order to achieve satire rather than jeremiad.

9. Letter to Evert Duyckinck (July 28, 1846). See Davis and Gilman, eds., *The Letters of Herman Melville* (item B248), p. 43.

10. Items P156 and P160.

11. Item P216.

12. See, for instance, Louise Barnett, *The Ignoble Savage* (1975, item B292) and H. Bruce Franklin, "Herman Melville: Artist of the Worker's World" (item B304).

13. Short title of the English edition. See Leon Howard's "Historical Note" for a presentation of the various titles of the book.

14. Melville first submitted the book to Harper and Brothers, who turned it down as much too literate for a common swab. Their reader enjoyed the book in a significant way: "This work," he reported, "if not as good as *Robinson Crusoe* seems to be not far behind it." See Howard's "Historical Note" and Gay Wilson Allen's *Melville and His World* (item B291), p. 86.

15. See "New Names for the Hall of Fame?" *The Publishers' Weekly*, 117 (March 8, 1930), 1334–35. For "*Redfern*," see Mary Ritchie, "Herman Melville" (item P432).

16. The essay on *Typee* and *Omoo* in *A Reader's Guide to Herman Melville* (item B277), for instance, begins with this first sentence: "*Typee* (1846) and *Omoo* (1847) are not only Melville's first but also his most neglected works" (p. 18, 1973 ed.).

17. For an overview of Melville's general reputation, see Watson G. Branch, ed., *Melville* (item B295), and Hershel Parker, ed., *The Recognition of Herman Melville* (item B282).

The Publication of *Typee:* A Chronology

Milton R. Stern*

January 3, 1841. Jobless during a financial depression, young Herman Melville left his mother's house in Lansingburgh, New York, and shipped as a common seaman aboard the whaleship *Acushnet*, Captain Valentine Pease commanding, out of Fairhaven, Massachusetts.

July 9, 1842. Together with shipmate Richard Tobias Greene, a sign-painter from Buffalo, New York, and known to him only as "Toby," Melville jumped ship at Anna Maria Bay in Nukuheva in the Marquesa Isles. Seeking the valley of the Happar tribe, they mistakenly fled to the valley of the Typees. Toby was allowed to leave the valley to find medical aid for Melville, who had injured his leg during the flight inland. Toby never returned.

August 9, 1842. Melville was rescued by the *Lucy Ann*, an Australian whaler out of Sydney.

September 25, 1842. Melville joined four fifths of the *Lucy Ann's* crew in mutiny at Papeete. With the others, Melville was put ashore at the British open air prison, where he was allowed to wander loose. He escaped from Tahiti on October 19 and beachcombed on the island of Eimeo. He shipped on the whaler *Charles and Henry* on November 3, and was honorably discharged at Lahaina, island of Maui, May 2, 1843. Melville wandered about the Hawaiian islands until August 17, when, in Honolulu, he signed on as an ordinary seaman aboard the U.S. Navy frigate, the *United States*, for the remainder of its voyage homeward bound.

October 14, 1844. Melville was honorably discharged in Boston. After almost four years, he returned to his mother's home in Lan-

---

*This chronology was written specifically for this volume and appears here for the first time. A splendid history of the publication of *Typee* is Leon Howard's "Historical Note" in volume 1 of *The Writings of Herman Melville* (Evanston: Northwestern University Press and the Newberry Library, 1968). Because the Northwestern University Press refuses permission to reprint the "Historical Note," this chronology appears in its place. The chronology is indebted at almost every point to the scholarship of Professor Howard, and follows the organization of the "Historical Note." It also owes a debt to Jay Leyda's *The Melville Log* and to Merrell R. Davis and William H. Gilman, eds., *The Letters of Herman Melville*. See note 5 of my "Introduction" to this volume.

singburgh. Encouraged by his family's delighted responses to his sailor yarns, at age twenty-five Melville began to write his first book—probably in December, 1844. In January, 1845, he moved to New York City to write his book while living with his brothers, Gansevoort and Allan.

July 31, 1845. Gansevoort sailed to London as secretary to the American legation in England. By that date, Herman had written a complete or an almost complete draft of *Typee*. The manuscript had been turned down by Harper, but was read by Thomas L. Nichols, a friend of Gansevoort. On the advice of Nichols, Gansevoort took a fair copy of the manuscript to London in order to try to enlist a British publisher. On August 20, Gansevoort arrived in London.

October 17, 1845. The English publisher, John Murray, finished reading the portion of *Typee* that Gansevoort had given him; he liked it and asked for the rest of the manuscript.

November 3, 1845. Gansevoort wrote Herman to send the remainder of the book. John Murray specialized in authentic travel adventures, and he was willing to publish *Typee* as a literally and completely factual piece of nonfiction which would add the South Seas to his *Colonial and Home Library* of travel narratives. These books were inexpensive and were aimed at a wide, popular readership in both the "Backwoods of America" and "the remotest cantonments" of Great Britain's "Indian dominions." But Murray was suspicious: the book seemed too good to be true. It was too well written to have been composed, as claimed, by a common seaman, a nonprofessional writer with little formal education. In response to letters from London, Herman wrote back that he would make whatever additions or revisions were necessary to reduce the taint of fiction, and he gave Gansevoort free rein in negotiating for the book's publication. Murray was assured that the book was not fiction.

December 6, 1845. Gansevoort sent Murray new portions of the manuscript (chapters 20, 21, and 27), containing materials intended to make the book seem more literally reportorial as well as descriptions of Marquesan dancing girls, which Murray considered too risqué and which he deleted. On December 20, withholding chapters 11 and 12 for some last minute checking, Gansevoort gave Murray the complete manuscript together with a few pages of emendation Herman had sent. Melville added more "ballast," factual materials about people, places, customs, and events, in order to avoid the semblance of fiction, which was taboo in the *Colonial and Home Library*. These additions probably influenced Melville's choice of materials for inclusion in almost every novel he wrote thereafter.

January 1, 1846. Gansevoort accepted £100 from Murray for payment, and on January 3 he sent Herman five pounds and the good news that *Typee* was going to become a book. William Clowes and Sons, the printers, sent Gansevoort the first batch of proofs on January 5. On January 7, Gansevoort read several pages to Washington Irving, with whom he had breakfasted. Irving liked what he heard and he escorted Gansevoort to the London office of Wiley and Putnam, his American publishers. On January 10, Gansevoort gave G. P. Putnam a sizeable sample of *Typee*, 107 proofsheets. Putnam was entranced by the book and offered to publish it in America.

January 16, 1846. Gansevoort completed arrangements for publication. In America the book would be offered in two volumes (they appeared in Wiley and Putnam's *Library of American Books*) at thirty seven and one half cents each, paperbacked, and one dollar each, clothbound. The first volume was to be published on February 28 or March 1; the second was to appear on April 1. In England the book would be published as two volumes in Murray's *Colonial and Home Library*, the first volume on February 27, the second volume to appear simultaneously with the American edition on April 1; both volumes were to sell at five shillings a set, clothbound. Murray would furnish proof sheets to Wiley and Putnam by February 3, and the American copyright would be in Herman's name. By February 3, Gansevoort had collected and corrected all proof, including the preface and the appendix, and had delivered two copies to Mr. Putnam on schedule for shipment to America. Herman, Gansevoort, and Murray's reader, Henry Milton, all made revisions and corrections before publication of the English edition, *Narrative of a Four Months' Residence Among the Natives of a Valley of the Marquesas Islands; or, A Peep at Polynesian Life*. It is unlikely that Melville had time to make any further changes for the American edition.

February 26, 1846. Wiley and Putnam placed the title of the book in copyright. On March 17 the American edition was published and deposited for copyright: *Typee: A Peep at Polynesian Life During a Four Months' Residence in a Valley of the Marquesas*. The English short title was *The Marquesas Islands*; the American, which Melville liked better, was *Typee*. The American edition showed several variations from the English proof sheets. It is likely that in America, Mr. Wiley, a man of unbending conventional morality and a strict observer of respectabilities, directed the revisions, which were bowdlerizing deletions of several sexual, religious, and political references. Gansevoort, who corrected proof up to the last minute for the English edition, most likely was unable to send changes to Mr. Wiley in time for the American first edition, which must account for some of the variations between the two transatlantic first editions. But the American first edition, with assent and some cooperative rewriting from Herman Melville himself, was, in effect, a deliberately expurgated version of the English text, a variation that was a foreshadowing of the bowdlerization yet to come.

February 21, 1846. Murray's edition came out ahead of time. Gansevoort received six copies on February 24. Wiley and Putnam's edition was delayed: it was copyrighted on March 17, but it was not bound before March 23.

May 7, 1846. Melville sent Wiley a copy of the book containing the further emendations he considered necessary for a new edition. On May 12 Gansevoort died (Melville and the family did not receive that news from England until June 4). Wiley replied to Melville with a strong request that the book be made more genteel and proper in its treatment of sexuality, missionary activity, and European imperialism in the South Seas. Melville removed the appendix and approximately thirty more pages of material that Wiley found objectionable. He also toned down the book's "raciness." On July 11, Wiley and Putnam gave Melville $150 ($63.74 more than the American edition had earned for him so far).

July 15, 1846. The revised text of the American edition went to the printers. While Wiley had been growing unhappy about *Typee*'s propriety, the reviews were making Murray unhappy about its authenticity. On July 1, Richard Tobias Greene, "the true and veritable 'Toby,' " had announced his existence. In his revelation in the *Buffalo Commercial Advertiser*, Toby explained his disappearance from the South Seas and his inability to find Melville thereafter, and he confirmed everything in *Typee* as fact. In the July 11 issue of the *Commercial Advertiser*, Toby published the account of his own adventures. Melville suggested that Murray publish the revised version, the American second edition, together with a "Sequel of Toby," under the American title, *Typee*. Because of delays in publication of the bowdlerized American second edition, on August 1 Melville sent Murray a copy of "The Story of Toby, A Sequel to *Typee* by the Author of that Work," but without a copy of the revised *Typee* itself. Melville delayed sending bowdlerized copies (even after they had become available) until September 2. The delay is curious. On the one hand, Melville acquiesced a bit more readily than a hero should to Wiley's demands for censorship and revision. On the other hand, Melville could have sent proof sheets of the American second edition to England in time for John Murray to consider them; yet, whether because of remissness or whatever conscious or subconscious revulsion to the bowdlerized version, Melville did not send Murray a copy before September 2. By that time, Murray had decided to reissue the unbowdlerized English first edition, which included the appendix (the cession to Lord George Paulet), deleted from the expurgated American second edition, together with "The Story of Toby" and the title, *Typee; or, A Narrative of a Four Months' Residence Among the Natives of a Valley of the Marquesas Islands; or, A Peep at Polynesian Life*. This second English edition was substantially the text of what is now the "received" version of *Typee*. In America, the bowdlerized edition became the basis for all further editions during Melville's lifetime. (In 1849 Melville bought the plates from Wiley and Putnam and gave them to his new publisher, Harper, for future printings.) Thus all the while Melville was alive, *Typee* continued to be internationally available, in both pirated and authorized editions, in two significantly different versions.[1]

February 13, 1849. *Typee* was transferred from Wiley and Putnam to Harper's; reissue by the new publisher commenced on June 15. The total income credited to Melville from all sales of *Typee* by Wiley and Putnam came to $732.75; when Melville bought the plates of the book to close out the account, which was lessened by what he had drawn from it, he ended up paying Wiley and Putnam $107.72.

June 23, 1876. In England, the Murray edition went out of print after a history of very good sales sapped by unauthorized editions offered by two pirating publishers, Routledge and Gibbs. Despite the consequent lawsuits and headaches, the Murray edition returned in a modest 1877 reprinting, which lasted until two years after Melville's death. According to Leon Howard, "*Typee* was never a best-seller, even by the standards of the 1840's. In round numbers, 6,500 copies were printed and sold by Wiley and Putnam, and 4,000 by the Harpers. Murray printed a total of 7,342 copies during Melville's lifetime . . . and a posthumous impression of 1,012 copies, making, in all, a profit of £245. 9s. 1d. on *Typee*. The English pirates may have printed at least as many more. But the total income Melville derived from the book during a period of 41 years (including the $708.40 he received from England) was approximately $2,000."[2]

1968. The definitive edition of *Typee*, volume 1 of *The Writings of Herman Melville*, edited by H. Hayford, H. Parker, and G. T. Tanselle—the "Northwestern-Newberry edition"—was published. Many nineteenth- and twentieth-century editions appeared after Melville's death, and several good editions were published after the Melville revival began in the 1920s. By 1968 the market offered (and still does) several good, perfectly reliable, inexpensive editions of *Typee* that are essentially the same version as the expensive Northwestern-Newberry edition.

Notes

1. For a discussion of the details of revisions made by Melville for both the first and second American editions, see Leon Howard's "Historical Note," section 4, pp. 288–93.

2. Howard, p. 298.

[Review of *Typee*]

[John Sullivan Dwight]*

In the middle of the Pacific Ocean, some nine or ten degrees south of the Equator, lie the Marquesas. Here where the heats of the tropical sun are mitigated by the influence of the vast surrounding expanse of waters, and the climate is perfect and free from excesses of every kind, Nature blooms in a genial and healthy luxuriance such as she can no where else display. No Hesperides ever wore the gorgeous beauty of this southern paradise. Its green valleys stretch away in a loveliness which cannot be described. Hidden in the recesses of rough volcanic hills, their varied features teem with a glory that the dweller in other regions never conceived of. Their precipitous sides, covered with vegetation and with flowers, gleam with silvery cascades; in their evergreen and lofty groves, the golden fruits which supply the wants of their inhabitants, ripen without the labor of man; and little lakes nestling amidst the exuberant foliage, reflect the sky and tempt the beholder into their cool, clear depths. Such are these gems of the ocean, in which Nature, prodigal and unhindered, has hinted the extent of her possibilities, and by a kind of material diffraction has prophecied her own future perfections;—perfections which she shall possess in infinite and universal variety when, through the combined industry and wealth and power of a United Race, she shall have become but the image and expression of the Kingdom of God abiding in the souls and societies of Man!

Of the inhabitants of these islands we have accounts quite as striking as of the islands themselves. All writers unite in declaring them to be most perfect specimens of physical beauty, symmetry and health. We copy from [*Typee*]. [There follow four long paragraphs describing the physical beauty and vigor of the islanders.]

Thus far there is no doubt of the facts; the assertions of the author are sustained by all the evidence relating to the subject. But in the course of his narrative, he makes some statements respecting the social condition and character of the tribe with which he was domesticated, of so remarkable a character that we cannot escape a slight suspicion that he

*Reprinted from the Brook Farm *Harbinger*, 2 (April 4, 1846), 263–66.

has embellished the facts from his own imagination, in other words, that there is an indefinite amount of romance mingled with the reality of his narrative.

We say this without knowing the author or how far he may be relied on. The name on the title page gives, we take it, no indication either of his what, or his whereabouts; there is, to be sure, a straight forward air in his preface which is worth something, and the fact that the book is dedicated to Chief Justice Shaw, is greatly in favor of the assumption that it is a true history, but yet we cannot avoid the possibility that it may be in the most important particulars, only an amusing fiction. Still there is a verisimilitude about it, which inclines us to the contrary opinion; it relates nothing which is in itself impossible, and, having made the foregoing deductions, we shall consider it as though its facts were not susceptible of doubt.

The scene of the adventures here related is Nukuheva, an island some sixty miles in circumference, one of that group of three, north-west of the Marquesas, which are sometimes called the Washington Islands, or Ingraham's Islands, but which the author regards as part of the Marquesas proper. "Typee," is the name of one of the valleys of this island and of the tribe by which it is inhabited. This tribe is, he tell us, noted throughout the South Seas for savage ferocity, and indeed the name "Typee," signifies a lover of human flesh. With the tribe dwelling around the bay of Nukuheva, which is the harbor generally visited by ships, they have always maintained an implacable hostility, which a warlike invasion of their valley by Commodore Porter some thirty years ago, had extended to foreigners in general. From this cause as well as from the comparative seclusion of their bay and valley, up to the time of our author's residence among them, no civilizees of any nation, except the warriors of Commodore Porter, had ever landed on their shores. Thus their native character and customs had been completely preserved, and they themselves saved from those civilized vices and diseases, which act upon the South Sea Islanders with the same fatality as upon the Indians of our continent.

The author went out to the Pacific in a whale ship. When they anchored in the bay of Nukuheva, dissatisfaction with the captain and the voyage, and a certain love of adventure, induced him to run away, with the design of secreting himself in the vicinity until the ship had gone, and then of remaining among the friendly natives of that tribe as long as he wished, or till a favorable chance of getting away should offer. In this undertaking he was joined by a ship mate, but the necessity of seeking some retreat where they could obtain the fruits which are to be had only on the sides of the valleys, without danger of being found by the captain, obliged them to go farther into the interior of the island than they had intended. Their wanderings over mountains and defiles are described with great skill, and indeed we will here say that the whole book is the work of an artist. Since Dana's "Two Years Before the Mast," we have had nothing to compare with it in point of fresh and natural interest. After great difficulties and sufferings, they at last made their way into the midst of a tribe which turned out to be the fearful and unsparing Typees! By good fortune they were received most kindly. After a short time, the companion of the author departs, with the design of returning to Nukuheva and procuring some remedy for a bodily injury which his friend had contracted from an unknown cause in their journey over the mountains. He departs with a company of the natives, who were drawn down to the sea by the report that boats were approaching the shore, but never returns, nor can any information respecting his fate be obtained. Thus left alone, the author remains for some four months in the valley. He is treated with the greatest kindness by the chiefs and by all the people, has an attendant devoted to his service, his wants are cared for with the most friendly solicitude, his person is made sacred by the "taboo," and as far as an indolent and aimless life with no duties and no anxieties, in the midst of the utmost natural beauty can go, nothing is wanting to his happiness. But he longs for the excitement of the world he has left and for home. His confidence in his savage friends is also not perfect. He has a vague fear that their kindness is only temporary, and that sooner or later they may subject him to some horrible death. He accordingly determines to leave them as soon as possible, but finds that they have no idea of allowing him to go. They will not even permit him to approach the sea. At last he hears that there is a boat at the coast. With great exertions he succeeds in reaching it, in getting on board and escaping, though not without the necessity of a deadly struggle with the Typee chief, who at first inclines to let him go, but afterwards endeavors to detain him.

What has most interested us in "Typee," is the social state which is described in the following extracts. [There follow eight paragraphs of quoted material describing the honesty, peacefulness, gentleness, and fraternal orderliness of the Typees in their communal life.]

This is certainly a noteworthy condition of social relations. Among these ignorant savages we behold order existing with liberty, and virtues of which, in civilized communities we find only the intellectual ideal, matters of every-day life. How is it that without our learning or our religion these cannibals can thus put to shame the most refined and Christian societies? How is it that in a mere state of nature they can live together in a degree of social harmony and freedom from vice, which all our jails, and scaffolds, and courts of justice, and police officers, and soldiers, and schoolmasters, and great philosophers, and immense politicians, and moral codes, and steam engines, material and spiritual, cannot procure for us? These are questions of some significance, but yet not difficult to answer. The great secret of the whole matter is that in Typee there is *abundance for every person*, and thus the most fruitful cause of the selfishness and crime of enlightened and philosophic civilization does not exist there. Here is the lesson which the leaders of this nineteenth century may learn from the Typees; here is the doctrine which our legislators and philosophers, aye! and our clergy and churches who *preach* the love of man, and ought to know what are its conditions, need a better understanding of. Said that Coryphaeus of our beneficent modern metaphysics, Victor Cousin, when the oppression and degradation of the laboring classes were urged upon his unwilling attention, "Eh! Give them good precepts! Give them good precepts! At least they can't abuse them, but if they get money they will only spend it in vice!"

To the winds with such shallow and selfish hypocrisy! Shame upon such intellectual inertia, such scepticism, as will not see that our Father who is in Heaven, has made it our duty to protect our brethren against the evils in which they are involved, and to discover and establish a social state of Justice and generous competence for all! Give them good precepts, but give them something else beside, if you wish to have your precepts effectual. Give them such an abundance of material things as bountiful nature in Typee bestows upon her children, and then when you bid them love each other, your words will not fall dead and unmeaning upon their ears. The peace and good will of that South Sea valley are as possible here as they are there; they are possible here in a far higher degree, on account of our greater refinement and intelligence, and our higher religious development. Here, indeed, in order to produce those blessings, we must in society create the material conditions which there are created by nature; we must have a social system which will produce and distribute to every member of society a complete abundance as the result of a healthy amount of labor, and not a niggardly, starving pittance to nineteen-twentieths of the population as the return for slavish and debasing toil, and enormous wealth to the other one-twentieth, as the fruit of grasping cunning or the wages of stupid and pitiable idleness. It is no deceitful phantasm when in some unknown and distant region we find a tribe of rude savages living in true social brotherhood; if we are wise we shall not hurry to the conclusion that such a state of things is impossible for us, but shall inquire what is the cause which produces it there, and how shall that cause be made to operate here. The cause is plain, and the means of putting it into effect with us not less so. The cause as we have said, is *universal abundance,* and the means of producing such abundance in civilized societies is the organization of industry and the distribution of its products according to principles of exact justice.

Let associated, coöperative labor once take the place of the drudgery of our gloomy manufactories, the dulness of our agriculture, and the poverty of our cities, and the word *want* thereby be banished from the language, and we shall no longer need to look to the islanders of the South Seas for examples of social virtues and happiness. But these virtues cannot prevail in society such as ours is now constituted. Their first requisite,—an abundant supply of the physical wants of every person is not possible in the midst of social and political institutions which are mostly forms of organized selfishness, where every thing is subjected to greedy, fraudulent and uncertain commerce, and where Slavery in some one of its disgusting and inhuman forms is a necessary and constant fact. The work of human regeneration has a foundation, the highest spiritual ends, a material basis. We press the whole matter on the most serious thought of every thinking man.

We had designed to bring forward some other considerations suggested by the above extracts, but we omit them to make room for a passage relating to the Sandwich Island Missions. [There follow four quoted paragraphs of an incident which contrasts the elegance of an American mission with the shabby and obtuse treatment with which the natives are abused by the missionaries.]

It is proper to say in behalf of the author, that he does not impeach the honesty with which this mission was planned, or the Christian character of the Missionaries in general. He merely avers that their designs have often been injudicious and that other influences than that of the New Testament have operated on the natives, which are undoubtedly the facts. It must however be remarked that the Sandwich Islands from their very locality, were doomed to be ravaged by the curses which commerce always inflicts on savage tribes. As the natural stoppingplace of all the shipping in the Pacific, it was impossible that they should do otherwise than afford an outlet for the vice and corruption gathered together for those long voyages, and intensified by absence from the restraints of society. How far the missions may have tended to delay the inevitable destruction of the islanders, we cannot say, but that they have not prevented it altogether is certainly not their fault. It is besides unreasonable to expect that the most sincere, judicious, and effectual efforts should produce there at once, or in any short period of time, a state of Christian morality. When we reflect that in many centuries of Christian instruction we have not attained to such a state, we can hardly demand it of a nation which has not emerged from the utmost darkness of heathenism above fifty years.

On first reading the above passage we were very painfully impressed by the fact that the conversion of the Sandwich Islanders to Christianity had also converted them into the slaves of their benefactors, and that even the wife of a missionary, a herald of the liberty of Christ, could drive them like beasts before her carriage. But a little thought soon showed us that such desecrations of our God-given human nature were not confined to that place. The fact of menial servitude, of artificial castes and distinctions, can also be found within the shadow of our metropolitan churches, nay, within those churches themselves. The ministers of the meek and lowly Jesus, here as well as there participate in this loathsome necessity, for as society now is, it is a necessity, and do not dream that they commit a sin. We do not presume to condemn them individually, but in God's name we condemn a social order which is founded on such contradictions of the Divine laws, and which devotes to a hopeless and miserable existence so large a majority of human creatures.

Four Months' Residence
in the Marquesas

Anonymous*

Mr. Murray's *Home and Colonial Library* does not furnish us with a more interesting book than this: hardly with a cleverer. It is full of the captivating matter upon which the general reader battens; and is endowed with freshness and originality to an extent that cannot fail to exhilarate the most enervated and *blasé* of circulating-library loungers.

A poor old ship is at sea. She has been at sea for six months, cruising after the sperm-whale "beneath the scorching sun of the Line, and tossed on the billows of the wide rolling Pacific—the sky above, the sea around, and nothing else!" The ship is an American, and one on board of her, a common sailor, the author of the words we have just quoted, and, in fact, the author of the volume, is vastly discontented with his tedious humdrum state of life. Joy to him when he hears that the ship shall shape her course to the *Marquesas.* "What strange visions of outlandish things does the very name spirit up! Naked houris—cannibal banquets—groves of cocoanut, coral reefs, tattooed chiefs, and bamboo temples; sunny valleys, planted with breadfruit trees, carved canoes dancing on the flashing blue waters, savage woodlands guarded by horrible idols,—*heathenish rites and human sacrifices.*" It was in the summer of 1842, and he arrived at the wished-for haven; but scarcely arrived before he was visited with an intense desire to quit the good ship Dolly once and for ever. The usage that Mr. Herman Melville had received on board had been of the order called tyrannical; the sick had been inhumanly neglected; the provisions had been doled out in scanty allowance; and, moreover, Dolly's cruises were unseasonably protracted. The replies of Captain Vange (horrible name!) to all complaints and remonstrances had been the butt end of a handspike, and "so conveniently administered as effectually to silence the aggrieved party." Mr. Melville was reflecting upon these various trials of his position, and upon the most effectual mode of escaping them, when he perceived—it was at night—one of the ship's company leaning over the bulwarks, "apparently plunged in a profound reverie." This was Toby; no ordinary character, truly!—a young fellow about the age of Mr. Melville,

*Reprinted from the *Times* (London), April 6, 1846, p. 3.

active, ready, obliging, of dauntless courage, and singularly open and fearless in the expression of his feelings. "He was one of that class of rovers you sometimes meet at sea, who never reveal their origin, never allude to home, and go rambling over the world as if pursued by some mysterious fate they cannot possibly elude." His dark complexion had been deepened by exposure to the tropical sun, "and a mass of jettylocks clustered about his temples, and threw a darker shade into his large black eyes." He was a strange wayward being, moody, fitful, and melancholy—at times almost morose. No one ever saw him laugh; he smiled, but it was sarcastically, and his dry humour only brought out into deeper shade his natural and almost imperturbable gravity. Toby, in a word, was a cut-and-dried hero of romance, strangely misnamed at his baptism, and the very companion for Herman Melville in the adventures he was bent upon undertaking. A tap on the shoulder and a few words sufficed for a mutual understanding. Preliminaries were arranged, and the engagement was ratified by a hearty shake of the hands.

The next day the starboard watch, to which both the seamen belonged, was sent ashore on liberty. The men had hardly effected a landing, when the rain poured down in torrents. The starboard watch fled for shelter under cover of an immense canoe-house, and there, conveniently enough for our history, fell fast asleep every one of them, with the exception, of course, of our heroes, who kept wide awake and took instant advantage of their companions' drowsiness to make their escape.

The fugitives were on the island of Nukuheva, which gives its name to the bay and village at which the starboard watch had just landed. A word or two of description is required before we proceed with our story. Besides this bay, the shores of the island are indented—Mr. Melville is our authority—by several other extensive inlets, into which descend broad and verdant valleys. These are inhabited by as many distinct tribes of savages, who, although speaking kindred dialects of a common language, and having the same religion and laws, have from time immemorial waged hereditary warfare against each other.

"The intervening mountains, generally 2,000 or 3,000 feet above the level of the sea, geographically define the territories of each of these hostile tribes, who never cross them, save on some expedition of war and plunder. Immediately adjacent to Nukuheva, and only separated from it by the mountains seen from the harbour, lies the lovely valley of Happar, whose inmates cherish the most friendly relations with the inhabitants of Nukuheva. On the other side of Happar, and closely adjoining it, is the magnificent valley of the dreaded Typees, the unappeasable enemies of both these tribes."

The object of Toby and his friend was to effect a passage to the mountains, and to remain amongst them, supporting themselves by such fruits as came in their way, until the dreaded ship should sail, and her prow be seen driving from the bay.

The sufferings of the runaways became painful in the extreme. They ascended the mountain with fearful difficulty, to find no broad and teeming vallies, but a series of ridges stretching away as far as they could see, their precipitous sides covered with the brightest verdure, and waving here and there with woodland—but with no fruit-trees to sustain them if they should advance. They did advance, under circumstances of appalling trial and danger; now clambering up an almost perpendicular and lofty height, now descending—Death staring them all the while in the face—its other jagged side, with a despairing courage that alone saved them from destruction; now burning with fever, now shivering with cold, lame and almost famished; passing nights, with no shelter, beneath a pitiless and raging sky,—and spending the day, in spite of hunger, illness, and fatigue, in exertions that mocked the hardships of the previous day, so gigantic and almost superhuman were they. The scenes are admirably told: simply and nervously. A week passes in such tremendous misery, and the unhappy men find themselves at length on a level spot in a fertile valley—amongst a living people. But what people? Friendly Happars or inimical and blood-thirsty Typees? Typees; but neither inimical nor bloodseeking. No; friends who invest the person of Herman with a peculiar sanctity, and for his sake treat Toby with all becoming hospitality. Mr. Melville, after all his troubles, is most agreeably surprised and sumptuously entertained. He is provided with provisions and attendants, a home is given to him, and the houris of whom he had dreamt on board the Dolly—but lovelier far than even his excited imagination had pictured them—hover around him, eager to enhance his bliss. Enviable Herman! A happier dog it is impossible to imagine than Herman in the Typee Valley.

To describe a day's existence would be to tell of the promised joys of the Mahomedan's paradise. Nothing but pure physical delight; sunny days, bright skies, absence of care, presence of lovely woman. Fayaway—who gave her that name?—is in herself sufficient to enchain a human heart to a dungeon for life, yet she failed to wed the soul of Herman to this happy valley. Like Rasselas, his pleasures palled. He wished to be beyond the mountains, to be freed from luscious imprisonment; for it has to be told that Herman is close prisoner in the valley, is well cared for, fed, and housed (not clothed), but, for some mysterious reason, *watched* during every hour of the day and night. As for Toby, he escaped a month or so after they reached the valley, although how he got away, and whither he went, are mysteries to the present hour. Mr. Melville thinks he was eaten by the Typees, but that by the way. Once or twice Herman asks leave to go back to his friends, but his request meets with a rebuke, and he asks no more. Four months pass away in a manner which will not fail to excite the worn out sensibilities of a modern tourist, and the valley is suddenly excited. A boat has arrived on the coast. The natives pour down the valley to meet it. Herman entreated the king of the Typees to suffer him to join them. The king frowned, but soon gave way and consented. When within a short distance of the sea, the companions of Herman suddenly repented their goodness, and shut the white man up in a roadside hut. He heard the roaring of the sea, was mad with impatience, but the savages were looking fiercely upon him, and he held his peace. A difference of opinion arose. Some of the chiefs pitied their captive, some were disposed to eat him. One fine old fellow, by name Marheyo, came to Herman's side (we can fancy Mr. T. P. Cooke playing the part at the Adelphi), and placing his arm upon the young man's shoulder, emphatically pronounced two English words—"Home," "Mother." Herman understood him, and thanked him, the lovely Fayaway weeping all the while. Lucky Melville! cruel Herman! why so anxious to depart? The friendly natives carry the mariner forward. He once more sees the billows, and is mad with joy. A boat is waiting to receive him. He presses on; Fayaway clings to him, sobbing audibly. The natives fight—the friendly and the inimical—and in the midst of the fray Herman reaches the boat. But is he safe? Not yet. He perceives Fayaway sitting disconsolately on the shingles, and a party of the inimicals dashing into the water to overtake him. If they reach him, he is speared and lost. A savage has neared the little boat. He is a friend; but, like many old friends, he is inclined to mischief for the present. Herman strikes at him with the boathook—aims at his throat—and hits it. Another savage has his hand upon the gunwale; a knife removes it; the little boat is already close to the vessel to which she belongs. Herman is safe, but, overpowered by agitation and strong excitement, he faints in the arms of his deliverer, recovering, happily, to write his adventures, and to add another volume to the 19 already issued of the *Colonial Library*.

We have been somewhat prolix in the narration of this history: first, because the book of Mr. Melville is really a very clever production; and, secondly, because it is introduced to the English public as authentic, which we by no means think it to be. We have called Mr. Melville a common sailor; but he is a very uncommon common sailor, even for America, whose mariners are better educated than our own. His reading has been extensive. In his own province, the voyages of Cook, Carteret, Byron, Kotzebue, and Vancouver are familiar to him; he can talk glibly of Count Bouffon and Baron Cuvier, and critically, when he likes, of Teniers. His descriptions of scenery are lifelike and vigorous, sometimes masterly, and his style throughout is rather that of an educated literary man than of a poor outcast working seaman on board of a South Sea whaler.

The book betrays itself. In the early part of the narrative, and during the frightful incidents of the flight, Mr. Melville has but a spoonful of sodden biscuit daily; his leg is fearfully swollen, his pains are most acute; he is suffering from a raging fever; yet on he goes, day after day, for a week, undergoing exertion and fatigue that would kill a giant in health, yet arriving at last in the happy valley in tolerably good plight notwithstanding.

It must have been impossible, under the circumstances, for the fugitives to have carried "luggage" with them, yet after two months' spent in the valley a large bundle turns up, which, it appears, Mr. Melville brought with him. After a week or two's sojourn the guest, ignorant of the Typee language when he first set foot in the valley, with most unaccountable facility understands all that is said to him, although the discourse of the chiefs comprehends abstruse points and very complex reasoning; and yet at the end of two or three months, forgetting what happened before, he informs us that gesticulation is required to enlighten him on the most ordinary subjects. At page 112 we find that "our Typee friends availed themselves of a disaster of Toby to exhort us to a due appreciation of the blessings we enjoyed amongst them, contrasting their own generous reception of us with the animosity of their neighbours. They likewise dwelt upon the cannibal propensities of the Happars, a subject which they were perfectly aware could not fail to alarm us, while, at the same time, they earnestly disclaimed all participation in so horrid a custom. *Nor did they omit to call upon us to admire the natural loveliness of their own abode and the lavish abundance with which it produced all manner of luxuriant fruits, exalting it in this particular above any of the surrounding valleys.*" Again, immediately afterwards, at page 119, when Herman inquires for the lost Toby, his earnest questions "appeared to embarrass the natives greatly. *All their accounts were contradictory;* one giving me to understand that Toby would be with me in a very short time; another, that he did not know where he was; while a third, violently inveighing against him, assured me that he had stolen away, and would never come back." Two months afterwards, when Mr. Melville's knowledge of Typee must have materially increased, we find—for so it is written at pp. 152 and 154—that he was so utterly ignorant of it as to be able to judge of the speaker's meaning only by signs, and very imperfectly by those. The getting rid of poor Toby, the only credible witness of these transactions, is of itself a most suspicious circumstance; so is the exquisite description of Fayaway; how different to what we elsewhere read of South Sea nymphs! So are the scenes that here and there end a chapter, like scenes of a play concluding an act with a *tableau vivant,* and bringing the curtain down in the midst of it—we refer especially to chapter 12, which gives us young girls, darting from surrounding groves, "hanging upon our skirts, and accompanying us with shouts of merriment and delight, which almost drowned the deep notes of the recitative."

The evidence against the authenticity of the book is more than sufficient to satisfy a court of justice. Our limits forbid us to prosecute it further. Of evidence against the smartness and talent of the production there is none. The author, be he American or Englishman, has written a charming little book, and, as it appears to us, with a laudable and Christian purpose. Let it be regarded as an apology for the Pagan; a plea for the South Sea Islanders, governments, and missionaries, who understand so little the sacred charge which God commits to them, when He places in their hands the children of His favoured sunny regions; may they learn from fiction a lesson which experience has hitherto failed to teach them— viz., that if it be needful for Christianity to approach the Heathen, it is equally necessary that it should approach him *reverently and tenderly.*

[Review of *Typee*]

[Nathaniel Hawthorne]*

WILEY & PUTNAM'S LIBRARY OF AMERICAN BOOKS, NOS. XIII. AND XIV. The present numbers of this excellent and popular series, contain a very remarkable work, entitled '*Typee, or a Peep at Polynesian Life.*' It records the adventures of a young American who ran away from a whale ship at the Marquesas, and spent some months as the guest, or captive, of a native tribe, of which scarcely anything had been hitherto known to the civilized world.—The book is lightly but vigorously written; and we are acquainted with no work that gives a freer and more effective picture of barbarian life, in that unadulterated state of which there are now so few specimens remaining. The gentleness of disposition that seems akin to the delicious climate, is shown in contrast with traits of savage fierceness;—on one page, we read of manners and modes of life that indicate a whole system of innocence and peace; and on the next, we catch a glimpse of a smoked human head, and the half-picked skeleton of what had been (in a culinary sense) a *well-dressed* man. The author's descriptions of the native girls are voluptuously colored, yet not more so than the exigencies of the subject appear to require. He has that freedom of view—it would be too harsh to call it laxity of principle—which renders him tolerant of codes or morals that may be little in accordance with our own; a spirit proper enough to a young and adventurous sailor, and which makes his book the more wholesome to our staid landsmen. The narrative is skillfully managed, and in a literary point of view, the execution of the work is worthy of the novelty and interest of its subject.

*Reprinted from the *Salem Advertiser* (March 25, 1846).

[Review of *Typee*]

Anonymous*

Is there any one whose eye may fall on this page, weary of the conventionalities of civilised life—some toil-worn Sisyphus bowed to the earth with his never-ending task of rolling up the hill of life the stone that ever threatens to fall back on himself—dispirited with the energies he has wasted on unrewarded or uncongenial pursuits—cheated with Hope until he regard her as a baffled impostor who shall cheat him no more; whose heart beats no longer high for the future; but whose best affections are chilled, and loftiest aspirations thrown back on themselves. Is there any one sick of the petty animosities, the paltry heartburnings and jealousies, and low-thoughted cares of what is called, in bitter mockery, society?— Oh! 'if such man there be,' let him take the 'wings of a dove,' or what perhaps will bear safer the weight of himself and his woes—a berth in a South-sea whaler, and try the effects of a 'Residence in the Marquesas,' and take a 'Peep at Polynesian life,' and if he likes the peep make that life his own.

Here, and we call Mr. Herman Melville into court, he need not fear the single rap at the door which dissipates his day-dreams as surely as the kite in the air scares away the feathered minstrelsy of the grove; nor the postman's knock that peradventure brings the letter of the impatient dun or threatening attorney; nor butchers' nor bakers' bills; nor quarter-days with griping landlord and brutal brokers; nor tax-gatherer; nor income-tax collectors gauging with greedy exactness the drops that have fallen from his brow. Here, strange to say, he will find no money, no bargaining, no bankers with overdrawn accounts or dishonoured acceptances; no coin, and therefore no care; no misery, and therefore no crime. No corn-laws, no tariff, no union-workhouse, no bone-crushing, no spirit-crushing, no sponging-houses, no prisons. But he may live as the songster *wish'd*, but dar'd not even to hope he could live—

> in an isle of his own
> In a blue summer ocean far off;

*Reprinted from *Douglas Jerrold's Shilling Magazine* (London), 3 (April, 1846), 380–83.

but *not* 'alone.' For here are Houris even more graceful and lovely than the flowers they are perpetually weaving to adorn themselves with chaplets and necklaces, their only ornaments, but worthy of the court of Flora herself; inviting him to repose his weary limbs beneath the shadows of groves, on couches strewn with buds and fragrant blossoms.

Here the bosom of Nature unscarified by the plough, offers up spontaneously her goodliest gifts; food the most nutritious, and fruits the most refreshing. The original curse on man's destiny, appears here not to have fallen, 'the ground is *not* cursed for his sake;' nor 'in sorrow does he eat of it all the days of his life.'

In this garden of Eden, from which man is not yet an exile, there are no laws, and what is more agreeable still, no want of them; unless it be an Agrarian law, which works to every one's satisfaction. In this paradise of islands, you have only to fix the site of your house, and you will not be called upon to produce your title deeds; and you may call upon your neighbours to help you to build it, without any surveyor being called in to tax their bills. Here you may, instead of going to your office or ware-house, loiter away your morning beneath the loveliest and bluest of skies, on the margin of some fair lake, reflecting their hues yet more tenderly; or join the young men in their fishing-parties or more athletic sports; or if more quietly disposed, join the old men seated on their mats in the shade, in their 'talk' deprived of only one topic, your everlasting one, the weather; for where the climate is one tropical June day, 'melting into July,' it leaves you nothing to wish for, positively nothing to grumble at.

Such is life in the valley of the Typees; and surely Rasselas, if he had had the good luck to stumble on it, would not have gone further in his search after happiness.

There is, however, one trifling drawback—some shadows to temper the light of this glowing picture—the Typees are cannibals! The author makes an elaborate, but to our notion, a very unnecessary apology for this propensity of theirs. The Polynesians have the advantage of the cannibals of civilised life, for we have long since made the pleasant discovery, that man-eating is not confined to the Anthropophagi of the South Seas. The latter have undoubtedly one redeeming distinction—they only devour their enemies slain in battle: there is nothing which man in a civilised state has a keener appetite for than his particular friend. Go to any race-course, and you will find some scented Damon picking his teeth with a silver tooth-pick after devouring his Pythias, as if he had relished the re-past. Go to Tattersal's or Cockford's, and you will find that in a single night a man has devoured his own wife and children—having been disap-pointed in supping off his intimate friends. We know instances of highly respected country gentlemen swallowing at a single election the whole of their posterity; and could quote one huge Ogre who can gorge in his mighty maw a few millions of 'the finest peasantry'—nothing, indeed, civilised men are more expert in than picking their neighbours' bones!

Possibly, we may have pushed the parallel to the furthest; but it is impossible to read this pleasant volume without being startled at the oft-recurring doubt, has civilization made man better, and therefore happier? If she has brought much to him, she has taken much away; and wherever she has trod, disease, misery and crime have tracked her footsteps. She finds man a rude but happy savage, and leaves him a repulsive outcast, whose only relation to humanity consists in the vices which stain it!

We have dwelt more on the subject of Mr. Melville's 'Narrative,' and the reflections it excites, than on the book itself, which is one of the most captivating we have ever read. What will our juvenile readers say to a *real* Robinson Crusoe, with a *real* man Friday?—one Kory-Kory, with whom we will venture to say they will be delighted in five minutes from his introduction. The early part of the volume, narrating the author's escape from the prison ship—with his strange comrade Toby, whose mysterious fate, after baffling our curiosity and speculation, is yet to be developed—for the best of all possible reasons, that the author himself has not found it out!—is full of vivid excitement. The hair-breadth escapes of the adventurous seamen, their climbing up precipices and perpendicular rocks, their perilous leaps into cavernous retreats and gloomy ravines, are painted in vivid contrast to the voluptuous ease and tranquil enjoyments of the happy valley which they eventually reach. Although with little pretension to author-craft, there is a life and truth in the descriptions, and a freshness in the style of the narrative, which is in perfect keeping with the scenes and adventures it delineates. The volume forms a part of 'Murray's Home and Colonial Library,' and is worthy to follow Borrow's *Bible in Spain,* and Heber's *Indian Journals.* What traveller would wish for a higher distinction?

Typee: The Traducers of Missions

[William Oland Bourne]*

An apotheosis of barbarism! A panegyric on cannibal delights! An apostrophe to the spirit of savage felicity! Such are the exclamations instinctively springing from our lips as we close a book entitled "Typee: a Residence in the Marquesas," lately published in Wiley & Putnam's interesting "Library of American Books." It is even so, reader! A work coming from the press of one of the first houses in this country, and published simultaneously by the same house in London, gemmed with enthusiastic descriptions of the innocent felicity of a savage tribe—tinselled with ornate pencillings of cannibal enjoyments—drawing frequent contrasts between the disadvantages and miseries of civilization, and the uninterrupted paradisaical bliss of a tribe which has traced in ominous characters of blood on the outer battlements of its natural fortresses of rock and mountain that omnipotent and talismanic "TABU."

We do not purpose in our examination of this book to enter into an analysis of its contents, its literary execution, or its claims to fidelity in the general description it gives of the people among whom our author resided during a period of some four months. Such a "review" belongs properly to the acknowledged critical journals of the day, and would occupy far more space than we can appropriate to such a task. Nevertheless, we shall attempt to canvass some of its statements, wherein the cause of MISSIONS is assailed, with a pertinacity of misrepresentation and degree of *hatred*, which can only entitle the perpetrator to the just claim of traducer. We know what we are saying when we use these terms; we have read this book word by word; we have studied it carefully with reference to these very points, for to all that appertains to the missionary work we are sensitively alive; and were gladdened when we first saw it, with the prospect of learning something more from an impartial source concerning the practical operations of the missionary enterprise in that interesting region of the earth known as POLYNESIA. But we were soon disappointed; instead of a calm and unbiassed view, we have on every occasion a tissue of misrepresentation, and detraction of the labors of the devoted men and women who have exiled themselves for the purpose of carrying the bless-

*Reprinted from *Christian Parlor Magazine*, 3 (July, 1846), 74–83.

ings of the gospel to some of the most degraded and benighted children of Adam—who have been debased from the spiritual "image and likeness" of their God to naked and roving savages; and who, in the wildness of their character and the helplessness of their social condition, are but little exalted above the "brutes that perish."

We do not look at the history of the missionary work from the merely enthusiastic or poetic point of view. We do not view the overthrow of the system of idolatry, the destruction of *Maraes*, the burning of idols, the cessation of infanticide, the extinction of the Areoi, the abandonment of cannibalism, the termination of desolating wars, and the partial substitution of the arts of civilization and of peace—together with the construction of a written code of laws and the presentation of a written and printed language to the Polynesians, as a brilliant establishment of Christianity in the hearts of the people of those insulated tribes. These are but pulling down the outworks of the fortresses of idolatry and spiritual degradation, which have their foundations in the hearts and souls of the people. But these results are not the less brilliant because the soul, which has become inwrought in its inmost tissues with everything that is corrupt and degraded, has not been taken, as it were, by a Gabriel, and in a moment, by a stupendous miracle of all-sanctifying grace, washed from its impurities and prepared for the fullest beamings of unsullied bliss: they are not the less splendid because the laborers have not been able to pour the broad beam of day upon every soul, and extirpate every vestige of barbarism and sin. No! the history of the world furnishes no parallel to the reformation in the South Seas, except under the preaching of the inspired apostles, when the enlightened and refined idolators of Rome and Greece forsook the temples of their gods, both known and unknown, and offered up the daily incense of praise from the altars of sanctified hearts, and sang round their wide domains the songs of a purer faith.

The results of the missionary enterprise are to be measured not by what is to be done, but by what has been achieved; and when a contrast is made between the present condition of the Polynesians, and that in which they were found by the early navigators, and even only thirty years ago, callous indeed must be the heart of that man who would not rejoice with every lover of the gospel, in the change which has been made in their political and social condition—deeply stained with depravity must he be who would not be gladdened by the improvement in their moral and spiritual aspects. Partial the change certainly is, and it could not, in the short space of one generation, be much more extensive under the circumstances, than we see it; but the work has been begun—the citadel has been thrown down, the altars destroyed, and the Christian religion acknowledged as infinitely superior to the ancient and bloody superstitions.

It would occupy too much space for us to present these contrasts now; we shall incidentally allude to them, and as we have future occasion shall endeavor to make known to the Christian public the past, the present, and the future of the missionary work. And here we revert to the task before us.

The book whose title we have given may be called a respectable publication. The author seems to possess a cultivated taste and a fair education, but a deficient reading, and to this latter cause we assign many of his errors of general fact, as well as gross misstatements concerning the missionaries. With a lively imagination and a good and often graceful description, together with a somewhat happy strain of narrative, he has written an attractive history of personal adventure and unwilling *abandon* among the happy and sequestered Typees.

Come, oh celestial Spirit of Primitive Bliss! and waft me on thy golden pinions to the lovely abodes of the Typeeans! Bear me, oh genial spirit of unrefined progression, to the eternal landmarks of thy tabued groves! Waft me, benignant genius of undisturbed repose, to the over-hanging peaks of thy untainted solitudes, where the dulcet strains of an uncaring minstrel shall thrill the sighing spirit with the newer life of a "healthful physical enjoyment!" Come, oh yearning soul of the angelic FAYAWAY! let me henceforth be the chosen partner of thy tabued pleasures! let me bask beneath the mild ray of thine azure eye, and repose on the swelling oval of thy graceful form! No lingering love for the griefs of a civilized home shall tempt *me* to leave thy presence! no profane desires for the pains and miseries of these pent-up cities, and sin-cursed streets, and fashion-worshipping crowds, shall distract my sighing heart, and cause me to leave thee weeping amid the dashing waters of thine entrancing abode. With thee let me sport on the mirror-surface of thy sacred waters, and ramble beneath the refreshing shades of the cocoa and the palm! No recreant will I be to thy matchless love—no reckless fugitive from thy twining arms! So let me rest, and no palaces of earth, or lands of other names and customs more refined, shall tempt me to flee thy loved abodes!

We have remarked that this is a respectable book, but yet we have doubted whether it were worth a notice. To give circulation to such statements as our author makes may seem unwise, but as extracts from it of the nature we condemn are obtaining a channel through the public journals, we have determined to do our part in the work of making him known to the public. Although ordinarily we should not have regarded it as being worth an extended notice, we think the mode of its publication and the rank it holds, deserve a passing remark. In the first place it is dedicated to HON. LEMUEL SHAW, *Chief Justice of Massachusetts;* it is published by WILEY & PUTNAM, in *New York* and *London;* and it is permanently lettered XIII. and XIV. in their *Library of American Books.* These considerations serve, then, to give the book a respectability and an influence which it could not have without them, and without which we should probably have passed it by.

Before proceeding to our investigation of his statements concerning the missionaries, we remark of the book generally: 1. It is filled with the most palpable and absurd contradictions; 2. These contradictions are so carelessly put together as to occur in consecutive paragraphs; 3. It is throughout laudatory of the innocence and freedom from care of the barbarians of the South Seas, particularly the Marquesans; 4. It compares their condition with civilized society as being the more desirable of the two; 5. It either excuses and wilfully palliates the cannibalism and savage vices of the Polynesians, or is guilty of as great a crime in such a writer, that of ignorance of his subject; and, 6. It is redundant with bitter charges against the missionaries, piles obloquy upon their labor and its results, and broadly accuses them of being the cause of the vice, misery, destitution, and unhappiness of the Polynesians wherever they have penetrated.

Brevity requires us to keep close to the point indicated in the title of our article, or we could furnish numerous extracts to justify these charges. On page 30 we have an account of a vessel whose crew was decoyed by the natives to a secluded spot and barbarously murdered. On page 31, we are told "the 'savages' are made to deserve the title. When the inhabitants of some sequestered island discover the 'big canoe' of the European, they rush down to the beach in crowds, and stand ready, with open arms, to embrace the stranger. Fatal embrace! They fold the viper to their bosom." We give the following paragraphs as they follow each other on page 32. The innocence of these islanders implied in the first is well sustained, according to our author's opinion, in the second, where we find that very aged men have never crossed the confines of their native vale from a fear of being murdered!

How often is the term "savages" incorrectly applied! None really deserving of it were ever yet discovered by voyagers or by travellers. They have discovered heathens and barbarians, whom by horrible cruelties they have exasperated into savages. It may be asserted without fear of contradiction, that in all the cases of outrages committed by Polynesians, Europeans have at some time or other been the aggressors, and that *the cruel and bloodthirsty disposition of some of the islanders is mainly to be ascribed to the influence of such examples.*

But to return. Owing to the *mutual hostilities* of the different tribes I have mentioned, the mountainous tracts which separate their respective territories remain altogether uninhabited; the natives invariably dwelling in the depths of the valleys, with a view of securing themselves from the predatory incursions of their enemies, who often lurk along their borders, ready to cut off any imprudent straggler, or make a descent upon the inmates of some sequestered habitation. I several times met with *very aged men, who from this cause had never passed the confines of their native vale, some of them having never even ascended midway up the mountains in the whole course of their lives,* and who, accordingly, had little idea of the appearance of any other part of the island, the whole of which is not perhaps more than sixty miles in circuit. The little space in which some of these clans pass away their days would seem almost incredible.

It will be admitted by our readers that this is a charming picture of the innocent Typees, "among whom, without being clamorously invoked, virtue is unconsciously practised."—Vol. ii., p. 245.

This state of society dates back long years anterior to the visits of Captain Cook in 1774, or Marchand in 1789, or Lieut. Hergest, in the Daedalus, when on his voyage from the Falkland Islands to Hawaii, in 1792. These navigators having preceded the missionaries many years, the latter cannot be responsible any more than the former for this affection among the Marquesans. "Coming events cast their shadows before," and so we suppose Mr. Melville will attribute the "mutual hostilities" of the islanders to be the foreshadowing, through some magnetic sympathy, of the coming of the missionaries. The transient visit of Alvaro Mendano, in 1595, had probably long been forgotten by the Marquesans, as we find that the profound Kory-Kory, the royal Mehevi, and the gentle and incomparable FAYAWAY, were alike ignorant of that remarkable event.

We are inclined to doubt seriously whether our author ever saw the Marquesas; or, if he did, whether he ever resided among the Typees; or, if he did, whether this book is not a sort of romantic satire at the expense of the poor savages who are too far removed ever to give "TOMMO" the benefit of another *taupiti*, or feast. "Tommo"—for so our author ycleped himself for their unlettered convenience, the Polynesians being unable, in obedience to the genius of their dialects, to pronounce the liquid appellative of "Herman Melville"—"Tommo," gives such enthusiastic descriptions of their happiness and exemption from care, that we think he is a poor commentator upon his insatiable desire to escape from the abodes of bliss and return to the vices and miseries of civilization. We presume, however, this desire is covertly hinted at in the following paragraph:

> The term "Savage" is, I conceive, often misapplied, and indeed, when I consider the vices, cruelties, and enormities of every kind that spring up in the tainted atmosphere of a feverish civilisation, I am inclined to think that so far as the relative wickedness of the parties is concerned, four or five Marquesan Islanders sent to the United States as missionaries, might be quite as useful as an equal number of Americans despatched to the Islands in a similar capacity.

Were we to say his anxiety to return was only one of those evidences of incurable depravity fostered by Christianity among a civilized people, we might commit a mistake: we must therefore impute it to a zeal to act as one of "the four or five missionaries from the Marquesas to the United States." Native missionaries are generally the best pioneers in evangelising and enlightening a people; and here, American "Savage!" is one of our own countrymen, from the renowned valley of Typee in the Marquesas, who has sacrificed his happiness with an unparalleled devotion to your welfare to convert you to Typeeism! All hail! Apostle of Cannibalism!

Welcome, self-immolated herald of classic barbarism! Thou hast published the ritual, how soon shall we be initiated into the high masonry of savage enjoyment with the perpetual seal of the picturesque tattoo!

The worst feature of the book is the undisguised attempt to decry the missionary work in its every feature. Here is a paragraph which condenses the matter into a trifling compass:

> The naked wretch who shivers beneath the bleak skies, and starves among the inhospitable wilds of Terra-del-Fuego, might indeed be made happier by civilization, for it would alleviate his physical wants. But the voluptuous Indian, with every desire supplied, whom Providence has bountifully provided with all the sources of pure and natural enjoyment, and from whom are removed so many of the ills and pains of life—what has he to desire at the hands of Civilisation? She may "cultivate his mind,"—may "elevate his thoughts,"—these I believe are the established phrases—but will he be the happier? Let the once smiling and populous Hawaiian islands, with their now diseased, starving, and dying natives, answer the question. The missionaries may seek to disguise the matter as they will, but the facts are incontrovertible; and the devoutest Christian who visits that group with an unbiased mind, must go away mournfully asking—"Are these, alas! the fruits of twenty-five years of enlightening?"

There are several classes of men who compose the grand order of antagonists to missions. We roughly classify as follows:

1. The merchants, traders, speculators, and others, who go to the South Seas for the purpose of engaging in mercantile pursuits.

2. Masters and crews of whaling and trading vessels, who stop a day or two, or longer, at the islands, for supplies and refits.

3. Deserters from vessels of every description, of which class our author is a lively specimen.

4. Adventurers and passengers who are on their route to distant points, and who are prejudiced against religion anywhere.

5. Convicts escaped from Botany Bay and other parts of New South Wales.

These, it will be perceived, are all directly interested parties. Attracted by purely selfish motives, and often as reckless of virtue and as abandoned as the most depraved of the Polynesians, they find their schemes of aggrandizement at the expense of the ignorant tribes, or their gross and corrupt appetites checked by the presence of the missionary establishments, and the, at least partial, establishment of Christianity. Hence the continual and virulent attempts to throw *infamy* upon the laborers in the remote Pacific. We make one short quotation here in passing, to show that our author has given a true representation in one instance, of an evil universally complained of by all the missionaries:

> Our ship was now wholly given up to every species of riot and debauchery. The grossest licentiousness and the most shameful inebriety

prevailed, with occasional and but short-lived interruptions, through the whole period of her stay. Alas for the poor savages when exposed to the influence of these polluting examples! Unsophisticated and confiding, they are easily led into every vice, and humanity weeps over the ruin thus remorselessly inflicted upon them by their European civilizers. Thrice happy are they who, inhabiting some yet undiscovered island in the midst of the ocean, have never been brought into contaminating contact with the white man.—Vol. i., p. 17.

Had our romantic adventurer been as candid in regard to the rest of the South Sea Islands, he could not have thrown the burden of *"licentiousness and misery"* upon the bearers of the gospel. It will be remembered that a mission was commenced in the Marquesas by Mr. Crook, on the island of Tahuata, in 1798, but he was obliged to abandon it about a year afterwards. In 1825, another attempt was made, and in 1828 still another, by English missionaries, aided by native assistants; but owing to the ferocious and corrupt character of the tribes they were successively abandoned. In 1833, some American missionaries, a deputation from the Sandwich Islands, undertook a mission, but the following year they, too, were obliged to withdraw—the foreign and native teachers living under continual apprehension of being devoured by the irreclaimable savages. The Tahitians, taken to the Marquesas in 1825 by Mr. Crook, although accustomed to the corrupt and brutal life of a former heathenism, after laboring some time, were so disheartened with the horrible state of the islanders, that they abandoned the group in despair. Only two natives remained at the island of Uahou. A mission has been abandoned on the island of Nukuheva, where the licentious revelry above described occurred.

To prevent any charge of unfairness in our quotations, we give the following pencillings, which embody a full expression of the sentiments of the author. [Here follow twelve paragraphs of quotation citing the evils of missionary presence among the primitive peoples of the South Seas. The cited passages include the instance in which the red-faced wife of a missionary, to whom Melville sarcastically refers as a "paragon of humility," goads two naked natives who are harnessed to her carriage and draw her uphill like tired draft horses.]

With all these evils, if they exist, would Mr. Melville consent to have the Polynesians relapse again to what they were one hundred years since—withdraw the foreign population—recall the missionaries—burn up the Bible and the various works in the dialects of the Pacific—destroy the written languages, with the written constitutions, and abrogate codes of printed laws—rebuild the Maraes—reinstate the idols, Oro, Taaro, Tangaroa, and a thousand others—re-organize the Areoi—rekindle the sacred fires—slay new victims for sacrifice—and then join in celebrating the restoration of the Polynesians to their blissful condition, in a feast of a thousand human victims, moistened with an inspiriting draught of the oblivious ava? If not, Mr. Melville deserves the scorn of an intelligent community.

In the perusal of these volumes the reader would inevitably arrive at the conclusion that the presence and the influence of the missionaries are the predominant causes of all the deplorable evils of the South Sea Islands. If the missionary work had achieved nothing more, the abolition of the Areois, than whom a more loathsome and demoralizing band probably never existed—who swept the islands with a periodical pestilence of pollution and crime, would be reward for the labors of a quarter of a century; the abolition of infanticide would have been alone a splendid work—but these, with the extinction of the bloody rites, the impure orgies, and the thousand crimes of heathenism, are countless benefits resulting from the progress of Christianity. Says this remarkably consistent author on p. 245:

> The Areoi Society—one of the most *singular*(!) institutions that ever existed in any part of the world—spread universal licentiousness over the island. It was the voluptuous character of these people which rendered the disease introduced among them by De Bougainville's ships, in 1768, doubly destructive. It visited them like a plague, sweeping them off by hundreds.

Shades of all the classic anachronisms! 1768! Why, Mr. Melville, that was only *thirty years* before the first missionary doubled Cape Horn! and tradition does not furnish a date for the foundation of the Areoi! Do you not know that the good ship *Duff*, Capt. WILSON, did not reach Tahiti with its first band of missionaries until the 6th of March, 1797, when she anchored in the Bay of Matavai? Do you not know this was the deplorable condition of the Sandwich Islands when the American missionaries first rested there, in 1820, and which they have in some measure reformed? If the exaltation of these nations would be effected by the withdrawal of the missionaries, let us blot out Polynesia from our maps, and bid the elevating influence of heathenism restore the islanders to their "paradisaical condition." If Mr. Melville would not do this for the "ill-fated people," he has less of the milk of human kindness than his lachrymose whinings over their civilization would lead the reader to suppose.

We have no room to speak of the caricature he gives us of tea-parties, and the "red-faced" "paragon of humility." The reader can judge of the value of the author's observations, and make his own estimate of his claims for common truth and intelligence. For the "red-faced lady," we refer to OLMSTED's *"Incidents of a Whaling Voyage,"* where the popular custom is referred to, and to WILKES' *Exploring Expedition,* vol. iii. We see for ourselves no reason why public porters should not draw a cwt. of humanity as well as a cwt. of goods, if circumstances make it expedient. But why need our author go to the Pacific to find "evangelized draught-horses?" He may find them every day in front of nursery-wagons—even young girls dragging the children of their employers through the streets! He may find "civilized beasts of burden," in the shape of public porters, drawing heavily loaded hand-carts after them in every city of the United States! Why, we even recollect when the evangelized and refined citizens of Baltimore took a pair of elegant draught horses from the carriage of a foreign *danseuse* of somewhat questionable reputation, and "harnessing" some hundreds to it, actually dragged the "*divine* Fanny" through the streets of that refined city! We venture a modest opinion that, had our author been present, he would have volunteered a prominent position as a draught-*horse* (?) on that occasion. But the whole thing is too contemptible to notice, were it not that it seems to have some weight in the minds of readers, as though the Hawaiians had been *evangelized into draught-horses for their spiritual instructors alone.* Better to earn a subsistence by industry as porters than to slaughter and devour each other!

The little coral villas which excite the author's jealousy in contrast with the residences of the natives, are necessary. They are an advanced standard which the natives are encouraged to reach—and although the work must be slow, it will probably be finally attained. Were it not for the men who visit and frequent these seas and impede the progress, the work of evangelizing would be synonymous with civilizing the people. To elevate nations of indolent barbarians in one generation from the depths of brutalization to a civilized, faultless, and industrious community, will not be realized in this world; it is a progressive work—painful and laborious—and from the nature of the case must be slow and toilsome. To change the intellectual and moral character of savages is not the work of a day. Capt. WILKES says, vol. ii., p. 12,

> No one can visit the islands without perceiving on every side the most positive evidence of the great benefits they [the missionaries] have already bestowed, and are daily conferring upon the inhabitants.

We have one brief answer in the words of the MARTYR MISSIONARY, WILLIAMS, in his remarks on *Raratonga:*

> The graceful foliage of the banana, young bread fruit, and cocoa-nut trees, by which they are surrounded, invests our premises with an appearance of neatness and elegance. *It was my determination when I originally left England to have as respectable a dwelling as I could erect;* for the missionary does not go to barbarize himself, but to civilize the heathen. He ought not, therefore, to sink down to their standard, but to elevate them to his.—*Miss. Enterprises*, p. 429.

Capt. Wilkes, whom we must select from a host of witnesses, and who had frequent opportunities of becoming familiar, by his protracted visits to many of the groups of islands, with the missionaries and their labors, says in his remarks on Tahiti (the Italics are our own),

All this good has been done in the face of many and great difficulties. The most serious of these is the evil influence of the other foreign residents. Although among these are some who are truly respectable, the majority is made up of runaways from the English convict settlements, and *deserters from vessels.* These men, the outcasts and refuse of every maritime nation, are addicted to every description of vice, and would be a pest even in a civilized community. It may easily be conceived what an injurious influence such a band of vagabonds, without trade or occupation by which they can support themselves, guilty of every species of profanity and crime, must exert upon the morals of the natives, and what a barrier they must oppose to their improvement in morals and religion.

Tahiti, *when first visited,* was proverbial for its licentiousness, and it would be asking too much to require that, after so short an enjoyment of the means of instruction, and in the face of such obstacles, its inhabitants should, as a body, have become patterns of good morals. Licentiousness does still exist among them, but the foreign residents and visitors are in a great degree the cause of its continuance, and an unbridled intercourse with them serves to perpetuate it. Severe laws have been enacted, but they cannot be put in force in cases where one of the parties is a foreigner. I see no reason, however, why this island should be pointed out as conspicuous for licentiousness. When compared with other parts of the world that arrogate a superior civilization, it appears almost in an advantageous light. Vice, at any rate, does not stalk abroad in the open day, as it did in some places we had lately visited upon the American continent. It would be unfair to judge of these natives before they had received instruction, by our rules of propriety; and now many of those who bear testimony to the laxity of their morals, visit their shores for the very purpose of enticing them into guilt, and of rioting without fear or hindrance in debauchery. Coming with such intentions, and finding themselves checked by the influence of the missionaries, they rail against them because they have put an end to the obscene dances and games of the natives, and procured the enactment of laws forbidding illicit intercourse.—*Narrative of the Exploring Expedition,* vol. ii., pp. 12–13.

I cannot pass without notice, the untiring efforts of many of the foreign residents to disparage the missionaries and vilify the natives. They endeavor on all occasions to prepossess the minds of visitors against both. These efforts, however, generally fail of success; for no reflecting mind can fail to perceive how devoid they are of any foundation, nor avoid noticing the baneful effects these residents are themselves producing, by inculcating principles for which many of them have been compelled to fly their own countries, or teaching the practice of crimes from whose penalty they have made their escape.—*Ex. Expedition,* vol. ii., p. 13.

We recommend Capt. Wilkes' Narrative to the author of Typee, where he will doubtless find a portrait photographed from life, which he will be able instantly to recognize.

We are not "bigoted," although we are by anticipation placed in that category by our adventurer. "Facts are facts, and will remain such, notwithstanding all that the bigoted and incredulous may write to the contrary." In an appendix, which is the refined essence of all that is mean and hateful, he says:

> It is needless to rehearse all the abuse that for some time previous to the spring of 1843 had been heaped upon the British residents, especially upon Captain Charlton, her Britannic Majesty's consul-general, by the native authorities of the Sandwich Islands. High in the favor of the imbecile king at this time was one Dr. Judd, a sanctimonious apothecary adventurer, who, with other kindred and influential spirits, were animated by an inveterate dislike to England. The ascendancy of a junto of ignorant and designing Methodist elders in the councils of a half-civilized king, ruling with absolute sway over a nation just poised between barbarism and civilization, and exposed by the peculiarities of its relations with foreign states to unusual difficulties, was not precisely calculated to impart a healthy tone to the policy of the government.

Capt. Wilkes' position as an official representative of the United States government, afforded him facilities of observation and opportunities for inquiry which enabled him to arrive at a candid opinion after hearing every complaint and statement, from every party, of every complexion and pursuit. Of the events which transpired at Tahiti, he says:

> Much complaint has been made of the influence which the missionaries, and Mr. Pritchard in particular, exercise over the government. They have, unquestionably, great influence; BUT I AM SATISFIED THAT THEY ARE JUSTLY ENTITLED TO IT. *Indeed, I cannot but consider it as part of their duty, nay,* THE GREAT OBJECT OF THEIR MISSION, to acquire and exercise a salutary control over their converts, both of high and low degree.— WILKES' *Narrative*, vol. ii., p. 12.

Once more, concerning the Sandwich Islands. When speaking of the difficulties with Laplace, he says:

> The foreigners, both residents and missionaries, keep aloof from him [the king], although now was a juncture at which the true friends of this people might have acted to advantage, by stepping forward in support of the laws under which they lived. *They cannot be too much blamed for* [their neglect], &c. THE MISSIONARIES, IN PARTICULAR, LOST A GLORIOUS OPPORTUNITY. (!!)—*Ex. Expedition*, vol. iv., p. 17.

Our space will not permit extracts from Byron's Narrative of visits to many of the Polynesian Islands, in the Blonde, in 1824–5; of Capt. Waldegrave, in the Seringapatam, and a host of others, whose responsibilities pledged them to candor, and we must pass them by. Among the latest authorities, however, and contemporaneous with the Residence in Typee, we mention "Darwin's Voyage of a Naturalist," and Russell's Polynesia, for a lucid condensation of many valuable facts. These and other merely scientific and historical works are of interest and value with reference to a fair view of the missionary work.

Capt. Wilkes again, in reference to the difficulties between foreigners and the government, in which he introduces those of English vessels of war, makes these declarations;

> In this state of things it became evident to the king and chiefs that they were in want of information in regard to international law, and they in consequence desired to obtain a competent person to give them advice on that subject. For this purpose they endeavored to procure a suitable counsellor from the United States. Failing in this attempt, they requested Rev. Mr. Richards, one of the missionaries, to undertake this duty.
>
> The missionaries, as a body, seem to have thought it a duty to abstain from meddling with any temporal matters, but Mr. Richards was prevailed upon to serve. As respects the internal policy of the island, no better guide could have been chosen. But, like the missionaries, he was but little versed, and had no experience in the affairs of government. He was unused to the petty squabbling of foreign officials, and his mind was far above the ignoble task of disputing with the revilers of all law and religion.
>
> I had the pleasure of becoming intimately acquainted with Mr. Richards in his private capacity, and enjoyed an opportunity of judging as to the manner in which he performed his public functions; and I cannot but felicitate the government and people of Hawaii upon their fortune in obtaining the services of one who has made such exertions in their behalf, and who is so well qualified for the responsible position he holds.
>
> Mr. Richards had, as a missionary, been for some years a resident of these islands, and was thus in close connection with the king and chiefs in their spiritual concerns. That they should have desired his counsel in their temporal affairs, is a strong proof of the affection and esteem with which they regarded him, and is alike creditable to their character and the soundness of their judgment. It was not, however, to be received as an evidence of any undue influence of the missionaries in political questions; and from a close examination I am satisfied that no such influence exists.

If anything more positive is required, the following will probably reach the point. It is extracted from the correspondence between P. A. BRINSMADE, U. S. Commercial Agent at the Hawaiian group, and Kamehameha III.

U. S. CONSULATE,
SANDWICH ISLANDS, Oct. 26, 1839.

As the opinion seems to be to some extent entertained that American citizens residing in the Sandwich Islands as missionaries, under the patronage of an incorporated institution in the United States, have exerted a controlling influence upon the framers of the laws of this country, I have very respectfully to inquire if they have ever had any voice in the passage of laws affecting the interests of other foreigners, and particularly whether they have ever had anything to do in the measures adopted by your government for the prevention of the introduction of the Catholic religion into your country; and whether, in the treatment which has been shown to any subject of the government of France, they have directly or indirectly recommended the course pursued by your govern-ment?   *   *   P. A. BRINSMADE.

To this the king replied, under date of Oct. 28th, in a letter, from which we must only quote as follows:

I have received your letter asking questions respecting the American missionaries, supposed by some to regulate the acts of my government under me; I, together with the chiefs under me, now declare to you that we do not see anything in which your questions are applicable to the American missionaries. From the time the missionaries first arrived, they have asked liberty to dwell in these islands. Communicating instructions in letters and delivering the word of God has been their business. * * * * *
But that thing which you speak to me of, that they act with us, or overrule our acts, we deny it; it is not so.   KAMEHAMEHA III.

The correspondence in full may be found in the appendix to "Jarves' History of the Sandwich Islands."

It is enough. We regret that our limits prevent our entering farther into the details of the various questions relating to the "temporal destruction" of the Polynesians, charged by our author to the account of the missionary establishments in the Pacific. We reserve these for future consideration.

For the rest, we must content ourselves with saying that he is either unfortunately ignorant, or barely worthy of that civilization which has alone been the means of preserving him from being made a sacrifice upon the altar of a bloody superstition.

Here is a gentle palliative for cannibalism:

Cannibalism to a certain moderate extent is practised among several of the primitive tribes in the Pacific, but it is upon the bodies of slain enemies alone; and horrible and fearful as the custom is, immeasurably as it is to be abhorred and condemned, still I assert that those who indulge in it are in other respects humane and virtuous.—p. 262.

If Mr. Melville's idea of humanity and virtue were to be measured by his regard for facts, we would be sufficiently curious to see his system of ethics. Doubtless the Areoi Society would be the legitimate expounders of the canon law of such a system—while the infanticide which universally prevailed prior to the introduction of the gospel, would be the highest and most authoritative evidence of their humanity. One chief of Raiatea, at a public meeting in 1824, bitterly mourned while he confessed he had destroyed *nineteen* children. Three women of whom Mr. Williams speaks, had destroyed *twenty-one* between them—while another mother on her death-bed confessed to the slaughtering of *sixteen* children. The "humane and virtuous" lives of depraved and polluted cannibals!

On the 11th of February, 1840, Messrs. Hunt and Lythe, with their ladies, missionaries to Carolib or Goat Island, were witnesses to a cannibal entertainment. The circumstances are briefly these: The king had sent a servant to Lauthala, and a quarrel arising, he was killed. An order was given to attack the town, when, according to some reports, *three hundred,* according to others, *thirty* persons, without respect to age, sex, or condition, were slain and eaten on the spot. *Eleven* bodies were brought to the king's square, immediately in front of the missionaries' dwelling. *Mr. Hunt stood within his garden fence and saw the bodies distributed, and one cut up and cooked within two or three yards of it,* and eaten—Wilkes' *Narrative,* vol. iii., 153, 155. This is being *"primitive"* with a *witness!*

The following tragic events recently transpired in Viti Levui, the principal island of the Feejee group, between Ambua, Mbua, or Bau and Rewa districts. Rev. John Marston gives these among other facts:

> We have found that the cruelties and cannibalism of Feejee exceed all the description which has been given; not one half has been told. The whole cannot be told. The war between Bau and Rewa is still carried on. Some towns have been burned, and many persons have been killed and eaten, since we last wrote; and it is more than probable that hundreds more will follow them ere the war terminates. At Bau, perhaps, more human beings are eaten than anywhere else. A few weeks ago they ate twenty-eight in one day. They had seized their wretched victims while fishing, and brought them alive to Bau, and there half-killed them, and then put them into their ovens. Some of them made several vain attempts to escape from the scorching flame. It makes our hearts bleed to hear of their fiend-like cruelty; and we pray God, and beseech the Christian world to pray with us, that the wickedness of this cruel people may soon come to an end.

The above specimens of "moderation" among the anthropophagi need not be followed by an account of the murder of Rev. John Williams and his colleague Harris, on the 20th of November, 1839, and the subsequent events at Erromanga.

Some of our readers will perhaps be surprised at our review of "Typee: or Residence in the Marquesas." It is matter of surprise to us that such a work could have obtained the name of Lemuel Shaw, and such a press as that of Wiley & Putnam. The author manifests a palpable ignorance in regard to every question of interest, and redeems that feature by laying his tribute upon the altar of cannibal felicity and barbaric society. He looks at the savage life with a captivated eye, and seals his approbation with a constant phrenzy to be freed from this happy vale—being in almost daily fear of finding himself hashed in the most approved style of Typee epicurean rites, or tenderly roasted and served up in calabashes for "the regal and noble Mehevi" and his chiefs!

We have borne with the pretensions of this book as though it were a narrative of real events. It may be, and likely is, though somewhat highly colored. But whether true or false, the real or pseudonymic author deserves a pointed and severe rebuke for his flagrant outrages against civilization, and particularly the missionary work. The abuse he heaps upon the latter belongs to the vagabonds, fugitives, convicts, and deserters of every grade—and there let it rest. We have meditated nothing in a spirit of harshness or "bigotry." We have sought only to present the other side of the case to the public, with the hope of rendering at least a little service to the cause of truth; while we regret that a book possessed of such high merit in other respects, should have been made the vehicle of so many prejudiced misstatements concerning missions.

We purpose on some future occasion to take a view of the present state of the missionary work, and what is needed to make it more efficient and exceptionless than it is, and shall endeavor to give every side a fair hearing. We shall probably give Typee a glance among the authorities, as a specimen of that genus of writers whose poetry and poetic feelings lead them to admire only what is savage, and condemn, under assumed pretexts, the ripening fruit of the gospel of Christ. The author having anticipated and challenged investigation, will doubtless duly appreciate our pains-taking in comparing his statements with the contemporaneous reports of Capt. Wilkes and other authorities.

[From "The Island Nukuheva"]

William Ellery Channing [the Younger]*

In that sweet vale where Nature serves her lord,
The land is equal, sounds no Tyrant's word;
Upon the doors no padlocks shall you see,
The Warrior's spear stands out against the tree,
The maiden's brooch hangs careless from the roof,
The door is open, but the heart is proof.
There is no prison, neither fence nor road,
The land is but the man's desired abode,
What there is worth is freely shared by all,
No man is sad, and life a festival.
Within the forests ne'er the Lion's hum,
No wild beasts from the mountain-deserts come,
No snakes crawl hissing o'er the fruitful ground,
But sportive lizards golden-hued abound,
And purple-azure birds flit freely by,
Or crimson, white, and black, and gold come nigh,
Fly not at man's approach, and fear no harm,
Sometimes alight upon the extended arm,
But trill no reedy notes in those high woods,
Silent save roar of Falls those solitudes.

And in this happy vale the "Taboo" rites,
Cast a religious awe o'er many sites,
And feasts of Calabash are freely set,
In "Hoolah-Hoolah" grounds the men are met;
The delicate fair maids are all forbid
To enter there, and cannot be Priest-rid.

---

*Reprinted from William Ellery Channing, *Poems, Second Series* (Boston: James Munroes, 1847), pp. 144–52. This selection, taken from pp. 151–52, excerpts the most significant rather than the most representative portion of the poem. Of nine tedious pages of heroic couplets, seven are devoted to the paradisiac and picturesque aspects of the South Seas: *Typee* as exotic travelogue; for Channing, as for many of the book's contemporary readers, that clearly was the charm and point of the book. However, as the last one and one half pages of the poem indicate (reprinted here), even the devotees of travelogue sensed that there was something more than guidebook material in the volume.

Ah! lovely vale, why art thou called that name,
The land of Cannibals,—did nature tame
Thy happy groups, and Paradise make thee
In some forgetful moment, savagely
Turning, and for her frolics bid thee eat
Her Happar children, yon the mountain's feet?

Marquesan Melville

H. S. Salt*

Has America a literature? I am inclined to think it a grave mistake to argue seriously with those afflicted persons who periodically exercise themselves over this idlest of academic questions. It is wiser to meet them with a practical counter-thrust, and pointedly inquire, for example, whether they are familiar with the writings of Herman Melville. Whereupon, confusion will in most cases ensue, and you will go on to suggest that to criticise "Hamlet," with the prince's part omitted, would be no whit more fatuous than to demonstrate the non-existence of an American literature, while taking no account of its true intellectual giants. When it was announced, a few months ago, that "Mr. Herman Melville, the author," had just died in New York at the age of seventy-two, the news excited but little interest on this side of the Atlantic; yet, forty years ago, his name was familiar to English, as to American readers, and there is little or no exaggeration in Robert Buchanan's remark, that he is "the one great imaginative writer fit to stand shoulder to shoulder with Whitman on that continent."

It was in 1846 that Melville fairly took the world by storm with his "Typee: the Narrative of a four months' residence in the Marquesas Islands," the first of a brilliant series of volumes of adventure, in which reality was so deftly encircled with a halo of romance that readers were at once captivated by the force and freshness of the style and puzzled as to the personality of the author. Who and what was this mysterious sojourner in the far islands of the Pacific—this "Marquesan Melville," as a writer in *Blackwood* denominated him? Speculation was rife, and not unaccompanied by suspicion; for there were some critics who not only questioned the veracity of Herman Melville's "Narratives," but declared his very name to be fictitious. "Separately," remarked one sagacious reviewer, "the names are not uncommon; we can urge no valid reason against their juncture; yet in this instance they fall suspiciously on our ear."

Herman Melville, however, was far from being a mythical personage, though in his early life, as in his later, he seems to have instinc-

*Reprinted from *Gentleman's Magazine*, 272 (March, 1892), 248–57. This selection is taken from pp. 248–55.

tively shrunk from any other publicity than that which was brought him by his books. He was a genuine child of nature, a sort of nautical George Borrow, on whom the irresistible sea-passion had descended in his boyhood, and won him away from the ordinary routine of respectable civilised life, until, to quote his own words, to travel had become a necessity of his existence, "a way of driving off the spleen and regulating the circulation." The son of a cultured American merchant, of Scotch extraction, he had early imbibed from his father's anecdotes a romantic attachment to the sea. "Of winter evenings," he says, "by the well-remembered sea-coal fires in old Greenwich Street, New York, he used to tell my brother and me of the monstrous waves at sea, mountain-high, and of the masts bending like twigs." At the age of eighteen, his father having died in bankruptcy, he found himself unexpectedly face to face with poverty and disappointment, and was forced to embark as a common seaman in a merchant vessel bound to Liverpool, a voyage of disillusionment and bitter experience, of which he has left us what is apparently an authentic record in one of his early volumes.[1]

Returned from this expedition, he essayed for a time to gain a quiet livelihood as a teacher. But destiny and his natural genius had willed it otherwise; it was no academic lecture-room, but the deck of a whale-ship, that was to be "his Yale College and his Harvard." "Oh, give me again the rover's life," he exclaims, "the joy, the thrill, the whirl! Let me feel thee again, old sea! Let me leap into thy saddle once more! I am sick of these *terra firma* toils and cares, sick of the dust and reek of towns. Let me snuff thee up, sea-breeze, and whinny in thy spray!" So in 1841 the child of nature was again aboard, and off to the Pacific on a whaler; and it was the adventures that befell him, during this absence of nearly four years' duration, that subsequently furnished the material for the chief series of his volumes. In "Typee" he related the story of his romantic captivity among a tribe of noble savages in the Marquesas; in "Omoo" we have his further wanderings in the Society and Sandwich Islands; in "White Jacket," his return voyage as a common sailor in a man-of-war. "Mardi," on the other hand, is a phantasy, in which the imaginative element, having slipped from the control of the narrative, runs riot in the wildest and most extravagant luxuriance.

"Typee" must be regarded as, on the whole, the most charming of Melville's writings, and the one which may most surely count on lasting popularity; it is certainly the masterpiece of his earlier period, during which the artistic sense was still predominant over those transcendental tendencies which characterised his later volumes. Coming at a time when men's minds were filled with a vague, undefined interest in the wonders of the Pacific, and when the French annexation of Tahiti, of which Melville was an eyewitness, had drawn universal attention to that quarter of the globe, it gained an instantaneous and wide-spread success, both in America and England, and was quickly translated into several European tongues. Alike in the calm beauty of its descriptive passages, and in the intense vividness of its character-sketches, it was, and is, and must ever be, a most powerful and fascinating work. Indeed, I think I speak within the mark in saying that nothing better of its kind is to be found in English literature, so firm and clear is it in outline, yet so dreamily suggestive in the dim mystic atmosphere which pervades it. Here is a passage from one of the early chapters, itself as rhythmical as the rhythmical drifting of the whaler "Dolly" under the trade-winds of the Pacific:

> The sky presented a clear expanse of the most delicate blue, except along the skirts of the horizon, where you might see a thin drapery of pale clouds which never varied their form or colour. The long, measured, dirge-like swell of the Pacific came rolling along with its surface broken by little tiny waves, sparkling in the sunshine. Every now and then a shoal of flying fish, scared from the water under the bows, would leap into the air, and fall the next moment like a shower of silver into the sea. Then you would see the superb albicore, with his glittering sides, sailing aloft, and, often describing an arc in his descent, disappear on the surface of the water. Far off, the lofty jet of the whale might be seen, and nearer at hand the prowling shark, that villainous foot-pad of the seas, would come skulking along, and at a wary distance regard us with his evil eye. At times some shapeless monster of the deep, floating on the surface, would, as we approached, sink slowly into the blue waters, and fade away from the sight. But the most impressive feature of the scene was the almost un broken silence that reigned over sky and water. Scarcely a sound could be heard but the occasional breathing of the grampus and the rippling at the cutwater.

And Typee itself, the scene of Melville's detention, when he and a companion sailor had deserted from the whale-ship—what a fairyland of tropical valleys, and crystal streams, and groves of cocoa-palms and bread-fruit trees, is here magically depicted for us! How life-like the portraiture of the innocent, placid, happy islanders, who, albeit cannibals at times, were yet far superior to civilised nations in many of the best qualities by which civilisation is supposed to be distinguished! And Fayaway—surely never was Indian maiden so glorified by poet or romancer[2] as is the gentle, beautiful, faithful Fayaway in Melville's marvellous tale! The strongest and tenderest pictures that George Borrow has drawn for us of his friendly relations with the wandering gipsy-folk by roadside or dingle are not more strong and tender than Melville's reminiscences of this "peep at Polynesian life." As Borrow possessed the secret of winning the confidence of the gipsies, so Melville, by the same talisman of utter simplicity and naturalness, was able to fraternise in perfect good fellowship with the so-called savages of the Pacific.

It is, furthermore, significant that Melville's familiarity with these "noble savages" was productive of a feeling the very opposite of contempt; he bears repeated and explicit testimony to the enviable healthfulness and happiness of the uncivilised society in which he so-journed so long. "The continual happiness," he says, "which, so far as I was able to judge, appeared to prevail in the valley, sprung principally from that all-pervading sensation which Rousseau has told us he at one time experienced, the mere buoyant sense of a healthful, physical existence. And indeed, in this particular, the Typees had ample reason to felicitate themselves, for sickness was almost unknown. During the whole period of my stay, I saw but one invalid among them; and on their smooth, clear skins you observed no blemish or mark of disease." Still more emphatic is his tribute to their moral qualities. "Civilisation does not engross all the virtues of humanity: she has not even her full share of them. . . . If truth and justice, and the better principles of our nature, cannot exist unless enforced by the statute-book, how are we to account for the social condition of the Typees? So pure and upright were they in all the relations of life, that entering their valley, as I did, under the most erroneous impressions of their character, I was soon led to exclaim in amazement: Are these the ferocious savages, the blood-thirsty cannibals, of whom I have heard such frightful tales! . . . I will frankly declare that after passing a few weeks in this valley of the Marquesas, I formed a higher estimate of human nature than I had ever before entertained. But, alas! since then I have been one of the crew of a man-of-war, and the pent-up wickedness of five hundred men has nearly overturned all my previous theories."

But here it may be asked by later, as by earlier readers, "Was Melville's narrative a true one? Is his testimony on these subjects a testimony of any scientific value?" The answer to this question, despite the suspicion of the critics, is a decided affirmative. Not only is Melville's account of Typee in close agreement with that of earlier voyagers, as, for example, Captain Porter's "Journal of a Cruise to the Pacific Ocean," published in 1822, but it has been expressly corroborated by later adventurers. "I cannot resist," wrote an American naval officer,[3] "paying the faint tribute of my own individual admiration to Mr. Melville. Apart from the innate beauty and charming tone of his narratives, the delineations of island life and scenery, from my own personal observation, are most correctly and faithfully drawn." Another witness, who has recently been cited, was the Rev. Titus Coan, of the Hawaiian Islands, who "had personally visited the Marquesas group, found the Typee valley, and verified in every detail the romantic descriptions of the gentle but man-devouring islanders."[4]

After the publication of "Typee" Melville married the daughter of Chief Justice Shaw, to whom the book was dedicated, and made his home, from 1850 to 1863, in an old spacious farmhouse at Pittsfield, Massachusetts, commanding picturesque views of Greylock and the other Berkshire mountains. He was here a neighbour of Nathaniel Hawthorne, who was then living at Lenox, and there are records of many friendly intimacies between the two authors, whose intellects were in many ways akin. We read in the Hawthorne diaries of "Mr. Omoo's visits," and how he came accompanied by "his great dog," and how he held transcendental conversations with Hawthorne "about time and eternity, things of this world and of the next, and books, and publishers, and all possible and impossible matters, that lasted pretty deep into the night." It is during this residence at Pittsfield, the adventurous struggles of his early life being now concluded, that we note the commencement of the second, the transcendental period of Melville's literary career. It has been truly said of him that "he had all the metaphysical tendencies which belong so eminently to the American mind;" and it is interesting to observe in this, as in other cases, the conjunction of the practical with the metaphysical temperament. "The chief characteristic of Herman Melville's writings"— so I have elsewhere remarked[5]—"is this attempted union of the practical with the ideal. Commencing with a basis of solid fact, he loves to build up a fantastic structure, which is finally lost in the cloudland of metaphysical speculation."

As "Typee" is the best production of the earlier and simpler phase of Melville's authorship, so undoubtedly is "The Whale" (or "Moby Dick," as it is sometimes styled) the crown and glory of the later phase; less shapely and artistic than "Typee," it far surpasses it in immensity of scope and triumphant energy of execution.[6] It is in "The Whale" that we see Melville casting to the winds all conventional restrictions, and rioting in the prodigality of his imaginative vigour. . . .

The increasing transcendentalism of Melville's later thought was accompanied and reflected by a corresponding complexity of language, the limpid simplicity so remarkable in "Typee" and "Omoo," and "White Jacket" being now succeeded by a habit of gorgeous and fantastic word-painting, which, though brilliantly effective at its best, degenerated, at its worst, into mere bombast and rhetoric, a process which had already been discernible in the concluding portions of "Mardi," while in "Pierre" (or "The Ambiguities," as it was appropriately designated) it reached the fatal climax of its development. This unfortunate book, published in 1852, was to a great extent the ruin of its author's reputation; for the critics not unfairly protested against the perversity of "a man born to create, who resolves to anatomise; a man born to see, who insists upon speculating." Of "The Confidence Man" (1857), and Melville's later books in general, it is not necessary to speak; though it is noticeable that in his narrative of "Israel Potter" (1855), and one or two of the short stories in "The Piazza Tales" (1856), he partly recovered his old firmness of touch and delicacy of workmanship.

For, in spite of all the obscurities and mannerisms which confessedly deform his later writings, it remains true that *naturalness* is, on the whole, Melville's prime characteristic, both in the tone and in the style of his productions. His narratives are as racy and vigorous as those of Defoe or Smollett or Marryat; his character-sketches are such as only a man of keen observation, and as keen a sense of humour, could have realised and depicted. His seamen and his seacaptains all, his savages ashore or aboard, from the noble unsophisticated Mehevi in "Typee" to the semi-civilised comical Queequeg in "The Whale," are admirably vivid and impressive, and the reader who shall once have made their acquaintance will thenceforward in no wise be persuaded that they are not real and living personages. Moreover, there is a large-souled humanity in Melville—the direct outcome of his generous, emotional, yet uniformly sane temperament—which differentiates him entirely from the mere artist or *littérateur*. "I stand for the heart," he writes, in one of his letters to Nathaniel Hawthorne, a statement fully substantiated by the many humane sentiments that find expression in his pages, whether on the subject of modern warfare, or negro slavery, or the barbarities of naval discipline, or the cruel treatment of the harmless "savages" of the Pacific by the more savage apostles of "civilisation." For the rest of it, Melville appears as a frank, simple believer in common human nature, and so little a respecter of persons that his democracy was described by Hawthorne as "ruthless." "With no son of man," says Melville, "do I stand upon any etiquette or ceremony, except the Christian ones of charity and honesty . . . . A thief in jail is as honourable a personage as General George Washington."

It may be surmised that this uncompromising attitude was scarcely calculated to win the favour of society. A friend who visited Melville at Pittsfield described him as an Ishmael who was "apparently considered by the good people of Pittsfield as little better than a cannibal or a beachcomber." "In vain," he says,[7] "I sought to hear of Typee and those Paradise islands; he preferred to pour forth his philosophy and his theories of life. The shade of Aristotle arose like a cold mist between myself and Fayaway. But what a talk it was! Melville is transformed from a Marquesan to a gipsy student, the gipsy element still remaining strong in him. And this contradiction gives him the air of one who has suffered from opposition, both literary and social." . . .

Notes

1. *Redburn, his First Voyage: Being the Sailor-boy Confessions and Reminiscences of the Son of a Gentleman in the Merchant Service*, 1849.

2. Unless it be Paquita, in Joaquin Miller's *Life among the Modocs*.

3. Lieut. Wise, in *Los Gringos*, a volume of travels published in 1849.

4. For this and other particulars I am indebted to the courtesy of Mr. Arthur Stedman of New York, the friend and literary executor of Herman Melville.

5. *Art Review*, November 1889.

6. *The Whale* was dedicated to Hawthorne, and is referred to in his "Wonder Book." "On the hither side of Pittsfield sits Herman Melville, shaping out the gigantic conception of his 'White Whale,' while the gigantic shadow of Greylock looms upon him from his study window."

7. Dr. Titus Coan's letter, quoted in the *New York World's* obituary notice of Melville.

[Noble Savages]

Raymond M. Weaver*

Literature was, of course, already elaborated with fantastic patterns drawn from barbarism, and the Indians of Aphra Behn and Voltaire had given place to the redmen of Cooper. Earlier than this, however, the great discoverers, in their wealth of records, had given many an account of their contacts with savage peoples. But one searches in vain among these records for any very vivid sense that the savage and the Christian belong to the same order of nature. At best, one gathers the impression that in savagery God's image had been multiplied in an excess of contemptible counterfeits. Melville reports that as late as his day "wanton acts of cruelty are not unusual on the part of sea captains landing at islands comparatively unknown. Indeed, it is almost incredible, the light in which many sailors regard these naked heathens. They hardly consider them human. But it is a curious fact, that the more ignorant and degraded men are, the more contemptuously they look upon those whom they deem their inferiors." John G. Paton records in his *Autobiography* how, in 1860, three traders gleefully told him that to humble the natives of Tanna, and to diminish their numbers, they had let out on shore at different ports, four men ill with the measles—an exceedingly virulent disease among savage peoples. "Our watchwords are," these jolly traders said, " 'sweep the creatures into the sea, and let white men occupy the soil.' " This sentiment belongs more to a fixed human type, than to a period, of course: and that type has frequently taken to sailing strange seas. In treachery, cruelty, and profligacy, the exploits of European discoverers contain some of the rosiest pages in the history of villainy.

These sickening pages of civilised barbarism soon won to the savage ardent apologists, however, who applied an old technique of libel by imputing to the unbreeched heathen a touching array of the superior virtues. Montaigne was among the first to come forward in this capacity. "We may call them barbarous in regard to reasons rules," he said, "but not in respect to us that exceed them in all kinde of barbarisme. Their warres are noble and generous, and have as much excuse and beautie, as this humane

*Reprinted from Raymond M. Weaver, *Herman Melville, Mariner and Mystic* (New York: George H. Doran, 1921), pp. 203–14, by permission of Sidney A. Burrell.

infirmitie may admit: they ayme at nought so much, and have no other foundation amongst them, but the meere jelousie of vertue." Once in full current of idealisation Montaigne goes on to write as if he soberly believed that savage peoples were descended from a stock that Eve had conceived by an angel before the fall. In his dithyramb on the nobilities of savagery, Montaigne was unhampered by any first-hand dealings with savages, and he was far too wise ever to betray the remotest inclination to improve his state by migrating into the bosom of their uncorrupted nobility.

The myth of the "noble savage" was a taking conceit, however, and when Rousseau taught the world the art of reverie, he taught it also an easy vagabondage into the virgin forest and into the pure heart of the "natural man." In describing Rousseau's influence on the drawing rooms, Taine says that "The fops dreamed between two madrigals of the happiness of sleeping naked in the virgin forest." Rousseau's savage, "attached to no place, having no prescribed task, obeying no one, having no other law than his own will," was, of course, a wilful backward glance to the vanished paradise of childhood, not a finding of ethnology. Yet ethnology may prate as it will, the "noble savage" is a myth especially diverting to the over-sophisticated, and like dreams of the virgin forest, thrives irrepressibly among the upholsterings of civilisation. The soft and ardent dreamer, no less than the sleek and parched imagination of Main Street, find compensation for the defeats of civilisation in dreams of a primitive Arcadia. While the kettle is boiling they relax into slippers and make the grand tour. Chateaubriand—whose life, according to Lemaître, was a "magnificent series of attitudes"—showed incredible hardihood of attitudinising in crossing the Atlantic in actual quest of the primitive. In the forest west of Albany he did pretend to find some satisfaction in wild landscape. He showed his "intoxication" at the beauties of wild nature by taking pains to do "various wilful things that made my guide furious." But Chateaubriand was less fortunate in his contact with savagery than he was with nature. His first savages he found under a shed taking dancing lessons from a little Frenchman, who, "bepowdered and befrizzled" was scraping on a pocket fiddle to the prancings of "ces messieurs sauvages et ces dames sauvagesses." Chateaubriand concludes with a reflection: "Was it not a crushing circumstance for a disciple of Rousseau?" And it is an indubitable fact that if the present-day disciples of the South Sea myth would show Chateaubriand's hardihood and migrate to Polynesia, they would find themselves in circumstances no less "crushing."

Melville was the first competent literary artist to write with authority about the South Seas. In his day, a voyage to those distant parts was a jaunt not lightly to be undertaken. In the Pacific there were islands to be discovered, islands to be annexed, and whales to be lanced. As for the incidental savage life encountered in such enterprise, that, in Montaigne's phrase, was there to be bastardised, by applying it to the pleasures of our corrupted taste. These attractions of whaling and patriotism—with incidental rites to Priapus—had tempted more than one man away from the comfort of his muffins, and more than one returned to give an inventory of the fruits of the temptation. The knowledge that these men had of Polynesia was ridiculously slight: the regular procedure was to shoot a few cannibals, to make several marriages after the manner of Loti. The result is a monotonous series of reports of the glorious accomplishments of Christians: varied on occasions with lengthy and learned dissertations on heathendom. But they are invariably writers with insular imagination, telling us much of the writer, but never violating the heart of Polynesia.

The Missionaries, discreetly scandalised at the exploitation of unholy flesh, went valiantly forth to fight the battle of righteousness in the midst of the enemy. The missionaries came to be qualified by long first-hand contact to write intimately of the heathen: but their records are redolent with sanctity, not sympathy. The South Sea vagabonds were the best hope of letters: but they all seem to have died without dictating their memoirs. William Mariner, it is true, thanks to a mutiny at the Tongo Islands in 1805, was "several years resident in those islands:" and upon Mariner's return, Dr. John Martin spent infinite patience in recording every detail of savage life he could draw from Mariner. Dr. Martin's book is still a classic in its way: detailed, sober, and naked of literary pretensions. This book is the nearest approach to *Typee* that came out of the South Seas before Melville's time. So numerous have been the imitators of Melville, so popular has been the manner that he originated, that it is difficult at the present day to appreciate the novelty of *Typee* at the time of its appearance. When we read Mr. Frederick O'Brien we do not always remember that Mr. O'Brien is playing "sedulous ape"—there is here intended no discourtesy to Mr. O'Brien—to Melville, but that in *Typee* and *Omoo* Melville was playing "sedulous ape" to nobody. Only when *Typee* is seen against the background of *A Missionary Voyage to the Southern Pacific Ocean performed in the years 1796, 1797, 1798 in the Ship Duff* (1799) and Mariner's *Tonga* (1816) (fittingly dedicated to Sir Joseph Banks, President of the Royal Society, and companion of Captain Cook in the South Seas) can Melville's originality begin to transpire.

This originality lies partly, of course, in the novelty of Melville's experience, partly in the temperament through which this experience was refracted. Melville himself believed his only originality was his loyalty to fact. He bows himself out of the Preface "trusting that his anxious desire to speak the ungarnished truth will gain him the confidence of his readers."

When Melville's brother Gansevoort offered *Typee* for publication in England, it was accepted not as fiction but as ethnology, and was published as *Melville's Marquesas* only after Melville had vouched for its entire veracity.

Though Melville published *Typee* upright in the conviction that he had in its composition been loyal both to veracity and truth, his critics were not prone to take him at his word. And he was to learn, too, that veracity and truth are not interchangeable terms. Men do, in fact, believe pretty much what they find it most advantageous to believe. We live by prejudices, not by syllogisms. In *Typee*, Melville undertook to show from first-hand observation the obvious fact that there are two sides both to civilisation and to savagery. He was among the earliest of literary travellers to see in barbarians anything but queer folk. He intuitively understood them, caught their point of view, respected and often admired it. He measured the life of the Marquesans against that of civilisation, and wrote: "The term 'savage' is, I conceive, often misapplied, and indeed when I consider the vices, cruelties, and enormities of every kind that spring up in the tainted atmosphere of a feverish civilisation, I am inclined to think that so far as the relative wickedness of the parties is concerned, four or five Marquesan Islanders sent to the United States as missionaries, might be quite as useful as an equal number of Americans dispatched to the Islands in a similar capacity." Civilisation is so inured to anathema,—so reassured by it, indeed,—that Melville could write a vague and sentimental attack upon its obvious imperfections with the cool assurance that each of his readers, applying the charges to some neighbour, would approve in self-righteousness. But one ventures the "ungarnished truth" about any of the vested interests of civilisation at the peril of his peace in this world and the next. It was when Melville focussed his charge and wrote "a few passages which may be thought to bear rather hard upon a reverend order of men" with incidental reflections upon "that glorious cause which has not always been served by the proceedings of some of its advocates," that all the musketry of the soldiers of the Prince of Peace was aimed at his head. Melville himself was a man whose tolerance provoked those who sat in jealous monopoly upon warring sureties to accuse him of license. He specifies his delight in finding in the valley of Typee that "an unbounded liberty of conscience seemed to prevail. Those who were pleased to do so were allowed to repose implicit faith in an ill-favoured god with a large bottle-nose and fat shapeless arms crossed upon his breast; whilst others worshipped an image which, having no likeness either in heaven or on earth, could hardly be called an idol. As the islanders always maintained a discrete reserve with regard to my own peculiar views on religion. I thought it would be excessively ill-bred in me to pry into theirs." This boast of delicacy did not pass unnoticed by "a reverend order of men." The vitriolic rejoinder of the London Missionary Society would seem to indicate that there may be two versions of "the ungarnished truth." It should be stated, however, that the English editions of *Typee* contain strictures against the Missionaries that were omitted in the American editions. But even Melville's unsanctified critics showed an anxiety to repudiate him. Both *Typee* and *Omoo* were scouted as impertinent inventions, defying belief in their "cool sneering wit and perfect want of heart." Melville's name was suspiciously examined as being a *nom de plume* used to cover a cowardly and supercilious libel. A gentleman signing himself G. W. P. and writing in the *American Review* (1847, Vol. IV, pp. 36–46) was scandalised by Melville's habit of presenting "voluptuous pictures, and with cool deliberate art breaking off always at the right point, so as without offending decency, he may excite unchaste desire." After discovering in Melville's writing a boastful lechery, this gentleman undertakes to discountenance Melville on three scores: (1) only the impotent make amorous boasts; (2) Melville had none of Sir Epicure Mammon's wished-for elixir; (3) the beauty of Polynesian women is all myth.

Unshaken in the conviction of his loyalty to fact, Melville discovered that the essence of originality lies in reporting "the ungarnished truth."

On the subject of "originality" in literature, Melville says in *Pierre:* "In the inferior instances of an immediate literary success, in very young writers, it would be almost invariably observable, that for that instant success they were chiefly indebted to some rich and peculiar experience in life, embodied in a book, which because, for that cause, containing original matter, the author himself, forsooth, is to be considered original; in this way, many very original books being the product of very unoriginal minds." It is none the less true, however, that though Melville and Toby both lived among the cannibals, it was Melville, not Toby, who wrote *Typee*. . . .

While Melville had the companionship of Toby in Typee, he was even then eager to get back to civilisation. That savagery was good for savages he never wearied of contending. But despite the idyllic delights of Typee—an idyll with a sombre background, however—Melville was never tempted to resign himself to its vacant animal felicity. Melville, unlike Baudelaire and Whitman, was not stirred by the advantages of "living with the animals." While among them, he evinced a desire neither to adopt their ways, nor to change them. He made them pop-guns, he astonished them by exhibiting the miracle of sewing. He tried to teach them to box. "As not one of the natives had soul enough in him to stand up like a man, and allow me to hammer away at him, for my own personal satisfaction and that of the king, I was necessitated to fight with an imaginary enemy, whom I invariably made to knock under to my superior prowess."

Though later, when Melville was a sailor in the United States Navy, he touched at the Marquesas, he never again set foot within the valley of Typee. Melville had known the Typees in their uncorrupted glory—strong, wicked, laughter-loving and clean. Mr. O'Brien visited Typee not many years ago, to find it pathetically fallen from its high estate. "I found myself," he says, "in a loneliness indescribable and terrible. No sound but that of a waterfall at a distance parted the sombre silence. . . . Humanity was not so much absent as gone, and a feeling of doom and death was in the motionless air, which lay like a weight, upon leaf and flower. The thin, sharp buzzing of the *nonos* was incessant." Mr. O'Brien discovered in the heart of the valley fewer than a dozen people who sat within the houses by cocoanut-husk fires, the acrid smoke of which daunted the *nonos*. "They have clung to their lonely *paepaes* despite their poverty of numbers and the ferocity of the *nonos*. They had clearings with cocoanuts and breadfruits, but they cared no longer to cultivate them, preferring rather to sit sadly in the curling fumes and dream of the past. One old man read aloud the *Gospel of St. John* in Marquesan, and the others listlessly listened, seeming to drink in little comfort from the verses, which he recited in the chanting monotone of their *uta*. . . . Nine miles in length is Typee, from a glorious cataract that leaps over the dark buttress wall where the mountain bounds the valley, to the blazing beach. And in all this extent of marvellously rich land, there are now this wretched dozen natives, too old or listless to gather their own food."

Thou hast conquered, O Galilean!

Herman Melville's *Typee* and *Omoo*

D. H. Lawrence*

The greatest seer and poet of the sea for me is Melville. His vision is more real than Swinburne's, because he doesn't personify the sea, and far sounder than Joseph Conrad's, because Melville doesn't sentimentalize the ocean and the sea's unfortunates. Snivel in a wet hanky like Lord Jim.

Melville has the strange, uncanny magic of sea-creatures, and some of their repulsiveness. He isn't quite a land animal. There is something slithery about him. Something always half-seas-over. In his life they said he was mad—or crazy. He was neither mad nor crazy. But he was over the border. He was half a water animal, like those terrible yellow-bearded Vikings who broke out of the waves in beaked ships.

He was a modern Viking. There is something curious about real blue-eyed people. They are never quite human, in the good classic sense, human as brown-eyed people are human: the human of the living humus. About a real blue-eyed person there is usually something abstract, elemental. Brown-eyed people are, as it were, like the earth, which is tissue of bygone life, organic, compound. In blue eyes there is sun and rain and abstract, uncreate element, water, ice, air, space, but not humanity. Brown-eyed people are people of the old, old world: *Allzu menschlich*. Blue-eyed people tend to be too keen and abstract.

Melville is like a Viking going home to the sea, encumbered with age and memories, and a sort of accomplished despair, almost madness. For he cannot accept humanity. He can't belong to humanity. Cannot.

The great Northern cycle of which he is the returning unit has almost completed its round, accomplished itself. Balder the beautiful is mystically dead, and by this time he stinketh. Forget-me-nots and sea-poppies fall into water. The man who came from the sea to live among men can stand it no longer. He hears the horror of the cracked church bell, and goes back down the shore, back into the ocean again, home, into the salt water. Human life won't do. He turns back to the elements. And all the vast sun-and-wheat consciousness of his day he plunges back into the deeps, burying the flame in the deep, self-conscious and deliberate. As blue flax and sea-poppies fall into the waters and give back their created sun-stuff to the dissolution of the flood.

The sea-born people, who can meet and mingle no longer: who turn away from life, to the abstract, to the elements: the sea receives her own.

Let life come asunder, they say. Let water conceive no more with fire. Let mating finish. Let the elements leave off kissing, and turn their backs on one another. Let the merman turn away from his human wife and children, let the seal-woman forget the world of men, remembering only the waters.

So they go down to the sea, the sea-born people. The Vikings are wandering again. Homes are broken up. Cross the seas, cross the seas, urges the heart. Leave love and home. Leave love and home. Love and home are a deadly illusion. Woman, what have I to do with thee? It is finished. *Consummatum est.* The crucifixion into humanity is over. Let us go back to the fierce, uncanny elements: the corrosive vast sea. Or Fire.

Basta! It is enough. It is enough of life. Let us have the vast elements. Let us get out of this loathsome complication of living humanly with humans. Let the sea wash us clean of the leprosy of our humanity and humanness.

Melville was a northerner, sea-born. So the sea claimed him. We are most of us, who use the English language, water-people, sea-derived.

Melville went back to the oldest of all the oceans, to the Pacific. *Der Grosse oder Stille Ozean.*

Without doubt the Pacific Ocean is aeons older than the Atlantic or the Indian Oceans. When we say older, we mean it has not come to any modern consciousness. Strange convulsions have convulsed the Atlantic and Mediterranean peoples into phase after phase of consciousness, while the Pacific and the Pacific peoples have slept. To sleep is to dream: you can't stay unconscious. And, oh heaven, for how many thousands of years has the true Pacific been dreaming, turning over in its sleep and dreaming again: idylls: nightmares.

The Maoris, the Tongans, the Marquesans, the Fijians, the Polynesians: holy God, how long have they been turning over in the same sleep, with varying dreams? Perhaps, to a sensitive imagination, those islands in the middle of the Pacific are the most unbearable places on earth. It simply stops the heart, to be translated there, unknown ages back, back into that life, that pulse, that rhythm. The scientists say the South Sea Islanders belong to the Stone Age. It seems absurd to class people according to their implements. And yet there is something in it. The heart of the Pacific is still the Stone Age; in spite of steamers. The heart of the Pacific seems like a vast vacuum, in which, mirage-like, continues the life of myriads of ages back. It is a phantom-persistence of human beings who should have died, by our chronology, in the Stone Age. It is a phantom, illusion-like trick of reality: the glamorous South Seas.

Even Japan and China have been turning over in their sleep for countless centuries. Their blood is the old blood, their tissue the old soft tissue. Their busy day was myriads of years ago, when the world was a softer place, more moisture in the air, more warm mud on the face of the earth, and the lotus was always in flower. The great bygone world, before Egypt. And Japan and China have been turning over in their sleep, while we have "advanced." And now they are starting up into nightmare.

The world isn't what it seems.

The Pacific Ocean holds the dream of immemorial centuries. It is the great blue twilight of the vastest of all evenings: perhaps of the most wonderful of all dawns. Who knows?

It must once have been a vast basin of soft, lotus-warm civilization, the Pacific. Never was such a huge man-day swung down into slow disintegration, as here. And now the waters are blue and ghostly with the end of immemorial peoples. And phantom-like the islands rise out of it, illusions of the glamorous Stone Age.

To this phantom, Melville returned. Back, back, away from life. Never man instinctively hated human life, our human life, as we have it, more than Melville did. And never was a man so passionately filled with the sense of vastness and mystery of life which is non-human. He was mad to look over our horizons. Anywhere, anywhere out of *our* world. To get away. To get away, out!

To get away, out of our life. To cross a horizon into another life. No matter what life, so long as it is another life.

Away, away from humanity. To the sea. The naked salt, elemental sea. To go to sea, to escape humanity.

The human heart gets into a frenzy at last, in its desire to dehumanize itself.

So he finds himself in the middle of the Pacific. Truly over a horizon. In another world. In another epoch. Back, far back, in the days of palm trees and lizards and stone implements. The sunny Stone Age.

Samoa, Tahiti, Raratonga, Nukuheva: the very names are a sleep and a forgetting. The sleep-forgotten past magnificence of human history. "Trailing clouds of glory."

Melville hated the world: was born hating it. But he was looking for heaven. That is, choosingly. Choosingly, he was looking for paradise. Unchoosingly, he was mad with hatred of the world.

Well, the world is hateful. It is as hateful as Melville found it. He was not wrong in hating the world. *Delenda est Chicago*. He hated it to a pitch of madness, and not without reason.

But it's no good *persisting* in looking for paradise "regained".

Melville at his best invariably wrote from a sort of dream-self, so that events which he relates as actual fact have indeed a far deeper reference to his own soul, his own inner life.

So in *Typee* when he tells of his entry into the valley of the dread cannibals of Nukuheva. Down this narrow, steep, horrible dark gorge he slides and struggles as we struggle in a dream, or in the act of birth, to emerge in the green Eden of the Golden Age, the valley of the cannibal savages. This is a bit of birth-myth, or re-birth myth, on Melville's part—unconscious, no doubt, because his running underconsciousness was always mystical and symbolical. He wasn't aware that he was being mystical.

There he is then, in Typee, among the dreaded cannibal savages. And they are gentle and generous with him, and he is truly in a sort of Eden.

Here at last is Rousseau's Child of Nature and Chateaubriand's Noble Savage called upon and found at home. Yes, Melville loves his savage hosts. He finds them gentle, laughing lambs compared to the ravening wolves of his white brothers, left behind in America and on an American whaleship.

The ugliest beast on earth is the white man, says Melville.

In short, Herman found in Typee the paradise he was looking for. It is true, the Marquesans were "immoral", but he rather liked that. Morality was too white a trick to take him in. Then again, they were cannibals. And it filled him with horror even to think of this. But the savages were very private and even fiercely reserved in their cannibalism, and he might have spared himself his shudder. No doubt he had partaken of the Christian Sacraments many a time. "This is my body, take and eat. This is my blood. Drink it in remembrance of me." And if the savages liked to partake of their sacrament without raising the transubstantiation quibble, and if they liked to say, directly: "This is thy body, which I take from thee and eat. This is thy blood, which I sip in annihilation of thee", why surely their sacred ceremony was as awe-inspiring as the one Jesus substituted. But Herman chose to be horrified. I confess, I am not horrified; though, of course, I am not on the spot. But the savage sacrament seems to me more valid than the Christian: less side-tracking about it. Thirdly, he was shocked by their wild methods of warfare. He died before the great European war, so his shock was comfortable.

Three little quibbles: morality, cannibal sacrament, and stone axes. You must have a fly even in Paradisal ointment. And the first was a ladybird.

But Paradise. He insists on it. Paradise. He could even go stark naked, as before the Apple episode. And his Fayaway, a laughing little Eve, naked with him, and hankering after no apple of knowledge, so long as he would just love her when he felt like it. Plenty to eat, needing no clothes to wear, sunny, happy people, sweet water to swim in: everything a man can want. Then why wasn't he happy along with the savages?

Because he wasn't.

He grizzled in secret, and wanted to escape.

He even pined for Home and Mother, the two things he had run away from as far as ships would carry him. HOME and MOTHER. The two things that were his damnation.

There on the island, where the golden-green great palmtrees chinked in the sun, and the elegant reed houses let the sea-breeze through, and people went naked and laughed a great deal, and Fayaway put flowers in his hair for him—great red hibiscus flowers, and frangipani—O God, why wasn't he happy? Why wasn't he?

Because he wasn't.

Well, it's hard to make a man happy.

But I should not have been happy either. One's soul seems under a vacuum, in the South Seas.

The truth of the matter is, one cannot go back. Some men can: renegade. But Melville couldn't go back: and Gauguin couldn't really go back: and I know now that I could never go back. Back towards the past, savage life. One cannot go back. It is one's destiny inside one.

There are these peoples, these "savages". One does not despise them. One does not feel superior. But there is a gulf. There is a gulf in time and being. I cannot commingle my being with theirs.

There they are, these South Sea Islanders, beautiful big men with their golden limbs and their laughing, graceful laziness. And they will call you brother, choose you as a brother. But why cannot one truly be brother?

There is an invisible hand grasps my heart and prevents it opening too much to these strangers. They are beautiful, they are like children, they are generous: but they are more than this. They are far off, and in their eyes is an easy darkness of the soft, uncreate past. In a way, they are uncreate. Far be it from me to assume any "white" superiority. But they are savages. They are gentle and laughing and physically very handsome. But it seems to me, that in living so far, through all our bitter centuries of civilization, we have still been living onwards, forwards. God knows it looks like a *cul de sac* now. But turn to the first negro, and then listen to your own soul. And your own soul will tell you that however false and foul our forms and systems are now, still, through the many centuries since Egypt, we have been living and struggling forwards along some road that is no road, and yet is a great life-development. We have struggled on, and on we must still go. We may have to smash things. Then let us smash. And our road may have to take a great swerve, that seems a retrogression.

But we can't go back. Whatever else the South Sea Islander is, he is centuries and centuries behind us in the life-struggle, the consciousness-struggle, the struggle of the soul into fulness. There is his woman, with her knotted hair and her dark, inchoate, slightly sardonic eyes. I like her, she is nice. But I would never want to touch her. I could not go back on myself so far. Back to their uncreate condition.

She has soft warm flesh, like warm mud. Nearer the reptile, the Saurian age. *Noli me tangere.*

We can't go back. We can't go back to the savages: not a stride. We can be in sympathy with them. We can take a great curve in their direction, onwards. But we cannot turn the current of our life backwards, back towards their soft warm twilight and uncreate mud. Not for a moment. If we do it for a moment, it makes us sick.

We can only do it when we are renegade. The renegade hates life itself. He wants the death of life. So these many "reformers" and "idealists" who glorify the savages in America. They are death-birds, life-haters. Renegades.

We can't go back, and Melville couldn't. Much as he hated the civilized humanity he knew. He couldn't go back to the savages; he wanted to, he tried to, and he couldn't.

Because, in the first place, it made him sick; it made him physically ill. He had something wrong with his leg, and this would not heal. It got worse and worse, during his four months on the island. When he escaped, he was in a deplorable condition—sick and miserable, ill, very ill.

Paradise!

But there you are. Try to go back to the savages, and you feel as if your very soul was decomposing inside you. That is what you feel in the South Seas, anyhow: as if your soul was decomposing inside you. And with any savages the same, if you try to go their way, take their current of sympathy.

Yet, as I say, we must make a great swerve in our onward-going life-course now, to gather up again the savage mysteries. But this does not mean going back on ourselves.

Going back to the savages made Melville sicker than anything. It made him feel as if he were decomposing. Worse even than Home and Mother.

And that is what really happens. If you prostitute your psyche by returning to the savages, you gradually go to pieces. Before you can go back, you *have* to decompose. And a white man decomposing is a ghastly sight. Even Melville in Typee.

We have to go on, on, on, even if we must smash a way ahead.

So Melville escaped, and threw a boat-hook full in the throat of one of his dearest savage friends, and sank him, because that savage was swimming in pursuit. That's how he felt about the savages when they wanted to detain him. He'd have murdered them one and all, vividly, rather than be kept from escaping. Away from them—he must get away from them—at any price.

And once he has escaped, immediately he begins to sigh and pine for the "Paradise"—Home and Mother being at the other end even of a whaling voyage.

When he really was Home with Mother, he found it Purgatory. But Typee must have been even worse than Purgatory, a soft hell, judging from the murderous frenzy which possessed him to escape.

But once aboard the whaler that carried him off from Nukuheva, he looked back and sighed for the Paradise he had just escaped from in such a fever.

Poor Melville! He was determined Paradise existed. So he was always in Purgatory.

He was born for Purgatory. Some souls are purgatorial by destiny.

The very freedom of his Typee was a torture to him. Its ease was slowly horrible to him. This time *he* was the fly in the odorous tropical ointment.

He needed to fight. It was no good to him, the relaxation of the non-moral tropics. He didn't really want Eden. He wanted to fight. Like every American. To fight. But with weapons of the spirit, not the flesh.

That was the top and bottom of it. His soul was in revolt, writhing for ever in revolt. When he had something definite to rebel against—like the bad conditions on a whaling ship—then he was much happier in his miseries. The mills of God were grinding inside him, and they needed something to grind on.

When they could grind on the injustice and folly of missionaries, or of brutal sea-captains, or of governments, he was easier. The mills of God were grinding inside him.

They are grinding inside every American. And they grind exceeding small.

Why? Heaven knows. But we've got to grind down our old forms, our old selves, grind them very very small, to nothingness. Whether a new somethingness will ever start, who knows? Meanwhile the mills of God grind on, in American Melville, and it was himself he ground small: himself and his wife, when he was married. For the present, the South Seas.

He escapes on to the craziest, most impossible of whaling ships. Lucky for us Melville makes it fantastic. It must have been pretty sordid.

And anyhow, on the crazy *Julia*, his leg, that would never heal in the paradise of Typee, began quickly to get well. His life was falling into its normal pulse. The drain back into past centuries was over.

Yet, oh, as he sails away from Nukuheva, on the voyage that will ultimately take him to America, oh, the acute and intolerable nostalgia he feels for the island he has left.

The past, the Golden Age of the past—what a nostalgia we all feel for it. Yet we don't want it when we get it. Try the South Seas.

Melville had to fight, fight against the existing world, against his own very self. Only he would never quite put the knife in the heart of his paradisal ideal. Somehow, somewhere, somewhen, love should be a fulfilment, and life should be a thing of bliss. That was his fixed ideal. Fata Morgana.

That was the pin he tortured himself on, like a pinned-down butterfly.

Love is never a fulfilment. Life is never a thing of continuous bliss. There is no paradise. Fight and laugh and feel bitter and feel bliss: and fight again. Fight, fight. That is life.

Why pin ourselves down on a paradisal ideal? It is only ourselves we torture.

Melville did have one great experience, getting away from humanity: the experience of the sea.

The South Sea Islands were not his great experience. They were a glamorous world outside New England. Outside. But it was the sea that was both outside and inside: the universal experience.

The book that follows on from *Typee* is *Omoo*.

Omoo is a fascinating book; picaresque, rascally, roving. Melville, as a bit of a beachcomber. The crazy ship *Julia* sails to Tahiti, and the mutinous crew are put ashore. Put in the Tahitian prison. It is good reading.

Perhaps Melville is at his best, his happiest, in *Omoo*. For once he is really reckless. For once he takes life as it comes. For once he is the gallant rascally epicurean, eating the world like a snipe, dirt and all baked into one *bonne bouche*.

For once he is really careless, roving with that scamp, Doctor Long Ghost. For once he is careless of his actions, careless of his morals, careless of his ideals: ironic, as the epicurean must be. The deep irony of your real scamp: your real epicurean of the moment.

But it was under the influence of the Long Doctor. This long and bony Scotsman was not a mere ne'er-do-well. He was a man of humorous desperation, throwing his life ironically away. Not a mere loose-kneed loafer, such as the South Seas seem to attract.

That is good about Melville: he never repents. Whatever he did, in Typee or in Doctor Long Ghost's wicked society, he never repented. If he ate his snipe, dirt and all, and enjoyed it at the time, he didn't have bilious bouts afterwards, which is good.

But it wasn't enough. The Long Doctor was really knocking about in a sort of despair. He let his ship drift rudderless.

Melville couldn't do this. For a time, yes. For a time, in this Long Doctor's company, he was rudderless and reckless. Good as an experience. But a man who will not abandon himself to despair or indifference cannot keep it up.

Melville would never abandon himself either to despair or indifference. He always cared. He always cared enough to hate missionaries, and to be touched by a real act of kindness. He always cared.

When he saw a white man really "gone savage," a white man with a blue shark tattooed over his brow, gone over to the savages, then Herman's whole being revolted. He couldn't bear it. He could not bear a renegade.

He enlisted at last on an American man-of-war. You have the record in *White Jacket*. He was back in civilization, but still at sea. He was in America, yet loose in the seas. Good regular days, after Doctor Long Ghost and the *Julia*.

As a matter of fact, a long thin chain was round Melville's ankle all the time, binding him to America, to civilization, to democracy, to the ideal world. It was a long chain, and it never broke. It pulled him back.

By the time he was twenty-five his wild oats were sown; his reckless wanderings were over. At the age of twenty-five he came back to Home and Mother, to fight it out at close quarters. For you can't fight it out by running away. When you have run a long way from Home and Mother, then you realize that the earth is round, and if you keep on running you'll be back on the same old doorstep,—like a fatality.

Melville came home to face out the long rest of his life. He married and had an ecstasy of a courtship and fifty years of disillusion.

He had just furnished his home with disillusions. No more Typees. No more paradises. No more Fayaways. A mother: a gorgon. A home: a torture box. A wife: a thing with clay feet. Life: a sort of disgrace. Fame: another disgrace, being patronized by common snobs who just know how to read.

The whole shameful business just making a man writhe.

Melville writhed for eighty years.

In his soul he was proud and savage.

But in his mind and will he wanted the perfect fulfilment of love; he wanted the lovey-doveyness of perfect mutual understanding.

A proud savage-souled man doesn't really want any perfect lovey-dovey fulfilment in love: no such nonsense. A mountain lion doesn't mate with a Persian cat; and when a grizzly bear roars after a mate, it is a she-grizzly he roars after—not after a silky sheep.

But Melville stuck to his ideal. He wrote *Pierre* to show that the more you try to be good the more you make a mess of things: that following righteousness is just disastrous. The better you are, the worse things turn out with you. The better you try to be, the bigger mess you make. Your very striving after righteousness only causes your own slow degeneration.

Well, it is true. No men are so evil to-day as the idealists, and no women half so evil as your earnest woman, who feels herself a power for good. It is inevitable. After a certain point, the ideal goes dead and rotten. The old pure ideal becomes in itself an impure thing of evil. Charity becomes pernicious, the spirit itself becomes foul. The meek are evil. The pure in heart have base, subtle revulsions: like Dostoevsky's Idiot. The whole Sermon on the Mount becomes a litany of white vice.

What then?

It's our own fault. It was *we* who set up the ideals. And if we are such fools, that we aren't able to kick over our ideals in time, the worse for us.

Look at Melville's eighty long years of writhing. And to the end he writhed on the ideal pin.

From the "perfect woman lover" he passed on to the "perfect friend". He looked and looked for the perfect man friend.

Couldn't find him.

Marriage was a ghastly disillusion to him, because he looked for perfect marriage.

Friendship never even made a real start in him—save perhaps his half-sentimental love for Jack Chase, in *White Jacket.*

Yet to the end he pined for this: a perfect relationship; perfect mating; perfect mutual understanding. A perfect friend.

Right to the end he could never accept the fact that *perfect* relationships cannot be. Each soul is alone, and the aloneness of each soul is a double barrier to perfect relationship between two beings.

Each soul *should* be alone. And in the end the desire for a "perfect relationship" is just a vicious, unmanly craving. *"Tous nos malheurs viennent de ne pouvoir être seuls."*

Melville, however, refused to draw his conclusion. *Life* was wrong, he said. He refused Life. But he stuck to his ideal of perfect relationship, possible perfect love. The world *ought* to be a harmonious loving place. And it *can't* be. So life itself is wrong.

It is silly arguing. Because, after all, only temporary man sets up the "oughts".

The world ought *not* to be a harmonious loving place. It ought to be a place of fierce discord and intermittent harmonies: which it is.

Love ought *not* to be perfect. It ought to have perfect moments, and wildernesses of thorn bushes—which it has.

A "perfect" relationship ought *not* to be possible. Every relationship should have its absolute limits, its absolute reserves, essential to the singleness of the soul in each person. A truly perfect relationship is one in which each party leaves great tracts unknown in the other party.

No two persons can meet at more than a few points, consciously. If two people can just be together fairly often, so that the presence of each is a sort of balance to the other, that is the basis of perfect relationship. There must be true separatenesses as well.

Melville was, at the core, a mystic and an idealist.

Perhaps, so am I.

And he stuck to his ideal guns.

I abandon mine.

He was a mystic who raved because the old ideal guns snot havoc. The guns of the "noble spirit." Of "ideal love."

I say, let the old guns rot.

Get new ones, and shoot straight.

Herman Melville

Fred Lewis Pattee*

Home from his amazing adventure, the boy of twenty-five settled to a career of authorship—one of his youthful dreams. There had been no apprenticeship in letters: his four years in the forecastle had been anything but literary. Mark Twain had had preliminary training at a printer's case, and so had Whitman, but the young Melville, scarcely out of his sailor's slops, without practice and without models, sat down to tell his story in his own words. Time and again he had told it in the forecastle groups and to eager relatives. Varnished unquestionably it was, spiced freely with the marvelous, and worked always to a surprising climax, but it squared at every point with forecastle knowledge and nautical technique: his early audiences were imperious here. The result was "Typee," one of the most original books of the mid-century, as completely without prototype as "Roughing It" and "Huckleberry Finn."

It was as much a product of New York as "Knickerbocker's History," or Cooper's novels, or "Leaves of Grass." None of them could have come from New England. The original creations of American literature, our genuinely *American* classics, have with few exceptions been extra-New England in origin. For flouters of the old order, whether in religion or in literature, the Puritan had only damnation. The novel from the first he despised, and as a result, to the present day, Hawthorne alone excepted, no great piece of fiction has come from New England. "Uncle Tom's Cabin" would never have been written but for its author's seventeen years in the Middle West. The *North American Review*, inspired voice of the Brahmins, never once in its whole New England career mentioned Whitman or Melville. Even Hawthorne had to fight twenty-five years for recognition, and he received it at last only because "The Scarlet Letter" seemed to be a Puritan document and sermonic at heart.

But even cosmopolitan New York hesitated at "Typee": the English edition was pruned of its anti-missionary sentences before the Putnams dared issue it. The book was scarcely off the press when both in England

*This essay originally appeared in *American Mercury*, 10 (January, 1927), 33–43 and was republished in the "Revaluations" chapter of *The New American Literature, 1890–1930* (New York: Cooper Square Publishers, 1930), pp. 366–71.

and America it was attacked with ferocity. It was lecherous, it was blasphemous, it was deliberately untrue. The man by his own confession was a vile outcast, one who naturally would have no sympathy with missions or with anything else that stood for decency. Leading magazines, widely circulated, such as the *Living Age*, lashed him with superlatives:

> With this tribe he remained about four months, during which he cohabited with a native girl, named Fayaway. We shall not pollute our pages by transferring to them the scenes in which this wretched profligate appears, self-confessed as the chief actor. . . . When they left jail no captain in the harbor would have anything to do with them on account of their desperate character. They even leagued with a reckless gang of seamen known in the Pacific as "Beachcombers."

Thus was Herman Melville first presented to the reading world. Fitz-James O'Brien, New York Bohemian, was the first adequately to review the book. It was its utter originality, he declared, that was damning it, its frank sensuousness in an age of mawkishness and religiosity. No later critic has surpassed some phases of his diagnosis:

> The man is essentially exotical in feeling. Matter is his god. His dreams are material. His philosophy is sensual. Beautiful women, shadowy lakes, nodding plumy trees, and succulent banquets make Melville's scenery, unless his theme utterly preclude all such. His language is rich and heavy with a plating of imagery. He has a barbaric love of ornament and does not mind how much it is put on. Swept away by his sensual longing, he frequently writes at random. One can see that he uses certain words only because they roll off his pen lusciously and roundly.

But even O'Brien missed the fundamental secret of "Typee." The book is woven of three strands. One, as O'Brien discovered, is the realistic and sensuous. Everywhere first-hand observation: the manufacture of poee-poeee, and tappa; the laws of the taboo; the personal habits and daily life of the natives; and so on and on. Some have seen only this element, and have classified "Typee" as a book of travel. But the book fundamentally is a romance. Its affinity is with "Robinson Crusoe": the infernal whale ship, the exciting escape, the desert island with its unheard-of flora and fauna, the cannibals, the man Friday, the final escape. Everything is heightened even to melodrama; everywhere the marvellous; everywhere the hero central. The landscape through which he flees, itself melodramatic, with the mighty waterfalls in a series, three hundred feet high; the final break from captivity with the death of the villain Mow-Mow at the hero's hands, all seems carefully planned romance.

Consider the beauty of Fayaway. Three pages of superlatives he lavishes upon her: "I would have matched the charming Fayaway against any beauty in the world. . . . Her figure was the very perfection of feminine grace and beauty, . . . her rosy mouth with teeth of dazzling whiteness, . . . her hands soft and delicate as those of any countess." A

Bertha M. Clay heroine could not be more perfect. But this is not enough: *all* the maidens of Typee are beautiful: "To compare them with the gallery of coronation beauties in Westminster Abbey: it would be the Venus de Medici placed beside a milliner's doll." Mere superlatives, indeed, are too feeble to embody his dream. To see a Peruvian lady inhale a *cigarro* under orange trees, he declares, is ravishment, "but Fayaway, holding in her delicately-formed olive hand the long yellow reed of her pipe, with its quaintly carved bowl, and every few moments languishingly giving forth light wreaths of vapor from her mouth and nostrils, looks still more engaging. . . . To the mild fumes of the tobacco her rosy breath added a fresh perfume." It is too much: we begin to be suspicious of the whole story. "I boldly pronounce the teeth of the Typees to be far more beautiful than ivory itself. . . . Nearly every individual of their number might have been taken for a sculptor's model." This is not a book of travels, a record of mere fact: it is romance, it is rhapsody.

Which leads directly to the third strand, the heart of the book. Starting as a "Robinson Crusoe" it ends as a "Utopia." The Knickerbocker romancer is interrupted by the Puritan. The perfection of the savage Typees is but a foil for the rottenness of civilization. The book is a Carlylean sermon. In that little valley ten miles long, there are only physical perfection, ideal symmetry, radiant health, but "stripped of the cunning artifices of the tailor and standing forth in the garb of Eden, what a sorry set of round-shouldered, spindled shanked, crane-necked varlets would civilized men appear!" Life is elementally simple among the happy Typees, "No mortgages, no protested notes, no bills payable, no debts of honor in Typee; no unreasonable tailors and shoemakers, perversely bent on being paid; no duns of any description; no assault and battery attorneys to foment discord, backing their clients up in a quarrel, and then knocking their heads together; no poor relations everlastingly occupying the spare bedchamber, and diminishing the elbow room at the family table; no destitute widows with their children starving on the cold charities of the world; no beggars; no debtor's prisons; no proud and hardhearted nabobs in Typee; or to sum up all in one word—no Money!"

The book was completely in the key of the reforming forties—the era of the Transcendental ferment. It should be placed on the same shelf as "Walden," Emerson's "The New England Reformers," the Brook Farm story, "The Blithedale Romance," and Cooper's "The Crater," written in supreme contempt of all the New England gospels. Thoreau would lessen the denominator of civilization by the practice of New England parsimony and by using nature as a cathartic and a balm, but the young Melville would go to the utter extreme: he would return to the savagery from which the race sprang, to primitive morals when mankind was naked and unashamed, and to primitive health of body and soul.

Typee

William Ellery Sedgwick*

The story of *Typee* is so familiar that it needs only the briefest repetition here. It is based, as everyone knows who knows anything about Herman Melville, on his experiences in the course of a long and diversified voyage into the Pacific which began on board a whaler out of New Bedford early in January, 1841, and ended more than three and a half years later, when as a member of the crew of a United States man-of-war Melville sailed into Boston harbor and was honorably discharged. Skipping the voyage out around Cape Horn, *Typee* begins at the point where his ship, the *Dolly* as Melville calls her, turned away from a usual cruising ground of whalers and pointed to Nukaheva, in the group of islands in the South Seas known as the Marquesas. In the harbor of Nukaheva, Melville deserted and with a single companion from the crew, Toby, made his way to the valley of Typee.

According to the story as Melville wrote it, he and Toby struggled desperately to get beyond the mountains to where they would be safe from pursuit. They meant to take refuge among the Happars, a tribe of the island of Nukaheva who enjoyed a reputation for kindness to white strangers. Unluckily, as it turned out, they followed the wrong trail and descended into the valley of Typee, the inhabitants of which were reputed to be cannibals of a particularly virulent stripe, and as their reluctant guests Toby and Melville were pressed to stay. To make matters worse, Melville had hurt his leg in the descent from the steep mountains and the use of it caused him severe pain. In the course of time, Toby was allowed to make his way to the harbor as best he could on the excuse of getting medical assistance for Melville. He never came back. Melville remained alone among the Typees, until, at the end of four months, he made a perilous escape in a little boat sent to fetch him from a whaler that was in need of sailors to man her.

Melville's escape is the high point of the yarn he spins in his first book. As his rescuers rowed to the beach, the Typees, suspecting some-

*Reprinted from William Ellery Sedgwick, *Herman Melville: The Tragedy of Mind* (Cambridge: Harvard University Press, 1944), chap. 2, pp. 19–35. Copyright 1944, © 1972 by the President and Fellows of Harvard College.

thing was up, gathered around. Melville suddenly broke from his guards and waded to the boat, which put about as soon as he reached her and started for the open sea. The savages, running to a point, plunged into the water and swam out to head her off. One, with a tomahawk in his teeth, almost reached the boat and was on the point of grabbing one of the oars. Melville, whose hands were free, seized a boat hook. "Even at the moment," he wrote, "I felt horror at the act I was about to commit; but it was no time for pity or compunction, and with a true aim and exerting all my strength, I dashed the boat hook at him." The savage sank under the blow and when he reappeared he was helpless. "Never," Melville wrote, "shall I forget the ferocious expression of his countenance."

The passage shows that here already Melville was in command of his great gift for describing action. We are made to feel an excitement that almost hurts in this final scene of *Typee* and the issue of it. Nevertheless, as soon as the excitement subsides and the book as a whole comes back to mind, we cannot help feeling that the narrative climax is deeply at odds with a great part of the book, and that the excitement it gives us grates on the feelings which the rest of the book has stirred up. For the natives of Typee, as Melville has described them at length, are hardly the kind of people from whom a man would have to fly for his life, or, for that matter, a man would care to take leave of under any circumstances whatever.

The little, far out-of-the-way world of Typee, which we have shared vicariously, is a world of almost visionary loveliness, luxurious peace and unbroken joy. At his first sight of the valley, Melville tells us that, had a glimpse of the gardens of Paradise been revealed to him, he could scarcely have been more ravished with the sight. "I looked straight down into the bosom of a valley, which swept away in long wavy undulations to the blue waters in the distance. Midway toward the sea, and peering here and there amidst the foliage, might be seen palmetto-thatched houses of its inhabitants, glittering in the sun that had bleached them to a dazzling whiteness. . . . On either side of it appeared hemmed in by steep green acclivities, which, uniting near the spot where I lay, formed an abrupt and semicircular termination of grassy cliffs and precipices hundreds of feet in height, over which flowed numberless small cascades. But the crowning beauty of the prospect was its universal verdure." With this for the outline, there follow many passages that complete the lovely picture: "Birds—bright and beautiful birds—fly over the valley of Typee. You see them perched aloft among the immovable boughs of the majestic breadfruit trees, or gently swaying on the elastic branches of the Omoo; skimming over the palmetto thatching of the bamboo huts; passing like spirits on the wing through the shadows of the grove, and sometimes descending into the bosom of the valley in gleaming flights. . . . Their plumage is purple and azure, crimson and white, black and gold. . . . They go sailing through the air in starry throngs."

And of this green paradise the Typees are the worthy denizens. Their physical appearance by itself would seem a goodly enough heritage from nature: "In beauty of form they surpassed anything I had ever seen. Not a single instance of natural deformity was observable. . . . The men, in almost every instance, are of lofty stature, scarcely ever less than six feet in height. . . ." Except for here and there a scar from a wound received in battle, "every individual appeared free from those blemishes which sometimes mar the effect of an otherwise perfect form."

Mixing harmoniously with the moulded elegance of the men is the volatile charm and beauty of the women. Their type is best seen in the lovely maiden Fayaway, whom Melville describes at length, remarking afterwards, "Though in my eyes, at least, Fayaway was indisputably the loveliest female I saw in Typee, yet the description I have given of her will in some measure apply to nearly all the youthful portion of her sex in the valley. Judge ye then, reader, what beautiful creatures they must have been." With Fayaway, Melville tells us, he lived on terms of enchanting intimacy, such terms of intimacy as were to shock some of his readers in a faraway nineteenth-century America. "Her free pliant figure was the very perfection of female grace and beauty. Her complexion was a rich and mantling olive. . . . The face of this girl was a rounded oval, and each feature as perfectly formed as the heart or imagination of man could desire. Her full lips, when parted with a smile, disclosed teeth of a dazzling whiteness; and when her rosy mouth opened with a burst of merriment, they looked like the milk-white seeds of the 'arta,' a fruit of the valley. . . . Fayaway—I must avow the fact—for the most part clung to the primitive and summer garb of Eden. But how becoming the costume!"

Fayaway's little vanities which she shared with the companions of her sex were gay and ever so ingratiating: "Flora was their jeweler. Sometimes they wore necklaces of small carnation flowers . . . or displayed in their ears a single white bud . . . the delicate petals folded together in a beautiful sphere, and looking like a drop of the purest pearl." They crowned their heads with chaplets like strawberry coronals, or put on bracelets and anklets of intertwined leaves and blossoms. "Indeed, the maidens of the island were passionately fond of flowers and never wearied of decorating their persons with them; a lovely trait in their character. . . ." Yes, surely.

A blessed people, these natives of Typee appear to be; beautiful girls and young men with magnificent bodies, living in an environment of green valley and blue sky and distant blue sea; nowhere at all, as Melville adds, the concerns and anxieties which we think of as inseparable from middle age, nor any of the usual disappointments and deformities of old age. Physical beauty is not unsupported by moral well-being but is linked—a point I shall return to—to beauties of sincere feeling and spontaneous affections. Yet from this world and from this people Melville tells us he had to fly for his life, and he did not hesitate to practice deception and make use of physical violence in order to effect his escape.

2

What accounts for the paradox that is forced upon us here? I do not think we can easily convince ourselves that it lies in the facts themselves which Melville undertook to report. Was it then that he was divided between his instinct for exciting climax while he told a story and his romantic love of the exotic, showing in lavish and exaggerated descriptions? That is partly the case. Yet the paradox that glares so on the surface of the book reaches up from far below the level on which artistic intentions can be discriminated. It reached out of realizations that grew upon Melville as he wrote *Typee* and which were to impel him to his later books.

Melville swore to the literal truth of *Typee*. According to common report, the book was accepted for publication in London only after Melville had vouched for its entire veracity. Afterwards he was irritated by the incredulity of many of its readers. Nevertheless, it seems certain that as a yarn of personal adventure, *Typee* does not always stick to the literal truth.

A recent biographer of Melville during his years of vagabondage in the Pacific has tracked his devious wanderings and outlined the literal truth about them.[1] He shows that Melville's sojourn in the valley of Typee was closer to four weeks in duration than the four months that Melville said and he casts doubts on the circumstances of his escape as Melville recounted it. He proves that Melville borrowed from the accounts of other travellers to fill out his picture of the natives and that he exaggerated their reputation for ferocity. He also exaggerated the good traits of their character: "Following a long and ample tradition, both literary and philosophical, Melville consistently adopts a romantic attitude in his account of the Noble Savages he found in Typee Valley."

As ethnology I am willing to leave the book to others. As to its literal autobiographical truth, I am concerned with it only incidentally. What I am concerned with is a third aspect of the truth of *Typee*—its truth to Melville's mind at the time he wrote it and, beyond this, its truth to the experience of universal human nature. It is under this aspect that we can best account for the paradox in the book which forces itself on our attention.

When Melville wrote *Typee* he was twenty-five, just the age when, as he wrote to Hawthorne some years later, he began to unfold within himself. While he was writing it the impressions received in the course of his travels began to work in his mind and take on new overtones of meaning precisely because his mind was coming to a sense of itself. Certain observations generally connected with Typee had made a deep impression on his mind. But this is not as interesting, in my opinion, as the indisputable fact that while he was writing his mind was impressing itself on this body of observations. Being intelligent and curious, he naturally supplemented his own observations of Polynesian life with whatever reading on the subject he could get at. That does not alter the case. From my point of view it is immaterial in what proportions Melville drew (a) from his own observations, (b) from his reading, (c) from his imagination. In the book as we have it his reading and his observations have fused into a single substance which was cast in the image of his mind just when he had arrived at a self-conscious view of life.

In *Typee* there are two perspectives. There is the perspective of the story proper, or of the events at the time they happened; and there is the broader perspective of the book as a whole, in which the events of the story and their circumstances are seen at a distance of four years across all the light and shadow of Melville's experience in the interim. Accordingly Melville wrote, "I will frankly declare, that after passing a few weeks in this valley of the Marquesas, I formed a higher estimate of human nature than I had ever before entertained. But alas! since then I have been one of a crew of a man-of-war, and the pent-up wickedness of five hundred men has nearly overturned all my previous theories." It was a year after he quitted Typee that he enlisted on the man-of-war, the *United States*, which was to return him to America after fourteen long months of the rigors of life in the navy. His experiences on board the *United States* and his repugnance at the severities and the brutalities of naval life are on record in his book *White Jacket* (1850). In this book, too, his thoughts reaching out beyond his immediate subject matter, he reflected not once but many times on this "man-of-war world" of ours, where, under professions of adoration of the Prince of Peace, the great civilized nations behave like a pack of armed ruffians. This insight into the civilized world, which so plumes itself on its superiority and lords it over the weaker members of the race, was a present influence in Melville's mind when he wrote his first book. In the murky moral obliquities of the civilization to which he had come home, the island valley of Typee shone brighter and brighter in the distance of four crowded years and across thousands of miles of sanitary ocean.

As well known as the story of Melville's captivity among the Typees in his first book is his indictment there of civilization. It need not be rehearsed at length, but something of the tone and temper of it may be recalled. It will be objected, Melville wrote, that these unprincipled islanders are cannibals: "Very true; and a rather bad trait in their character, it must be allowed. But they are such only when they seek to gratify the passion of revenge upon their enemies," and, he asks, does this eating of human flesh exceed the barbarity of some forms of capital punishment in the civilized nations? "The fiend-like skill we display in the invention of all manner of death-dealing engines, the vindictiveness with which we carry on our wars, and the misery and desolation that follow in their train, are enough of themselves to distinguish the white civilized man as the most ferocious animal on the face of the earth." The term "savage" is too often misapplied—"and indeed when I consider the vices, cruelties, and enormities of every kind that spring up in the tainted atmosphere of feverish civilization, I am inclined to think that so far as the relative wickedness of the parties is concerned, four or five Marquesan islanders sent to the United States as missionaries might be quite as useful as an equal number of Americans dispatched to the islands in a similar capacity."

Of course it will be insisted by critics of a certain stamp that in this contrast between civilized and savage life Melville is still following "a long and ample tradition, both literary and philosophical," namely, the exaltation of the Noble Savage at the expense of his civilized opposite. True as this may be, it is not the whole truth nor the most interesting part of it. If there is a literary convention here there is the pressure of personal responses to animate it. In Melville's exaltation of the savage in *Typee* we come on the first of many instances in which Melville instinctively took the side of the underdog. Besides, in his idealization of the savage of Typee there are certain traits peculiar to him which are worth considering.

In view of his deep-seated and life-long preoccupation with religion, it is significant of more than his aversion for professional missionaries that he should have viewed the irreligion of the Typees with such sympathetic amusement. "They are sunk in religious sloth, and require a spiritual revival. A long prosperity of breadfruit and cocoa-nuts has rendered them remiss in the performance of their higher obligations. The wood-rot malady is spreading among the idols—the temples themselves need rethatching—the tattoed clergy are altogether too light-hearted and lazy—and their flocks are going astray." Elsewhere, Melville, dissenting from other "scientific voyagers," lets out the truth about the islanders, that "they are a community of lusty savages, who are leading a merry, idle, innocent life. . . . For my own part, I am free to confess my almost entire inability to gratify any curiosity that may be felt with regard to the theology of the valley. I doubt whether the inhabitants themselves could do so. They are either too lazy or too sensible to worry themselves about abstract points of religious belief."

Melville was delighting in the light-hearted hedonism of these savages. Their life of luxurious sleeping, healthy appetite and undisguised impulses touched a very sympathetic chord in him. Yet partly out of fidelity to the facts and partly under the stress of another trait in Melville's character, the colors of hedonism in his painting of Typee are softened by a gentle radiance of spiritual well-being. He insisted that truth and justice were the mainstay of the Typees' social and political life. They approximated a lovely ideal of democracy; and the individual among them was remarkable for his freedom from arrogance and social pretentiousness, and for his kindliness and generosity: "They deal more kindly with each other, and are more humane, than many who study essays on virtue and benevolence, and who repeat every night that beautiful prayer breathed first by the lips of the divine and gentle Jesus."

Melville's delight in sensuous life and his love of goodness, of goodness as it is set forth in the *New Testament,* contend in his idealization of the Typees. Yet the joyous sensual life and the simple, spontaneous virtue which he pictures have something very deep in common. They unite in standing apart, both of them, from the complications of intellectual reflections and from the anxieties of moral and spiritual self-consciousness. They stand together in the sunlight and freedom outside the "shades of the prison-house" that begin to close about a man's maturity.

It appears more and more that the picture painted of Typee valley was not at last view an adoption and adaptation to himself of an external literary ideal. It has far too much warmth and flowing fulness to have been that at bottom. It came from within, out of personal recollections, and out of recollections far more integral in Melville's consciousness than the literal facts about an outlandish people he had chanced to visit. What Melville is finally expressing in *Typee* is an inward and universal phase of human experience, obtaining in individuals and peoples alike;—the phase in which life lies along the easy slopes of spontaneous, instinctive being, in which human consciousness is a simple and happy undertaking of rudimentary sensations and simple sensuous impressions; in which physical health and good animal spirits have a large preponderance; in which the impulses and affections of the human heart suffer no disguise nor any distortion; the phase, finally, in which as yet no painful cleavage is felt dividing a happy animality from the gentlest and most guileless impulses of the heart.

As we feel our way into the book, it comes over us more and more that we have all been to Typee, and that under one set or another of associations and images, it lies in all our minds. It is an embodiment of the world as we have all felt it in the glow and rapture of youthful love, whatever the object of that love. To one person it is one thing, to another something else. As one poet looks back on it, it is the "blue, remembered hills" of his boyhood, the "land of lost content"; while to another poet it stands under a wholly different train of associations:—

> *Thou wast that all to me, love,*
> *For which my soul did pine—*
> *A green isle in the sea, love,*
> *A fountain and a shrine. . . .*

In this light Melville looked back on Typee valley. Perhaps he had been in love with Fayaway; perhaps she was his first love. But the literal truth about it is not important. Somewhere, sometime or at different times, Melville had experienced the first just-ensanguined raptures of young love, and from an association of actual circumstances, or by a transfer in his imagination, that rapture gives his picture of Typee its warmth and incandescence.

The phase of his life which he identified with Typee is not present in the book, but it is recollected there. It is a recollection not remembered in tranquillity, but amidst all the stresses of a consciousness which has expanded far beyond the simplicities of sensuous, instinctive being. Yet in his imagination he returns to the Typee phase of life and embraces it. Furthermore, by this identification of a phase of his inward experience with an island people of the South Seas whom he had undertaken to describe, he did not sacrifice the objective reality of his picture. The objective reality of *Typee* held itself intact. While being the occasion for emotions that sprang from deeply felt personal recollections, it clarified them by drawing them forth and embodying them anew in concrete forms, at the same time that it invigorated itself on them. By this identification, simply, a dimension of being was added to Melville's picture. And far from detracting from the objective truth of the picture, it extended it, adding to the truth about a particular people a universal truth about human consciousness.

The labored antithesis, then, which Melville drew between savage life and civilization goes deeper than differences of place and lies between youth and maturity, between the carefree vagabondage of mostly sensuous being and the rigors of intellectual and spiritual self-consciousness. And how lovely by contrast, how infinitely lovely and ingratiating, is the former! "In the secluded abode of happiness"—the green valley that so rejoiced him—Melville writes, "All was mirth, fun, and high good humor. Blue devils, hypochondria, and doleful dumps went and hid themselves among the nooks and crannies of the rocks"; and again, "One peculiarity that fixed my admiration was the perpetual hilarity reigning through the whole extent of the vale. There seemed to be no cares, griefs, troubles, or vexations in all Typee. The hours tripped along as gayly as the laughing couples down a country dance." What has such a child of the sun as a native of Typee, "what he to desire at the hands of civilization? She may 'cultivate his mind,'—may 'elevate his thoughts,'—these I believe are the established phrases—but will he be happier?" "When I looked around the verdant recess in which I was buried, and gazed up to the summits of the lofty eminence that hemmed me in, I was well disposed to think that I was in the 'Happy Valley,' and that beyond those heights there was naught but a world of care and anxiety."

Praise it and delight in it as one will, nevertheless one cannot reënter into full possession of the "Happy Valley." One cannot stay long. There are intimations of the mind that will not be shut out; thoughts, they may seem, of a "dry brain in a dry season." It is forced upon us to know that Typee is not the human thing itself, and a man cannot duck his human destiny. For all its loveliness it is wanting in the elements of man's intellectual and spiritual consciousness. Its fawn-like impulses of affection, although they are ever so engaging, do not amount to the ties through which the heart fulfills itself. Fayaway showed more human than the rest: "I was almost led to believe that her mind was swayed by gentle impulses hardly to be anticipated from one in her condition." When news went around that a boat was coming for him and Melville begged to be taken to the beach, only one native in the whole crowd, an old man, could understand the human necessity he was under to escape.

It is a necessity of our human life that we should sojourn in Typee, and that we should open to it with all the pores of our sensuous being and that we should cherish it for the refreshment which it alone can give. Lovely, easy-lying, green valley! surrounded as it is by the veiled heights and the appalling ocean vastnesses of man's completer consciousness, it will grow lovelier and more and more desirable the further it is left behind. But it is a dark necessity of our being human that a time comes when we must escape from it for our lives.

Yet, after all, it is not so much that a man leaves Typee behind him as that he passes on to other aspects of life while Typee remains one element among others in his consciousness. The man in whom this element does not persist, or in whom it has been reduced to a few scraps of memory, is very much the poorer. He has lost a range of impressionability, as also a source within himself at which to bathe his whole emotional being. And of all men it is the artist, of course, who counts most on the survival of this element as a living principle. It remained strong in Melville, and I believe it might be pointed out that, because of the compact, objectified expression of it in his first book, it was all the more viable and resourceful in representing itself in the later ones, showing in his vivid visualization of things and in adding to such effects as meet the eye a bodily sense of textures and of the heft of things and of the tug-of-war play of elemental forces.

There is a deep-flowing continuity between *Typee* and *Moby Dick*, as also between *Typee* and the books which preceded and followed *Moby Dick*. This is to be observed in the way that facts written down as such in *Typee* keep recurring in its successors in strange contexts and with a new figurative or symbolic accentuation. For instance, a whaler is mentioned in *Typee* which had been many years at sea and was thought lost, but which turned up in a harbor in the South Seas, her hull all encased in barnacles and "three pet sharks" in her wake. The description of this ship is repeated in the much more elaborate description of the *Pequod* in *Moby Dick;* and the three pet sharks reappear with a new sinister connotation in the wake of Melville's canoe in *Mardi*. Again, at the very beginning of *Typee*, Melville is expressing how parched he felt after months spent out of sight of land: "Oh! for a refreshing glimpse of one blade of grass—for a snuff at the fragrance of a handful of the loamy earth! Is there nothing fresh around us? Is there no green thing to be seen?" At once we are reminded of the many references in *Moby Dick* to farms and fields in summer time, connoting growth and nourishment—April butter, for instance, and smells of meadows at hay-making—which make up an imagery of life in contrast to the salt, bleached imagery of the sea.

The significance which Melville attached in his first book to the island valley of Typee continued to unfold the further it dropped behind him in point of fact and as the perspective in which he looked back at it continued to open and to fill in with further realizations of life. The meaning of Typee varied as Melville reflected on it under the various pressures of his human make-up. Now it wore the complexion of joyous bodily living identified with Rabelais; now it wore the colors of the heart's deeper affections; and yet again it wore the subtilized colors of the soul. Still, for all this variation, the meaning that Typee had for Melville remained within recognizable limits. Whether Rabelaisian or spiritualized, and spiritualized, as we shall see it in some instances, in the likeness of Ralph Waldo Emerson, it was never out of reach of the idea of natural goodness, and always in Melville's dramatic view of life and his dramatic experience of what it is to be a human being it had for Melville the relish of salvation in it.

The outwardness or extroversion of the senses grew to include the outwardness of human ties and affections and, beyond that, the outwardness of religious faith. Thus, I believe, the significance of Typee was reëmbodied in Lucy, the good angel of *Pierre*, which is the most desperate and the least outward and objective of all Melville's books. Thus, too, the meaning of Typee grew into the symbolic significance of the land in *Moby Dick*, as opposed to the sea—the land being the sphere not only of sensuous and affectionate being, but also that in which men share together in worship and practical pursuits. Against this common continent of man stands the sea—"a foe to man, who is an alien to it." "The first boat we have read of floated on an ocean, that with Portuguese vengeance had whelmed the whole world without leaving so much as a widow. That same ocean rolls now . . ." and "however baby man may brag of his science and skill, and however much, in a flattering future, that science and skill may augment; yet forever and forever, to the crack of doom, the sea will insult and murder him, and pulverise the stateliest, stiffest frigate he can make. . . ."

While taking its place in this comprehensive and impersonal view of man, Typee retained its place in the perspective of the individual's consciousness, lying there a green island valley of sensuous and instinctive being against the arduous heights and ocean vastnesses of man's tremendous intellectual and spiritual nature. Its significance of outwardness, beginning with the outwardness of the senses and reaching to love and faith, is flashed against its terrible opposite in the words, almost the most impressive in all *Moby Dick*, "Though in many of its aspects this visible world seemed formed in love, the invisible spheres were formed in fright." It retained its place in the perspective of the individual's consciousness. That is to say, it retained its place in Melville's personal spiritual drama as representing his vital need, in the teeth of opposite needs almost as vital, to hold on to and to find his way back to those resources of life which he included under the significance of Typee. In that great act of being which was his life, which we are to see reflected in his books, so long as he might keep touch with Typee and might repair thither to refresh his sensuous and affectionate and spiritual nature, then no matter how far he might press into the invisible spheres of man's thought and consciousness it would be well with him. In the last view to take here of the meaning Typee came to have for Melville it appears under its original image, although, a point of no importance, the name is different: "Consider them both," wrote Melville, "the sea and the land; and do you not find a strange analogy to something in yourself? For as this appalling ocean surrounds the verdant land, so in the soul of man there lies one insular Tahiti, full of peace and joy, but encompassed by all the horrors of the half-known life. God keep thee! Push not off from that isle, thou canst never return."

3

Melville was nothing if not individualistic. Bodily as well as intellectually and spiritually he travelled a wide eccentric orbit. True as this was, there was much that he had in common with such Americans of his time as Emerson, Thoreau, Hawthorne, Whitman and Poe. For they were each and all of them individualistic and eccentric, some of them almost as much so as he. Going off in their separate directions, they were in accord in that they were all facing off at tangents to American orthodoxy and respectability. Melville and these others were at odds with America. That is, they were at odds with their nineteenth-century America of the industrial revolution which was spreading its rigor mortis of standardization and gentility over the face of the land.

In a larger view of things, however, it was not they but the solid mass of their respectable compatriots who were at odds with the main American movement and experience. Looking back to the seventeenth and eighteenth centuries one sees that a dominant impulse in American history was to break away from authority and to step free of the shackles of traditional society. That impulse was embodied in the Puritan and the pioneer alike. In the nineteenth century, all the way from the Atlantic seaboard almost up to the frontier, it was opposed by a growing dead weight of conventionalism and gentility. Nevertheless it persisted. It existed chiefly beyond the frontier and it signalized itself in some of the most moving events and greatest creations in American literature and literary history. For example, there is Leatherstocking, to whose spirit Cooper was never so loyal as at the end of *The Pioneers*. Civilization and society in the person of Judge Temple would persuade the old hunter to stay the remainder of his days where he had been all his life. True, these lands have become the judge's vast domain which he is parcelling out to hundreds of tenant farmers. No matter: the old hunter may feel himself as much at home as of old. But Leatherstocking will not accept the judge's kindness. Between the impulse which he represents and the circumspections and circumventions and circumscriptions impersonated by Judge Temple there is no reconciliation. Old as he is, he leaves his familiar hunting grounds and presses alone into the western wilderness where he dies. So, too, at the end of *Huckleberry Finn*, Mark Twain was true to the impulse which created the hero of his finest book. Huck will not be fooled a second time by Tom Sawyer's slick salesmanship that would persuade him that he can be free—free as it was in his soul to understand freedom—and remain a respectable member of society with good prospects of amassing a reputable fortune. This time Huck will not submit; he will not be tamed: "I reckon I got to light out . . . because Aunt Sally says she's going to adopt me and sivilize me and I can't stand it. I been there before."

"I am a free companion." "I confront peace, security, and all the settled laws, to unsettle them. . . ." Walt Whitman's revolt against the restraints of society and his vagabondage was the same as Huck's but on a cosmic scale. And how close, by the way, to Melville's response to the graceful insouciance of the Typees was Walt's response to the animals, "so placid and self-contain'd":

> They do not lie awake in the dark and weep for their sins,
> They do not make me sick discussing their duty to God,
> Not one is dissatisfied, not one is demented with the mania of
>   owning things,
>
> .   .   .   .   .
>
> Not one is respectable or industrious over the whole earth.

Emerson experienced the conflict between society and solitude, as he called it—the restraints of the one and the freedom of the other. His heart chose solitude. Thoreau turned his back more boldly on society. "They who know of no purer sources of truth," he wrote, "who have traced up its stream no higher, stand, and wisely stand, by the Bible and the Constitution, and drink at it there with reverence and humility; but they who behold where it comes trickling into this lake or that pool, gird up their loins once more, and continue their pilgrimage toward its fountainhead." It is as if the long process of revolt which originated in England in the seventeenth century and was carried forward by successive generations of Puritans and pioneers, which dissented from the Church of England and broke away from the British government, came to a climax when Thoreau turned his back on civilization and went to live alone at Walden Pond. There was nothing closer dramatically and spiritually to Thoreau's action than Melville's, in giving up the respectable occupations of clerk and schoolteacher to sail off in the crew of a disreputable whaler and find an earthly paradise among the cannibals of Typee.

Note

1. C. R. Anderson, *Melville in the South Seas* (New York, 1935).

[The Maimed Man in the Glen]

Richard Chase*

The hero of *Typee* presumably suffered the same kind of alienation aboard his whaler as did Redburn aboard his merchantman. He found the crew mean-spirited and "dastardly." The captain was a vengeful "Lord of the Plank." The young hero and his companion, Toby, jumped ship in the Marquesas and fled inland. From then on the story describes another kind of alienation: the more pleasurable but more terrible alienation of one who was coddled and worshiped and at the same time inscrutably held prisoner by one's benefactors. Redburn was the young man who, though poignantly remembering the past, matured and began to accept the conditions of maturity. The young hero of *Typee* withdrew into the past, his anxieties and his pleasures were archaic, and he could finally break out of the prison of the past—his own past—only by a violent and tortured assertion of a nearly paralyzed will.

Having left the ship, the young hero and his companion fought their way into the mountainous interior of the island, painfully cutting a path through growths of yellow reeds, strong as steel rods, that thickly blocked their way. They scaled steep sunlit mountains by day and retreated into damp, wild glens by night. After much suffering from hunger and fatigue, they made a nightmarishly dangerous descent into a deep gorge which they hoped was Happar Valley and not Typee Valley—for though the Happars were rumored to be mild and friendly, the Typees were notorious for their cannibalism. As it happened, they made the wrong choice. But, surprisingly, the Typees turned out to be ostensibly as kind and temperate as possible.

The descent into the valley of Typee was a withdrawal from the world, and the valley was, for the young hero, a sanctuary containing unknown but enticing treasures. The chief enticement, which gives its character to the whole experience, was a mild, somnolent eroticism, tinged, however, with vague intimations of "frightful contingencies."

*Reprinted with permission of Macmillan Publishing Co., Inc., from *Herman Melville: A Critical Study*, by Richard Chase. Copyright 1949 by Richard Chase, renewed 1977 by Frances W. Chase.

The first human beings the hero saw in the valley were a naked boy and girl, the boy's arm placed fondly about the girl's shoulders.

The young hero, who had left a fatherless family at home, was accepted into a native family, with whom he lived during his four months' stay. The family consisted of Marheyo, the patriarch who had once been a splendid warrior and now tried to make the hero happy with an abundance of touchingly foolish deeds of kindness; Tinor, the affectionate matriarch who bustled about like a benevolently officious housewife; Kory-Kory, a bizarre but endlessly thoughtful young savage who was appointed to be the hero's constant attendant; and Fayaway, a beautiful girl with whom the hero soon fell in love. There were various other young men and women in the household, but the blood relationship of all of these people was equivocal: they were not said to be brothers and sisters or sons and daughters (beyond the explicit statement that Kory-Kory was the son of Marheyo).

At first the hero was painfully ill; he had a "mysterious malady" in his leg, presumably the result of an injury sustained in the long climb over the mountains. He was overcome by dark forebodings and a profound melancholy which he recognized as being far in excess of a natural response to his physical injury and for which, therefore, he could not account. The hero's low state of spirits and his paralysis of will were, however, justified by at least two outward circumstances: the Typees might yet prove to be cannibals, and Toby, who had fled over the mountains to summon help, might have met a violent end, or so, with a placid impenetrability, the natives vaguely hinted.

But on the whole the natives were gay and kindly. They ministered to the hero's needs, and Kory-Kory carried him around on his shoulders. His body was anointed every day by the young girls of the family, and soon he was able, with the help of Kory-Kory, to bathe with the girls in an idyllic lake set enchantingly in the midst of the valley and fed with fresh waters. Gradually the hero lost all sense of time and anxiety. He sank into a pleasantly hedonistic apathy. His leg improved and he began to enjoy a sort of passive happiness, a muted and continuous erotic ecstasy. Swimming with the girls, he dove under the water and playfully tried to pull them under. Fayaway, whose blue eyes and soft tawny skin enchanted him, became his constant companion. They bathed together; they lounged long hours together in a canoe paddled by Kory-Kory; or the young hero steered the canoe while Fayaway, having slipped off her mantle, unfurled it as a sail and stood gracefully in the center of the canoe, her straight body serving as a mast. He admired Fayaway; he admired the natives and their way of life, finding "the tranquillizing influences of beautiful scenery and the exhibition of human life under so novel and charming an aspect" a great consolation. And he admired himself; his own beloved image appealed to him with persistent eroticism. He came to feel that he was quite "the belle of the season, in the pride of her beauty and power"; and the charming, naïve natives, who reacted as surely as reflexes to his impulses, became less real external objects than extensions of his own personality. When he had first joined the household of Marheyo, Kory-Kory had insisted on feeding poi to the young hero with his own fingers. It was an appropriately symbolic act, for the hero, with a sad gaiety, was reliving his childhood in terms of the entrancingly fitting symbolic objects of which Typee Valley so expertly consisted.

But the sense of guilt and foreboding which the indulgences of his archaic emotions gave the hero could not be entirely avoided. They became sharply recrudescent when the natives insisted that he should be tattooed; it was a religious rite whose sanctions no one could do without. But Karky, the tattoo artist, with his slender instrument tipped with a shark's tooth and his small wooden mallet, aroused in the hero a deep revulsion, which proceeded far more from a fear that his body might be mutilated than from a realization that the pagan rite of tattooing would be sacrilege for a Christian. Shortly after meeting Karky, the pain in his leg returned so violently that he felt "unmanned." And this calamity was followed by the chance discovery that three tapa bundles which hung from the ridgepole of Marheyo's house contained three human heads, one of a white man, two of natives.

The hero's escape from Typee Valley was sudden and violent. An Australian whaler, in need of men, put a boat ashore, and with a terrible effort the hero limped down to the beach, eluded the hostile natives, taking advantage of a dispute among them as to whether he should be allowed to go or not, and leaving Marheyo, Kory-Kory, and Fayaway weeping in the surf, managed to fall exhausted into the boat.

In *Redburn* the young man, still a boy, learned to master the feelings aroused in him by hunger, discomfort, excrement, obscenity, cruelty, death, and alienation from his kind; and he began to see that somehow human life—personality and society—had to be based upon these things. It was an act of growing up. In *Typee* the young man performed a further act. With a great effort and much suffering, he withdrew into the recesses of his own infantile sexuality and then escaped to a higher level. He feared cannibalism in general; but specifically he feared castration. This was the real content of the nameless foreboding which he felt when he descended into Typee Valley and when he was about to escape. He did not feel this fear during the time when he was able to give himself over to the mild eroticism of the valley. To leave the archaic level of personality and civilization represented by Typee Valley was to face and suffer and overcome the fears which accompanied maturing sexuality. This figure, the hero suffering the fear of castration, became a common one in Melville's books. We can call him "the Maimed Man in the Glen"; and we shall discover him again in Ahab, in Pierre Glendinning (whose surname means "dweller in a glen"), in the "invalid Titan" of *The Confidence Man*, and in other of Melville's characters.

The hero's attachment to Fayaway cannot be regarded as a completely sexualized one. She remained a wraith of youthful erotic fantasies, as her name indicated. From the departing whaleboat the hero threw a bolt of colored cloth to Fayaway—an intolerably callous act, the reader thinks, until he begins to reflect that the young man, having taken his decisive step, now sincerely and perhaps correctly regarded Fayaway as a child or a wraith, not as a mature lover. It is by no means clear that the hero's act hurt Fayaway. . . .

The young man who had observed society in the forecastles of a merchantman and a whaler and who had seen the injustices of industrial civilization in Liverpool had begun to develop political ideas. Longing for the ideal society, where affairs are conducted with compassion and noble simplicity, he was very much impressed by the Typees. He compared Western civilization unfavorably with Typee Valley, and openly deplored the inevitable arrival of French military forces with their cruelty, corruption, and syphilis and the missionaries with their self-righteous hypocrisy. "Civilization," he decided, "does not engross all the virtues of humanity." The Typees

> deal more kindly with each other, and are more humane, than many who study essays on virtue and benevolence, and who repeat every night that beautiful prayer breathed first by the lips of the divine and gentle Jesus. I will frankly declare that after passing a few weeks in this valley of the Marquesas, I formed a higher estimate of human nature than I had ever before entertained.

In Typee the young man found mild and dignified chiefs but no police and no courts of law. There was, to be sure, an extensive system of taboo, but it was seldom oppressive and did not interfere with the harmony of daily life. The natives generally conducted themselves according to an indwelling sense of virtue and honor which kept them free of the weight of social protocol and confusion. They were, in the best sense, "carefree." Eros, far from being the malign demon that often goads and worries civilized society, conspired harmoniously with the social institutions of Typee.

Still, as the young man realized, it was part of the process of growing up to force oneself to grow beyond the Typee society. There was an unintegrated part of Typee which its bland social institutions and its benevolence either ignored or could not control: cannibalism. And cannibalism might at any moment overturn and destroy Typee society. In Typee, Eros was an emasculated god and so was its political god; he was a god who remained a child, who was content to make his social arrangements at too low a level of maturity, a god who could not face, understand, and accept the tragic realities or the larger ecstasies of human life. The tendency of Western civilization was to take cognizance of these tragic realities and to try, at least, to arrange social institutions accord-

ingly. And so the young man had to return to it, though he was so sad-
dened at the thought of the undeniable advantages of Typee society.

As the author of *Mardi* intimated, "no past time is lost time." The
past must be studied and understood, to keep it from playing on one its
monstrous tricks of seduction. For those who could not understand their
own past, or themselves as products of it, there was the danger that they
would be betrayed into thinking that a reversion was really a standing in
the present or a motion toward the future. In *Moby-Dick* the young man
at the helm of the *Pequod* was to feel this danger one night when the crew
was boiling blubber in the vats and the ship seemed to be "freighted with
savages, and laden with fire, and burning a corpse, and plunging into the
blackness of darkness." The young man succumbed to a momentary
drowsiness and lost consciousness in an inexpressible dream. Then

> starting from a brief, standing sleep, I was horribly conscious of some-
> thing fatally wrong. The jaw-bone tiller smote my side, which leaned
> against it; in my ears was the low hum of sails just beginning to shake in
> the wind. . . . I could see no compass before me to steer by . . . Nothing
> seemed before me but a jet gloom, now and then made ghastly by flashes
> of redness. Uppermost was the impression, that whatever swift, rushing
> thing I stood on was not so much bound for any haven ahead as rushing
> from all havens astern.

The young man realized, with a "stark, bewildered feeling, as of death,"
that in his sleep he had turned around so that he faced astern and that in
letting go of the tiller he had almost brought the ship up into the wind and
capsized her. He had lost his bearings, for, facing backward, he could not
see the compass. Momentarily the relation of past, present, and future
was confused. He feared the present and the probably disastrous future;
even more he feared the past, under whose sudden influence he had
turned around and almost turned the little world of the *Pequod* with him:
he was gripped at this moment, as D. H. Lawrence says in his study of
Moby-Dick, with the "horror of reversion, or undoing." In a later episode
the same confusion of time is again symbolized: the *Pequod*'s compass is
magnetically inverted during an electric storm in the night, and the next
morning finds the ship running precisely opposite to the course that had
been set for her.

Typee was Melville's most adequately symbolized study of the past.
But the memory of the past was not always accompanied by horror. In
a love poem, written in later times, Melville could use such a wistful
image as:

> I yearn, I yearn, reverting turn,
> My heart it streams in wake astern.

Again he could call himself and Ned Bunn (a mythical companion)
"Typee-truants" who once as "pleasure-hunters broke loose"

>   for our pantheistic ports:
>   Marquesas and glenned isles that be
>   Authentic Edens in a Pagan sea.

And with mildly sardonic wisdom he could indulge his nostalgia for the "authentic Edens" and at the same time observe that "Adam advances."

The Author of *Typee, Omoo,* &c.

Newton Arvin*

Most modern writers have come to the literary career in response to a vocation of which they have been conscious from boyhood on; if they have not lisped in numbers, they have at any rate filled their adolescence with plans for novels, for ambitious poems, for plays. One cannot say flatly that this was not true of Melville; we do not know whether it was or not. But in spite of the "Fragments from a Writing-Desk," one's impression is that Melville came to literature, not after long and conscious preparation, but with a kind of inadvertence. He speaks of having dreamed as a boy of becoming a great traveler and even of becoming a famous orator but never of becoming an author. The need for movement, for flight, for the coarse stuff of experience was stronger in him in his earliest youth than the need for expression. The germ of what was creative in him needed to ripen, not in solitude or in intellectual labor, but in the push and stir of action. In the beginning, for Melville, was decidedly not the word, but the deed. Not until he had to come to terms with the dense material world and the actualities of the human struggle was he prepared to give himself out in language and form. His development, in that sense, as he recognized, had been abnormally postponed, and when it came, it came with a rush and a force that had the menace of quick exhaustion in it. Could it possibly be maintained at that pitch over the span of a long career?

That remained to be seen, but meanwhile, in just this respect, in the postponement of creation to action, Melville makes one think, not of the representative modern man of letters, for whom action has been either secondary or without significance, but of a heterogeneous list of writers, as different from one another as from him in power and in character, writers like Smollett or Stendhal or Fenimore Cooper or Tolstoy, who spent their earliest years, not at their writing desks, but on the deck of a ship or in the train of a marching army. Bookish as Melville had always been and was increasingly to be, he came to the profession of letters as a

*Reprinted from Newton Arvin, *Herman Melville* (New York: William Sloane Associates, 1950), pp. 77–88, with permission of William Morrow and Co.

kind of brilliant amateur, and he was never quite to take on, whether for better or for worse, the mentality of the professional.

This is hardly to say that he was a lesser writer than those who did. Nor certainly is it to say, on a more superficial level, that he was not, once he had found his tongue, almost unaccountably productive. One imagines him writing *Typee* in much the same spirit in which Dana had written *Two Years* or in which the young Englishman Kinglake was writing *Eothen:* because he had seen a bit of the world, because his head was stored with fresh impressions and entertaining circumstances, and because his relatives and friends had drawn him out in conversation in a way that aroused and ignited him. No doubt he wrote *Typee* almost casually; it turned into a great success before his eyes; his powerful literary instincts were fully awakened, and there followed, during the next five or six years, at a breathless pace, four other books—*Omoo, Mardi, Redburn,* and *White-Jacket*—in the composition of which he can hardly have paused or deliberated. Neither Dana nor Kinglake had done anything of the sort, and that is one difference between them and Melville.

This was the school of writing, nevertheless, that furnished Melville his springboard as an artist. It was no mere accident that it did so, but a characteristic fact that holds for no other nineteenth-century writer of his stature. He did not begin at once, like most of them, as a writer of tales, sketches, or novels for the periodicals or the booksellers' libraries of the era; he did not begin as a successor of Sterne or Godwin or Scott, of Mrs. Radcliffe or Hoffmann. He began as one more writer of travel narrative, and the books from which he took off were not *Tristram Shandy* or *Waverly* but Mungo Park's *Travels in the Interior of Africa,* the Rev. C. S. Stewart's *Visit to the South Seas,* and of course the book he called "my friend Dana's unmatchable *Two Years Before the Mast.*" Saying this is something like saying that George Eliot began as a writer of critical and philosophical articles for the *Westminster Review;* no other writer of just that sort has gone on to write books like *Middlemarch,* and none of the other writers of "travels" or "journals" or "narratives" went on to write books like *Moby Dick.* But George Eliot's whole work is pervaded by the attitudes of the moralist and critic, and Melville, for his part, was always to be an imaginative writer for whom the facts of movement through space, of change of site, of physical unrestingness and the forward push were basic. The voyage or quest was not simply a subject or an occasion for him; it was an archetypal pattern of experience to which his whole nature instinctively turned, and he was to lose half his strength not when he lost contact with the earth but when he stood still upon it.

Typee and *Omoo,* to be sure, were books that he wrote, if not off the top of his mind, at any rate off its less profound levels, and it is idle to look for great depths or difficulties in them; to do so would be to miss their special quality of spontaneity and youthfulness. Yet there are intimations of complexity in them, and in a purely literary sense, easy though they seem, they are curiously many-faceted. They owe something, in a general way, to the whole tradition of travel literature since the modern age of discovery began, and particularly to the voyages of the eighteenth century, to the writers of the age of Cook and Carteret and Bougainville, whose aim was always to be lucid, impersonal, informative; to suppress *themselves* and to convey the facts, however novel or strange, with the most reasonable and enlightened objectivity. A love of information for its own sake was one of the aspects of Melville's complex mind, as every reader of *Moby Dick* knows; and when, in *Typee*, he describes the process of making tapa or the operations of the system of tabu, or when, in *Omoo*, he dilates on the botany and the economy of the coco-palm, his tone and manner are not easily distinguishable from those in which Captain Cook or Bougainville or Langsdorff had expatiated on exactly similar subjects. Melville's first two books have been quoted by anthropologists since his time, by Sir James Frazer for example, as having at least some claim to trustworthiness, despite Melville's very small comprehension of the language of Taipi or Tahiti. The fact is that, whenever his imagination was at work most freely and naturally, it sought for and found the factual, prosaic counterpoise to the inwardness and ideality that were its essential expression; and *Typee* and *Omoo* owe much of their vitality to their apparently unpoetic ballast of facts.

A transformation, however, had taken place in the literature of travel since the eighteenth century, just as it had done in literature generally, and such books could no longer be written sustainedly in the old manner, any more than novels could be written in the manner of Diderot or Smollett. The dry, clear, sober impersonality of the older writers had given place to a more and more frankly personal and subjective style, whimsical, humorous, lyrical, sentimental, or poetic; Melville began writing in a period that had formed its taste on such lighthearted and charming books as Heine's *Pictures of Travel*, Irving's *Alhambra*, Kinglake's *Eothen*, and Gautier's *Travels in Spain*. Information of a kind does indeed appear in books like these, but what really counts in them is not that but feeling, fancy, atmosphere, and the effort to evoke as many and as brilliant pictures as possible. The sense of the painterly has usurped the place of the older interest in fact.

Even in a writer like Mungo Park, at the turn of the nineteenth century, one detects already a strain of personal feeling and even a sense of the pictorial that is by no means merely "eighteenth century"; and Mungo Park was almost certainly one of Melville's literary masters. There are deeply moving passages in Park's *Travels*, but what happened to travel writing after his time becomes evident when one turns to Melville abruptly from a writer of his sort. Here is a passage, quite typical of Park's ordinary narrative style, from his account of a night spent at an African town in the kingdom of Kajaaga:

I found a great crowd surrounding a party who were dancing by the light of some large fires, to the music of four drums, which were beat with great exactness and uniformity. The dances, however, consisted more in wanton gestures than in muscular exertion or graceful attitudes. The ladies vied with each other in displaying the most voluptuous movements imaginable.

Compare with this—in its quiet, taciturn failure to realize a potentially quite wonderful picture—compare with it Melville's description in *Omoo* of the dancing girls at Tamai or, better yet, this description in *Typee* of a fishing party returning from the beach at night:

Once, I remember, the party arrived at midnight; but the unseasonableness of the hour did not repress the impatience of the islanders. The carriers dispatched from the Ti were to be seen hurrying in all directions through the deep groves; each individual preceded by a boy bearing a flaming torch of dried cocoa-nut boughs, which from time to time was replenished from the materials scattered along the path. The wild glare of these enormous flambeaux, lighting up with a startling brilliancy the innermost recesses of the vale, and seen moving rapidly along beneath the canopy of leaves, the savage shout of the excited messengers sounding the news of their approach, which was answered on all sides, and the strange appearance of their naked bodies, seen against the gloomy background, produced altogether an effect upon my mind that I shall long remember.

Naturally this is not yet Melville in his great evocative vein, and Stevenson was later to outdo him, just here, in finish and precision of brush stroke, but the passage will serve as a fair example of Melville's painterliness in *Typee* and *Omoo*. Like some other passages in those books, it hints to us—with its romantic chiaroscuro, its violent contrast of deep shadow and high flaring lights, the uncanniness of its moving figures, and its dependence on words like "wild," "startling," "strange," and "gloomy"—hints to us that Melville, in looking at the scenes that passed before him and in reinvoking them, had learned something from such Gothic writers as Mrs. Radcliffe and "Monk" Lewis, and that through them, perhaps also independently, his landscape sense had been formed by the Baroque painters they were always echoing, by Claude Lorrain and Salvator Rosa. Salvator in the Marquesas might have done the nocturne of the fishing party. Baroque, at any rate, most of Melville's landscapes and seascapes certainly are, as well as many of the other scenes he composes like pictures. The hours he spent as a boy poring over the portfolios of prints Allan Melville had brought home had worked a permanent influence on his imagination.

His first two books abound in pictorial effects that can only be described as in some sense romantic; wild and fearful like the gorges, ravines, and chasms of Nuku-Hiva through which he and Toby make their painful way in *Typee*; solemn, deeply shaded, and awe-inspiring, like the tabu groves in Taipi-Vai; uncannily beautiful like another fishing party by torchlight, in *Omoo*, in the sullen surf off Moorea; or in a wholly different vein—the vein of Claude rather than of Salvator—pastoral, Arcadian, richly reposeful, like the first breathless glimpse of the Paradisal valley of Taipi. Already in these early, experimental books, with varying degrees of success, Melville knows how to cover a gamut of painterly and emotional effects that ranges all the way from the broad and serene to the wild, the grim, and even the grotesque. And indeed it is evident that these contrasts of tone and feeling, especially marked in *Typee*, are conscious and artful, not merely inadvertent, and that they express a native feeling for structure and style that already suggests how much farther Melville may go as an imaginative writer than any of the narrators he is emulating. *Two Years Before the Mast* is a greater book than either *Typee* or *Omoo*, in its strong, sustained austerity of style as well as in its grandeur of feeling; but Melville's books are the unmistakable products of a far more complex and ductile mind than Dana's, and potentially, of course, of a richer creative power. Dana's great book suggests no artistic mode beyond itself; *Typee* and *Omoo* hint constantly at the freer and more plastic form of fiction.

When they first appeared, indeed, they were taxed, or credited, by many readers with being *pure* fiction, and some of these readers, at least, were more imaginative than those who took them for sober fact. It is not only that we now know how long a bow Melville was drawing in both books, especially *Typee*; how freely he was improvising on the mere actualities of his experience; that is an external and mechanical sort of check. The books themselves need only to be read responsively in order to uncover their real quality—their real and equivocal quality of narrative that is constantly vibrating between the poles of "truthfulness" and fantasy. The proportion of sober truthfulness in *Omoo* is doubtless greater than in *Typee*, and the free, fanciful strains in it take the form of playfulness, gay exaggeration, and grotesqueness rather than, as they mostly do in *Typee*, of a heightened "anxiety," on the one hand, and a deliberate idyllism, on the other. But in both books Melville is far too much the born artist not to keep bathing the plain truth in a medium of imaginative intensity.

A few weeks after *Typee* was published, as we have seen, Toby Greene unexpectedly turned up in Buffalo to testify to the veracity of those chapters for which he could vouch, but we must not take his evidence too literally. Melville's story of what happened after he and Toby plunged into the interior of Nuku-Hiva, of the hardships and sufferings they underwent before they arrived in Taipi—this story bears on the face of it the hallmarks of poetic sublimation. Plenty of travelers have undergone greater ordeals than Melville's was at its worst, and one has only, again, to read Mungo Park's account of some of his solitary vicissitudes in order to observe how calmly and even barely the thing can be done. There is nothing calm or bare and certainly nothing austere in

Melville's narrative. It is frankly and volubly a tale of tribulation: it abounds in the imagery of physical and mental misery. At the outset Melville and Toby are drenched by a downpour of tropical rain; they find themselves trapped in a thicket of dense, resistant reeds; they are baked by the heat of midday; they scramble up a steep cliff and crawl along a ridge on their bellies to evade detection; they are confronted by a series of "dark and fearful chasms, separated by sharp-crested and perpendicular ridges," up and down which they painfully clamber; they spend the nights in gloomy ravines, shivering with the chill and dampness; and at last they make their way down into the valley by falling, rather than descending, from ledge to ledge of a horridly high, steep precipice. Throughout, they suffer from hunger and raging thirst; Melville, from a painful injury to his leg; and both of them, from "frightful anticipations of evil." We move, in all this, not over the solid terrain of even a romantic island but amidst a dream-imagery of deadly apprehensiveness, baffled and dismayed by obstacle after obstacle, and oppressed continually by a dread of what is before us. Such writing is far less reminiscent of *Two Years* than it is of Mrs. Radcliffe or Poe.

The note of nightmarish foreboding, in any case, is struck recurrently in *Typee*, where it reaches a culmination of intensity in the last chapters, with Melville's gruesome discoveries and his horror lest he should be powerless to escape. It alternates, however, like a theme in music, with the strongly contrasted note of contentment and peace; the contentment and peace of daydreaming. The conflict between wishful revery and the anxiety that springs from a feeling of guilt, in short, goes on throughout the book. In *Omoo*, on the other hand, perhaps because it was written in a period of emotional freedom and effervescence, there is no such inner drama and no such stylistic musicality. The contrasts of tone in the book are furnished partly by the simple alternation between personal narrative and impersonal informativeness, but also by the relatively prosaic setting-off of the hardships and exasperations of life aboard the *Julia* (Melville's name for the *Lucy Ann*) or in the Calabooza Beretanee against the heady pleasures of freedom and vagrancy. The play of fantasy in *Omoo* takes the form not of nightmarishness or even of daydreaming but of an easy and emotionally liberating current of humorous narrative, always slightly in excess, as one sees with half an eye, of the sober autobiographical facts. It usually has the satisfactory effect of throwing a ludicrous light on the representatives of order and authority—captains and mates, consuls and missionaries, resident physicians and native constables. There is still, as a result, an emotional release in reading *Omoo*, as in reading any such book; we take our own revenge on respectability by contemplating the discomfiture of the feeble Captain Guy and the bullying consul Wilson, or by listening to the wily sermon of the Chadband whom Melville describes himself as hearing in the church at Papeete.

It is true that, compared with the billows of almost demoniac humor on which *Moby Dick* is so incredibly sustained, the humor of *Typee* and even of *Omoo* seems gentle and rather tame. Yet one feels at once that it is the expression of a genuinely humorous fancy. One feels it in such accounts as that of the popgun war in *Typee* or of Long Ghost's jolly philanderings in *Omoo*. One feels it even verbally in such remarks as that Captain Guy was "no more meant for the sea than a hairdresser," or in the observation on the ugliness of the ship's carpenter on the *Julia:* "There was no absolute deformity about the man; he was symmetrically ugly." One feels this youthful humor chiefly, however, in the individual characters in whom both books abound, and who are treated with a freedom far closer to fiction than to mere reminiscence. The difference is easily evident when one puts one of Dana's characters—say the young Hawaiian, Hope, or the English sailor, George P. Marsh, a decayed gentleman—side by side with characters like Melville's Kory-Kory or Long Ghost. Dana's portraits have the sobriety and the realism of Copley's in another medium; Melville's come closer to suggesting Cruikshank or Phiz. For the rest, in the period when he was writing *Typee* and *Omoo*, it was mostly the amusing, even lovable oddities and humors of human character that engaged him, not its darknesses and depravities. There are shadows of some intensity here and there; in the brutal Captain Vangs and in the dark, moody, vindictive Maori harpooner, Bembo; but mostly the scene is animated by such gently comic personages as fussy old Marheyo in Taipi, or the grotesque-looking Kory-Kory, or the poor landlubber sailor, Ropey, on the *Julia*.

Most of them are mere sketches, lightly and hastily drawn; and the most fully realized feminine character, the exquisite Fayaway, is not so much drawn as vaguely and dreamily evoked in wishful water colors. Only one personage among them all is painted at full length; this is the demoted ship's surgeon, Long Ghost, who is the real protagonist of *Omoo* (Melville himself is the protagonist of *Typee*), and who embodies the complete footlooseness, the perfect irresponsibility, which Melville, on one side of his nature, would have liked to attain. A ruined gentleman, well-read and well-mannered, but lazy, mischievous, reckless, amorous, and rascally, Long Ghost appears in the forecastle of the *Julia* as if he were a personal materialization of all Melville's longings for a really unbraced and ungirded freedom. So long as the mood lasts, Long Ghost sticks by his side, a perfect companion, indeed another self, but at length the mood passes, the fundamental seriousness in Melville reasserts itself, and about to join the crew of the *Leviathan* he takes leave both of the waggish doctor and, to all intents and purposes, of the beachcomber in himself.

The gesture has an almost allegorical quality. Lighthearted and unprofound as on the whole they are, *Typee* and *Omoo* have an undertone of serious meaning. Taken together they tell the story of a quest or pilgrimage—a pilgrimage not, certainly, "from this world to that which is to come," but from the world of enlightened rationality, technical progress, and cultural complexity backward and downward and, so to say, inward to the primordial world that *was* before metals, before the alphabet, before cities; the slower, graver, nakeder world of stone, of carved wood, of the tribe, of the ritual dance and human sacrifice and the prerational myth. It was a pilgrimage that led to no all-answering oracle or consummatory revelation; in that sense it was a failure. But it was a pilgrimage that Melville's deepest needs had driven him to make, and he did not return from it empty-handed. There are passages in *Typee* especially that tell us how really intense, how far from merely fashionable, was his animus against "civilized barbarity," against "the tainted atmosphere of a feverish civilization." He returned to civilization in the end, but he had had a long gaze at a simpler, freer, gayer, and yet also statelier mode of life, and this was to serve him, in memory, as a stabilizing and fortifying image. His own creative power, moreover, at its height, was primeval and myth-making in a sense that, in his day, was of the rarest: it could never have been set free, just as it was, if he himself had not made his descent into the canyon of the past. In touching the body of Fayaway, Melville had regained contact with the almost vanished life of myth.

His instincts had guided him rightly when they sent him wandering into the young Pacific world, and they guided him rightly when they drove him away from it again and back to civilized society, to resume a burden he had temporarily laid down—the burden of consciousness, of the full and anguished consciousness of modern man. He had taken a long plunge into the realm of the preconscious and the instinctual, the realm of heedless impulse and irreflective drift; he had been refreshed, indeed remade, by it; but he had found there no ultimate resolution of his difficulties. Not in avoiding the clash between consciousness and the unconscious, between mind and emotion, between anxious doubt and confident belief, but in confronting these antinomies head-on and, hopefully, transcending them—in that direction, as Melville intuitively saw, lay his right future as an adult person. The alternative was a lifetime of raffish vagrancy with the seedy Long Ghost, and a kind of Conradian dilapidation at the end. In the last chapter of *Omoo*, saying good-bye to this companion, he insists on Long Ghost's taking half the Spanish dollars which the captain of the *Leviathan* has given him as an advance; a generous but also a proper payment for the wisdom he has acquired in Long Ghost's society. A new cruise awaits him, on another vessel; and in fact, when Melville finished the writing of *Omoo*, he had come to the end of one expedition, in the intellectual and literary sense, and was ready to set out again in a quite different direction.

Eden Revisited

Lawrance Thompson*

> Ah, paddle away, brave chieftain, to the land of spirits! To the material eye thou makest but little progress; but with the eye of faith, I see thy canoe cleaving the bright waves, which die away on those dimly looming shores of Paradise.
>
> This strange superstition affords another evidence of the fact, that however ignorant man may be, he still feels within him his immortal spirit yearning after the unknown futuro.
>
> MELVILLE, *Typee*

So rich and varied were Melville's youthful adventures that they provided abundant raw materials for seven book-length narratives, which he wrote and published during the first seven years of his literary career. Such an extraordinary demonstration of sheer energy (not to mention talent) is not easily matched in the history of American letters; but there is a restricted aspect of that demonstration which is even more extraordinary. In most of those narratives, Melville consciously arranged his picturesque subject matter to represent, in specific or symbolic forms, different aspects of his own religious disillusionment.

Pierre, the seventh of these narratives, is easily recognized as a fictional projection of the author's spiritual autobiography during the progressive phases of his youth. *Moby-Dick,* the sixth, is centered symbolically on a limited aspect of Captain Ahab's religious disillusionment, which has much in common with a parallel aspect of Melville's own story. Although the other five narratives should be viewed as apprentice works in which Melville was making elaborate experiments with style, structure, form, as he sought to discover his own idiom, they all deal with disillusionment, in either subject matter or theme. Of these, the fifth, *White-Jacket,* carried in its very title the central image of a homemade garment (symbolically a garment of the conscience) which the owner improvises, patches, discards. The fourth, *Redburn,* is a story of a young man's initial and disillusioning contact with the world when he leaves

*"Eden Revisited," in Lawrence Thompson, *Melville's Quarrel with God* (copyright 1952, copyright renewed © 1980 by Princeton University Press), pp. 42–55. Reprinted by permission of Princeton University Press.

home for the first time. The third, *Mardi,* approaches the subject of disillusionment in terms of conventional moral allegory.

A careful progression through these narratives, in chronological order of writing, will also reveal that Melville's spiritual idiom (in part the cause and in part the effect of his disillusionment) was the major factor which shaped and controlled and determined his mature artistic idiom. The complexities of that involved relationship are only suggested by the demonstrable fact that his cumulative revulsion against orthodox Christian doctrine made him so self-conscious that he began, in *Mardi,* to experiment with riddling techniques, insinuative symbolism, satirical allegory, to protect himself from, and to retaliate against, those orthodox readers who were his enemies.

For purposes of clarification, three distinct phases of Melville's blended artistic and spiritual development may be suggested, somewhat arbitrarily. The first phase, reflected in his first two books, *Typee* (1846) and *Omoo* (1847), reveals his apprentice preoccupation with mere travel-narrative (essentially factual in nature), written during a period when he still clung to his jolted belief in the fundamentals of his Calvinistic religious heritage. The second phase, reflected in his third book, *Mardi* (1849), reveals his more sophisticated artistic preoccupation with moral allegory, written during a period when his own heart and mind had suddenly become a battleground across which his growing skepticism counterattacked his deeply ingrained mystical faith. Defensively, Melville arranged an alliance between Christian and Platonic concepts, in *Mardi,* to resist that counterattack. The third phase, reflected in his next two books, *Redburn* (1849) and *White-Jacket* (1850), reveals his modified use of fictionalized travel-narrative (blended with ambivalent allegorical connotations in *White-Jacket*), during a period when he began to take increasingly crafty and covert delight in asserting his skepticism; when he became increasingly preoccupied with glorifying Rousseau's concepts of man-centered man's inalienable rights, and with ridiculing Calvinistic concepts of God-centered man.

I am aware that this arbitrary representation of these so-called phases is much too pat, in that it oversimplifies the fluctuations and complexities of Melville's aesthetic and spiritual responses to his own experience. Nevertheless, some form of oversimplification is necessary in order to clarify the fact that the tug of war in Melville's heart and mind did have a recognizable outcome, and did not end in a stalemate. Matthew Arnold's "Dover Beach" image (tidal ebb, as symbolic of religious disillusionment) may be modified to serve us here. By the time Melville came to write *Typee* and *Omoo,* he himself was apparently aware that his own Sea of Faith (which had been at the full during the years before he left home) had begun to ebb; yet he tried to resist that ebb. Although the immediate sea-level, during an ebb tide, moves slowly and irresistibly out and down, the waves move in exactly the opposite direction. And each wave leaves briefly the distinct mark of its attainment on the beach. Melville's resistance to the ebb of his own belief may be represented by that wave-versus-tide siege of contraries. During the first two phases of Melville's apprenticeship disillusionment, his response differed from Arnold's, in that Melville refused to surrender to the tide's "melancholy, long, withdrawing roar, retreating." His reaction was one of wavelike resistance, temporarily, and the brief attainment of these waves may be viewed in all these early narratives.

2

In planning to write his first narrative, just after his twenty-fifth birthday, Melville chose to present a slightly fictionalized version of a picturesque personal experience still quite fresh in his mind. Approximately four years earlier, he had shipped out of New Bedford aboard the whaler *Acushnet* for the Pacific, and had grown so dissatisfied with drudgery that he had jumped ship at Nukuhiva Harbor in the South Seas. He and his shipmate-companion in the escapade decided to hide away in a native valley, but by accident they entered the wrong valley and were forced to accept the dubious hospitality of cannibals. In retrospect, Melville viewed these primitive people as proof that Rousseau's glorification of the "noble savage" was to some degree valid. And before he returned home from the South Seas he was able to observe the contrast between the dignified serenity of that primitive pagan society and the degenerate slavery to which some of the more easily accessible natives had been reduced by misguided Christian missionary enterprises, intent on "civilizing" the noble savage.

In *Typee*, Melville chose to elaborate this contrast between the blessings of primitive life, as he had shared them with the so-called cannibals in the valley of Typee, and the evils of that so-called Christian civilization which the missionaries had forced on the natives. Still believing in the essential rightness of well-conducted missionary enterprises, Melville worked into *Typee* several out-spoken attacks on the way in which so many of the missionaries whom he had seen had corrupted and disgraced not only the natives but also those teachings of Christ which lay behind the missionary profession. As his preface to *Typee* indicates, Melville offered his narrative of travels, and his commentaries on what he had seen, as an accurate "peep at Polynesian life," apparently believing that such slight artistic liberties as he had taken in presenting the story would not invalidate his primary intent to represent the truth. Fearing, however, that his interspersed attacks on the behavior of both Protestant and Catholic missionaries would arouse misunderstanding as to the sincerity of his attempt to work for a purification of missionary activities, Melville tried to make his viewpoint and purpose quite clear in the preface, thus:

"There are a few passages in the ensuing chapters which may be thought to bear rather hard upon a reverend order of men, the account of whose proceedings in different quarters of the globe—transmitted to us through their hands—very generally, and often very deservedly, receive high commendation. Such passages will be found, however, to be based upon facts admitting of no contradiction, and which have come immediately under the writer's cognisance. The conclusions deduced from these facts are unavoidable, and in stating them the author has been influenced by no feeling of animosity, either to the individuals themselves or to that glorious cause which has not always been served by the proceedings of some of its advocates."[1]

Anyone familiar with Melville's later pleasure in irony and sarcasm might suspect that his use of the term, "that glorious cause," might be sarcastic. As we shall see, however, the larger context makes it quite clear that Melville is here speaking earnestly and sincerely. Another passage which touches on his assumption that his serious purpose in this regard may be misunderstood, occurs late in *Typee:*

"Lest the slightest misconception should arise from anything thrown out in this chapter, or indeed in any other part of the volume, let me here observe, that against the cause of missions in the abstract no Christian can possibly be opposed; it is in truth a just and holy cause. But if the great end proposed by it be spiritual, the agency employed to accomplish that end is purely earthly; and although the object in view be the achievement of much good, that agency may nevertheless be productive of evil. In short, missionary undertaking, however it may be blessed by Heaven, is in itself but human; and subject, like everything else, to errors and abuses . . . subject as Christianity is to the assaults of unprincipled foes, we are naturally disposed to regard everything like an exposure of ecclesiastical misconduct as the offspring of malevolence or irreligious feeling. Not even this last consideration, however, shall deter me from the honest expression of my sentiments."[2]

Melville felt justified in dealing harshly with the misconduct of the missionaries, not only because of his own deeply-ingrained Puritanism, which was offended by religious delinquencies, but also because of his ardent belief that the Polynesians in their primitive state came close to existing in an Earthly Paradise, deliberately and divinely designed for them. Having already come under the influence of Rousseau, Melville seems to be aware of the conflict in his own mind between the rightness of missionary enterprises, in pure form, and the opposed rights of natural man. At times he implies that all missionary endeavors in the South Seas cannot help but be corrupting and degrading influences, because they attempt to superimpose "civilization" on innocence. At other times, he resolves the Calvin-Rousseau conflict by insisting that God has these primitive children in his especial care; that the Eden-like settings were divinely ordered to permit these noble savages to live in accordance with God's plan. For example, in one place he alludes to the "spontaneous fruits of the earth, which God in His wisdom had ordained for the support of the indolent natives." Again, in describing another ideal aspect of Polynesian life, he comments, "This would seem expressly ordained by Providence." In another place, he makes this summary statement: "But the voluptuous Indian, with every desire supplied, whom Providence has bountifully provided with all the sources of pure and natural enjoyment, and from whom are removed so many of the ills and pains of life—what has he to desire at the hands of civilisation?"[3]

Although Melville seems partially able to resolve the conflict in his own mind between his inherited belief in the essential rightness of Calvinistic teaching and his newly acquired belief in Rousseau's teachings as to the rights of natural man, we as readers may recognize the problem as one which may later cause Melville trouble and force him to resolve it in another way. For the present, however, it is important for us to see and hear and feel the intense sincerity of Melville's dominantly Christian viewpoint, even when he arranges to include within this viewpoint references to the rights of natural man:

"The penalty of the Fall presses very lightly upon the valley of Typee. . . . Nature had planted the bread-fruit and the banana, and in her own good time she brings them to maturity, when the idle savage stretches forth his hand and satisfies his appetite.

"Ill-fated people! I shudder when I think of the change a few years will produce in their paradisiacal abode; and probably when the most destructive vices, and the worst attendance on civilisation, shall have driven all peace and happiness from the valley, the magnanimous French will proclaim to the world that the Marquesas Islands have been converted to Christianity! and this the Catholic world will doubtless consider as a glorious event. Heaven help the 'Isles of the Sea'!—The sympathy which Christendom feels for them has, alas! in too many instances proved their bane.

"How little do some of these poor islanders comprehend when they look around them, that no inconsiderable part of their disasters originate in certain tea-party excitements, under the influence of which benevolent-looking gentlemen in white cravats solicit alms, and old ladies in spectacles, and young ladies in sober russet low gowns, contribute sixpences toward the creation of a fund, the object of which is to ameliorate the spiritual condition of the Polynesians, but whose end has almost invariably been to accomplish their temporal destruction!

"Let the savages be civilised, but civilise them with benefits, and not with evils; and let heathenism be destroyed, but not by destroying the heathen. The Anglo-Saxon hive have extirpated Paganism from the greater part of the North American continent; but with it they have likewise extirpated the greater portion of the Red race. Civilisation is gradually sweeping from the earth the lingering vestiges of Paganism, and at the same time the shrinking forms of the unhappy worshippers.

"Among the islands of Polynesia, no sooner are the images over-turned, the temples demolished, and the idolaters converted into *nominal* Christians, than disease, vice, and premature death make their appearance. The depopulated land is then recruited from the rapacious hordes of enlightened individuals who settle themselves within its borders, and clamorously announce the progress of the Truth. Neat villas, trim gardens, shaven lawns, spires, and cupolas arise, while the poor savage soon finds himself an interloper in the country of his fathers, and that too on the very site of the hut where he was born. The spontaneous fruits of the earth, which God in His wisdom had ordained for the support of the indolent natives, remorsely seized upon and appropriated by the stranger, are devoured before the eyes of the starving inhabitants, or sent on board the numerous vessels which now touch at their shores. . . .

"But what matters all this? Behold the glorious result!—The abominations of Paganism have given way to the pure rites of the Christian worship—the ignorant savage has been supplanted by the refined European! Look at Honolulu, the metropolis of the Sandwich Islands!—A community of disinterested merchants, and devoted self-exiled heralds of the Cross, located on the very spot that twenty years ago was defiled by the presence of idolatry. What a subject for an eloquent Bible-meeting orator! Nor has such an opportunity for a display of missionary rhetoric been allowed to pass by unimproved! But when these philanthropists send us such glowing accounts of one half of their labours, why does their modesty restrain them from publishing the other half of the good they have wrought?—Nor until I visited Honolulu was I aware of the fact that the small remnant of the natives had been civilised into draught horses, and evangelised into beasts of burden. But so it is. They have been literally broken into the traces, and are harnessed to the vehicles of their spiritual instructors like so many dumb brutes!"[4]

Because we shall later pay much attention to *how* Melville says *what* he says, it should be pointed out here that his intensely angry use of irony and sarcasm throughout that passage forces us to hear the tone of voice, as determined by the context. Furthermore, it should be noticed that Melville's meaning, throughout these passages, suggests his belief that the savages in their primitive state more nearly exemplify Christian virtues than do the unconsciously corrupt but so-called "Christian" and "civilised" missionaries:

"Civilisation does not engross all the virtues of humanity: she has not even her full share of them. They flourish in greater abundance and attain greater strength among many barbarous people. The hospitality of the wild Arab, the courage of the North American Indian, and the faithful friendships of some of the Polynesian nations, far surpass anything of a similar kind among the polished communities of Europe. If truth and justice, and the better principles of our nature, cannot exist unless enforced by the statute-book, how are we to account for the social condition of the Typees? So pure and upright were they in all the relations of life, that entering their valley, as I did, under the most erroneous impressions of their character, I was soon led to exclaim in amazement: 'Are these the ferocious savages, the blood-thirsty cannibals of whom I have heard such frightful tales! They deal more kindly with each other, and are more humane, than many who study essays on virtue and benevolence, and who repeat every night that beautiful prayer breathed first by the lips of the divine and gentle Jesus.' I will frankly declare, that after passing a few weeks in this valley of the Marquesas, I formed a higher estimate of human nature than I had ever before entertained. But alas! since then I have been one of the crew of a man-of-war, and the pent-up wickedness of five hundred men has nearly overturned all of my previous theories."[5]

There is fair warning! For arbitrary purposes, we have over-simplified the complexity of Melville's viewpoint as reflected in his travel-narrative *Typee*. But it is clear that Melville's adventures on sea and land had already brought him into contact with enough "wickedness" to jolt his "previous theories," and his mind is already on the move as he writes *Typee*, and its sequel *Omoo* (which need not concern us here). It is therefore difficult to describe which effect was most important to Melville from his experiences in the Eden-like valley of the Typees. But it does not seem difficult to recognize that many previous interpretations have missed some of the most important aspects of those complex effects. For example, Richard Chase insists that Melville's fear of cannibalism symbolizes his fear of castration; that his escape from the natives symbolizes his ability to leave "the archaic level of personality and civilization represented by Typee Valley" and his further ability "to face and suffer and overcome the fears which accompanied maturing sexuality."[6] Is that an accurate interpretation? I am inclined to be merely bored with the monomaniac Freudian emphasis on "maturing sexuality"; but I do seriously doubt whether Melville's experience among the Typees did indeed teach him to leave the "archaic level of personality." Isn't *Typee* itself a kind of proof that Melville, while writing it, was actually moving closer to an archaic level of personality, rather than away from one; that he had come to idealize that primitive life in recollection, some time after he had left it in fact? Consider another interpretation. Newton Arvin, equally charmed by Freud and Jung, finds that the experience meant to Melville a symbolic "descent into the canyon of the past," from which he returned with a "stabilizing and fortifying image."[7] But, whatever that "image" may be said to have been, was it either "stabilizing" or "fortifying"? Let us consider another possible interpretation.

Because the Freudians like to start with causes, in terms of early family relationships, and with questions as to whether an individual was loved too much or too little during early childhood, why not concede that Melville's troubles started not from his being loved too little but from his being loved too much, and by his mother: he was spoiled. The details are unimportant. Somehow he developed a habit of mind which was not only proud and haughty but also demanding. At a very early age, he got into the habit of asking too much of life. There is the crux of it.

Although the result was always the same, it took various protean forms. Whenever he was made aware of the discrepancy between whatever he wanted and whatever he could have, he started looking around for someone to blame for having been so mean as to deny him what he wanted. And the more he was denied, by experiences, the further out he reached for compensations, which were also denied to him.

Come at it another way. The Melville who jumped ship in Nukuhiva Harbor was "tormented with an everlasting itch for things remote," just as surely as was Ishmael in the first chapter of *Moby-Dick*, and all of his major works provide us with ample evidence as to the different forms taken by his peculiar "itch." Long before Freud, many authors described the basic and reflexive human recoil from various kinds of discomfort or, as we like to call it today, maladjustment. That basic recoil sets in motion a progressive series of physical and mental and emotional actions calculated to achieve some form of rest or peace or serenity (Melville's favorite word, in this context, was "serenity"), no matter how temporary or illusory. For our immediate purposes, it does not matter whether these actions be described as escapes or pursuits: either way, they are impelled by the same "itch" for rest, peace, serenity. Each of Melville's reactions to his itches represented another recoil from some kind of experience which denied him what he wanted in his here-and-now. As a result, he went to sea. His running away to sea, at the age of eighteen, was an early example of such recoil, as one plainly gathers from the early chapters of its fictional projection in *Redburn*. During that first voyage, however, Melville's new sense of maladjustment produced a new recoil, violent enough to drive him back to the relative comfort of his discomforts at home! Within a short time, of course, his injured sensitivities drove him back to sea, in search of some new adventure which might serve as new adjustment. And just how persistently this basic pattern of human response repeated itself in Melville's early life, the first chapters of each of his first seven books indicate. Our immediate concern is with *Typee*, which begins by describing the intolerable life aboard a whaler and the consequent need for jumping ship and taking refuge among the natives, but, quite by accident, in the wrong valley.

Quite by accident? Melville later became bitterly fond of blaming God, of making a scapegoat of God and of calling God a Practical Joker. Let us pretend, for the moment, that Melville's God did indeed play some kind of joke on him by letting him assert his predestined free will in entering the valley of the Typees; that God did it, just to let Melville refuse to learn the implicit object lesson as to the fallacy of his protean itch. According to Melville's own words, that Typee valley was a veritable Earthly Paradise, a Garden of Eden, a Heaven on Earth. It was ideal. By contrast, civilization came close to being pure evil, which could be blamed for much. In that Earthly Paradise of Typee, Melville found that the noble savage lived in an uncorrupted state, strikingly different from that civilized "here-and-now" from which he had fled. How did he react to this blissful serenity? As soon as that Eden became his here-and-now, Melville felt trapped, imprisoned: he longed for anything except Eden. The first chapter of *Typee* is entitled, "The Sea—Longings for Shore" and the last chapter is entitled, "Escape" or (by implication) "The Shore—Longings for Sea." There is no hint in the context that Melville, already fond of ironies, recognized the irony implicit in these two chapter titles: the object lesson was wasted on him.

If Melville fought so hard to get away from that Earthly Paradise, how could he ever have idealized it? The answer is fairly easy: the Typee valley became Paradise for him only after he had left it, only after it had again become remote. Then he could look back at it wistfully, and glorify it as a symbol of something highly desirable but unobtainable, remote in both the past and the future: Paradise. While sampling this ultimate serenity, Melville had suffered egregiously and had longed to escape. But as soon as he had gotten far enough away from it, he suffered egregiously to think that there was no other place on earth quite like it.

There is a revealing passage in *Typee* which had one value for Melville, and which has another value for us, as we try to understand him. It foreshadows his subsequent pilgrimages into the remote of time and space, during his various quests for serenity. While wandering about the valley of Typee, he tells us, he discovered a mausoleum erected in memory of a celebrated leader. Placed conspicuously was a carven effigy of the dead chieftain seated in the stern of a canoe and holding a paddle in his hands. He seemed in the act of driving the canoe swiftly ahead, "leaning forward and inclining his head, as if eager to hurry on his voyage." But again a symbolic want-versus-denial image, or life-versus-death antithesis, of the sort which Melville loved: "Glaring at him forever, and face to face, was a polished human skull which crowned the prow of the canoe. The spectral figure-head, reversed in its position, glancing backward, seemed to mock the impatient attitude of the warrior." Having established the emblematic life-death relationship, Melville added:

"Whenever, in the course of my rambles through the valley, I happened to be near the chief's mausoleum, I always turned aside to visit it. The place had a peculiar charm for me; I hardly know why, but so it was. As I leaned over the railing and gazed upon the strange effigy, and watched the play of the feathery headdress, stirred by the same breeze which in low tones breathed amidst the lofty palm-trees, I loved to yield myself up to the fanciful superstition of the islanders, and could almost believe that the grim warrior was bound heavenward. In this mood, when I turned to depart, I bade him 'God speed, and a pleasant voyage.' Ah, paddle away, brave chieftain, to the land of spirits! To the material eye thou makest but little progress; but with the eye of faith, I see thy canoe cleaving the bright waves, which die away on those dimly looming shores of Paradise.

"This strange superstition affords another evidence of the fact, that however ignorant man may be, he still feels within him his immortal spirit yearning after the unknown future."[8]

For present purposes, *Typee* is particularly interesting because it reflects Melville's first phase of disillusionment, from several different angles, all closely related. His undisciplined and self-indulgent impatience with life as he found it prompted him to go to sea and then to jump ship; that same impatience was partly a cause and partly an effect of his itch for the unknown and the unknowable, in both time and space: the mariner and the mystic in him were correlated in their spoiled-child motivation. And even his Puritanical impulse to purify missionary enterprises, by calling attention to the discrepancy between the ideal and actuality, suggests the yearning of his own spirit for a personal religious belief which would correct and transcend the narrowness of his Calvinistic heritage. The "eye of faith" was still so undimmed in him, however, that he had consciously dedicated himself, as a man of letters, to the related ideal of discovering and revealing God's truth, even though he might suffer opprobrium, as did the Old Testament prophets.

But his disillusionment was heightened when some sectarian reviewers of *Typee* denied the truth of his attacks on Christian missionaries in the South Seas, and accused him of being an atheistical liar. That hurt enough to make him say in his preface to *Mardi*, "Not long ago, having published two narratives of voyages in the Pacific, which, in many quarters, were received with incredulity, the thought occurred to me of indeed writing a romance of Polynesian adventure, and publishing it as such; to see whether the fiction might not possibly be received for a verity: in some degree the reverse of my previous experience."[9]

Notes

1. *Typee* (London: Constable and Co., Ltd., 1922), pp. viii–ix.

2. *Typee*, pp. 266–67.

3. *Typee*, pp. 264, 259, 165.

4. *Typee*, pp. 262–67.

5. *Typee*, p. 273.

6. Richard Chase, *Herman Melville: A Critical Study* (New York: Macmillan Co., 1949), p. 12.

7. Newton Arvin, *Herman Melville* (New York: William Sloane Associates, 1950), p. 87.

8. *Typee*, pp. 231–233.

9. Herman Melville, *Mardi* (London: Constable and Co., Ltd., 1922), I, vii.

Typee

Milton R. Stern*

> And man rebounds whole aeons back in nature.
> —Melville, "The House-Top"

Typee does not seem to belong in the same class with the consciously symbolic "metaphysical" novels like *Mardi, Pierre,* and *Billy Budd.* And, in many ways, of course, it does not. But, like a Melvillean character, its face is deceptively bland. Seeing only the face, when a transcendentalist reviewer wished to tell his readers about a new book called, *Typee, the Narrative of a Four Month's Residence among the Natives of a Valley of the Marquesas Islands: or a Peep at Polynesian Life,* he wrote of the Marquesas which Melville had visited as "these gems of the ocean, in which Nature . . . has hinted the extent of her possibilities . . . perfections which she shall possess in infinite and universal variety when, through the combined industry and wealth and power of a united Race, she shall have become but the image and expression of the Kingdom of God abiding in the souls and societies of Man. . . ."[1] The reviewer went on to explain that the secret of the good social state is abundance; that, contrary to Victor Cousin's beliefs, man must have more than good precepts; that industrialized America, with a more equitable social order of production and distribution, can have a stronger peace and more profound good will than have the Typees. When the writer touched upon the issue raised by Melville's treatment of the missionaries, he said that

> It is proper to say in behalf of the author that he does not impeach the . . . Christian character of the missionaries in general. He merely avers that their designs have often been injudicious and that other influences than that of the New Testament have operated on the natives, which are undoubtedly the facts. . . . We do not presume to condemn [the missionaries] individually, but in God's name we condemn a social order which is founded on such contradictions of the Divine laws, and which devotes to a hopeless and miserable existence so large a majority of human creatures.[2]

*This essay is reprinted from *The Fine Hammered Steel of Herman Melville,* by Milton R. Stern, © 1957 by the Board of Trustees of the University of Illinois, and is reprinted with the permission of the University of Illinois Press.

117

In some ways this pronouncement is typical of the nineteenth-century reaction to Melville. It interprets the book according to its own predetermined findings, and uses the "charming travelogue" as a point of departure into its own advocations. Yet the *Harbinger* notice does discuss some of the book's basic themes, at least those of universal human brotherhood, the aspects of western civilization which are inhuman, and the obvious discrepancies between the preachments or intentions and the actions of militant Christianity.[3]

But when it does touch upon the book's themes, it does so either in a doctrinaire fashion, or accidentally, or indirectly. Consequently, even the friendly *Harbinger* review, like most of the other contemporary critiques, did not come to grips with *Typee's* symbolic implications. Melville's reviewers were not accustomed to find in popular literature the methods and meanings which Melville was to put into travelogue. In this sense, it is fair to say that as early as the publication of his first book, after which he was, for a while, a very successful and popular young author, Melville was "misunderstood."[4] Indeed, almost without exception, the amusingly literal-minded critics considered his book in terms of whether or not it was authentic (some even going so far as to wonder if there were any such person as Herman Melville), or in terms of enchanting escapism, or in terms of whether he was to be praised, tolerated, or jailed for his treatment of the missionaries.[5] But more recent scholarship has made it increasingly clear that however authentic his works may or may not be, it is less and less possible to deny the actuality of symbolic experience in Melville's early books.[6]

There is no way to prove that Melville consciously set out to create a symbolic work in his first book. But the themes arising from *Typee's* symbolic construction do become a point of embarkation for Melville's philosophical voyage into the sea of relationships between the western world, the primitive world, the quester, and the lure. The apparent vehicle for those relationships is the occasional treatment of the contact between Christianity and the Marquesans. The more important and less apparent vehicle is an opposition of mind and body, mind and heart, communication and lack of communication. And again and again, as Melville dives into the depths of his later books, he is to hook these thematic leviathans by the nose, subject them to the tryworks of his mind, and boil every last drop of suggestion out of them.

As little as we know about Melville's (or any man's) own feelings and stated intentions, there is some historical evidence that he was not as interested in the factual reporting of his experience as he was in what he could accomplish thematically using those experiences. For instance, when source books like C. S. Stewart's *A Visit to the South Seas* are examined,[7] it becomes clear that the "significance of the discovery of this source material lies in the fact that it constitutes another step in solving the problem of the relationship between Melville's technique of composition and the use of his source materials. . . . At times he borrowed extensively without alteration; at other times he made significant alterations for the purpose of producing a dominant mood or impression . . . again, he seems to be deliberately planning to throw us off the trail."[8] Indeed, in *Typee* the crew of the *Dolly* is painted in heavily uncomplimentary colors. Tommo voices extreme dissatisfaction with his lot aboard ship and with the crew—a gang of debauched immoralists, roughnecks, and ignorant, craven sneaks and bullies. Yet, in a letter to Lemuel Shaw, in which Gansevoort Melville relays news from Herman during the factual period of Melville's "*Dolly*" trip to the Marquesas aboard the whaler *Acushnet*, Gansevoort says: "I am in receipt of a letter from my brother Herman dated August 1841 at Santa Martha, coast of Peru—He was then in perfect health, and not dissatisfied with his lot—the fact of his being one of a crew so much superior in morals and early advantages to the ordinary run of whaling crews affords him constant gratification. By the paper I see that his ship—the Acushnet—Pease [the captain]—was spoken in Dec last—at sea—all well. . . ."[9] There is no reason to doubt that even at this early date, Melville was consciously prepared to utilize experience in a sacrifice of fact for thematic purpose. As the London *Athenaeum* put it, "*si non e vero e ben trovato*. . . . We vouch for the verisimilitude, but not the verity."[10] It is not only Melville's desire to spin a good yarn for commercial success that keeps *Typee*, in its heightened color and drama, from being a "true" story. The verity was also manipulated by symbolic creation of theme. Nor is this impossible for a brand-new, twenty-six-year-old author. "Until I was twenty-five, I had no development at all," he wrote to Hawthorne. "From my twenty-fifth year I date my life. Three weeks have scarcely passed, at any time between then and now [June 1, 1851], that I have not unfolded within myself. But I feel that I am now come to the inmost leaf of the bulb, and that shortly the flower must fall to the mould. It seems to me now that Solomon was the truest man who ever spoke, and yet that he a little *managed* the truth with a view to popular conservatism. . . ."[11]

And back "then," in 1846 (or 1845, when Melville was composing the book), the author makes a statement about the author in the "Preface" to *Typee*. "In his account of the singular and interesting people among whom he was thrown, it will be observed that he chiefly treats of their more obvious peculiarities; and, in describing their customs, refrains in most cases from entering into explanations concerning their origin and purposes. As writers of travels among barbarous communities are generally very diffuse on these subjects, he deems it right to advert to what may be considered a culpable omission."[12] Melville is twitting and protecting himself. Whatever literary sins he may have had, he was hardly ever guilty of sparseness or humility in his books. More important, he did not spend as much time among the Typees as he pretended: he never had time to learn the "explanations" from which he "refrains."[13] This defensiveness is not a mildly humorous deference to the audience as much as it is a thinly veiled excuse for thematic organization rather than entertaining journalism. As Melville complains, whenever the aspiring writer looking for markets wrote the familiar and fashionable travel book, he crammed his account with as much detail as possible.[14] Yet in his own utilization of event, Melville rejected the limitation of factual and chronological exactness of detail, even though his contemporaries considered him to be an anthropologist of sorts and an expert on the Marquesas.[15] Melville was not ultimately concerned with the reception of his South Seas books as works of ethnological value, for after he was fully aware of the favorable reception of his two South Seas books (*Typee* and *Omoo*), he proceeded to write *Mardi*, a "South Seas" book which sacrificed for theme any accuracy of ethnological detail whatever. Melville's commercial and artistic interests were by no means similar. Prodded by fears and doubts and insecurities, he was always trying to talk his publishers into the most advantageous terms. While he remained sober with the American publishers, Wiley and Putnam, Harper and Brothers, he kept assuring his English publishers, John Murray and Richard Bentley, that his projected books were factual, or historical, or "very much more calculated for popularity than anything . . . yet published of mine."[16] But in intimate letters, he wrote to his friends that, "I shall write such things as the Great Publisher of Mankind ordained ages before he published 'The World'—this planet, I mean—not the Literary Globe."[17] And, "So far as I am individually concerned, & independent of my pocket, it is my earnest desire to write those sort of books which are said to 'fail.' "[18] And, "Dollars damn me; and the malicious Devil is forever grinning in on me, holding the door ajar. . . . What I feel most moved to write, that is banned,—it will not pay. Yet altogether write the *other* way I cannot. So the product is a final hash, and all my books are botches."[19]

Moreover, if, as the "Preface" says, much detail has been deleted, the questions of what has been retained, and why, remain. In the case of the missionaries, for instance, the "Preface" continues, "The conclusions deduced from these facts [about the missionaries] are unavoidable, and in stating them the author has been influenced by no feeling of animosity, either to the individuals themselves or to that glorious cause which has not always been served by the proceedings of some of its advocates." But Melville had just said that it was *easy* to avoid certain other facts and details. Yet not only in *Typee*, but in *Omoo*, *Mardi* and *White-Jacket* as well, there is charge after charge against the inhumanities of "that glorious cause" of militant or coercive religion, with some animus reserved for the glory of the cause itself. One suspects the "Preface" of being a good liar. Like any craftsman, Melville did select which of the "unavoidable" facts he would avoid. Further, Melville says, "The great interest with which the important events lately occurring at the Sandwich, Marquesas, and Society Islands, have been regarded in America and England, and indeed throughout the world, will, he trusts, justify a few otherwise unwarrantable digressions." Those "unwarrantable digressions" prove themselves to be an integral part of the book's theme of human behavior in contrasting civilizations.

Whether we approach the book according to what has been deleted or according to what has been reinforced (as is the case here), the conclusion remains the same: *Typee* is a symbolically created thematic construct rather than a haphazard piece of reporting or a tale which is merely picaresque adventure.

II

Immediately after extended statements about the barrenness of sea-life, *Typee* begins with yearning for the lush and exotic land. "The Marquesas! What strange visions of outlandish things does the very name spirit up! Naked houris—cannibal banquets—groves of cocoa-nut—coral reefs—tattooed chiefs—and bamboo temples; sunny valleys planted with bread-fruit trees—carved canoes dancing on the flashing blue waters—savage woodlands guarded by horrible idols—*heathenish rites and human sacrifices.*" Two features of Polynesia oppose the sterility of life at sea, with which the book opens. One is the physicality and fertility of Marquesan life, and the other is the primitive simplicity, which is barbaric enough to serve as an image of the most basic, pristine human life. The Marquesas are the very beginnings and first curve in the human life cycle, and have not kept pace with western history. "The group for which we were now steering (although among the earliest of European discoveries in the South Seas, having first been visited in the year 1595) still continues to be tenanted by beings as strange and barbarous as ever." The Typee valley itself is further set off from even this primitive group of peoples. Melville's insistence upon the vale's seclusion and isolation increases the dramatic interest; it also makes Typee the constant and unspoiled laboratory test case from which is universalized a general statement about man's primitive life in nature.

The west, with its seamen, missionaries, and French and English conquerors, also represents a single level of value. But it is a level of conquest which clashes with the blissful animal existence of the islanders. The opposition of the two civilizations furnishes the tension in *Typee*, both in the theme and the rising action of conflict. So clear are the tensions in this relatively straightforward story, that the reader can quickly extract a list of opposing characteristics even before he is aware of what Melville is doing in his redefinition of Eden.

WESTERN CIVILIZATION (Mind)	MARQUESAN CIVILIZATION (Body)
1. Heartlessness	1. Heartfulness
2. Conquest	2. Submission, ultimate doom
3. Quest, mobility	3. Seclusion, immobility
4. Consciousness	4. Unconsciousness
5. Sea	5. Land
6. Communication with other worlds	6. Inability to communicate with other worlds
7. Inability to communicate with Typee	7. Spontaneous, childlike, meaningless chatter among selves
8. Sparse food, little sleep, technology	8. Physical gratification, somnolence, unaided nature
9. Planning, scheming, technological and military foresight	9. Spontaneity of animal spirits, innocence
10. Attempt to conquer natural environment	10. Integration with natural environment
11. Artificiality, complexity	11. Naturalness, simplicity

The simplicity of *Typee's* action and characterization can be gauged by the starkness of the list. However, it is in the evaluation of opposing forces that Melville creates the book's complexity of relationships. To do this, once the oppositions were settled, Melville had to give the literal level of action a kinetic thematic energy; he had to hitch "adventure" to the potential symbolism of the motifs. He did this in *Typee* as he did in all his first-person narratives—through the plight and observations of the protagonist.

At the very first, Melville indicated the evaluative relationship of the narrator to both sea and land. To Tommo, the sea is a monotone of time and work, and everything about it is repugnant. In his anxiety to leave the whaler, he plans to jump ship. He thinks of the sunny valleys planted with breadfruit groves and of the heathenish rites, and he muses that "Such were the strangely jumbled anticipations that haunted me during our passage from the cruising ground. I felt an irresistable curiosity to see those islands which the olden voyagers had so glowingly described." He is in a fever very similar to that of Ishmael, who, before he set foot on the *Pequod*, was haunted by the image of a humped and hooded phantom like a snow-hill in the air. Compulsively, Tommo is drawn to the objects of tension before the particulars of that tension are introduced either to him or the reader.

Searching for a rationalization which will justify his actions, Tommo offers a legalistic argument for abandoning ship. Although the actions of the captain and the conditions aboard ship form part of the thread of deceit which weaves through the book, Tommo's legalities are really irrelevant. Imaginatively, he is incorrect, for his legal sensitivity has nothing to do with the realities of his desire or the consequences of his actions. While he makes up his own morality as he goes along, Tommo's argument only touches upon its strongest motivation—the simpler and more elemental urge to reintegrate self in the physical and emotional satisfactions of human life. And Tommo has ample emotional inducement. The deceit and brutality of the captain have reduced Tommo's life to a business of elementary survival. Each man thinks that his own comfort is contingent upon his toadying to the captain's despotism. The crew, or populace, has neither realization of, nor courage for, united action, and the sailors blindly accept the consequences of their each-man-for-himself attitudes. Though much degraded, this is the crew of Captain Vere's *Indomitable*. But unlike the enlightened and purposeful rule of the *Indomitable*, the government of the *Dolly* is reduced to all the possible blind egoism and viciousness of western life—the Typee savages are never so debased. Simple savagery in civilized man only results in brutishness. On the *Dolly*, the artificialities of rule do not check and balance each other. The captain's government is not the "law and equity" whereby western society maintains itself. "[The captain's] prompt reply to all complaints and remonstrances was—the butt end of a handspike, so convincingly administered as effectually to silence the aggrieved party.

"To whom could we apply for redress? We had left both law and equity on the other side of the Cape; and unfortunately, with a very few exceptions, our crew was composed of a parcel of dastardly and mean-spirited wretches, divided among themselves, and only united in enduring without resistance the unmitigated tyranny of the captain." The laws of the west do not apply to Marquesan waters. And when we first meet Tommo, he has already dissociated himself from the crew and from the ship.[20] He is enraged by the thought that he is merely another anonymous member of the *Dolly's* doll-like and sick society. Giving up the sniveling and anarchic crew as a hopeless job, he no longer even toys with ideas of union or social betterment. Unlike Vere, he certainly will not risk sacrifice of self for the good of the community. His solution is evasion, withdrawal from the actualities of his world as he knows it. Consequently he loses his only possible individual identity: he becomes like all the other crew members by dedicating himself to the proposition that as long as life is such an elemental thing, he might as well make himself as comfortable as possible. At this point Tommo has no more realization, and no more ability to change or control fate, than any of the Ancient Mariner's crew. He rejects and escapes from the inhumanity of quest (the sea, whaling) and the inhumanity of western man (the dominance of the captain). He tries to find both comfort and individual identity by submerging himself in a reintroduction to humanity in the unconsciousness of its very beginnings (Nukuheva's hinterlands). By the end of the book he discovers that a man does not capture his identity by such means, because individual identity is contingent upon the individual's place in the human community of his own history. To Typee, as a social concept, Tommo is another pig for slaughter.

But supposing, as Tommo does, that the captain might be endured; what are the added conditions of sea life that make the Marquesas so attractive in the first place? As if in answer, the very first chapter introduces a note of hideously parched living. There is no food for the freshness and completeness of life. The chapter subheadings begin, "The Sea—Longings for Shore—A Land-Sick Ship. . . ." And the introductory paragraph continues the lament: "Six months at sea! . . . six months out of sight of land . . . the sky above, the sea around, and nothing else! Weeks and weeks ago our fresh provisions were all exhausted. There is not a sweet potato left; not a single yam. Those glorious bunches of banannas which once decorated our stern and quarter-deck have, alas, disappeared! and the delicious oranges which hung suspended from our tops and stays—they, too, are gone! Yes, they are all departed, and there is nothing left us but salt-horse and sea-bisquit." The very food of life offered at sea serves merely to continue the departure from land and world. Tommo describes the prodigious preparations for sailing, during which quantities of stale bread, poor meat and roachy water are stored in the hold; and as long as the stores last, the ship remains at sea. "But not to speak of the quality of these articles of sailors' fare, the abundance in which they are put on board a whaling vessel is almost incredible. Oftentimes, when we had occasion to break out in the hold, and I beheld the successive tiers of casks and barrels, whose contents were all destined to be consumed in due course by the ship's company, my heart has sunk within me." Adding to Tommo's heartsickness is the story about the good ship *Perseverance*, whose skipper simply touched port for food and then headed back to whaling grounds. The ship becomes a veritable Flying Dutchman, always seeking, never returning to world and time. Fearing a similar fate, Tommo notes that the meals of salt pork and sea-bisquit are scanty so that the stores will last even longer. At the outset Tommo renounces sea and search and sterility. "Is there nothing fresh around us? Is there no green thing to be seen? Yes, the inside of our bulwarks is painted green; but what a vile and sickly hue it is, as if nothing bearing even the semblence of verdure could flourish this weary way from land."

What the sea says is that like the world of land and body, this life of quest and mind, when limited to a monotone existence, is a cannibal life. It fattens off its opposite member. In its exploitation and scorn of the more elementary levels of natural, animal living, it kills and devours, sucking life and sustenance from land. Western spoilation and cannibalism are presented directly after Tommo bewails the lack of green things. "Even the bark that once clung to the wood we use for fuel has been gnawed off and devoured by the captain's pig; and so long ago, too, that the pig himself has in turn been devoured." Tommo and Toby, when they fight and conquer nature in their struggle to reach the isolated valley, must also live, like the pig, on the bark they can chew off twigs: in the inversion caused by change of worlds, the provisions and foresights of the western man are all lost on Typeean existence. The natives also rape nature, but nature willingly allows the defloration at her own pleasure. Her Typeean seducers never attempt to conquer her. The *Dolly*, however, like the *Perseverance*, will continue to sail until the last reminder of land and animal life, Pedro the rooster, is devoured—and then the ship will touch land again, taking from it the provisions for life which it never replaces in the South Pacific's eternal cycles of growth.

This kind of single-level existence is unmistakably associated with western civilization. All the men who come to the Marquesas from the sea are alien. They are always whalers, traders, conquerors; they are always Americans, Englishmen, Frenchmen; and they come to exploit either the resources of the waters, or the peoples, or the lands. They display behavior values which become represented by a restless striving for conquest, a quest summed up on the personal and philosophical level by Taji and Ahab, and on the political and military level by the missionaries and by Admiral Du Petit Thouars. Totally, this striving is an attempt to extend human power, for all the wrong reasons, over all creation. The argument, however, is not with an extension of human power. Melville does not imply that there should be no ship's captains or French military men as much as he does imply that captain or soldier must make a realistic and humanitarian extension governed by social insight into what he is doing. Realistic because it proceeds from a tactical understanding of the instruments demanded by time and place, rather than proceeding from an external and superimposed set of values. Humanitarian because its goal is what Vere sees as the "lasting peace and welfare of mankind" rather than privilege or power per se. The western, or present-day world—Melville's "world of mind"—is really two worlds in relation to the primitive. It is the philosophical world of mind, and it is the shrewd or technological world of mind. Melville's philosophical characters may set out with social goals, but their cosmic view and their tactics are wrong. His shrewd characters have no cosmic view at all, or if they do it is hypocritical and conventional. Like the "town" characters in *Huckleberry Finn*, their morality does not arise from a firsthand evaluation of experience. They do not care about possible relationships between their own selfishness and the social good. They have technological minds, or political minds, or military minds, but they have no historical and social vision. They are the "practical" men of the world, whose practicality, because visionless and therefore isolated, is ultimately unrealistic and absurd. When Melville devotes his artistic concentration to the world of mind as such, this latter, shrewd quality becomes an element of mindlessness. But in contrast to the primitive, it is the shrewd world of mind, largely, that operates in *Typee*, presenting the semi-picaresque surface which can so easily be mistaken for the totality.

In *Typee*, mind often is objectified in the physical object of the human head, just as mindlessness is objectified in the human body. The sailors know the technics of whaling and the politics of shipboard life. But they eat sparsely of stale food. The Typees, on the other hand, have no technology, and are always feasting. Their food is a profusion of fresh fruits and vegetables, or newly killed and freshly roasted pork. They offer nothing to the world of mind. When the alien western sailors approach the vicinity of the Marquesas, mental activity, toil, and sea-consciousness also become alien, and virtually disappear. Animal existence and somnolence become the only possibility, as though the sailors were approaching a realm of lotus-eaters.

> We abandoned the fore-peak altogether, and spreading an awning over the forecastle, slept, ate, and lounged under it the live-long day. Every one seemed to be under the influence of some narcotic. Even the officers aft, whose duty required them never to be seated while keeping a deck watch, vainly endeavored to keep on their pins; and were obliged invariably to compromise the matter by leaning up against the bulwarks, and gazing abstractedly over the side. Reading was out of the question; take a book in your hand, and you were asleep in an instant [p. 473].

And if the "insular green Tahiti" offers no mental refreshment, it reinvigorates and replenishes all the physical and emotional stores robbed by search and consciousness. For instance, Tommo dives from the parching heat of the sea-sun into Polynesia's verdure, which allows oblivion and relief from the perspiration of toil and conflict with nature.

> I had come from Nukuheva by water in the ship's boat, and when we entered the bay of Tior it was high noon. The heat had been intense . . . the sun's rays had expended all their fury upon us; and to add to our discomfort, we had omitted to supply ourselves with water previous to starting. What with heat and thirst together, I became . . . impatient to get ashore . . . I rushed forward across *the open ground in the vicinity of the sea,* and plunged, diver fashion, into the recesses of the first grove that offered.
>
> What a delightful sensation did I experience! I felt *as if floating in some new element* while all sorts of gurgling, trickling, liquid sounds fell upon my ear. People may say what they will about the refreshing influences of a cold-water bath, but commend me when in a persperation to the shade baths of Tior, beneath the cocoa-nut tree, and amidst the cool, delightful atmosphere which surrounds them [pp. 497–98, italics mine].

The Marquesas pile mountainous reaches of verdure into a monumental, beckoning emblem of Eden, which stands green and fresh in the sweaty, barren contemporary wasteland of a world, as a cool reminder of the lost

Golden Age when life was not touched by time and had not yet become history. The Typee natives, who never leave their homes, are the children of nature, the noble savages of primitivism. They have nothing to do with the deep-sea ships except to bring innocence and physical and emotional gratification. That Typeeans are as much at home in the water as on land is an indication of fertility and integration with physical nature rather than an indication of toil and contemporary quest. Their water is lake or inland stream: it is not sea. The Typees prefer sea fish and sea salt and seaweed as the three delicacies they prize above all else, yet Tommo is surprised that these sea-girt people make only rare excursions to the ocean for those abundant delicacies. Women, who more in *Typee* than in any other Melville book, are representatives of land and land values (particularly body and safety), are not permitted by native taboo to even enter a canoe. It is Tommo, the western alien, who effects the beginning dissolution of native order by effecting the change which allows his mistress Fayaway to break the taboo.

The very first picture of even those Marquesans who are not so isolated as the Typees is an introduction of mindless physicality and simple innocence. The male natives swim up to the *Dolly* surrounded by rings of floating coconuts, which they bring as gifts. At first the *heads* of the natives are indistinguishable from *coconuts*, and when Tommo exhausts this poor pun, he notices that the natives "use their heads" only as a means to push the coconuts through the water. The native females are at first indistinguishable from so many shoals of fish, and when they climb out of the water, they are described as frolicking, cavorting animals.

> We were still some distance from the beach, and under slow headway, when we sailed right into the midst of these swimming nymphs, and they boarded us at every quarter; many seizing hold of the chain-plates and springing into the chains, others, at the peril of being run over by the vessel in her course, catching at the bob-stays, and wreathing their slender forms about the ropes, hung suspended in the air. All of them at length succeeded in getting up the ship's side, where they hung dripping with the brine and glowing from the bath, their jet-black tresses streaming over their shoulders, and half enveloping their otherwise naked forms. There they hung, sparkling with savage vivacity, laughing gaily at one another, and chattering away with infinite glee. Nor were they idle the while, for each one performed the simple office of the toilette for the other. Their luxuriant locks, wound up and twisted into the smallest possible compass, were freed from the briny element; the whole person carefully dried, and from a little round shell that passed from hand to hand, anointed with a fragrant oil: their adornments were completed by passing a few loose folds of white tappa, in a modest cincture, around the waist. Thus arrayed they no longer hesitated, but flung themselves lightly over the bulwarks, and were quickly frolicking about the decks. Many of them went forward, perching upon the head-rails or running out upon the bowsprit, while others seated themselves upon the taffrail, or reclined at

full length upon the boats. What a sight for us bachelor sailors! how avoid so dire a temptation? For who could think of tumbling these artless creatures overboard, when they had swam miles to welcome us?

Their appearance perfectly amazed me; their extreme youth, the light clear brown of their complexions, their delicate features, and inexpressibly graceful figures, their softly moulded limbs, and free unstudied action, seemed as strange as beautiful.

The "Dolly" was fairly captured; and never I will say was vessel carried before by such a dashing and irresistible party of boarders! The ship taken, we could not do otherwise than yield ourselves prisoners, and for the whole period that she remained in the bay, the "Dolly," as well as her crew, were completely in the hands of the mermaids.

In the evening after we had come to anchor the deck was illuminated with lanterns, and this picturesque band of sylphs, tricked out with flowers, and dressed in robes of variegated tappa, got up a ball in great style. These females were passionately fond of dancing, and the wild grace and spirit of their style excel everything that I have ever seen. The varied dances of the Marquesan girls are beautiful in the extreme, but there is an abandoned volptuousness in their character which I dare not attempt to describe.

Our ship was now wholly given up to every species of riot and debauchery. Not the feeblest barrier was interposed between the unholy passions of the crew and their unlimited gratification. The grossest licentiousness and the most shameful inebriety prevailed, with occasional and but short-lived interruptions, through the whole period of her stay. Alas for the poor savages when exposed to the influence of these polluting examples! Unsophisticated and confiding, they are easily led into every vice, and humanity weeps over the ruin thus remorselessly inflicted upon them by their European civilizers. Thrice happy are they who, inhabiting some yet undiscovered island in the midst of the ocean, have never been brought into contaminating contact with the white man [pp. 480–81].

This passage would seem to serve as another statement of demarcation between the qualities of primitive and contemporary man. So far there is a stark division between the regenerative Adamic life and the destructive sea life of present western history. But as the distinctions between mind and body lead one to suspect, this passage is more than a statement of opposites, for although the "good" natives are distinct from the "bad" crewmen (Melville discreetly avoids the fact that it takes two to make a bargain), and although they are magnificent animals, they are somehow less than human. Now the relationships between worlds are introduced, and the black-and-whiteness of "good" and "bad" begins to disappear as the worlds are evaluated further. Here is the first hint that the applicability, or correctness, of the elements of man's mysterious nature change as the elements of man's historical condition change. The crew surrenders to the savage which is in all men, and the savage in the civilized character is not purity or artless innocence as it is in the natives. The bestiality of the sailors indicates that what Typee represents is not peculiar to the Marquesas alone; it becomes a universal for the animal in all mankind. Thus Typee is isolated not because it is simply different, but because it serves as an unvitiated example of the animal in pure and innocent state. The Marquesans are the epitome of unsophisticated confidence, and they are doomed in their pure isolation. As Tommo discovers, a man's most important facts are the facts of historical realities. He cannot change his world by jumping back into the past. The present world demands its claim to present life, and the process of adjusting life to contemporaneous reality is historically inevitable. As with individuals, if societies do not recognize this, they forfeit all possible control of their own destinies. If the pitiable and victimized natives share any responsibility for their debased condition, it is only because their level of development and their passive relationship with nature have not allowed them anything but a passive relationship with the impinging world of the present. With a sigh, Tommo notes that it is only a matter of time until the French have their gunboats and troops on the lovely bay and valley, and what has been presented in the extended quote above will occur all over again. Thus *Typee* presents the germ of *Billy Budd's* major argument: the purity of innocence may be beauty, but in the complete inversion that naturalism makes of idealistic tenets, innocence, not knowledge, is a murderous impossibility that becomes original sin.

Eden is deceptive because it is indefensible as a state of being. It is open to all the incursions of history once life has become subject to time. Indeed, Eden is not Eden, but, as historical land, has already been corrupted by the western world of the present. In *Typee* the first visible signs of land, almost immediately contrasted with luxurious and inviting somnolence, are the portentous seafowl led by "That piratical-looking fellow, appropriately named the man-of-war's hawk, with his blood-red bill and raven plumage. . . ." Perhaps Eden was never Eden. Further suspicions are cast upon the state of primitive, pure, and natural life by hints about the quality of its still unspoiled state. Melville is to find that any isolated state of being—mind, body, or heart—which does not review all states of being is untenable. Land in itself is not to be equated with safety or infallible human happiness. The Melville of a story like "The Lightning Rod Man," for instance, envisions the inevitability of fate as something equally embracing whether one is in a howling onshore gale or in the comfort of his easy chair. And particularly in terms of Typee existence, the single luxury of mindless body is bloody murder, a process of rot, a practice of cannibalism; *Typee's* scattered bits of reminders about cannibalism do more than merely sharpen anticipation and suspense. Says Tommo, before he ever lands in Nukuheva,

> I had heard too of an English vessel that many years ago, after a weary cruize, sought to enter the bay of Nukuheva, and arriving within two or three miles of the land, was met by a large canoe filled with natives, who

offered to lead the way to their place of destination. The captain, unacquainted with the localities of the island, joyfully accepted to the proposition—the canoe paddled on and the ship followed. Soon she was conducted to a beautiful inlet, and dropped her anchor in its waters beneath the shadows of the lofty shore. That same night the perfidious Typees, who had thus inveigled her into their fatal bay, flocked aboard the doomed vessel by hundreds, and at a given signal murdered every soul on board [pp. 493–94].

If untainted natural man in constant communion with nature is Adamic, then this Eden is vastly changed in concept. Rather it is only a different kind of the sharkishness of *Redburn's* land, or the deceptive safety of *Moby-Dick's* Aunt Charity and "The Lee Shore." The initial picture of salvation and pure regeneration associated with Edenic primitivism becomes suspect as only partly true, as factually inaccurate.

Simplicity, innocence, seclusion, isolation, passivity, and avoidance of historical knowledge are not the virtues that either the Christian tradition or transcendentalism thought they were. Melville strengthens this suspicion by adding another detail to the consequences of conflict between the two worlds. The first human who comes aboard ship from the Marquesan land is a tottering, almost comatose, and aged native. He is a drunken old vagabond who "was utterly unable to stand erect or to navigate his body across the deck." And—he is the official pilot for the bay of Nukuheva! He is the man appointed to navigate the microcosm of one entire world into communication with another. The activities of one world simply cannot be bundled into the activities of another without the dehumanization which results from the loss of function and identity. The murder works both ways. Not only is the representative of Eden a ruin to the west, but the west also ruins the representative of Eden. This will not be the only time that Melville is to suggest that the oppressor becomes more debased than the oppressed he debases. As long as the western, contemporary world of mind is the visionless world of "practicality" and selfish conquest, and as long as the values of the primitive world of heart and body remain isolated from contemporary experience, the two can never be joined correctly. The final product is an inability to navigate life, for neither Typee alone nor the *Dolly* alone provide the necessary fullness for complete, correct human behavior. These early hints prepare for the demonstration of Eden's failure, which is the purpose of the rest of the book.

In the purity of Typee terms, the main tasks of body seem to be an innocent partaking of nature's munificence and an avoidance of conflict. For Ahab, in his departure from nature, the area of conflict is imaged in the depths of the ocean. For Pierre, in his departure from nature, the area of conflict is epitomized in the scaling of the Mount of Titans. The Typees avoid both ocean and mountain. Conflict is in ocean, whence come intruders and invaders, and is in mountain, where there is none of the nature that gives sustenance, and where there is the chance to meet battle and death from hostile tribesmen. The Typee existence is so diametrically opposed to toil and conflict, quest and consciousness, that its limitations preclude any hope for human aspiration in western terms, any hope for a widening of man's horizons.

> The mountainous tracts which separated their respective territories remain altogether uninhabited; the natives invariably dwelling in the depths of the valleys, with a view of securing themselves from the predatory incursions of their enemies, who often lurk along their borders . . . I several times met with very aged men, who from this cause had never passed the confines of their native vale, some of them having never even ascended midway up the mountains in the whole course of their lives, and who, accordingly, had little idea of the appearance of any other part of the island, the whole of which is not perhaps more than sixty miles in circuit. The little space in which some of these clans pass away their days would seem almost incredible [pp. 496–97].

Isolation and seclusion become not only some of the perfecting charms of the sequestered vale, but also some of its major limitations and defects. *Typee* becomes a natural starting point for themes which will illuminate men who would see all the known world and the infinities beyond it. But always the striking through to infinities is validly meaningful (even if the meaning is negative) only when it is motivated by broad experience in life.

Tommo is impressed by the wholeness, wholesomeness, and perfect magnificence of the islanders' bodies. At the same time, the conscious and injured isolato describes the mindlessness of the Typees. They cannot communicate with or understand the rest of humanity from which they are isolated. They can hear news from outlying valleys only through the agency of itinerant and taboo "communicados" like Marnoo and Jimmy. When the Typees talk—as they always do chatter chatter chatter—the talk is always spontaneous, unplanned, childlike and inconsequential. The Typee's only communication system but serves to continue isolation; the human telegraph system of natives shouting from tree to tree, from the beach to the inmost glen of the valley, announces invasion from either mountain or sea. The very animals of the glen, the physically brilliant lizards and birds, can make no sound. Always, except in its own primitive terms, which are not the terms of Tommo's life, childlike Typee can neither see, talk, nor hear; like Baby Budd, it is beautiful, mindless and blind.[21]

When Tommo does escape to the sea, his greatest opposition comes from a warrior chief, Mow-Mow, who is characterized by a gigantic and wonderfully powerful body, and by the fact that he has only one eye. On the other hand, the leader of the faction which would allow Tommo to leave unharmed is the old man, Marheyo, who (with his daughter Fayaway) is among the few Typees to understand Tommo's plight to the point of compassion. It is true that others (Mehevi the chief and Kory-Kory the valet) also are fond of Tommo, but when the values of Typee conflict with Tommo's values, these others refuse Tommo's wishes, with few exceptions. When they do grant his wishes, they do so believing that his injured body will make him ineffectual in the attainment of his goals—that he will be unable to effect his own destiny. Fayaway has love and sympathy for Tommo because she is his mistress. But it is Marheyo who has the compassion of understanding, and he is the only native aware that there may be in non-Typeean worlds values which also have claim upon human behavior. When Tommo tries to escape, Marheyo consequently is in the van of those who see Tommo as a human being—they have been able to make that much of an extension beyond their own world into history. Those who wish to head Tommo off see him from the ahuman perspective of a single and isolated world. They wish only to maintain patterns of belief and behavior which have remained secluded from the history Tommo represents, and if they were to have their way, his identity and destiny would alike be consigned to the sacred "pork" dishes of a Feast of Calabashes. To them Tommo is not a human being as much as he is a sacrificial subject for cannibal rites. Tommo is pursued by the blind, magnificent animal and by the religion of the hidden valley, by Mow-Mow and the priests. As they rush onto the beach in furious chase, the shout "Roo-ne! Roo-ne!" which, judging by its effect upon Tommo, is a reference to the cannibalistic death which he must not be allowed to escape. "In the midst of this tumult old Marheyo came to my side," says Tommo, "and I shall never forget the benevolent expression of his countenance. He placed his arm upon my shoulder, and emphatically pronounced the only two English words I had taught him—'Home' and 'Mother.' I at once understood what he meant, and eagerly expressed my thanks to him." Whether Melville so intended it or not, this is more than a sop to nineteenth-century sentimentality. For suddenly, with no warning Marheyo is the only Typeean who can communicate in the tongue of another history, and the time of departure from Typee is the only moment in the entire book in which he does speak the words he knows. The Typeean Marheyo of the Typeean social group could not have been at all sentimental or lugubrious in his evocation of home and mother, for an entire chapter was devoted to pointing out that family relationships among the Typees were extremely loose and flexible, and that homes are only houses, open to all. Significantly, in the frozen instant of Marheyo's communication, he states a realization of the need common to all mortality, the need for identification with one's world. He is capitulating to worlds which can offer Tommo his identity, something that Marheyo's beloved Typee can never do. This capitulation is crucial not only to an understanding of Tommo's salvation, but also to Melville's naturalism. If isms split on the rock of the problem of man's identity, then it is central to recognize that in Melville's books human identity is attained by its relationship to its historical and social world, and not to any set of ideals which exist outside time.

Marheyo's sorrow when he takes leave of Tommo represents many things. His loss of Tommo on the literal level is the loss of a friend and a son. His loss of Tommo is also a yielding to the claims of consciousness, and is the first drumbeat of Eden's doom. The world moves on beyond Typee, and here is the first intimation for Marheyo that there may be greater areas of being which impinge upon Typee. The loss of Tommo becomes a portent of a loss of Typee's ability to control its own future. As in the climax of all Melville novels, characters and incidents take on added significance in the suddenly quickened tumble of events which bring the action to a close; and here Marheyo, a harmlessly puttering old savage who cannot even build a tiny hut, almost becomes a figure of transition in time. Marheyo and Fayaway tearfully aid Tommo's escape only because they realize that their desires are not consonant with the larger, predatory world outside.

Tommo recognizes the human and emotional meaning of their action, and he would reward their love. He gives to them and to Kory-Kory the cloth and musket which were used as ransom by his deliverers. But just as Marheyo buys his realizations with sacrifice, so Tommo too cannot buy his own deliverance with the fortuitous gun and calico, which are a bogus reprieve because they are external to his own commitments. He had had to translate commitment into action in order to be free of the *Dolly*. He must yet prove in action his own rejection of the level of Typee existence which shouts "Roo-ne!" rather than "Home" and "Mother." The complete deliverance, the consequence, is dependent upon his own manipulation of events, and his personal sorrow over a loss of idealized, innocent, Edenic sexuality and love must not be permitted to bar his choice of histories. In order to capsize the rowboat which carries Tommo out to sea, Mow-Mow swims after his fleeing victim. "After a few breathless moments I discerned Mow-Mow. The athletic islander, with his tomahawk between his teeth, was dashing the water before him till it foamed again. He was the nearest to us, and in another instant he would have seized one of the oars. Even at the moment I felt horror at the act I was about to commit; but it was no time for pity or compunction, and with true aim, and exerting all my strength, I dashed the boat-hook at him. It struck him just below the throat, and forced him downwards." Melville could not have chosen a better representative of Typee to be the last real obstacle between Tommo and his freedom. Tommo's action here is an acutely conscious thing rather than mere physical reflex. In the pitch of the fray he weighs worlds and actions, compassion or force. He is aware of his horror—his action is not spontaneous on every level as is that of the islanders. Also, by this time Tommo's bad leg has almost crippled him, in contrast to the "athletic islander" who opposed him. But the excitement of conscious will, of self-preservation, overcomes his disabilities.

With identity itself staked upon the outcome, the world of mind physically utilizes sheer will in order to defeat the physical world of external circumstance. "The strong excitement which had thus far kept me up, now left me, and I fell back fainting into the arms of Karakoee." Finally then, Tommo rejects isolation and his own former escapist role. His horror, like his sorrow, is on a personal level of human pity. He must override this in order to remove Mow-Mow the symbol, although he is pained at the thought of hurting Mow-Mow the man. Yet because his choice is so central to man's historical destiny, he must take the same action which looks forward, over the haze of years, to the actions of Captain the Honourable Edward Fairfax Vere. What makes Melville's meaning especially clear is the clinching detail of Tommo's salvation. He is rescued not by a Typeean, not even Marheyo or Fayaway, but by Karakoee, a tabooed *communicado*, a native who has rejected isolation and primitive existence, a man who can communicate with both worlds. His native Marquesan physical and linguistic abilities are brought to the present world of whalers, which is the world in which he chooses to live. Man cannot run from the present to the past without murder and loss of identity. Tommo will swear to this. Man cannot be abruptly flashed from one history to another without dehumanization. The pilot of the bay of Nukuheva will attest to this. Motion is one-directional. Man can only educate himself from the past to the present in order to find his fullest self. Melville, Tommo, Karakoee, *and* the transcendentalist will honor this.

Communication and isolation, as shaped by the literal characteristics of Marquesan geography, are concentrated in the story of Tommo's and Toby's attempt to reach an inland valley of Nukuheva. The secondary character in these chapters (VI–IX) is physical nature, which battles the intruders every inch of the way. Moreover, the captain of the *Dolly* had offered rewards to the natives for the capture of the two renegade sailors. Tommo and Toby are doubly isolated. As individuals who attempt to transfer into different worlds of space and time, they are met with rebuffs on every hand. As isolatoes, their individualism can never be as overwhelming as the pride and identity of either world. The world to which they flee will not have them (and when it does, there must be unconditional surrender), and the world from which they flee will not let them go.[22]

Tommo and Toby have brought some slight provisions with them, but those provisions turn out to be almost useless in the new environment. Escape into the alien environment only hurts Tommo's body. Tommo's identity at once becomes a residual rather than a complete quality, an emblem of consciousness in a purely physical world, and the body is the only weapon of that world. Once transferred in time, Tommo's consciousness is not only of no help, but it is a danger. Whenever Tommo begins to feel a sharp awareness of his isolation in Typee, and particularly whenever he meditates on the possible meanings of that isolation, at that precise moment Melville always reintroduces the injured leg; and also at that precise moment the leg becomes more acutely inflamed and painful. The failure of Tommo's body is symbolic of his entire plight. The man who evaluates his actions individualistically rather than historically is ground to a pulp in the warfare between historical conditions. This germinal suggestion is fulfilled in *Pierre,* and is one of the keys to an understanding of that book. The world is not integrated. As Pierre discovers, the world's segments become "banded" only in the act of turning against the man who would withdraw from his historical identity. Tommo's plight sounds the first note in Melville's thematic call to integration and completion. Body needs consciousness (Tommo can strike a Lucifer match, but Kory-Kory must struggle to produce a flame), and consciousness needs body (Kory-Kory must carry the injured Tommo) lest man become an invalid in the undeniable world of physical nature or a childlike animal in the undeniable world of the human mind. Segmentation makes suicide a dual thing: it is visited upon society by the individual who tries to remake the world in the image of his own individual disintegration (Ahab), and it is visited upon the individual by the disintegrated world which tries to deny border-crossing (Pierre). Each segment is more aware of its own absolutist concepts than of the relativistic view demanding integration, and Melville uses this folly to satirize religious dogma, hypocritical social mores, and thoughtless nationalism. Thus there is the need for the complete man, the Vere-hero, whose reinforming vision is historical and communal, and who can effect a border-crossing eclecticism according to what is pertinent to his time and civilization rather than according to a preconceived ideality. It is this crying human need which is the polemical stimulus for Melville's themes of universal brotherhood, cultural relativism, and social democracy, even in the experimental spawn of *Typee.*[23]

Certainly Melville's position was not completed, or perhaps even formed, by 1845–46. For the remaining forty-six years of his life, Melville was to wrestle with his "ontological heroics." But the relativistic mind is observable in *Typee* if only in the embryonic qualities of the hints and possibilities which are to grow to full stature in the later books. In *Typee* the relativism, or early and simple Melvillean "duality," is best realized in the scene wherein Admiral Du Petit Thouars, western conqueror of the Marquesans, meets the chief of the natives of Tior, who have just capitulated to the French.

> It so happened that the very day I was in Tior the French admiral, attended by all the boats of his squadron, came down in state from Nukuheva to take formal possession of the place. He remained in the valley about two hours, during which time he had a ceremonious interview with the king.
> The patriarch-sovereign of Tior was a man very far advanced in years; but though age had bowed his form and rendered him almost decrepid,

his gigantic frame retained all his original magnitude and grandeur of appearance. He advanced slowly and with evident pain, assisting his tottering steps with the heavy war-spear he held in his hand, and attended by a group of grey-bearded chiefs, on one of whom he occasionally leaned for support. The admiral came forward with head uncovered and extended hand, while the old king saluted him by a stately flourish of his weapon. The next moment they stood side by side, these two extremes of the social scale,—the polished, splendid Frenchman, and the poor, tattooed savage. They were both tall and noble-looking men; but in other respects how strikingly contrasted! Du Petit Thouars exhibited upon his person all the paraphernalia of his naval rank. He wore a richly decorated admiral's frockcoat, a laced chapeau bras, and upon his breast were a variety of ribbons and orders; while the simple islander, with the exception of a slight cincture about his loins, appeared in all the nakedness of nature.

At what an immeasurable distance, thought I, are these two beings removed from each other. In the one is shown the result of long centuries of progressive civilization and refinement, which have gradually converted the mere creature into the semblance of all that is elevated and grand; while the other, after the lapse of the same period, has not advanced one step in the career of improvement. "Yet, after all," quoth I to myself, "insensible as he is to a thousand wants, and removed from harassing cares, may not the savage be the happier man of the two?" Such were the thoughts that arose in my mind as I gazed upon the novel spectacle before me. In truth it was an impressive one, and little likely to be effaced. I can recall even now with vivid distinctness every feature of the scene. The umbrageous shades where the interview took place—the glorious tropical vegetation around—the picturesque grouping of the mingled throng of soldiery and natives—and even the golden-hued bunch of banannas that I held in my hand at the time, and of which I occasionally partook while making the aforesaid philosophical reflections [pp. 498–99].

The cliché, the flip "philosophy" about the undressed-savage-as-happier-man-than-beribboned-admiral is relatively unimportant. It is glib and traditional, and as it appears here, cheap and shoddy. It cannot be believed completely in the context of Tommo's total relations with the savages, nor even in the context of the tone of this particular passage—and tone is always one of Melville's most obvious clues. Tommo lounges and chews bananas while he "philosophizes"; he is not greatly bowed under the weight of his thought. What is important is that the "social" differences between the two men are differences in time and levels of development. Although this passage devotes itself to appearance—the apparent evil of civilization's artificiality and the apparent good of primitivism's honesty—what does emerge is the total force of the contrast, the snapshot of the two disjoined segments of the world under analysis at the moment. By calling attention to the Frenchman's lack of nakedness and the native's lack of surface artificiality, the point of view creates expectations for a symbolism of clothing, as it were. It prepares for a statement of modifications, for more than the external relationships between the civilized and uncivilized world.

For instance, there is a modification created by a contrast (which is somewhat extrinsic, appearing in the Appendix) between the westerner, the Englishman Paulet, and the westerner, the Frenchman Thouars. Paulet, also a uniformed man, introduces civilization to primitivism in terms of the primitive world which is to be affected. He attempts to understand, to wisely control, rather than merely to rule this aspect of human existence. Thouars and the missionaries, on the other hand, prove that rule without understanding is not a guiding control, but chaos. It is consequently a denial of the very consciousness which present history represents and which makes control possible. It is only an imposing of the technology and mores of the western world on a world which cannot cope with them, and it becomes a mirror of civilization's sins. Once again the elements of the book return us to Melville's controlling point of view: the government of human affairs must deny mere conquest and utilize consciousness for social goals. The primitive must be evaluated by a cumulative racial experience rather than by that one aspect of it which is called respectability. As a segment of that experience, the natives in a most basic sense are not divorced from western man, and a view of cultural differences which is not motivated by an attempt to guide the civilization from which the differences are seen, simply continues a wrongful and artificial segmentation. As "ethnologist" Melville insists that anthropology must be descriptive only so that it may be properly prescriptive, for "prescriptions" will be forthcoming in any case.

The universality of Typee is suggested not only by its debased manifestation in the primitive savagery of the western ship's crews, but also in Melville's description of the natives on their home grounds. The young men lounge around trying to look important and trying to avoid work. They are interested in weapons, athletics, and girls. The girls are interested in cosmetics and flirtations. The men at the bachelor quarters are interested in eating, drinking, smoking, discussing current events and making casual small talk of male affairs. The description of Tinor is the description of any good middle-class Lansingburgh or Albany or New York or Berkshire housewife—although in conformity to the life symbolized by Typee, Tommo takes care to point out that old Tinor is the only conscientious worker in the entire valley. Melville describes characteristics in these instances as typical not of Typees particularly, but as typical of one's youth, sex, marital status, or office. Except on the literal, narrative level, the Typeean is not unconnected with the you's and me's of Melville's and Tommo's current world. Symbolically he is that ultimately murderous part of all men which is unconscious, spontaneous, and comfortable. Like the sea self, the Typee self is also a robber, and both selves are cannibalistic because in their incompleteness they set man to devouring man. The Typee simply takes. He never plants or plans, never enters into conflict with nature in order to grasp the control that the quest figure constantly seeks. There are times when the breadfruit trees do not bear food, and only the haphazardly stored fruits of past crops sustain the natives, or else they go hungry. For unlike the whaleman, the savage does not store food with any plan, sufficiency, or foresight. This unconsciousness is simple and childlike and beautiful, but it is a luxury which can be afforded only in the limited area of existence wherein man can allow himself to be submissively integrated with nature. And that is the limited quality of Eden. Like Tommo's legal arguments at the beginning of the book, the unconsciousness is inapplicable to the realities of history. It is a fortuitous thing, like the Typeean attributes of Mrs. Glendinning's riches in *Pierre*. The blithe unconsciousness is necessary for the honest and inescapably animal functions of body, and consequently Melville uses it in his exposure of western respectability. It is a necessary part of man's relationship with external physical nature, and cannot be omitted if such a relationship is to be successful. But this primitivism must be recognized as only a part of the necessary human completion, and not as something to be mistakenly adored as the purity which cures the sweat and toil of the life of conscious relationship with both nature and man.

In his praise of the islanders and their happiness, and to the extent that he insists upon a human integration with physical nature, Melville agrees with the Rousseauism that appeared in so many modified and contradictory forms during the era of the transcendentalists. But by no means is his agreement a back-to-nature movement, transcendental or otherwise. For the transcendental back-to-nature doctrine was predicated upon idealistic rather than physical growth. Melville felt that the idealists used the wrong means for given goals. Indeed, Thoreau went to the woods to rid himself of his "scurvy, empirical self." Melville rejects sheer physicality as well as doctrines for human behavior that minimize the physical and the empirical. He never departs from his historical evaluation of primitivism, for his area of concern is that of social integration. Given that integration, man uses time and is not used by it. Given that, the cosmic will follow—at least for man. "We must first succeed alone, that we may enjoy our success together," said Thoreau.[24] Melville inverts the dogma. In presenting his happy Typee community, he says that true individual happiness can never exist unless and until it is conditioned by and given a frame of reference by social happiness. A man alone in a world of woe can find truth but not happiness. The truth must be applied to the world in which the truth is born, or else mere truth becomes a silent and selfish accomplice of murder, as it does with *Pierre's* Plinlimmon and *Billy Budd's* Dansker. This approach to morality and identity in *Typee* is at once a foreshadowing of Melville's naturalism and a reinforcement of Tommo's final desire to regain his own self's true place. The rejection of Typee, despite all of Typee's own kind of happiness, is the flight from the unmodified natural level of man's existence. Man must step above the unselfconsciousness of elemental living, yet must not reject the physical world as reality. The foreshadowing suggests the distinctive qualities of Melville's naturalism: William Faulkner, for instance, is naturalistic in his acceptance of the physical world as reality, yet is in tactical disagreement with the view that man must rise above an unselfconscious assimilation into elemental life.[25] The very answer that is needed by Faulkner's haunted heroes is the answer Tommo learns to distrust. For Faulkner, nature is something that man must emulate, something that is man's positive tutor and moral surrogate. For Melville, nature is something that man must reshape and modify according to his own needs, i.e. the needs of his own society.

Consciousness of self has characterized Tommo from the beginning. He is an exponent of conscious will. He reviews alternatives and makes choices concerning his own destiny. Then he withdraws from the *Dolly*. He forces himself to an act he cannot physically sustain when he uses his body to crush the barriers of physical nature as he and Toby labor through the reed tangles on the slopes. It is Tommo who conceives the plan for use of body in the first place. Even when compared to Toby, who is himself a representative of western civilization, it is always Tommo who prevails in council. It is he who decides where they shall camp, which path they shall follow, into which valley they shall descend. Toby prevails in action, in spontaneous physical endeavor, and he does not communicate to Tommo except in those terms. Whereas Tommo discusses alternatives with Toby, Toby simply moves when the next move is up to him: he falls off the cliff into the palm tree in the last descent into the Typee valley, leaving the startled Tommo gasping behind him. It is Tommo who first communicates to Toby his own plans for desertion, whereas Toby had been harboring similar thoughts in silence, telling no one.

There are, of course, ample instances of Toby's conscious will. After all, he too is alien to pure Typee existence, and it would be surprising indeed to find symbolic subtleties of characterization fulfilled in this first novel. But the relationship between Tommo and Toby (Tommo is always the more enterprising, even in the first, comic introduction to Polynesian food: "By my soul, it is baked baby!" exclaims Toby, while Tommo sets to with epicurean gusto) makes it clear that it is the more spontaneous Toby who is best fitted for existence in Typee. His body is unimpaired by Typee. His conversion would not demonstrate the meaning of Typee ethics as much as would Tommo's conversion; Melville permits the natives to be willing to part with Toby—but they will not allow Tommo so much as a glimpse of the sea. These considerations lead one to expect to find not the Tommo and Toby that *Typee* actually presents, but an Ahab and a Flask, a Faust and a happy-go-lucky companion. And it remains true that until Tommo longs to return to his own world, his quality of mind remains "practical," and shrewd, and uninformed by philosophy. But once his attitudes do change, and they do, the implication is that he does begin to think deeply. His "philosophy" must be extrapolated by the reader, because Melville suggests the underlying meaning of Tommo's rejection of Typee only in terms of action. Had Melville been fully conscious of what he actually was doing, he certainly would have given Tommo opportunity for Ahabian soliloquy or dialogue. One can only conclude the obvious: thematically and artistically, Melville was as yet unprepared to express his controlling perception on many levels.

Still, the barrier to the sea presented by *Typee* prepares for the difference between the quester and the lee shore. As demonstrated by Tommo and Typee, the difference is intensified in Tommo's and Kory-Kory's variant reactions to the effigy of the warrior chief in the canoe of death.

> In one of the most secluded portions of the valley . . . was the mausoleum of a deceased warrior chief. Like all the other edifices of any note, it was raised upon a small pi-pi of stones, which, being of unusual height, was a conspicuous object from a distance. . . . The sanctity of the spot appeared never to have been violated. The stillness of the grave was there, and the calm solitude around was beautiful and touching. The soft shadows of those lofty palm-trees!—I can see them now—hanging over the little temple, as if to keep out the intrusive sun.
>
> On all sides as you approached this silent spot you caught sight of the dead chief's effigy, seated in the stern of a canoe, which was raised on a light frame a few inches above the level of the pi-pi. The canoe was about seven feet in length; of a rich, dark colored wood, handsomely carved and adorned in many places with variegated bindings of stained sinnate, into which were wrought a number of sparkling seashells, and a belt of the same shells ran all around it. The body of the figure—of whatever material it might have been made—was effectually concealed in a heavy robe of brown tappa, revealing only the hands and head; the latter skillfully carved in wood, and surmounted by a superb arch of plumes. These plumes, in the subdued and gentle gales which found access to this sequestered spot, were never for one moment at rest, but kept nodding and waving over the chief's brow. The long leaves of the palmetto dropped over the eaves, and through them you saw the warrior holding his paddle with both hands in the act of rowing, leaning forward and inclining his head, as if eager to hurry on his voyage. Glaring at him forever, and face to face, was a polished human skull, which crowned the prow of the canoe. The spectral figurehead, reversed in its position, glancing backwards, seemed to mock the impatient attitude of the warrior [pp. 678–80].

Here is a touch which could be right out of the later Melville. The muffled figure is immediately recognizable as the model of all Melville's questers, and the antithesis of Typee life. His body is hidden; his head demands notice. He is voyaging. He is impatient. He is mounted on an aspiring structure. He is water-bound, sea-traveling, surrounded by and ornamented with emblems of another life than the land's. He is Taji in his canoe, with the backward-mocking specter in the prow grinning out the message that time is more absolute than ideal. He is Ahab furiously staring into the ever gaping mask of the white whale. He is Pierre struggling to complete the rebellious journey of Enceladus. He sees no Heaven, no God, no Answer—as long as he quests, ever trying to streak past the symbol of impossibility, he sees nothing but the face of time: mortality, transiency, death. At this point Tommo becomes momentarily separated from the narrator. The narrator notes that the skull "seemed to mock the impatient attitude. . . ." But how does Tommo react?

> Whenever in the course of my rambles through the valley I happened to be near the chief's mausoleum. I always turned aside to visit it. The place has a peculiar charm for me; I hardly know why; but so it was. As I leaned over the railing and gazed upon the strange effigy and watched the play of the feathery head-dress, stirred by the same breeze which in low tones breathed amidst the lofty palm-trees, I loved to yield myself up to the fanciful superstition of the islanders, and could almost believe that the grim warrior was bound heavenward. In this mood when I turned to depart, I bade him, "God speed, and a pleasant voyage." Aye, paddle away, brave chieftain, to the land of the spirits! To the material eye thou makest but little progress; but with the eye of faith, I see thy canoe cleaving the bright waves, which die away on the dimly looming shores of Paradise [p. 681].

It is the material eye which sees the skull. It is the idealistic eye which sees the dimly looming shores of Paradise. Not only is this at the core of the pessimism which often characterizes naturalism (yet which is not necessarily one of naturalism's identities), but it is a significant insight into Melville's perception. For it is at the moment that the idealistic eye and the material eye are differentiated that the figures of Tommo and the narrator barely perceptibly slide apart, like two identical, photographed figures whose outlines momentarily fail to merge on the screen. If the warrior is a symbol of general human aspiration, then there need be no blurring of identities—the naturalist may have his own Faith and Belief. But here the figure represents to Tommo a kind of idealistic faith, for his reaction to the effigy is couched in obvious suggestions of Christian theology. And Tommo sympathizes; he understands the everlasting trip to another world; he himself is a changeling. But the quester as such is not yet. Tommo does not wish to plunge beyond the human world, and wishes only to return to his own true home.

Melville proceeds to use the reactions of Tommo and Kory-Kory to further divide the perceptions of the material and idealistic eye. The innocent animality of the islanders had at first been presented as apparently enviable. Then the relationship of Tommo to Typee presented the same quality as murderous. Now, when the physicality of the native is presented in its hardheaded, simple and materialistic aspects, the tone of the book becomes jocularly sympathetic. If Tommo, who empathizes with the warrior chief, has strong reservations about leaving the human world, Kory-Kory is completely empirical about the whole business, and his vision of the warrior and voyage is projected completely in the matter-of-fact terms of body.

> When I first visited this singular place with Kory-Kory, he told me—or at least so I understood him—that the chief was paddling his way to the realm of bliss, and bread-fruit—the Polynesian heaven—where every moment the bread-fruit trees dropped their ripened spheres to the ground, and where there was no end to the cocoa-nuts and banannas: there they reposed through the live-long eternity upon mats much finer than those of Typee; and every day bathed their glowing limbs in rivers of cocoa-nut oil. In that happy land there were plenty of plumes and feathers, and boars'-tusks and sperm-whale teeth, far preferable to all the shining trinkets and gay tappa of the white man; and, best of all, women far lovelier than the daughters of earth were there in abundance. "A very pleasant place," Kory-Kory said it was; "but after all, not much pleasanter," he thought, "than Typee." "Did he not then," I asked him, "wish to accompany the warrior?" "Oh, no: he was very happy where he was; but supposed that some time or other he would go in his own canoe."
>
> Thus far, I think, I clearly comprehended Kory-Kory. But there was a singular expression he made use of at the time, enforced by as singular a gesture, the meaning of which I would have given much to penetrate. I am inclined to believe it must have been a proverb he uttered; for I afterwards heard him repeat the same words several times, and in what appeared to me to be a somewhat similar sense. Indeed, Kory-Kory had a great variety of short, smart-sounding sentences, with which he frequently enlivened his discourse; and he introduced them with an air which plainly intimated, that, in his opinion, they settled the matter in question, whatever it might be.
>
> Could it have been then, that when I asked him whether he desired to go to this heaven of bread-fruit, cocoa-nuts, and young ladies, which he had been describing, he answered by saying something equivalent to our old adage—"A bird in the hand is worth two in the bush?"—if he did, Kory-Kory was a discreet and sensible fellow, and I cannot sufficiently admire his shrewdness [pp. 680–81].

When the ideal is subjected to the empirical view, the blurring between the narrator and Tommo disappears. The incipient naturalism is manifest in the sympathy the Tommo-narrator has with Kory-Kory's implicit suspicion that this life is reality and when it is surrendered, all is surrendered. Melville does here what he is to do in all the books to follow: he suggests the discrepancy between the idealistic belief (especially when institutionalized) and the empirical evidence which makes even the pious man afraid to die. The way is prepared for *Mardi's* bitter "Marmora" passages on the hypocrisy, blindness (the idealistic eye of Pani is literally closed to the naturalist's basic truth), and idiocy of institutionalized religion. Melville as naturalist does have a Truth and a Belief, but it is born of the material eye: he is religious, but cannot be pious. The material eye of Melville's perception explains the idealist's, Hawthorne's, statement that "If he [Melville] were a religious [in context, a pious] man, he would be one of the most truly religious and reverential;"[26] and also explains the "Rabelaisian" quality that all readers notice in Melville. This common-sensical, physical *joie de vivre* stems from the assumption underlying Kory-Kory's doubts, that is, that the purpose of life is not a dying into another life, but the living of the present life. In an impish passage in which Tommo, through satiric tone, again identifies himself with an impious, common-sense attitude, Kory-Kory further displays the primacy he places upon the physical realities of this world. The Typee far exceeds the American in accentuating earthliness and in confining all areas of being to the realm of body.

> On the whole, I am inclined to believe, that the islanders in the Pacific have no fixed and definite ideas whatever on the subject of religion . . . In truth, the Typees, so far as their actions evince, submitted to no laws human or divine—always excepting the thrice mysterious taboo. The "independent electors" of the valley were not to be brow-beaten by chiefs, priests, idols, or devils. As for the luckless idols, they received more hard knocks than supplications. . . .
> . . . Walking with Kory-Kory through the deepest recesses of the groves, I perceived a curious looking image, about six feet in height, which originally had been placed upright against a low pi-pi, surmounted by a ruinous bamboo temple, but having become fatigued and weak in the knees, was now carelessly leaning against it. The idol was partly concealed by the foliage of a tree which stood near, and whose leafy boughs drooped over the pile of stones, as if to protect the rude fane from the decay to which it was rapidly hastening. The image itself was nothing more than a grotesquely shaped log, carved in the likeness of a portly naked man with the arms clasped over the head, the jaws thrown wide apart, and its thick shapeless legs bowed in to an arch. It was much decayed. The lower part was overgrown with a bright silky moss. Thin spears of grass sprouted from the distended mouth and fringed the outline of the head and arms. His godship had literally attained a green old age. All its prominent points were bruised and battered, or entirely rotted away. The nose had taken its departure, and from the general appearance of the head it might have been supposed that the wooden divinity, in despair at the neglect of its worshippers, had been trying to beat its own brains out against the surrounding trees.
> I drew near to inspect more closely this strange object of idolatry; but halted reverently at the distance of two or three paces, out of regard to the religion of my valet. As soon, however, as Kory-Kory perceived that I was in one of my inquiring, scientific moods, to my astonishment, he sprang to the side of the idol, and pushing it away from the stones against which it rested, endeavored to make it stand upon its legs. But the divinity had lost the use of them altogether; and while Kory-Kory was trying to prop it up, by placing a stick between it and the pi-pi, the monster fell clumsily to the ground, and would infallibly have broken its neck had not Kory-Kory

providentially broken its fall by receiving its whole weight on his own
half-crushed back. I never saw the honest fellow in such a rage before. He
leaped furiously to his feet, and seizing the stick, began beating the poor
image: every moment or two pausing and talking to it in the most violent
manner, as if upbraiding it for the accident. When his indignation had
subsided a little he whirled the idol about most profanely, so as to give me
an opportunity of examining it on all sides. I am quite sure I never should
have presumed to have taken such liberties with the god myself, and I was
not a little shocked at Kory-Kory's impiety [pp. 687–89].

Kory-Kory is a simple, earthbound, unphilosophical Ahab who furiously
seeks vengeance against any god who would crush him. The Typee, of
course, does not function on a metaphysical level, and for just that reason
underscores the irony of Ahab's mistake: God is a dumb block of wood
whose hurts to man really have nothing to do with any intentional relationship between heaven and earth. It is man who "providentially" keeps
the "infallible" god from falling and breaking his neck. Typee's incompleteness, on the other hand, is manifested in Kory-Kory's complete
lack of recognition of the god as a concept, as an emblem of human
aspiration. Typee is death to informing vision, and thus Tommo has a certain amount of nostalgic sympathy for the dead warrior-chief. Once
again, Typee is universalized, for the savage's "practicality" and mindless
materialism result in the same limitation as does the shrewd "practicality"
of the west, even though it is not the same qualitatively. And every time
the universal limitations of Typee are suggested, there is also a focus of
Tommo's change. The contemporary world he has abandoned, with all its
savage denials and perversions of its own possibilities, is the world of
man's largest potentialities. This is Tommo's driving force for an identity
which explains action that "Home" and "Mother" on the merely sentimental level cannot justify at all. Significantly, it is Kory-Kory who, as a
representative Typee and Tommo's friendly valet and warden, is the man
assigned by the islanders to keep the American from breaking taboos or
from fleeing toward the sea.

When Karky the tattooer wishes to practice his craft on Tommo, the
injured man refuses in horror. At first his refusal is based upon a relatively
superficial fear that once he has been decorated, he will no longer have
the "face" for western society. But Karky will not be satisfied with a com-
mission to work on Tommo's arm—he wishes to attack the face. The
Typee tattoos of the face all include a line which runs across the eyes
(either horizontally or vertically, like *prison bars* [Melville's image], or
diagonally as part of the two inclines of an equilateral triangle with the
base line running across the *mouth*). The Typee designs for tattoo of the
head all include a hiding of the agents of communication and understanding. The designs for the body are—as would be expected—animals or
vegetable growth. When all the natives, even Kory-Kory and the high
chief Mehevi evidence their strong desire to have Tommo's face tattooed,

and when all the priests join vehemently in agreement, Tommo realizes that the basis of their desire is conversion. None of the Typees understands why Tommo refuses the tattoo. They are all amazed that the values, symbols, and commitments of luxurious Typee can be refused by anyone. So there is a more basic meaning to Tommo's fear that his face will thereafter be unfit for western society. It is the book's fundamental suspense, the tension between mind and mindlessness. At this moment Tommo's desire to escape mounts to panic. And again the point is made that Tommo is inoperative in Typee; the pain in his useless leg becomes unbearable; his body cannot compete. His will and mind are useless because they cannot communicate the truth of Tommo's position. The truth enrages and insults the Typees. When will and mind do communicate at all, they only betray the wish to escape, and the guard is further alerted. If Tommo remains in Eden, either his will and mind will be altered by the overlay of Typee values, or else they will be consigned to death by the cannibal festivals. To retain physical existence, he must consent to the extinguishing of his mind, the loss of his own identity. The plight of Tommo in the death trap of alien values is summed up in a bit of dialogue with Marnoo. When Tommo pleads with Marnoo to try to get him out of the valley—thus endangering Marnoo's life as well as his own—Marnoo cuts him short. " 'Kannaka [natives] no let you go no where,' he said; 'you taboo. Why you no like stay? Plenty moee-moee (sleep)—plenty ki-ki (eat)—plenty whihenee (young girls)—Oh, very good place Typee! Suppose you no like this bay, why you come? You no hear about Typee? All white men afraid Typee, so no white men come.' " Marnoo's statement works in both major directions. First there is the Faulknerian hint about the universal savage which civilized man is afraid to admit is a truth about himself; secondly, the gravity of Tommo's sin is intensified. He cannot reply, in response to Marnoo's question, "Well, I guess I made a mistake." By the very legalities he claimed when he renounced his own world, he cannot claim the mistake and disclaim the consequence. Indeed Marnoo's conversation immediately heightens the suspense by revealing the symbolic meaning, or reality, beneath the appearance of Tommo's captivity: "Me no hear you talk any more; by by Kannaka get mad, kill you and me too. No you see he no want you to speak to me at all?—you see—ah! by by you no mind—you get well, he kill you, eat you, hang you head up there like Happar [enemy tribe] Kannaka! . . ."

Jealousy for the possession of Tommo, as indicated in the avidly proffered conversion, is a concentration of the conflict and isolation of the two worlds; Tommo has plunged back down into the primitive beginnings of human order only to find that man of the conscious, technological world has traveled too far beyond that Eden to find operation, completion, or even existence possible on that primary, mindless level. In short, man's history teaches that Eden and Adam must be redefined for every period of man's development; that if Eden is to be defined as a positive virtue for human aspiration, it lies not in the primitive past but somewhere in the completely conscious future, and is a goal, not a beginning. Marnoo, who is operative, and who, with his own broken communication, might connect the present with the past, is neither physically limited or debilitated like Tommo, nor isolated like the Typees. His tattooing sets him apart from the Typees: his head and face are clear of any tattoo. His body tattoo is not a collection of isolated items, like those of the Typees. His is one complete and integrated picture, and Tommo points this out quite emphatically. His level of existence is a transition, a hovering below the western world and above the Polynesian. Like Karakoee, he too has broken out of seclusion in time and space and has contacted the west and the sea. In a chronological sense but, significantly, not in the sense of political possibility, Marnoo comes close to the integration of polar values that will characterize the complete man. The real distances are distances of time.

There have been attempts to interpret Tommo's and Toby's literal descent and final fall into the valley as a parallel to the Fall from grace. Actually the parallel exists as a condensation of Tommo's entire voyage, the plunge from the world and time of civilization to the world and time of unconsciousness. It is a plunge that can no longer be accepted in terms of the Christian concept of the Fall from grace. Indeed the very fall in *Typee* is a fall from the barren uplands, which demand toil, into the cushioning verdure of the palm tree, down into greenness and plenty. The barriers of waters, mountains, and ravines are startlingly similar to the traditional barriers between worlds in the literature of Christian mythology.[27] And in inverse parallel to Christian mythology with its fabulous questing heroes, innocent purity and ignorance of worldly ways become a seeming thing. With the refructified lands and running waters, they bring death, for the appearance of innocence and the reality of its consequences are different things. And since the only time is world-time, the death is final, with no dying into anything but time's mocking, backward-glancing skull. This is the naturalist's view of the deadly paradox of limitations hidden beneath the smiling surfaces of Typee-Eden. Indeed it is Melville's consistent view of the deadly-funny grim jest, the lie, which hides beneath the occasionally smiling surfaces of an apparently benevolent universe.

Typee's very use of the luxuriant land reinforces this ironic note. The constant reference to verdure looks forward to the symbolic function of green in *Pierre*, where the color there too merges with the theme of time. In *Typee* green is related to decay in time. The first close view that Tommo and the crew have of land is the bay of Nukuheva, which is described in language vitally cognizant of the time motif: "Nothing can exceed the imposing scenery of this bay. Viewed from our ship as she lay at anchor in the middle of the harbour, it presented the appearance of a vast natural amphitheatre in decay, and overgrown with vines, the deep glens that furrowed its sides appearing like enormous fissures caused by the ravages of time." Closer to home in its application to humanity is the following use of green under the subheading (Chapter XII) "Timeworn Savages":

> As we advanced further along the building, we were struck with the aspect of four or five hideous old wretches, on whose decrepit forms time and tattooing seemed to have obliterated every trace of humanity. Owing to the continued operation of this latter process, which only terminates among the warriors of the island after all the figures stretched upon their limbs in youth have been blended together—an effect, however, produced only in cases of extreme longevity—the bodies of these men were of a uniform dull green color—the hue which the tattooing gradually assumes as the individual advances in age. Their skin had a frightful scaly appearance, which, united with its singular color, made their limbs not a little resemble dusty specimens of verde-antique [pp. 579–80].

The application of greenness and time has been made to man and nature; all that remains is to find the same applied to the divine. In the description of the idol beaten by Kory-Kory, the use of green-rot is made in just such a way, showing that the gods men worship are themselves decayed by time. That picture recalls the image of the verde-antique natives at the Ti, who always sit motionlessly, Tommo says, like so many idols. And later, at the Feast of the Calabashes, Tommo discovers that they are priests. Everything, including religion and man's conceptions of God, are subject to time. This theme is developed more completely and startlingly in *Pierre*, and is a basis for an understanding of Melville's view of history, religion, and Christ. It is for this reason, for instance, that Melville can dismiss Christian priests, ministers, and missionaries with the same amusement, the same devastatingly ironic tone, the same emphasis on futile and foolishly misdirected effort, that he employs for his treatment of pagan religion. Looked upon as timeless and permanent by its adherents, each religion, like each segment of the world, becomes an isolated caricature of each other religion and each other segment. One of the best examples again is found in the passage on Kory-Kory's beating of the idol:

> When one of the inferior order of natives could show such contempt for a venerable and decrepit God of the Groves, what the state of religion must be among the people in general is easily to be imagined. In truth I regard the Typees as a backslidden generation. They are sunk in religious sloth, and require a spiritual revival. A long prosperity of bread-fruit and cocoa-nuts has rendered them remiss in the performance of their higher obligations. The wood-rot malady is spreading among the idols—the fruit upon their altars is becoming offensive—the temples themselves need re-thatching—the tattooed clergy are altogether too light-hearted and lazy—and their flocks are going astray [p. 689].

Tommo, tongue in cheek, is assuming the attitude of the Christian missionary, and, of course, thus seems to blast those very aspects of Typee which have been found good. When the Tommo-narrator's sympathy for certain elements of Typeean materialism and empiricism is remembered, certainly we cannot believe aversion to Typee on *these* grounds. The puckish humor changes the "long prosperity" and the "blackslidden generation" into an obvious and satirical reference to the western-Christian—particularly American—world of Melville's day. Here again, Melville uses Typee not as a separate or ethnic grouping, but as a control for a general Type. Typee is not alone open to charges of decay. Time has affected all. It has reduced the once conscious, aspiring civilization which erected the monumental stone piles of the Typee valley into a memory confused by superstitions. That past civilization is one with all the great conquerors of nature whose works are now misunderstood and degraded to a level of support for a later, unconscious race which has not earned that support. *Mardi* is to state explicitly the implications of this idea; *Pierre* is to use the identical image of crumbling stones and past civilizations to recreate the idea; and *Billy Budd* is to center upon the historical monument perverted into superstitious myth, which becomes man's historical blindness and cannibalism. The idealistic presuppositions of religion repeatedly are seen as folly, not as man's truly highest aspirations. Consider the following savage indictment:

Mehevi and the chieftains of the Ti have just risen from their noontide slumbers. There are no affairs of state to dispose of; and having eaten two or three breakfasts in the course of the morning, the magnates of the valley feel no appetite as yet for dinner. How are their leisure moments to be occupied? They smoke, they chat, and at least one of their number makes a proposition to the rest, who joyfully acquiescing, he darts out of the house, leaps from the pi-pi, and disappears in the grove. Soon you see him returning with Kolory [a high priest], who bears the god Moa Artua in his arms, and carries in one hand a small trough, hollowed out in the likeness of a canoe. The priest comes along dandling his charge as if it were a lachrymose infant he was endeavoring to put into a good humor. Presently, entering the Ti, he seats himself on the mats as composedly as a juggler about to perform his sleight-of-hand tricks; and with the chiefs disposed in a circle about him, commences his ceremony.

In the first place he gives Moa Artua an affectionate hug, then caressingly lays him to his breast, and, finally, whispers something in his ear; the rest of the company listening eagerly for a reply. But the baby-god is deaf or dumb,—perhaps both, for never a word does he utter. At last Kolory speaks a little louder, and soon growing angry, comes boldly out with what he has to say and bawls to him. He put me in mind of a choleric fellow, who, after trying in vain to communicate a secret to a deaf man, all at once flies into a passion and screams it out so that every one may hear. Still Moa Artua remains as quiet as ever; and Kolory, seemingly loosing his temper, fetches him a box over the head, strips him of his tappa and red cloth, and laying him in a state of nudity in the little trough, covers him from sight. At this proceeding all present loudly applaud and signify their approval by uttering the adjective "mortarkee" with violent emphasis. Kolory, however, is so desirous his conduct should meet with unqualified approbation, that he inquires of each individual separately whether, under existing circumstances, he has not done perfectly right in shutting up Moa Artua. The invariable response is "Aa, Aa" (yes, yes), repeated over and over again in a manner which ought to quiet the scruples of the most conscientious. After a few moments Kolory brings forth his doll again, and while arraying it very carefully in the tappa and red cloth, alternately fondles and chides it. The toilet being completed, he once more speaks to it aloud. The whole company hereupon show the greatest interest; while the priest holding Moa Artua to his ear interprets to them what he pretends the god is confidentially communicating to him. Some items of intelligence appear to tickle all present amazingly; for one claps his hands in a rapture; another shouts with merriment; and a third leaps to his feet and capers about like a madman.

What under the sun Moa Artua on these occasions had to say to Kolory I never could find out; but I could not help thinking that the former showed a sad want of spirit in being disciplined into making disclosures, which at first he seemed bent on withholding. Whether the priest honestly interpreted what he believed the divinity said to him, or whether he was not all the while guilty of a vile humbug, I shall not presume to decide. At any rate, whatever as coming from the god was imparted to those present seemed to be generally of a complimentary nature: a fact which illustrates the sagacity of Kolory, or else the time-serving disposition of this hardly-used deity.

Moa Artua having nothing more to say, his bearer goes to nursing him again, in which occupation, however, he is soon interrupted by a question put by one of the warriors to the god. Kolory hereupon snatches it up to his ear again, and after listening attentively, once more officiates as the organ of communication. A multitude of questions and answers having passed between the parties, much to the satisfaction of those who propose them, the god is put tenderly to bed in the trough, and the whole company unites in a long chaunt, led off by Kolory. This ended, the ceremony is over; the chiefs rise to their feet in high good humour, and my Lord Archbishop, after chatting awhile, and regaling himself with a whiff or two from a pipe of tobacco, tucks the canoe under his arm and marches off with it.

The whole of these proceedings were like those of a parcel of children playing with dolls and baby houses [pp. 683–85].

Markedly, this is not the reportage of an "ethnologist." There is not any desire or attempt to understand the religious basis of the ceremony (Moa Artua is a High God, not an underling, Tommo explains); rather the religious ceremony is used as a foil for the narrator's observations of it. All the elements of unconsciousness unite in this incident. Except for the simple deceit which Kolory practices upon his parishioners—the same simple and transparent deceit which the natives practice upon Tommo—there is no disguise. Except for the "chaunt," all action is pictured as spontaneous, not ritualized. There is no attempt to pierce through appearances, no intellection. When Moa Artua is denuded in punishment, he is revealed as nothing more or less than what we are led to believe he is—a piece of wood. As Melville asks repeatedly in his later books, how can men get an answer from a stone, a voice from a silence, a guide from a zero? There is no directive connection between the absolute and the human, and no moral communication. There is only the fact of wood and the credulity, spontaneity, and unconsciousness of childish primitivism. The doll-playing members of Typee are no different from the doll-like crew of the *Dolly*. Religion becomes Melville's emblem of unquestioned values, unexamined behavior, and as a human institution it either demands submission (the missionaries and the natives) or unconsciousness (Kolory and Moa Artua).

The basic lack of communication, and the consequent need for it, returns Melville's thematic material directly to the cause of human brotherhood. Mere imposition of values is neither brotherhood nor integration. It denies communication. It may result in incongruity and farce: the visiting native queen of Mowanna, king of Nukuheva, getting into the spirit of the splendor and pomp of a military review, hoists her skirts to reciprocally display the splendor of her own brilliantly tattooed hindquarters. The French are scandalized and the incident is funny, like the joint-stock nature of the world presented in Queequeg's boarding the ferry to Nantucket, and his voyage to that island. But sometimes denial of real communication results in disease and death, as brought on by the ravages of venereal disease introduced by the western aliens. Often loss of brotherhood brings debasement, poverty, and death as introduced by the missionaries with their shifting, inapplicable laws and mores. Or incompleteness brings a denial of man's potentialities, and it is death as introduced by Typee with its cannibalism.

The treatment of isolation brings Melville's eclecticism to the fore. Tommo needs Kory-Kory: Ahab should have some of Queequeg's characteristics. Kory-Kory needs Tommo: Queequeg should have some of Ahab's. Thus, cultural relativism and democracy. The isolation also becomes part of Typee's social and historical orientation. Man must not tire of his world only to scorn it Byronically from an isolated mountain peak or to hide from it in the depths of an isolated valley. Before Tommo jumps ship he delightedly envisages the former and after he jumps ship he lives the latter. And once he learns the lesson of isolation he rejects both as single possibilities for behavior.

The element of heart has been mentioned, but only casually because it does not occupy much place in *Typee*. It is one of the foreshadowings in which the book so richly abounds. Heart, in Melville's books, is generally related to the Typee world rather than to the western, to the female rather than to the male, to the healthy body rather than to the self-consumed and driven man. As Taji, Ahab, and Pierre become more and more driven in their quests, and as their bodies waste away, their hearts harden. The complete-man hero will emphasize neither heart nor mind, but will subordinate either to the necessities and realities of his world. *Mardi's* Media will slacken his use of shrewdness and advantage, and will intensify and enlarge his heart. Captain Vere will submit to a necessary action of mind which breaks his heart. But like *Typee* itself, these heart-mind fractures can be only a preparation.

Not only because it is chronologically his first book, but also because it looks ahead to so much, *Typee* is the beginning of Melville's voyage. It is a book whose rich display of Melville's craft has been almost overlooked. Tommo's is indeed the central story, enriched by the roles of the characters who become enmeshed in his discoveries. There is never any real doubt about point of view, as there is in *Mardi*, or *Pierre*, or even *Moby-Dick*. *Typee* is not travelogue; its *raison d'être* is not "A Peep at Polynesian Life." Polynesia could have been the Arctic Circle or the Belgian Congo. *Typee* is the story of a man's discovery of his relationship to the world. The narrator enters different worlds, always retaining the consciousness of his original orientation, which is that of contemporary civilization. Focused through this constant consciousness, the forming views of Melville are expressed in Tommo's implied awareness. Perhaps it is the constant consciousness that does it; perhaps it is the external quality of that consciousness; *Typee* yet remains more cleanly readable than many contemporary literary productions which fashionably, and therefore contrivedly, also wrestle with the favorite theme which Melville called "the shock of recognition," the sudden mirror which forces a change of perception and an initiation of sensibility into reality.

Consciousness itself has not been explored by Melville. It has been glimpsed only in relation to the primitivism which is the center of *Typee* and which has been rejected as a way of life. From this beginning in time and ethical values, Melville points Tommo and reader toward the open sea again, wherein he will make the deepest explorations of his great, gliding theme.

Notes

1. Unsigned review by John Sullivan Dwight, *The Harbinger*, II (April 4, 1846), 263.

2. *Harbinger*, 266.

3. There is no need to reopen the arguments about the nineteenth-century missionaries in Polynesia. After reading many of the attacks and defenses, I am inclined to believe that Melville's "sailor's grudge," as Duyckinck called it, was at least justifiable and not necessarily limited to personal animus. One interesting item, a letter from one H. R. Hawkins, dated Honolulu, December 10, 1849, to his father Captain Esek Hawkins, Jr., of Lansingburgh, New York, sheds some light, but it is only one item among many divergent conclusions. The

letter says in part, "All that Melville ever told about the missionaries in this part of the world, you may take for gospel." Quoted by William Gilman, "A Note on Herman Melville in Honolulu," *AL* XIX (1947), 169.

4. For a discussion of the favorable public acceptance of *Typee*, see two articles by Charles Anderson, "Contemporary American Opinions of *Typee* and *Omoo*," *AL*, IX (1937), 1–25; and "Melville's English Debut," *AL*, XI (1939), 23–38. An earlier attempt at the same kind of evaluation is O. W. Riegel's "The Anatomy of Melville's Fame," *AL*, III (1931), 195–203. See also the unpublished dissertation (Michigan, 1933) by Hugh Hetherington, "The Reputation of Herman Melville in America."

5. For examples, see Anderson, "Melville's English Debut"; an unsigned review of *Typee, Douglas Jerrold's Shilling Magazine*, III (April, 1846), 380–83; and Daniel Aaron, "Melville and The Missionaries," *NEQ*, VIII (1935), 404–8.

6. William Gilman, *Melville's Early Life and Redburn* (New York, 1951) is an excellent demonstration and proof.

7. (New York, 1831), 2 vols.

8. Russell Thomas, "Yarn for Melville's *Typee*," *PQ*, XV (1936), 27.

9. New York, July 22, 1842. (Lemuel Shaw Collection, Massachusetts Historical Society.)

10. No. 988 (Oct. 3, 1846), 419.

11. Pittsfield (Spring, 1851). Quoted by Eleanor Metcalf, *Herman Melville, Cycle and Epicycle*, p. 110.

12. *Typee*, in *Selected Writings of Herman Melville* (New York, 1952), p. 457. The "Sequel" which this edition adds may be the text of the American third rather than second edition: see Bernard DeVoto, "Editions of *Typee*," *SRL*, V (1928), 406.

13. The best study of the authenticity of Melville's books in reporting his stay in the Pacific is Charles Anderson's *Melville in The South Seas* (New York, 1939). Also, Robert S. Forsythe demonstrated that Melville was in the T'aipi valley for four weeks rather than four months. After a painstaking tracing of the true chronology of events, Mr. Forsythe concludes that "Melville confidently believed [that criticism] would seriously impair the success of *Typee* as a genuine narrative. The maintenance of the credit of the volume as a true account of its author's experiences seems to be the object of Melville's solicitude. . . . He rather innocently extended the term of his stay among the Typees in order to make his account more effective . . . . And I do not suppose . . . that the literary seaman, Herman Melville, was deterred by any scruples concerning the veracity of a sailor's yarn from making his narrative more appealing or more dramatic through taking liberties with the time involved in it." "Herman Melville in the Marquesas," *PQ*, XV (1936), 1–15.

14. There is no doubt that Melville was received by his contemporaries as just such an author. One review of *Omoo*, correctly groping for the secret of Melville's selection of detail, and incorrectly reckoning the extent and purpose of his art, summed up an attitude thus: "Doubtless we shall hear more of the author's adventures:—for, though the *vraisemblance* of history is well preserved, there are in the style and about the narrative indications of romance that suggest a power of prolonging these adventures to any extent for which a public shall demand them." *The Athenaeum*, No. 1015 (London, April 10, 1847), 384. Recognizing Melville's different treatment of fact, a friendly magazine, in a notice of *Omoo*, said, "Treating as they do on familiar topics . . . that we thought had been exhausted by other authors, we are agreeably delighted to find so much of what is positively new in *Omoo*. There is a freshness and novelty in the graphic sketches of society as it now exists in these islands, that we look for in vain in the writings of other travellers. Mr. Melville contrives to throw around his personal adventures all the interest and charm of fictitious narrative. *Omoo* and *Typee* are actually delightful romances of real life, embellished with powers of description, and a graphic skill of hitting off characters little inferior to the highest order of novelist and romance

writers." In *Albion*, n.s., VI (New York, May 8, 1847), 228. See also the unpublished dissertation (Stanford, 1953), by Howard C. Key, "The Influence of Travel Literature upon Melville's Fictional Technique."

15. Arthur Stedman, in an obituarial review of Melville, said, "A reference to *Typee* as 'Melville's Marquesan Islands' under which title the book first appeared in England [actually this was the title of the second, expurgated edition], was given in the *Popular Science Monthly* as recently as two weeks before the author's death, and shows the ethnological value of the work." "Melville of Marquesas," *Review of Reviews*, IV (1891), 429.

16. To Richard Bentley (April 16, 1852). Metcalf, p. 135.

17. To Evert Duyckinck, London (Dec. 14, 1849). Metcalf, p. 71.

18. To Lemuel Shaw, New York (Oct. 6, 1849). Metcalf, p. 67.

19. To Nathaniel Hawthorne, Pittsfield (Spring, 1851). Metcalf, p. 108.

20. For an excellent discussion of isolation, see R. E. Watters, "Melville's 'Isolatoes'," *PMLA*, LX (1945), 1138–48. In periodical publication, Mr. Watters' articles are as keen as any and more so than most. See also "Melville's 'Sociality'," *AL*, XVII (1945), 33–49; and "Melville's Metaphysics of Evil," *Univ. of Toronto Q.*, IX (1940), 170–80.

21. Perhaps even when he was a pretentious nineteen-year-old author, Melville was concerned with the idea of apparent beauty marred by dehumanizing defects. The embarrassingly bad second installment of "Fragments from a Writing Desk" by "L.A.V." (*Democratic Press and Lansingburgh* [N.Y.] *Advertiser*, May 18, 1839), offers as a punch line the fact that the delicious "Inamorata" is dumb and deaf.

22. In every novel except *The Confidence Man* the Melvillean quester either slinks away from his world, or is torn from his world, or is barred from normal society.

23. I emphasize social because Melville had many reservations about political democracy. These reservations are implicit in almost everything he wrote, and are explicit in the Vivenza section of *Mardi* and in *Billy Budd*. Even in *Omoo* and *White-Jacket* there is an implied differentiation between order as a concept and the wrongful imposition of order.

24. "Paradise to Be (Regained)," *The Writings of Henry David Thoreau* (Houghton Mifflin, Boston and New York, 1906), IV, 299.

25. As is Ernest Hemingway. Unlike Melville, Hemingway insists that man must discipline himself to be himself, but must not indulge himself to see himself, for that way lies either madness or sloppy, posed behavior.

26. Metcalf, p. 161.

27. See Howard Rollin Patch, *The Other World* (Cambridge, Mass., 1950), *passim*.

[From "Melville's Search for Form" and "The Complex Figure in Melville's Carpet"]

James E. Miller, Jr.*

Rarely in America have we had a creative writer attempt such a variety of forms as those explored by Melville. His entire literary career may be characterized in a very real sense as a vision in search of embodiment, a theme in quest of a form. (It should be parenthetically inserted here that the term *form* is meant not in the narrow, organizational sense, but in the broad, generic sense in which it is determined by and ultimately indivisible from content.)

To suggest that Melville's theme remained constant while his form changed is to ask for a reversal of the common view—that he was throughout his life trying, with more or less success, to write novels to illustrate a constantly shifting moral view.

If we may for the moment agree on a brief statement, admittedly and grossly over-simplified, as representing the core of Melville's recurring theme, we may make a quick trip through all the books and wonder at their various shapes. Reduced to its lowest common denominator, Melville's obsessive idea may be defined: the necessity of man to abide by the human terms of this world as it is, not by the heavenly terms of another world as it might be. All of Melville's books, though varied in their form, dramatize the quest for this truth, or the catastrophe of ignoring it, or the glory of discovering it.

Melville's first two books . . . represent the search on this earth for the primitive society which might in its isolation have preserved the values long lost to "civilization." It is seriously relevant that Melville's first books made no claims whatsoever to being novels. Their full titles suggested their major intent: "*Typee*: A Peep at Polynesian Life. During a Four Months' Residence in A Valley of the Marquesas with notices of the French occupation of Tahiti and the provisional cession of the Sandwich Islands to Lord Paulet"; "*Omoo*: A Narrative of Adventures in the South

*Reprinted from "The Complex Figure in Melville's Carpet," *Arizona Quarterly*, 15 (Autumn, 1959), 197–210, by permission of *Arizona Quarterly* (selection taken from pp. 200–201); and from "Melville's Search for Form," *Bucknell Review*, 8, (1959), 260–76, by permission of Associated University Presses (selection taken from pp. 265–66, 276). The paragraph from "The Complex Figure" is followed by [CF] and is inserted into a selection of paragraphs from "Melville's Search for Form."

Seas." The British edition properly added to the title of *Omoo*: "being a sequel to The 'Residence in the Marquesas Islands' [British title of *Typee*]."

Typee (1846) and *Omoo* (1847) must be considered as two volumes of a single work, an extended quest for innocence by the Young Seeker, Tommo-Omoo. Throughout his search for the "uncontaminated island" in the South Seas, he constantly contrasts three states of society—the primitive level as represented by the pristine savage life, the primitive level as contaminated by merchant and missionary, and (indirectly) the civilized level of which the protagonist is a protesting product. From the very beginning of *Typee*, as he prepares to abandon ship, disillusioned Tommo directs his criticism at civilization, particularly as it is represented in miniature in the world of the ship. But his keenest criticism is saved for merchants and missionaries who bring misery and destruction in the guise of merchandise and the gospel to the innocent islands of the Pacific. These merchants of death and missionaries of sin perpetrate an evil which is increased in enormity by their pretensions to innocence and their protestations of Godliness. Tommo-Omoo's highest praise is saved for the purely primitive society in which he seems to believe—at first—that he has discovered natural goodness. But gradually he becomes aware that the primitive goodness exists on an instinctive level where dwells, too, alas primitive hostility that might flash forth at any moment. The central discovery of the protagonist in *Typee-Omoo* is that the happiness of the primitive life is peculiarly mindless and soulless, and that its attractive instinctive love can be matched by a terrifying instinctive hate. At the end of his search in *Omoo*, the Young Seeker sails out into the wide Pacific, still uncommitted in a world of apparently infinite possibilities. [CF]

In creating the unique form of *Typee-Omoo*, Melville drew from a number of traditions. Foremost of these is the tradition of travel literature. *Typee* and *Omoo* are travel books, related to any number of specimens of a form highly popular during the eighteenth and nineteenth centuries. But plunging beneath the surface of the travel book's semi-serious sociological examination of the various facets of a strange society, we find in *Typee* and *Omoo* the folk-material, the salty, earthy humor, which at times capriciously captures Melville's imagination and carries him beyond fact into fiction as he exaggerates character or heightens suspense. And as we go deeper into *Typee* and *Omoo*, we discover as the skeleton form holding all the disparate episodes together, the archetypal quest which relates the books to a tradition reaching from Homer's *Odyssey*, through the medieval romance and the search for the Holy Grail, to Rousseau and the romantic search for the noble society of savages.

. . . If in his search Melville did not invent a form which he could pass on to posterity inviolate, he still must be given credit for the very highest powers of inventive genius. He was not content to accept without question the dominant form of his day—the novel. Instead, he adopted the outward shape but constantly pushed beyond the apparent limits. There is hardly a kind of literature that he did not sample or assimilate: travel book, sea yarn, sociological study, philosophical tract, allegory, epic, domestic or historical romance, tragedy or comedy. Moreover, he expanded the horizons of art when he explored new worlds in search of meaningful, usable myth—the world of the South Sea islands, the world of whaling, the world of frontier folklore and humor. Both as heir and master of the old, and as explorer and discoverer of the new, Melville must be granted a shaping imagination of the very first rank. If our definitions do not allow him this rank, we must rewrite our definitions. It will not be the first time that genius has compelled criticism to look to its terms.

Herman Melville:
The New-World Voyageur

A. N. Kaul*

Even after a century *Typee* remains in some ways an angry young book. But that does not tell the whole story of its effectiveness. If this account of a brief Polynesian sojourn seems weightier than the narrative of beachcombing vagabondage in *Omoo*, the chief reason lies in the fact that its criticism of Western civilization is balanced by an alternative concept of social organization. It is a fiction which, like religion—to use Melville's own words quoted in the epigraph—presents "another world, and yet one to which we feel the tie." It is a singularly disarming if unsophisticated attempt on the part of a young writer to engage, in terms of readily available experience, a problem which is still among the profounder social problems of the West: the problem of "community lost and community to be gained." It is true that in this first book Melville traveled half the circumference of the globe, and a couple of millennia backward in time, from the American civilization of the day, to discover his ideal community. In his later work he was to bridge the spatial and temporal gap between the two sides of the drama, and to give a fugitive and fleeting expression to the community theme in the contemporary world of the here and now. But this fact does not make *Typee* an exercise in literary escapism; it only places it in the American imaginative tradition of total repudiation and radical quest. In terms of the values involved, this peep at Polynesian life does not turn away from the issues that are raised; it faces them squarely.

As a work of imagination, *Typee* can be compared with two distinct kinds of fictional narrative. In the first place, there is a whole body of literature—usually of second-rate writing and no thematic pretensions—which takes the reader out of this world and into an imaginary realm where the sun always shines and the rain never falls—never at least in such a way as to remind the reader of his wet feet. The whole purpose of this literature is to induce temporary forgetfulness of life and its problems. It has nothing to do with known human and social realities; in

*Reprinted from A. N. Kaul, *The American Vision: Actual and Ideal Society in Nineteenth Century Fiction* (New Haven: Yale Univ. Press, 1963), pp. 214–79. Selection taken from pp. 222–35. Reprinted with permission from Yale University Press.

Melville's terms, there is no recognizable tie between the world it creates
for us and our own world. At the other extreme from these Shangri-las
there is the serious kind of imaginary construct of which a notable example is Samuel Butler's *Erewhon*. The pretended unreality of such a realm
is only a strategic device. Whether the reader is carried into it by means of
a dream, an allegory, a boat, a balloon, or some other mode of literary
transportation that happens to be handy, he is in truth hardly moved an
inch from the reality he knows, be it of manners, morals, social institutions, or whatever it is that the writer wishes to reform. Butler's "Nowhere" is England still, but England with some of its institutions turned
upside down in order to shock the reader into a concern for their abuses.
For instance, consider what is perhaps the most effectively contrived inversion in Butler's satire: the Erewhon code which requires disease to be
punished but which maintains that crime is an unfortunate accident for
which the afflicted criminal deserves not blame but sympathy and con-
dolence. The purpose here obviously is not to hold up the Erewhonian
community as an ideal in any sense; it is merely to confront us with the
recognition that crime is after all a sort of disease and that society should
accordingly treat it in a more humane spirit. Such imaginary structures
are thus wholly satire-determined. To revert to Melville's words, they present not another world but our own in another light.

   Typee, needless to say, shares the impulse that lies behind both these
kinds of fiction. It is full of angry, if not very artful, denunciation of
civilization and its institutions. On the other hand, its portrayal of the
Happy Valley is not altogether innocent of a Shangri-la–like quality of
perpetual sunshine and exotic glamor. In this sense Melville was obviously
exploiting simultaneously, though not without honest reservations, the
taste for tropic-island bewitchment as well as the Rousseau-esque myth of
aboriginal perfection. But there is more to this book than the use of these
best-selling devices; there is all its seriousness. As William Ellery
Sedgwick has said: "Of course it will be insisted by critics of a certain
stamp that in this contrast between civilized and savage life Melville is
still following 'a long and ample tradition, both literary and philosophical,' namely, the exaltation of the Noble Savage at the expense of his
civilized opposite. True as this may be, it is not the whole truth nor the
most interesting part of it. If there is a literary convention here there is the
pressure of personal responses to animate it."[1] To this one can add that
over and above the animation of personal response, there are behind
Typee the force and confidence of an important American tradition, as
also the contemporary ferment that made this an age of millennial expectations. Melville's personal formulation of it apart, preoccupation with
the theme of perfect community was at this date shared by a large number
of American dreamers. George Ripley, for instance, hailed the novel in
the *Harbinger* for its portrayal of an "ideal society" whose perfection is
based on the fact that "there is *abundance for every person*, and thus the

most fruitful cause of the selfishness and crime of our enlightened and philosophic situation does not exist there. Here is the lesson which the leaders of this nineteenth century may learn from the Typee."[2]

The most important thing about *Typee*, then, is its social theme, and this theme turns out to be the traditional American theme of a corrupt civilization at one end—one end of the globe in this case—and the dream of a simple and well-integrated community at the other. The inhabitants of the valley are not altogether the creatures of a satirical purpose. They are not Americans standing on their heads. Unlike Erewhon, Typee does not treat its criminals better. There are no criminals in Typee. Nor are there a hundred other social evils with which the civilized narrator is only too familiar. This state of affairs, as we shall see, arises primarily from the fact that life in Typee is based upon fundamentally different social principles. It exhibits an organization that makes harmony in human relations not a state of exalted virtue but simply a matter of the ordinary every-day course of things. In this connection it is worth while to note that Melville, unlike a true celebrator of the Noble Savage, is far from depicting each individual of the Polynesian tribe as a paragon of moral perfection. Like Cooper, or more like Natty Bumppo, he too distinguishes firmly between "gifts" and "nature," and points out time and again how, underneath the different and decisive customs of the country the inhabitants of the valley share the usual impulses, more developed perhaps in one direction and less in another, which belong to the common nature of humanity everywhere. If the savages offer points of contrast with civilized men, they also offer points of comparison. Mehevi at the Ti, for instance, does the honors of the house with the warmth and hospitality of an English squire; like the gentlemen of Europe the men of Typee indulge their mirth freely after the cloth is drawn and the ladies retire; the women are as lavish with cosmetics and ointments as women anywhere in the world; and, more importantly, as Melville observes in connection with a local mausoleum, both the superstitions and the faith of the Typees afford "evidence of the fact, that however ignorant man may be, he still feels within him his immortal spirit yearning after the unknown future." Nor, at the other extreme, are the savages innocent of violence and bloodshed, though such impulses are wisely channeled into carefully regulated wars.

Their physical perfection apart, Melville admires the Typees finally not for individual merit but for being a harmonious community. The principle of their social organization is their true distinction and the decisive point of contrast between them and civilized men. It is the source of their virtue and the reason for Melville's extenuation of their vice. Melville, it must be remembered, was evoking the picture of the Happy Valley across a span of unusually disillusioning experience with various forms of civilized society: civil and military, afloat as well as ashore. As Sedgwick has pointed out: "In *Typee* there are two perspectives. There is the perspective of the story proper, or of the events at the time they happened; and there is the broader perspective of the book as a whole, in which the events of the story and their circumstances are seen at a distance of four years across all the light and shadow of Melville's experience in the interim."[3] Melville himself makes this plain when he declares that "after passing a few weeks in this valley of the Marquesas, I formed a higher estimate of human nature than I had ever before entertained. But alas! since then I have been one of the crew of a man-of-war, and the pent-up wickedness of five hundred men has nearly overturned all my previous theories."

One should accordingly refrain from looking with easy complacency upon the idealization of Typee. The overdrawn brightness of its image only reflects the darkness of civilized society in Melville's mind. The two images in fact mutually interpret each other. Though the valley of the Typees itself is comparatively untouched by contact with outsiders, civilization is judged in the book in terms of its effect upon other Polynesian peoples. Melville is far from claiming that the natives of these islands cannot derive immense advantage from being moved out of their Stone Age ignorance and lethargy. He is advocating not primitivism, but humanity. "Let the savages be civilised," he declares, "but civilise them with benefits, and not with evils; and let heathenism be destroyed, but not by destroying the heathen. The Anglo-Saxon hive have extirpated Paganism," he adds, pointing to the parallel in his own country, "from the greater part of the North American continent; but with it they have likewise extirpated the greater portion of the Red race."

The process of civilizing the Polynesians is spearheaded by ruthless army commanders, canting missionaries, and rapacious tradesmen, and the fruits of civilization for the natives consist of degradation and exploitation. As Melville observes with some irony about the state of affairs in the Sandwich Islands:

> Behold the glorious result!—The abominations of Paganism have given way to the pure rites of the Christian worship—the ignorant savage has been supplanted by the refined European! Look at Honolulu, the metropolis of the Sandwich Islands!—A community of disinterested merchants, and devoted self-exiled heralds of the Cross, located on the very spot that twenty years ago was defiled by the presence of idolatry. What a subject for an eloquent Bible-meeting orator! . . . Nor until I visited Honolulu was I aware of the fact that the small remnant of the natives had been civilised into draught horses, and evangelised into beasts of burden. But so it is. They have been literally broken into the traces, and are harnessed to the vehicles of their spiritual instructors like so many dumb brutes!

Add to the destructiveness of this form of Christian-capitalist civilization the desolation caused by invading European armies and, as Melville says, who "can wonder at the deadly hatred of the Typees to all foreigners after such unprovoked atrocities? Thus it is that they whom we denominate 'savages' are made to deserve the title." It is indeed in this change from the feeling of universal love to one of distrust and hate that Melville locates the worst legacy of a corrupt civilization: "When the inhabitants of some sequestered island first descry the 'big canoe' of the European rolling through the blue waters toward their shoes, they rush down to the beach in crowds, and with open arms stand ready to embrace the strangers. Fatal embrace! They fold to their bosoms the vipers whose sting is destined to poison all their joys; and the instinctive feeling of love within their breasts is soon converted into the bitterest hate."

It is against this background—the background of "the vices, cruelties, and enormities of every kind that spring up in the tainted atmosphere of a feverish civilisation"—that we must regard Melville's idealization of the Typee valley. This civilization is represented more concretely, though not extensively, by the ship *Dolly*, which the narrator, presumably like other "long-haired, bare-necked youths," had been forced to join by "the united influences of Captain Marryat and hard times." In this book Melville does not dwell much either on the representative capacity of the ship or on shipboard usage. Nevertheless, it is obvious that, whether or not the sailors' expectation of adventure has been fulfilled, their poverty has remained unalleviated. As a matter of fact, the ship has only exposed them further to tyranny and inhuman neglect. In this connection one can contrast the captain of the *Dolly*—the remote and vengeful "Lord of the Plank"—with the Typee chieftain Mehevi who, though a sovereign in his own right, is so unattended by any ceremony and so close to the common inhabitants of the valley that the narrator remains for a long time unaware of his true status. It is to protest against the conditions aboard that the two sailors decide to risk falling among notorious savages rather than have any further truck with the repudiated vessel. Familiar as this gesture is in American fiction, we must notice further that the narrator and his companion Toby belong, characteristically enough, to that class of men "who never reveal their origin, never allude to home, and go rambling over the world as if pursued by some mysterious fate they cannot possibly elude."

The mysterious fate in this particular case involves a hazardous journey through certain chasms, ravines, and gorges beyond which, as the runaway sailors are convinced, lies the desired sanctuary of the Happy Valley. The writing here is remarkable in its combination of symbolical overtones with the raciest and most straightforward narrative of physical adventure. As had been observed before, this journey constitutes a sort of descent into inferno—a Ulyssean detour to find the way home. The passage through the outlandish regions—described in chapter 7 in terms of death-like coldness, appalling darkness, and infernal torment—marks a process of dying, or a process of being born anew, or simply a necessary preparation for the different world that awaits the fugitives. When at last they view the sunny expanse of land toward which they have so painfully struggled over a period of several days, it is greeted as a revelation of Eden itself: "Had a glimpse of the gardens of Paradise been revealed to me, I could scarcely have been more ravished with the sight." *Typee* is undoubtedly a sea yarn, suitably stretched here and there as all sea yarns are, and handsomely overlaid with literary and other clichés. But it is also the first book of a great imaginative genius who started on his career at a time when his culture's experience was beginning to assume an articulate form—the form of an apprehensible and meaningful action. For all its lack of sophistication, or perhaps because of it, *Typee* captures with revealing simplicity one aspect of this action: the dialectical movement between a corrupt civilization and an ideal community, or the opposition between the dream and the reality of society in America. It is this over-all rhythm of the book which distinguishes its theme from its travel-diary method, and which constitutes its claim to serious consideration.

Having arrived in Paradise, what did Melville and Toby find there? They found sunshine and breadfruit; healthful aboriginal savages and long-haired beautiful women; nudity, dancing, and only occasional drapery of white tapa; ease and indolence, and quantities of sleep; in short, all that makes living among cannibals worth the risk. These were also the conditions that finally led Melville to despair and made him long for a speedy release from this subhuman existence. Such exotic novelties, however, do not exhaust the meaning that Melville projected into the image of Typee. He also recognized in this valley certain admirable possibilities, a social situation of which he gives a full account in chapters 17 and 27. The narrator begins in the earlier of these two chapters by saying that, having reconciled himself inwardly to an indefinite period of stay in the valley, his ailing limb seemed to heal suddenly and he entertained hope of a quick and complete recovery. "In the altered frame of mind," somewhat like Miles Coverdale after his illness at Blithedale, he now looks upon the surrounding world with fresh insight: "every object that presented itself to my notice in the valley struck me in a new light, and the opportunities I now enjoyed of observing the manners of its inmates tended to strengthen my favourable impressions." He is disposed to believe that he has found his way into the "Happy Valley" and that beyond its mountains there is "naught but a world of care and anxiety." Contrasting the Typee community with the society he has known, he is ready to extenuate even the worst abuses of the former. With regard to cannibalism, for example, he records at more than one place the horror and revulsion aroused in him by this primitive rite. This of course falls within the first of the book's two perspectives noted by Sedgwick. But we must not forget the other, the broader perspective in which the image of Typee is flatteringly refracted through Melville's experience with civilization. In this light he argues that cannibalism—"a rather bad trait"—is practiced only on the declared enemies of the tribe, whereas in civilized societies innocent men are tortured and executed with the utmost cruelty and for no apparent reason. "The fiend-like skill we display," he concludes in a passage reminiscent of Swiftian savagery, "in the invention of all manner of death-dealing engines, the vindictiveness with which we carry on our wars, and the misery and desolation that follow in their train, are enough of themselves to distinguish the white civilised man as the most ferocious animal on the face of the earth." His "remorseless cruelty," he goes on to add, can be seen in the penal institutions of "our own favoured land"; in particular the treatment of criminals "whom we mason up in the cells of our prisons, and condemn to perpetual solitude in the very heart of our population."

In Typee, on the other hand, no one is ever brought to trial and there are no lawyers or law courts. Like America, it enjoys an abundance of natural resources, but these are universally and equally shared. Hence there are no destitute widows, no starving children, no beggars, and therefore also no "cold charities." Liberty of conscience, merely promised in the narrator's own country, prevails here without limitation or hindrance. There is neither civil nor domestic disharmony of any sort: no foreclosures of mortgages, no debts or debtors' prisons, no bolts, bars, or padlocks, no jealousies in love and no divorce. The prevailing polyandry results in no discord, and "wedlock, as known among these Typees, seems to be of a more distinct and enduring nature than is usually the case with barbarous people. A baneful promiscuous intercourse of the sexes is hereby avoided, and virtue, without being clamorously invoked, is, as it were, unconsciously practised." Of course, the Typees, like the rest of humanity, are a warring people, but their battles, unlike those of a society based upon predatory competition, are not internecine. Surely, the narrator observes, "if our evil passions must find vent, it is far better to expend them on strangers and aliens, than in the bosom of the community in which we dwell. In many polished countries civil contentions, as well as domestic enmities, are prevalent, at the same time that the most atrocious foreign wars are waged. How much less guilty, then, are our islanders, who of these three sins are only chargeable with one, and that the least criminal!"

The harmonious community life of the Typees is characterized chiefly by the absence of three institutions. In the first place, money plays no part in the social relationships of these people: "That 'root of all evil' was not to be found in the valley." Likewise, there is no repressive police machinery, and, more important than these two, no property in land. In connection with private property, Melville's narrator makes the important distinction that was being blurred by Cooper's Littlepages around the same time in the history of American fiction. In chapter 27 he makes it clear that there was no "community of goods" in Typee and that, on the contrary, "personal property" was held inviolate and was in no case encroached upon by the inhabitants. But he observes that there is a vast difference between personal property and what he calls the "investment of 'real property' " or "real estate." "Whether the land of the valley was the joint property of its inhabitants, or whether it was parcelled out among a certain number of landed proprietors who allowed everybody to 'squat' and 'poach' as much as he or she pleased, I never could ascertain. At any rate, musty parchments and title deeds there were none on the island; and I am half inclined to believe that its inhabitants hold their broad valleys in fee simple from Nature herself; to have and to hold, so long as grass grows and water runs."

The question to which the narrator is led inevitably by this state of affairs is the one which was most pertinent to the fortunes of his own tradition, the tradition of a people who had sought to form a pure community in freedom from all repressive social institutions but who had found themselves developing instead into an anti-society of isolated individuals permanently warring against each other. How, he asks in more than one place, did the Typees manage, "without the aid of established law, to exhibit, in so eminent a degree, that social order which is the greatest blessing and highest pride of the social state?" If "the better principles of our nature, cannot exist unless enforced by the statute-book, how are we to account for the social condition of the Typees?" His answer is quite characteristic of the visionary cast of the whole body of imaginative literature with which I have been dealing. "Civilisation," he says, "does not engross all the virtues of humanity"; there are some natural capacities which, with its emphasis on individualism, property, and money, it has not even tried. Every man harbors a "fraternal feeling" toward other men and all human beings desire to act "in concert and good fellowship." Free from the motives which vitiate human relationships in civilized societies, the harmonious life of the Typees is based precisely upon these feelings.

> During my whole stay on the island I never witnessed a single quarrel, nor anything that in the slightest degree approached even to a dispute. The natives appeared to form one household, whose members were bound together by the ties of strong affection. The love of kindred I did not so much perceive, for it seemed blended in the general love; and where all were treated as brothers and sisters, it was hard to tell who were actually related to each other by blood.

Here, then, is Melville's image of the ideal community: the image of a sort of prelapsarian Blithedale. Like Miles Coverdale, the narrator of *Typee* also abandons the community in order to return eventually to society or civilization. The reasons for this action are quite simple. On the level of the story, it is quite natural that, after tasting of this alien Paradise, the adventurous sailor should want to go back home to his mother. Moreover, while in Typee, he cannot hope to procure medical attention for his illness. It is not true, as D. H. Lawrence seems to imply, that his diseased limb gets progressively worse in Typee and heals immediately on his return to shipboard in *Omoo*. But it is true that his illness is a projection of psychological dis-ease, for it gets better or worse as he resigns himself to his existence in the valley or revives hopes of escape from it; and herein lies the more important motivation for the escape. To reconcile oneself to Typee is to comfort oneself falsely with an impossible primitivism. Typee is at best a picture of "community lost"—lost for good reasons—and not the image of "community to be gained." To a man of the nineteenth-century Western world, it is more than happy but also less than human. The Typees do not hunt the whale, whether we interpret that symbol in economic, technological, intellectual, psychological, or spiritual terms. However painful it may prove to be, it is a necessary part of human destiny to accept the challenge of the Leviathan. By contrast, the somnolent Typees are content to make fire by rubbing two pieces of wood for hours on end, and the movement of their inward life is characterized by similar childishness.

So Melville makes his narrator leave the Happy Valley, but neither reconciled to civilization nor in repudiation of the social values which he has observed and endorsed in Typee. The idea of community—of people forming one harmonious household—continues to be a persistent, though not equally central, theme in Melville's succeeding novels.[4] And as for his continued denunciation of civilization, one has only to turn to *Omoo*.

Notes

1. William Ellery Sedgwick, *Herman Melville: The Tragedy of Mind* (Cambridge, Harvard University Press, 1944), p. 26.

2. Hugh W. Hetherington, *Melville's Reviewers: British and American: 1846–1891* (Chapel Hill, University of North Carolina Press, 1961), p. 52.

3. Sedgwick, *Herman Melville*, p. 24.

4. For the persistence of this idea—in the statements of various characters, in authorial comment, and in incident—throughout the whole body of Melville's work, see R. E. Watters, "Melville's 'Sociality,' " *American Literature*, 17 (1945), 33–49. My own treatment, more detailed on the one hand, is restricted on the other to those works where the idea of community possesses both thematic weight and structural importance. However, I am in agreement with Watters' general thesis, namely that Melville countered the transcendentalist approval of solitude and self-reliance by a "positive alternative": "the racial and social community of mankind, with its wealth of social virtues: love, sympathy, gratitude, friendliness, charity, kindness, companionship" (p. 49).

Melville in a World of Pagan Gods

H. Bruce Franklin*

Melville's knowledge of Polynesian religion has remained a matter of debate ever since the publication of *Typee*. He has been considered everything from a major authority to a mere literary pretender to a downright liar. Charles Anderson has pointed out that "Melville is cited as an authority in such studies as those of Sir James George Frazer, Robert Wood Williamson, and Louis Rollin," and Frazer alone "quotes *Typee* with approval more than a score of times."[1] But Anderson has also shown Melville's heavy reliance on literary sources, and he therefore tends to suspect the accuracy of Melville's knowledge, preferring to rely on the findings of modern anthropological expeditions, even if they in turn were forced to rely on the memories of the surviving natives. Melville did have probably the most intimate contact of any Westerner with the Marquesan tribal civilization, but, as Anderson observes, "Melville was the first to confess his lack of any real understanding of the theology of the Typees."[2] Melville's confession of ignorance is not, however, a simple one.

When Melville, after spending several weeks as a captive of the Typees and after later reading almost every available account of the Marquesas, confesses ignorance, he is making a statement more about knowledge than about the Typee valley. He saw in the Typee mythology and theology the fundamental enigmas of all mythology and all theology; that is, he saw the fundamental enigmas in all human knowledge. He saw all knowledge as partly mythic. For almost half a century, beginning in *Typee* and not ending until his death, Melville used the methods and vocabulary of comparative mythology to help his explorations of these enigmas.

When Melville recalls the gigantic stone terraces of Typee, he thinks "of Stonehenge and the architectural labours of the Druid"[3] and of "the mighty base of the Pyramid of Cheops." Melville receives the islanders' ex-

*Reprinted from *The Wake of the Gods: Melville's Mythology*, by H. Bruce Franklin, with the permission of the publishers, Stanford University Press. © 1963 by the Board of Trustees of the Leland Stanford Junior University. Text contains minor revisions made by Professor Franklin for this edition.

planation of the stones perhaps as astutely as some more recent Polynesian investigators:

> These structures bear every indication of a very high antiquity, and Kory-Kory, who was my authority in all matters of scientific research, gave me to understand that they were coeval with the creation of the world; that the great gods themselves were the builders; and that they would endure until time shall be no more. Kory-Kory's prompt explanation, and his attributing the work to a divine origin, at once convinced me that neither he nor the rest of his countrymen knew anything about them. (p. 658)

When Melville generalizes on the stones, he implicitly opposes the usual orthodox theory of comparative religion and mythology:

> These remains naturally suggest many interesting reflections. They establish the great age of the island, an opinion which the builders of theories concerning the creation of the various groups in the South Seas are not always inclined to admit. For my own part, I think it just as probable that human beings were living in the valleys of the Marquesas three thousand years ago as that they were inhabiting the land of Egypt. (p. 659)

Orthodox Christians were explaining the similarities among the world's religions with the theory of geographical diffusion and were insisting that this diffusion began in the Near East. The prior antiquity of Near Eastern religion depended upon the prior antiquity of the Near Eastern peoples. When Melville claims that the people of the Marquesas may have been coeval with the people of Egypt, he implicitly allies himself with those who were finding the travel of religions across half the world (mostly water either way they went) not necessarily the most plausible theory.

The lines of diffusionist and anti-diffusionist theories crisscross in complicated patterns throughout the nineteenth century at large and throughout Melville's work in particular. In the mid-eighteenth century the Christian apologists, hard pressed by the psychological theories of deists and skeptics, fortified themselves behind simple diffusionist theories, usually constructed from the Genesis account of Ham, Shem, and Japheth. Although the main attacks against this position continued to come from the skeptics' psychological and astronomical theories of religious belief, toward the close of the eighteenth century a new major assault began. The new discoveries in India, brought about by the Asiatic Society's pioneering work in Sanskrit, threatened to turn diffusionism itself against the apologists. For many of the Hindu Vedas seemed to be at least as old as the Old Testament and embarrassingly similar to the New. Sir William Jones, the Society's first president, advanced the rather desperate hypothesis that spurious gospels must have circulated in ancient Hindustan. Upon this hypothesis was built a major restatement of diffusionism, the seven quarto volumes of *Indian Antiquities* and three folio volumes of *The History of Hindostan* by the Reverend Thomas Maurice. Maurice's efforts to explain away the apparently prior antiquity of Hindu mythology were foredoomed. The diffusionist barricades built by the apologists were gradually taken over by the skeptics and heretics, who mounted upon them some of their most dangerous weapons. By the time Melville abandoned prose and turned to poetry, the revolution was practically complete. In *Clarel* (1876), it is Derwent the Anglican priest who offers mild psychological theories and Rolfe the heretic who darkly hints of diffusionism.

> [Derwent:] "Why question me?
> Why pound the text? Ah, modern be,
> And share the truth's munificence.
> Look now, one reasons thus: Immense
> Is tropic India; hence she breeds
> Brahma tremendous, gods like seeds.
> The genial clime of Hellas gay
> Begat Apollo. Take that way;
> Nor query—Ramayana true?
> The Iliad?"[4]

Rolfe does suggest one kind of psychological theory, one as old as the fear theory of Democritus and the gratitude theory of Proclus:

> Yea, long as children feel affright
> In darkness, men shall fear a God;
> And long as daisies yield delight
> Shall see His footprints in the sod.
> (I, xxxi, 191–94)

But as he goes on, Rolfe shows that for him, unlike Derwent, the history and geography of religion may make its truth equivocal. Although psychology may be the basis for the idea of God, geographical neighbors may do more to shape that idea than geographical structure or climate. Rolfe darkly hints that the proximity of the Osiris myth may have shaped the story of Christ:

> "Hint you," here asked Vine,
> "In Christ Osiris met decline
> Anew?"—[Rolfe:] "Nay, nay; and yet, past doubt,
> Strange is that text St. Matthew won
> From gray Hosea in sentence: *Out*
> *Of Egypt have I called my son.*"
> (I, xxxi, 223–28)

In the last year of his life, Melville in his own voice speaks of the geographical diffusion of the gods. In "The New Zealot to the Sun" (published in *Timoleon*, 1891) he addresses as "Arch type" a Persian who rises "aflame from climes of sacrifice" amidst "rites whose tenor trace all worship hitherto":

Mid terrors dinned
Gods too came conquerors from your Ind,
The brood of Brahma throve;
They came like to the scythed car,
Westward they rolled their empire far,
Of night their purple wove.
Chemist, you breed
In orient climes each sorcerous weed
That energizes dream—
Transmitted, spread in myths and creeds,
Houris and hells, delirious screeds
And Calvin's last extreme.[5]

After a lifetime of comparing religions, Melville sees Calvinism as only an extreme development of Persian sacrifice. And he suggests that each religion is a form of sorcerous opiate.

Typee and *Omoo* represent the first definable probings of Melville's ever widening and ever deepening exploration of comparative religion. In both books Melville apparently weighs primitive religious beliefs and practices against those of the Christianity practiced in Polynesia, and the scales seem very nearly level. Although some of the islanders' beliefs may be childishly simple and others incomprehensibly obscure and complicated, although some of their practices may be absurd and others dangerous, Melville's attitude toward these beliefs and practices more nearly resembles Rousseau's than a Christian missionary's. The narrators of *Typee* and *Omoo* profess an orthodox Christianity, but they weigh the beauty, happiness, health, and childish simplicity of the natives before Christianity comes to the islands against their deformities, misery, disease, and hypocrisy after. Still professing orthodox Christianity, the narrators seem to weigh jolly old fraudulent native priests, who possibly are cannibals, against viciously deceptive Christian priests, who certainly are rapacious predators. But the pagan and Christian religions described by the narrators are not in reality weighed against each other. They are both weighed against a persistently assumed religion which might be called anything from deism to a primitive Christianity. The weighing of each results in clearly writing out its *mene, mene, tekel, upharsin*. The strange mythology of the Typee Valley is found no more wanting than the sermon of the Tahitian missionary, with its myths of the "Wee-wees" (the French) and their wicked priests. In *Typee* Melville discovers that these two inadequate religions may be weighed by indicating their essential identity. The temples, myths, rituals, and priests of Typee therefore are metaphorically equated with those of the reader.

The Typee temples make the narrator think of Christian as well as Egyptian and Druidic temples:

> Here were situated the Taboo groves of the valley—the scene of many a prolonged feast, of many a horrid rite. Beneath the dark shadows of the consecrated bread-fruit trees there reigned a solemn twilight—a cathedral-like gloom. The frightful genius of pagan worship seemed to brood in silence over the place, breathing its spell upon every object around. Here and there, in the depths of these awful shades, half screened from sight by masses of overhanging foliage, rose the idolatrous altars of the savages, built on enormous blocks of black and polished stone, placed one upon another, without cement, to the height of twelve or fifteen feet, and surmounted by a rustic open temple, enclosed with a low picket of canes, within which might be seen, in various stages of decay, offerings of bread-fruit and cocoa-nuts, and the putrefying relics of some recent sacrifice. (p. 578)

When the narrator of *Typee* wishes to reach beyond the Typee valley for a comparison adequate to its ominous gloom, apparently by chance he seizes upon a cathedral. The narrator of "The Two Temples" sees the same relationship from the other side; imprisoned in a New York cathedral, he reaches back to the primitive wilderness for a comparison adequate to its ominous gloom:

> A strange trepidation of gloom and loneliness gradually stole over me. Hardly conscious of what I did, I reascended the stone steps: higher and higher still, and only paused, when once more I felt the hot-air blast from the wire-woven screen. Snatching another peep down into the vast arena, I started at its hushed desertness. The long ranges of grouped columns down the nave, and clusterings of them into copses about the corners of the transept; together with the subdued, dim-streaming light from the autumnal glasses; all assumed a secluded and deep-wooded air.[6]

The "cathedral-like gloom" of the secluded and deep-wooded Typee grove surrounds what Melville calls the "pulpits" of its priests:

> In the midst of the wood was the hallowed "hoolah hoolah" ground—set apart for the celebration of the fantastic religious ritual of these people—comprising an extensive oblong pi-pi, terminating at either end in a lofty terraced altar, guarded by ranks of hideous wooden idols . . . Vast trees, standing in the middle of this space, and throwing over it an umbrageous shade, had their massive trunks built round with slight stages, elevated a few feet above the ground, and railed in with canes, forming so many rustic pulpits, from which the priests harangued their devotees. (p. 578)

Melville made his metaphorical comparisons of primitive pagan priests and civilized Christian priests into a theme upon which he played many later variations.

In *Mardi*, much of the religious satire centers upon the Holy Island of Maramma, literally a Polynesian island replete with fetishistic idols, allegorically both the Vatican and Palestine. In *Moby-Dick*, the mincer, functioning as a primitive phallic priest, is offered as a candidate for an "archbishoprick" or Pope. In *Benito Cereno*, the African slaves persistently seem to the naïve narrator "monks" and "friars" in a Catholic monastery. In *Clarel*, "the Druid priest Melchizedeck" (I, iii, 41) of Genesis 14 creates what Walter Bezanson's note calls "a 'primeval' scene of Druidic rites to set the tone for contemporary rituals"; he foreshadows the Anglican priest, Derwent, etymologically and symbolically the descendant of the Druids. Daniel Orme, the title character of an unpublished sketch at first subtitled "A Druid," dies on Easter while musing on the crucifix cut into his chest. *Billy Budd*, as we shall see, finally resolves pagan and Christian priests into a complicated order. In *Typee* and *Omoo* the theme is more simple and conventional: pagan priests like Kolory, the "Lord Primate of Typee," play their "episcopal part" with good-natured, unconcerned, primitive humbuggery; Christian priests not only deceive the natives, but humiliate and enslave them while hypocritically deceiving the folks back home about the native religion and the progress of Christianity in Polynesia. The narrator of *Omoo* hears the malicious and self-seeking sermon of a Tahitian missionary; the narrator of *Typee* sees the line of wagons parked on Sunday before the elegant chapel of Christianity, each wagon drawn by two naked natives.

In *Typee*, Melville compares not only Christian and pagan temples, priests, and practices but also Christians' descriptions of paganism with his own observations. He is fascinated with three aspects of the Typee religion: its fetishism, the careless abandon with which the natives treat their fetish gods, and the complete inscrutability of the Typee "theology." Moa Artua, the most important god, who "could take the whole island of Nukuheva in his mouth and dive down to the bottom of the sea with it," is only a bandaged piece of wood which is abused and threatened. Mystified by Moa Artua's helpless omnipotence, by the generally inferior position of gods to worshipers, and by intricate rituals and explanations, Melville concludes not only that he "hardly knew what to make of the religion of the valley," but that he is "inclined to believe, that the islanders in the Pacific have no fixed and definite ideas whatever on the subject of religion." He sharply criticizes other Polynesian investigators, deriding as "a vast deal of unintentional humbuggery" the "scientific" accounts of Polynesian religion and implying that the missionaries' accounts are humbuggery which is anything but unintentional. Melville says that the writer of the typical treatise on Polynesian religion "enters into a very circumstantial and learned narrative of certain unaccountable superstitions and practices, about which he knows as little as the islanders themselves . . . were the book thus produced to be translated into the tongue of the people of whom it purports to give the history, it would appear quite as wonderful to them as it does to the American public, and much more improbable." When, four years later, Melville offered *Mardi* as his own learned treatise on Polynesian societies and religions, he wrote it in the language of the natives, who did indeed find it highly improbable. For *Mardi* presents all lands as a world of pagan gods.

Notes

1. *Melville in the South Seas* (New York, 1939), pp. 120, 168.

2. *Ibid.*, p. 168.

3. *Typee*, in *Selected Writings of Herman Melville* (New York: Modern Library, 1952), p. 657. (Subsequent references to this edition and to other editions of Melville's works will be given in parentheses in the text.) In viewing Stonehenge as the works of the Druids, Melville shares the usual nineteenth-century opinion, which is now generally discredited.

4. *Clarel*, ed. Walter E. Bezanson (New York: Hendricks House, Inc., 1960), III, vi, 81–90.

5. *Collected Poems of Herman Melville*, ed. Howard P. Vincent (Chicago: Packard and Co. and Hendricks House, 1947), p. 226.

6. In *Selected Writings of Herman Melville*, p. 155.

Portraits of the Artist as a Young Man

Edgar A. Dryden*

The fact that Melville's first five novels were first-person narratives assumes a special significance when viewed in the context of his insistence that the names of all fine authors are fictitious ones. The striking autobiographical elements in his fiction have long been of interest to his critics. Indeed, many find his use of personal experience important enough to make unnecessary, if not misleading, any critical distinction between writer and narrator. Nevertheless, the unusual names of Melville's author-heroes certainly suggest their fictive nature. Tommo, Taji, Wellingborough Redburn, White Jacket, and Ishmael seem unlike characters one meets "in the same old way every day in the same old street" (*C-M*, XXXIII, 206). That Melville's decision to combine personal experience and an obviously fictitious narrator is an attempt to deal with the problem of the discrepancy between man and the artist is suggested by Montaigne's discussion of this same issue. He too recognizes the fact that often "the work and the artificer contradict one another." For him, as for Melville, the world "eternally turns around, all things therein are incessantly moving; the earth, the rocks of Caucasus, and the pyramids of Egypt, both by public motion and their own." Because Montaigne is content to describe the world "as it is the instant I consider it," to "paint its passage," not "its being," he presents himself to the reader as "Michael de Montaigne, not as a grammarian, a poet or a lawyer."[1] Melville, however, is interested in discovering the truth which lies hidden beneath the shifting and turning surfaces of things, in describing the world's "being" rather than its "passage." For this reason he finds it necessary to distinguish between the private and the literary consciousness. This he accomplishes by the creation of a fictive first-person narrator who stands as a portrait of the artist *par excellence*.

All first-person narrators are, of course, artists. As one critic has remarked, "this is at once true and tautological."[2] Nonetheless, when Melville's preference for the first-person point of view is placed in the con-

*Reprinted from Edgar A. Dryden, *Melville's Thematics of Form: The Great Art of Telling the Truth* (Baltimore: Johns Hopkins Univ. Press, 1968), pp. 33–46, with permission from Johns Hopkins University Press.

text of his discussion of the art-life relationship in the Hawthorne essay, an obvious function of technique is charged with a special suggestiveness. His fictive narrators are embodiments of the magical creative power which "ubiquitously possesses men of genius." Although related through their experiences to their "ostensible author," they are in an important sense "foundlings," Ishmael-like creatures with no familial connections to the world of lies.

Parallel to the problem of the author's relationship to his hero is the more complex question of the narrator's tie to his own earlier experience. Like the later eighteenth-century and romantic poets, Melville was interested in the activities of memory. All of his first-person narrators are engaged in a conscious act of remembering: in their narratives there are always two landscapes present, an experienced one and a recollected one. The Melvilleian hero, however, endows the operation of memory with a complexity which distinguishes it from the faculty which was so widely discussed at the end of the eighteenth century. Like Hartly most of the poets and philosophers regarded memory as "that faculty by which traces of sensations and ideas recur, or are recalled, in the same order and proportion, accurately or nearly, as they were once presented."[3] At a time when associationism insisted on the successive character of experience, memory became the faculty which not only allowed man to organize his world, but provided him with his strongest argument for the existence of a personal identity. Thomas Reid writes in 1786:

> What evidence have you that there is such a permanent self which has a claim to all the thoughts, actions, and feelings which you call yours?
> To this I answer that the proper evidence I have of all this is remembrance. . . . My memory testifies not only that this [a conversation in the past] was done, but that it was done by me who now remember it. If it was done by me, I must have existed at that time, and continued to exist from that time to the present. . . .[4]

The pleasures of memory, then, derive largely from the power that that faculty has to constitute an orderly picture of a self and a world, which otherwise threaten to disintegrate into a series of disconnected and fragmented sensations and ideas. The tendency of the turn-of-the-century poet to invoke the memory of a past experience in order to lend vitality to a present one illustrates a literary implication of Reid's idea. In the prefatory argument to Part II of "The Pleasures of Memory" Samuel Rodgers writes that "even in madness itself, when the soul is resigned over to the tyranny of a distempered imagination, she [memory] revives past perceptions, and awakens that train of thought that was formerly most familiar."[5]

It is, however, just this emphasis on memory's ability to authenticate present experience which distinguishes Melville's use of the faculty from many of the earlier discussions of it. For the Melvilleian narrator memory is an imaginative act which makes the present a moment of creative understanding of a past adventure that was experienced initially as an unintelligible and frightening chaos of sensations. At time of writing—often years after the original experience—the mature writer fictionalizes his earlier experience in an attempt to define its truth or meaning to himself and to his reader. It is the creative remembering in the present which gives meaning to the past. The emphasis, in other words, is on the act of remembering rather than on the content of memory. The past self is distinguished from rather than substituted for the present self, and a literary landscape replaces the natural one in which the experience initially occurred. Melville would regard Cowper's attempt to

> retrace
> (As in a map the voyager his course)
> The windings of my way through many years[6]

as a futile exercise because it merely repeats the confusing fluctuations of the experience itself. The "white doe of truth," object of all the narrators' memorial quests, can be glimpsed only within the verbal landscape created at the time of writing from the materials of the past. For these men the only meaningful way of recapturing the past is to invent it, to turn it into a fiction.

Although this idea is best illustrated in Ishmael's vision of his whaling voyage as a symbolic drama, it is present in less obvious ways in the earlier books. Like the narrator of "Hawthorne and His Mosses" Ishmael and his progenitors understand the necessity of turning experience into a *story* if they are to face and survive the horrible truth implicit in it. Because of his double role of author-hero the Melvillean narrator is both creature and creator, man and artist. The story that he tells is both experienced and invented. The young man, who begins his quest by throwing himself into the destructive sea of experience, is caught up in all of the confused sensations of the moment. Although he is unable to recognize any order in the chaos to which he is exposed, his very involvement demands that he assume that one exists. To imagine that the apparent confusion is a real one would render his experience absurd. The quest would end before it began.

It is, of course, the realization that experience is indeed meaningless which lies at the center of the mature narrator's vision—a truth which makes ordinary human life impossible. But since he is telling a story rather than living an experience, he is able to see the truth and survive. As storyteller he is able to approach the events from an opposite direction, starting at the end of the experience rather than at the beginning. Hence he is able to give a spatial dimension to a series of successive temporal events. By the act of turning his experience into a story, he places himself outside of that experience—in effect, treats it as though it belonged to someone else.

The narrator's relation to his earlier experience, then, may be seen as a dramatization of the writer's relationship to his fiction. Just as Melville maintains the important distinction between art and life by the use of fictive first-person narrators, so these author-heroes affirm the importance of this distinction as they tell their stories. Both the author and the narrator (the author's portrait of himself) maintain their sanity and discover truth by the creation of a rational lie, a fiction.

> I am like one of those seeds taken out of the Egyptian Pyramids, which, after being three thousand years a seed and nothing but a seed, being planted in English soil, it developed itself, grew to greenness, and then fell to mould. So I. Until I was twenty-five, I had no development at all. From my twenty-fifth year I date my life. Three weeks have scarcely passed, at any time between then and now, that I have not unfolded within myself. But I feel that I am now come to the inmost leaf of the bulb, and that shortly the flower must fall to the mould. (*L*, 130)

Writing to Hawthorne in the throes of the labor which preceded the birth of *Moby-Dick*, his first great novel, Melville not only reveals his despair at approaching what he thought was the peak of his creative career, but he also establishes an important connection between artistic and inward growth. That he chooses the year in which he wrote *Typee* to date the beginning of his development is suggestive, for it implies that his fiction is an expression of the progressive unfolding of the self. To read Melville's fiction, then, is to encounter, in James's words, "the growth of his whole operative consciousness." *Typee*, along with *Mardi*, *Redburn*, and *White Jacket*, dramatizes the initial stages in the blooming of his creative vision.

Moby-Dick and the later fictions not only ensure that their author will not "go down to posterity . . . as a 'man who lived among the cannibals' " (*L*, 130), but they also help to identify the ways in which *Typee* is more than a "Peep at Polynesian Life." Tommo's assertions that "appearances all the world over are deceptive" (XXIV, 172) and that "I saw everything, but could comprehend nothing" (175), when they are seen in the light of the later fiction, assume a special significance which is only vaguely suggested by the context of the novel itself. Similarly, Moa Artua, the deaf and dumb baby god of the Typees with the "time-serving disposition" (174), becomes more than an interesting part of Polynesian culture when placed in the company of such figures as Plotinus Plinlimmon, the lamb-like man, and Billy Budd. *Typee* is the first expression of a vision which was to continue to grow and develop.

As with Melville's later more complex first-person narratives, the structure and meaning of his first book depend on an important distinction between the real and literary worlds. Juxtaposed in *Typee* are the vision of the young Tommo, who, immersed in the chaos of successive temporal moments, "saw everything, but could comprehend nothing," with that of the mature narrator, whose later experiences of "the pent-up wickedness" of civilized savages while "one of the crew of a man-of-war" (XXVII, 200) have allowed him to construct a place to stand in his effort to find the meaning of his earlier experiences. By taking the view of the detached anthropologist, the narrator is able to bridge both the smaller gap between the successive sensations of his Typee experience and the larger one between the primitive and civilized worlds.[7] In experience the past is partially lost because it is pushed aside by the demanding details of the present moment. Forced always to remain "distressingly alive to all the fearful circumstances of our present situation," the mind of the young Tommo is "oppressed" by "various and conflicting" thoughts (XI, 73). "In the midst of this tumult" the past exists for him only in the two English words which he teaches Marheyo, "Home" and "Mother" (XXXIV, 243). Within the spatial imagination of the narrator, however, the events of the Typee adventure as well as those of his western experience form a wide and symbolic panorama.

To the young hero, immersed in the sea of experience, life seems interminable and monotonous. Aboard the "Dolly," each day is an absurd repetition of its predecessor: each meal consists of "salt-horse and sea-biscuit"; each object is painted the same "vile and sickly hue" (I, 1); even the movement of the ship itself, "rolling and pitching about, never for one moment at rest" (3), adds to the overwhelming sense of dullness. It is the unrelieved tediousness of his life which drives Tommo out to seek new experiences. Tired of merely existing, he hopes by jumping ship to turn his dull, repetitive life into a meaningful and exciting adventure. Because he is familiar with the glowing accounts of "olden voyagers," the Marquesas seem rich with exciting possibilities. He sees himself as one of those "adventurous rover[s]" who "once in the course of a half century . . . would break in upon their peaceful repose, and, astonished at the unusual scene, would be almost tempted to claim the merit of a new discovery" (3).

Experience, however, fails to live up to Tommo's adventurous expectations. After leaving the ship, he and Toby find themselves imprisoned in an "interminable" thicket of canes (VI, 37). Lost in a world which "seemed one unbroken solitude," the young man is "almost unmanned" by the "dismal sense of our forlorn condition" (VII, 44). Although this sensation is momentarily relieved by the exciting discovery of Typee Valley, the sense of adventure is not sustained. As with his experience aboard the "Dolly," life among the Typees is "uniform and undiversified" (XX, 147). Here, as one day follows another without rhyme or reason, Tommo "gradually . . . lost all knowledge of the regular occurrence of the days of the week" (XVII, 120).

In the mind of the narrator, however, meaningless experience is transformed into suggestive adventure because he, like God, knows the story's end before its beginning. For him the characters and events have an inner consistency which makes them intelligible. Sensations and events do not pile up chaotically; each one is caught up and drawn on by the end of the story. In this selective account no detail is inconsequential, for everything exists as a part of a complete adventure and carries with it a promise that its meaning finally will be revealed. For Melville the meaning of a thing is the form of its coexistence with other things; it is the light which everything else casts over it. But because things in experience exist in isolation, discovering meaning involves a process of creating a structure for experience, an ideal landscape of interlocking parts.

In addition to giving his experience meaning by placing it within the traditional structure of the story of the Fall of man, the narrator isolates one sensation and uses it as the symbolic center of his structure.[8] Immediately after his initial glimpse of the Eden-like valley, Tommo experiences for the first time a malady which is to trouble him at several important times during his stay in Typee: "During the hour or two spent under the shelter of these bushes, I began to feel symptoms which I at once attributed to the exposure of the preceding night. Cold shiverings and a burning fever succeeded one another at intervals, while one of my legs was swelled to such a degree, and pained me so acutely, that I half suspected I had been bitten by some venomous reptile" (VII, 46–47). Since the Eden-like Typee is "free from the presence of any vipers" (47) the ailment—which inexplicably vanishes and returns—forms an important part of Tommo's irrational experience. The narrator, although still without a factual or medical explanation of the illness, understands its relation to his total experience. The symbolic leg is reintroduced whenever he discusses Tommo's plans for escaping from Typee. Not only does it prevent him from making an active effort to flee, but it becomes inflamed whenever escape is thought of or discussed:

> But, notwithstanding the kind treatment we received, I was too familiar with the fickle disposition of savages not to feel anxious to withdraw from the valley, and put myself beyond the reach of that fearful death which, under all these smiling appearances, might yet menace us. But here there was an obstacle in the way of doing so. It was idle for me to think of moving from the place until I should have recovered from the severe lameness that afflicted me; indeed my malady began seriously to alarm me; for, despite the herbal remedies of the natives, it continued to grow worse and worse. Their mild applications, though they soothed the pain, did not remove the disorder. . . . (XIII, 95)

Although the "rich profusion" of Typee Valley seems to imply that Tommo has escaped the "vile and sickly" world of the "Dolly," he has not been able to discard the prejudices of that world. His dissatisfaction with the fertile primitive environment, tied as it is to his horror of the "fearful death," is a reminder of the Captain's early warning to the sailors to "keep out of the way of the bloody cannibals altogether" (VI, 32). The frightening yarns of that "lying old son of a sea-cook" (33) now seem more valid than the "smiling appearances" of the Typee world. It is true that aboard the "Dolly" "the sick had been inhumanly neglected" and the healthy subjected to "the butt end of a handspike" (IV, 18). But in Typee, although the sick are cared for, the primitive herbal remedies are ineffective. The swollen leg can be cured only by the higher knowledge of the "surgeons of the French fleet" (XIII, 95). Moreover, it is impossible to escape the suspicion that the kind treatment may be part of a plan to fatten up the victim.

Tommo's problem is clearly tied to his desire both to possess and to escape from the past, to have the advantages of both the primitive and civilized worlds. Once he decides that escape from Typee is impossible and surrenders himself to the sensations of the moment, there is an important change in the condition of the injured leg:

> Day after day wore on, and still there was no perceptible change in the conduct of the islanders towards me. Gradually I lost all knowledge of the regular occurrence of the days of the week, and sunk insensibly into that kind of apathy which ensues after some violent outbreak of despair. My limb suddenly healed, the swelling went down, the pain subsided, and I had every reason to suppose I should soon completely recover from the affliction that had so long tormented me.
>
> As soon as I was enabled to ramble about the valley in company with the natives, troops of whom followed me whenever I sallied out of the house, I began to experience an elasticity of mind which placed me beyond the reach of those dismal forebodings to which I had so lately been a prey. (XVII, 120)

As long as Tommo sees the present moment in terms of the past and future—the world he has left behind and to which he will eventually return—the leg remains swollen. Like the swollen foot of Oedipus, it is a symbol of his inability to possess the past entirely or escape it completely. It is a measure of the distance between the present moment and the lost past, between the primitive and civilized worlds.

When Tommo gives himself up to the "perpetual hilarity reigning through the whole extent of the vale" (XVII, 123), his wound suddenly disappears. Because the present moment is no longer seen as either coming from the past or moving toward the future, time imposes no burden. He is now a new Adam with no dependence on the past and without responsibility for the future. "The hours tripped along as gaily as the laughing couples down a country dance" (123).

But Tommo's physical and mental health does not last. When Karky, a professor of the fine art of tattooing, develops an insatiable desire to decorate the hero's attractive skin, his awareness of time returns and with it his mysterious malady;

> From the time of my casual encounter with Karky the artist, my life was one of absolute wretchedness. Not a day passed but I was persecuted by the solicitations of some of the natives to subject myself to the odious operation of tattooing. . . .

It was during the period I was in this unhappy frame of mind that the painful malady under which I had been labouring—after having almost completely subsided—began again to show itself, and with symptoms as violent as ever. (XXXII, 226–27)

Because "the whole system of tattooing was . . . connected with their religion," Tommo is convinced that "they were resolved to make a convert of me" (XXX, 217). Conversion is a double act, implying both a rejection of the old self and an acceptance of the new. For this reason the tattooing is a threat to his identity which results in the revival of his sense of temporal duration. Faced with the possibility that he will be "disfigured in such a manner as never more to have the *face* to return to my countrymen, even should an opportunity offer" (215), Tommo is driven to define his identity by the life lived before and after the present moment. Paralleling this rebirth of self-consciousness is the return of his Oedipal-like symptoms, for to be aware of the past is to experience the pain of the distance between it and the present moment. Since Tommo is unwilling to have his old *face* destroyed, he must live with the burden which it entails.

It is significant that just after his crucial decision to preserve his old face Tommo discovers evidence that cannibalism is practiced by the natives, and this accident completes his alienation from the primitive society. From this point until he hobbles to the beach to be rescued, he is painfully aware of the passage of time. Ten days separate his horrible discovery from the second visit of Marnoo, the wandering native, and three weeks after his arrival Tommo finally escapes. The career of the young hero, then, moves from a total rejection of the civilized world as represented by the "Dolly" through a search for an adventurous life of sensation in the primitive world of Typee to a total rejection of that world and a return to civilization. This traditional circular pattern of the symbolic death and rebirth of the hero, however, is called into question by the narrator. Although he is writing "amidst all the bustle and stir of the proud and busy city" (XXXIII, 239), he is, in an important sense, removed from both the primitive and Western cultures. Just as he has been able to bridge the gaps between the successive moments of his earlier experience by taking one sensation (the painful leg) and making it the center of a symbolic structure, so he is able to join two cultures meaningfully by seeing them as related parts of a single world:

But it will be urged that these shocking unprincipled wretches are cannibals. Very true; and a rather bad trait in their character it must be allowed. But they are such only when they seek to gratify the passion of revenge upon their enemies; and I ask whether the mere eating of human flesh so very far exceeds in barbarity that custom which only a few years since was practised in enlightened England:—a convicted traitor, perhaps a man found guilty of honesty, patriotism, and such like heinous crimes, had his head lopped off with a huge axe, his bowels dragged out and thrown into a fire; while his body, carved into four quarters, was with his head exposed upon pikes, and permitted to rot and fester among the public haunts of men!

.   .   .   .   .

The term "Savage" is, I conceive, often misapplied, and indeed when I consider the vices, cruelties, and enormities of every kind that spring up in the tainted atmosphere of a feverish civilization, I am inclined to think that so far as the relative wickedness of the parties is concerned, four or five Marquesan Islanders sent to the United States as Missionaries might be quite as useful as an equal number of Americans dispatched to the Islands in a similar capacity. (XVII, 122–23)

As this passage implies, the recurrent "burning fever" to which the young Tommo is susceptible identifies a disease which he brings from the "feverish civilization" he is trying to escape. Like the syphilitic sailors who infect whole islands of healthy primitives, Tommo, too, ends by partially destroying the primitive society he has sought. He demonstrates the universal trait of savagery which the narrator finds in both cultures when, during his escape, he strikes a pursuing native in the throat with a boathook.

By creating a world in which the primitive and civilized, past and present, exist side by side and illuminate one another, the narrator is able to identify the truth which lies hidden beneath the discontinuous sensations of his earlier experience. Looking back from his time of writing in this perspective he can "scarcely understand how it was that, in the midst of so many consolatory circumstances, my mind should still have been consumed by the most dismal forebodings, and have remained a prey to the profoundest melancholy" (XVI, 115). Now from his position as detached social critic he is able to see and understand things that were, at the time of action, "a little curious to my unaccustomed sight" (XI, 81).

The extent to which the narrator sees beyond the limits of his earlier vision is revealed in his comparative treatment of the Polynesian culture. Every effort is made to associate apparently unique primitive practices with accepted civilized modes of behavior. Some of the more obvious examples include his discussion of the participants in primitive religious ceremonies, who seem "much like . . . a parcel of 'Freemasons' making secret signs to each other" (XXIV, 175); his description of arva, the native beverage, which is said to possess "medicinal qualities" (XXIII, 162); and that of Ti, gathering place of the Typee warriors, which seems a "sort of Bachelor's Hall," a "savage Exchange, where the rise and fall of Polynesian Stock was discussed" (XXII, 155).

It is, then, the narrator's detached spatial imagination which allows him to see the implications which underlie the confusion of his earlier experiences. The world is seen as inherently "wolfish" and man as essentially a savage. Civilization has succeeded only in magnifying and developing a basic savagery which is found in a less appalling form in a primitive culture. It is this basic truth about himself and his world which the narrator of *Typee* confronts and reveals through his account of his earlier "Peep at Polynesian Life. . . ."

Notes

1. *Works*, trans. W. Hazlitt (New York, 1861), 3:64–65. Melville bought his copy of Montaigne in January, 1848 (see Merton M. Sealts, Jr., *Melville's Reading* [Madison, Wis., 1966], entry 366, p. 80).

2. Joseph Riddel, "F. Scott Fitzgerald, the Jamesian Inheritance, and the Morality of Fiction," *Modern Fiction Studies* (Winter, 1965–66), 11:335.

3. David Hartly, *Observations on Man* (London, 1801), 1:iii.

4. *Essays on the Intellectual Powers of Man*, ed. A. D. Woozley (London, 1941), p. 203.

5. *The British Poets* (Philadelphia, 1844), p. 238.

6. "The Task," bk. 4, *English Poets* (London, 1810), 18:698.

7. Claude Lévi-Strauss advocates a similar procedure in *Tristes Tropiques* (trans. John Russell [New York, 1964]): "The study of these savages does not reveal a Utopian state of nature; nor does it make us aware of a perfect society hidden deep in the forests. It helps us to construct a theoretical model of a society which corresponds to none that can be observed in reality, but will help us to disentangle 'what in the present state of man is original, and what is artificial' " (p. 391).

8. For an account of Melville's use of the Fall myth in *Typee*, see Milton R. Stern, *The Fine Hammered Steel of Herman Melville* (Urbana, Ill., 1957), pp. 29–65.

Melville and the Fortunate Fall: Typee as Eden

Richard Ruland*

> He who hath more of joy than sorrow in him . . . cannot be true—not true, or undeveloped. *Moby-Dick*

The idyllic world of Typee has become part of the national legend, and nineteenth- and twentieth-century readers alike have shared Tommo's regret that the rest of the world cannot be more like Typee, that the purity of life there must soon give way to corrupting civilization. Tommo, like the great majority of the novel's readers, never questions the exemplary "social virtues and happiness" (George Ripley) of this "ocean Eden" (London *Morning Chronicle*), this "Utopia" (Lewis Mumford), this "paradise" (Jay Leyda).[1] Robert E. Shafer has recently decided that *Typee* "established Melville as a primitive."[2] Heaven, the native Kory-Kory remarks in what seems to have served as summation, is "a very pleasant place . . . but, after all, not much pleasanter . . . than Typee."[3]

Tommo, Melville's narrator, has a sense of what Typee is like long before he arrives there. "The Marquesas!" he cries, while his whaler is still far out to sea. "What strange visions of outlandish things does the very name spirit up! Naked houris— . . . groves of cocoa-nut—tatooed chiefs— . . . bamboo temples; sunny valleys planted with bread-fruit-trees . . ." (5). Tommo finds precisely what he is looking for. He is well aware that for him the ship represents the sterility of civilization. He knows he is civilized man yearning to lose himself in an exotic, primitive Paradise, and he even imagines the ship itself being drawn toward the life-giving luxuriance of the shore. The keynote of his entire adventure is struck when he speaks of the first girls who swim out to greet the ship as *mermaids*. Tommo is, in short, a deliberate fantasist, a prototype of the tired businessman.

The pattern Tommo imposes on his journey is easily summarized. He is a Pilgrim who leaves the wicked world behind, endures a trial of thick cane and treacherous mountain chasms, and eventually wins his way to an idyllic haven. When Tommo first sees the land of the Typees he sighs, "Had a glimpse of the gardens of Paradise been revealed to me I could

*© 1968 by the Regents of the University of California. Reprinted from *Nineteenth Century Fiction*, 23:3 (1968), 312–23, by permission of the Regents.

scarcely have been more ravished with the sight" (49). The beautiful young couple he meets on entering the valley repeat the motif (68 ff.), and Tommo—always in the accents of the disillusioned fugitive from civilization—tirelessly rehearses the perfections of Typee. "During my whole stay on the island," he marvels, "I never witnessed a single quarrel. . . . The natives appeared to form one household, whose members were bound together by the ties of strong affection" (204). Tommo concludes that the Typees are governed by what he calls a "universally diffused perception of what is *just* and *noble*" (201). How has this come about? "Money!" he cries, " 'That root of all evil' was not to be found in the valley" (126). There is "perpetual hilarity reigning through the whole extent of the vale" (126).

We need to be reminded at this point that Tommo, like Ishmael, is conscious of himself as a storyteller. He is fully aware that he is narrating an adventure tale with a social message. The literature of the eighteenth century has not been lost on him. He emulates Swift in setting up an exotic land to berate the shortcomings of life at home. He carefully contrasts the ornately uniformed French Admiral with the simple stateliness of the Polynesian King and suggests that the native is the happier of the two. He invokes Rousseau and speaks of noble savages. He links the natives' happiness directly to their freedom from western institutions, particularly commerce and corrupted Christianity. "Thrice happy are they," he cries, "who, inhabiting some yet undiscovered island . . . have never been brought into contaminating contact with the white man" (15).

This social critique is telling, but it is as far as Tommo goes. He only knows that he personally is not happy in Typee, despite the lovely Fayaway and dutiful Kory-Kory. He leaves to secure treatment for his ailing leg, to escape tattooing, to avoid learning once and for all whether the Typees are cannibals. If we have focused faithfully through his eyes, we are sorry to leave the Happy Valley, sorry we cannot adjust to its quiet rhythms, sorry its blissful peace cannot resist much longer the rapacity of the white man. And if we indulge ourselves still further and sentimentalize the Typees, we can share the horror of Victorian readers at the final ungrateful blow which sets Tommo free. Perhaps, like Tommo, we faint dead away.

II

Few modern readers share the view of the *Springfield Republican* for March 30, 1850, that Melville's first five novels, *Typee* through *White Jacket*, are simply tales which "bring out the beauties of humble natures, and deal in pictures so pure and simple that while they refresh the searcher after recreation, they leave no stain upon the lip and no bitterness on the tongue." Evart Duyckinck described *Typee* to Hawthorne as "a lively and pleasant book, not over philosophical perhaps," and

Hawthorne himself, surprisingly enough, found it "lightly written"—
added evidence for Hubert H. Hoeltje's recent assertion that the blackness
Melville found in Hawthorne existed primarily in the eye of the beholder.[4]
Only one contemporary reviewer, in the *Literary Gazette* for October 20,
1849, suggested that *Typee*, like *Mardi*, was an allegory; current insistence on a symbolic reading has been limited almost solely to the work
of Charles Feidelson, Richard Chase and Milton Stern. For F. O. Matthiessen it was a straightforward account of Melville's adventures, while
Willard Thorp finds it "as nearly artless as anything Melville wrote," and
Harry Levin can link it to the haphazard pot-boiler, *Omoo*, and sweep
over both as "breezy memoirs of travel."[5]

Gansevoort Melville must have read the book as some such memoir or
he would never have carried the unfinished manuscript to London's John
Murray. "The publisher's tastes being well known," writes George Paston, "innumerable travellers' tales poured into Albemarle Street . . . and
many were purchased for the Home and Colonial Library." Murray had
built his reputation publishing travel literature; the list of his Knapsack
Guides seems endless. When Gansevoort brought him his brother's
manuscript in the autumn of 1845, Murray was charmed by the "adventure book." "A connoisseur in this class of work," he "was attracted by the
dramatic interest of the narrative and the raciness of the style, but he
scented the forbidden thing—the taint of fiction."[6] Murray took no fiction
whatever, and with the exception of Scott's novels he did not even read
any. His prejudice was common knowledge, and Melville was aware of it:
"I fear you abhor romances," he remarked in a letter to the publisher.[7]

Murray accepted *Typee* for his Home and Colonial Library Series,
but only after Melville had added three chapters of anthropological
description, extended the title to suggest a scientific treatise, and supplied
a preface which insists that the book's purpose is to communicate
knowledge about the South Seas and the efforts of Christian missionaries
there, and that the author is anxious "to speak the unvarnished truth."
The new chapters, Gansevoort notes in submitting them to Murray,
"are . . . less amenable than the others to the faults you have pointed
out. . . . Their subject matter . . . will go far to give a more life-like air
to the whole, and parry the incredulity of those who may be disposed to
regard the work as an ingenious fiction."[8] Murray published *Typee*, but
he still scented fiction. When he asked for documentary proof, Melville
became jocular and insisted none was needed. "Mr. Murray," he purred
(with, I think, his tongue in his cheek) "Mr. Murray, I am ready to
swear, stands fast in the faith, believing *Typee* from preface to sequel."[9]
There is no record of Herman's instructions to Gansevoort on sending the
book to England, but he certainly had every reason to keep quiet about
any fictional intentions he might have had as he watched enthusiasm
mount on all sides. If he did feel that the book was accepted by Murray
and praised by the reviewers for all the wrong reasons, he could scarcely

help recalling his failure to place it with Harpers. There he had been told: it is impossible that the book could be true, and therefore it is without real value.[10]

Students of Melville have never known quite what to make of an anecdote quoted by the well-known and highly respected French critic, Philarète Chasles. In his review of *Typee*, translated and reprinted in the New York *Literary World* of August 11, 1849, Chasles tells of a conversation with an "honorable citizen of the United States, a man educated and *spirituel*, well acquainted with the literary affairs of his race. . . ." Chasles, that is, trusts his informant and believes what he says about Melville. The American, Thomas Gold Appleton, speaks as a friend of Melville's cousin, Robert Melvill,[11] and of Lemuel Shaw, his father-in-law, and he claims to have met Toby (Richard Greene). Melville, Appleton tells Chasles,

> is generally regarded as a narrator of well made up stories, but very daydreams withal. . . .
>
> The pleasant part of the story is, that charmed by his improvised reputation, he has not contradicted those who attribute to the brilliancy and creative fecundity of his imagination the merit which belongs only to the fidelity of his memory. He would be vexed if the essential truth of this curious episode in the life of a young sailor should be acknowledged. The re-appearance of his companion Toby . . . provoked him to some extent, by making him descend from the pedestal of the novelist to the ordinary level of a narrator.

Appleton, in short, sees *Typee* as Murray strained to see it, as literally true. But Charles Anderson's meticulous study of *Melville in the South Seas* demonstrates conclusively that Melville came to know very little of Typee during his brief stay. The book is rather the product both of earlier travel accounts and Melville's already considerable skill as a writer of fiction. "In view of the vast array of evidence which [shows] how largely Melville drew upon these authorities," Anderson concludes, "his wholesale disparagement of travel books in general is misleading, for it deliberately intimates that he eschewed them altogether."[12] There is, then, "brilliance and creative fecundity of . . . imagination." But there is no need for Appleton's irony, and no need for Melville to "descend from the pedestal of the novelist."

In 1850, writing of Hawthorne's stories, Melville remarks that "like many other geniuses, this Man of Mosses takes great delight in hoodwinking the world. . . ." Whatever the motive, "playful or profound, . . . it is certain that some [of Hawthorne's tales] are directly calculated to deceive—egregiously deceive—the superficial skimmer of pages. 'Who in the name of thunder' (as the country people say in this neighborhood) . . . would anticipate any marvel in a piece entitled "Young Goodman Brown"? You would of course suppose that it was a simple little tale. . . . Whereas, it is deep as Dante. . . ."[13] It seems equally unlikely that Melville himself was ever straightforward or artless. We know how often he said he was trying to be—with *Moby Dick* and with *Pierre*, for instance. It is sometimes said that Melville's interest in metaphysics was his greatest liability as a novelist. This is perhaps true, but metaphysician he was, from start to finish. And his mode of perception was symbolic. The symbolic imagination, that cast of mind which habitually sees life in terms of "correspondences," cannot be turned on and off at will. We have taken Melville's remark that he had not developed at all before his twenty-fifth year—that is, 1844—too literally (just as we have too readily accepted his professed ignorance of Shakespeare before 1849). *Typee* appeared in 1846. Within four years—to pass over books like *Mardi* and *White Jacket*—Melville was writing *Moby Dick*. His philosophic penetration might have been no deeper than Tommo's when he actually visited the Marquesas, but by the time he came to write of the experience I doubt that he would have chosen to limit his concerns until circumstances persuaded him he had better. Tommo is Murray's narrator, speaking to the vast public for informative, uplifting and escapist writing. There are, of course, long sections of *Typee* in which Melville and Tommo merge. Melville supports Tommo's criticism of commercialism and the fruits of missionary activity. But he understands the valley far better than Tommo does and he knows what Tommo does not: what is wrong with the life lived there and why Tommo must not stay. Melville would have us cheer when Tommo strikes his violent blow, for a life is thereby saved, the inner life which Tommo only vaguely senses has been in danger. "The penalty of the Fall presses very lightly upon the valley of Typee" (195), Tommo remarks. There is as little sign, Melville would add, of its fruits.

III

Tommo is no naive persona. He employs metaphoric and symbolic patterns of his own in making his points. But there are moments when he relates without comment, when he seems unaware of the implications of his observations. And he has highly emblematic experiences which are for him wholly without significance. Thus it is possible to read the journey of Tommo and Toby as Tommo does read it, as successful escape from civilization to Paradise. But when they find themselves trapped in the canes, Tommo remarks, "we were not certain but that we might have been going all the time in a wrong direction" (38). What they need, he suggests, is a pair of wings—and indeed it is wings they would have to have if they are to reach Paradise. What they *do* have however is their sheath-knives, and so, with the tools of civilization, they free themselves. It has been suggested that Tommo differs from Crusoe (whom he invokes) in that Crusoe carries Europe with him to *his* isle. But Tommo too remains throughout a man of civilization. He is persistently reminded of this by the chills, fever and swelling which plague him to the end of the novel. This illness he himself attributes to exposure. It suggests that he is out of his element; it is a reminder that through mutiny and flight he has broken his contract with the whaler, with civilization; it is in effect the burden of experience with which he must confront the innocence of Typee. "I recommend all adventurous youths who abandon vessels in romantic islands during the rainy season to provide themselves with umbrellas" (48), he remarks in a jocular moment. Because there was no umbrella there is a swollen leg; the two signify the same thing.

Lest we miss the point, Melville provides another occasion to illustrate that his sailor has indeed lost his direction, that he is not headed for perfect bliss. Suffering from his strange malady, Tommo welcomes a chance to refresh himself at a mountain stream. But, he says, "a single drop of the cold fluid seemed to freeze every drop of blood in my body; the fever that had been burning in my veins gave place . . . to death-like chills, which shook me one after another like so many shocks of electricity. . . . My thirst was gone, and I fairly loathed the water" (53). Like the valley which lies ahead, the water is elemental and innocent, but it is not for Tommo, and he is reminded of it in a pointed image from the world he seeks to escape: that is, *shocks of electricity*.

The valley at the end of Tommo's journey is not Paradise. Unlike Pilgrim and Gulliver, and contrary to what Tommo himself seems to assume and his readers to accept, his journey takes place entirely in the natural sphere. Tommo has not reached the realm of mermaids. What he has found is indeed innocence of the ways of the world, but it is innocence *in* the world—the innocence of Baby Budd. Melville's first novel and his last are comments on such innocence and for this reason should be read together. In *Typee*, he takes Tommo, complete with his baggage of experience, on a journey of philosophic inquiry. What would happen, he asks, if we could indeed be born again into the innocence of childhood. It would be Edenic and prelapsarian; but would it be heavenly or utopian?

The path into the valley is "indistinctly traced," for travellers who would test the value of innocence are rare, and the natives are innocent precisely because they never venture from their familiar surroundings. The hungry travellers make for the first fruits they spy. "But to our chagrin," Tommo says, "they proved to be much decayed; the rinds partly opened by birds, and their hearts half devoured" (67). They are, in fact, no better than the brackish food left aboard ship, yet Tommo can call them "ambrosia." Within moments the sailors encounter the young couple, "slender and graceful, and completely naked, with the exception of a slight girdle of bark, from which depended at opposite points two of the russet leaves of the bread-fruit tree."[14] Are these two appealing figures, framed as they are in bark and leaf, also destined to disappoint the primitivist seeker? The close juxtaposition of fruit and Typean couple in the crucial first moments of our introduction to the valley suggests that Melville means to raise the question.

"I was completely at a loss to understand them," Tommo remarks after meeting these first Typees. He never does understand any of them. He looks at their culture with western eyes and finds much to challenge the world he knows. But he has no insight into the quality of that culture or of the lives lived there. He is so dominated by his metaphor of Paradise that he never seems to realize that the Typees have nothing to live *for*. He can tell us that their happiness stems from a "mere buoyant sense of a healthful physical existence" (129). He can note their idleness, their lethargy: "To many of them, indeed," he says, "life is little else than an often interrupted and luxurious nap" (152). He can describe with painstaking care the central problem in Typee, the producing of a spark for fire. But Tommo never sees that the Typees are blissful in their innocence because they have no intellectual light, that they are like the beautiful birds he describes which cannot sing. Life in Typee is monotonous: "The history of a day," Tommo says, "is the history of a life" (149). The static equilibrium of its society is ensured by irrational taboos which no Typee understands or cares to understand.

Tommo's Edenic imagery is employed ironically by Melville; for the one its connotation is happiness, but for the other it suggests insulation from a necessary exploration of the human condition. A far more significant image sequence is the repeated reference to the natives as children or animals[15]—this, and the masterful double weighting of the three central factors in Tommo's story: his fear of tattooing, his ailing leg, and his unresolved suspicions of Typean cannibalism. Tommo resists being tattooed because, he quips, he would then not have the "face" to return home. The insistence of the natives that he let himself be decorated, the discovery of the three human heads, and the pressing need for medical attention combine to motivate his escape. But the real danger of the tattooing is not that Tommo will lose his good looks, but that his intellect will be shuttered. The Typees not only have great difficulty making fire, they also regard as the highest form of tattooing the drawing of intersecting lines across the eyes and face. Their most honored chiefs, the very leaders who support the unreflecting life the Typees lead, are fitted with decorative blinders of this sort.[16] Submission to this rite will bring Tommo one step closer to becoming a Typee. For the Typees are indeed cannibals. Whether they literally eat human flesh or not is beside the point. Far more significant for Melville is the fact that the Typees want to devour Tommo's identity, everything that makes him what he is: his curiosity, his desire for communication, his delight in contemplation, his awareness of time and sense of history—in short, his need to understand the complexity that is human life.

Tommo understands that his curiously ailing leg has been caused by the exposure he endured in his effort to escape from his ship, from, that is, his life in a corrupt commercial society. "I half suspected," he adds, that "I had been bitten by some venomous reptile" (48). Melville, however, treats the leg throughout as the means to his hero's salvation. Its throbbing saves Tommo from the valley; it is the objectification of all that makes him different from the Typees. For, we are told, "There are . . . no snakes of any description" in the valley (212)—there is no insistence that innocence be tested at the Tree of Knowledge. When Tommo is most the outsider, that is, most his own man, his wounded leg pains him severely.[17] (He realizes that in a civilized country it would soon respond to medical treatment—symbolically, he would no longer be exposing himself in a hostile land.) But when he feels most at home with the Typees, after his fellow alien Toby has made his escape, the leg troubles him not at all."[18] It is at this moment, when Tommo is most content, that Melville would have us worry for him most. He is least suspicious of Typean cannibalism. The idea of being tattooed has come to seem less frightful, and Tommo considers having his arms decorated. This is actually the climactic moment of the narrative, although the narrator does not realize it. It is only the discovery of the heads, the renewed fear of being eaten—and the return of that life-giving pain in the leg—which save Tommo from the bovine world of Typee.

IV

"I will frankly declare," runs Tommo's familiar conclusion, "that after passing a few weeks in this valley of the Marquesas, I formed a higher estimate of human nature than I had ever before entertained." But alas!, he sighs, "since then I have been one of the crew of a man-of-war, and the pent-up wickedness of five hundred men has nearly overturned all my previous theories" (203). Tommo clearly means to polarize the two experiences, and it is the temptation of the book to read the valley as good and civilization as evil. Yet readers of Melville seldom find such polarization; they find instead that the wickedness of the ship's world is a challenge Melville accepts, that he would launch us all onto his sea of the unknown. The irony with which Melville regards Tommo's fantasy is nowhere better highlighted than in an early description of the valley. When Toby notices the sheer cliffs which hem in the land of the Typees, Tommo remarks, "Yes . . . as steep as the sides of a line-of-battle ship, and *about a hundred times as high*."[19] This should lead Tommo to reconsider his notion than human nature is somehow different in Typee, but he never does. Melville, however, is clear enough. Typee is not only very much a part of the world, but its insulation and Edenic innocence make it an impossible place for men to live and still remain men.

"I love all men who *dive*," runs the famous letter to Duyckinck in 1849. "Any fish can swim near the surface. . . ." Melville was from the first one of those "corps of thought-divers, that have been diving & coming up again with bloodshot eyes since the world began."[29] He saved his Tommo for thought-diving by returning him at last to a ship, and by providing him with sufficient sense of his real danger to muster the violence necessary to break with the persistent enchantment of Typee. The escape is narrow enough to justify his swoon.

Notes

1. See Hugh W. Hetherington, *Melville's Reviewers* (Chapel Hill, 1961), pp. 52, 64 and 58, and Jay Leyda, "Biographical," *The Portable Melville* (New York, 1952), p. 7.

2. "Teaching Sequences in Hawthorne and Melville," *The Teacher and American Literature: Papers Presented at the 1964 Convention of the NCTE* (Champaign, 1965), p. 114. The primitivist label is most firmly affixed to Melville by James Baird in his *Ishmael* (New York, 1956), but Mr. Baird is careful to establish a singularly private definition of primitivism before applying it to Melville. See especially Part I, Section I.

3. Herman Melville, *Typee: A Peep at Polynesian Life* in *The Writings of Herman Melville*, eds. Harrison Hayford, Hershel Parker, G. Thomas Tanselle (Evanston and Chicago, 1968), I, 172. All quotations from *Typee* are from this edition. The edition appeared too late for me to draw upon the further supporting evidence in Leon Howard's careful Historical Note; see especially pp. 293–301.

4. Jay Leyda, *The Melville Log* (New York, 1951), pp. 206, 207. Hubert H. Hoeltje, "Hawthorne, Melville, and 'Blackness,' " *American Literature*, XXXVII (March, 1965), 41–51.

5. For the discussions referred to, see the indices of Charles Feidelson, *Symbolism and American Literature* (Chicago, 1953), Richard Chase, *Herman Melville* (New York, 1949), Milton R. Stern, *The Fine Hammered Steel of Herman Melville* (Urbana, 1957), F. O. Matthiessen, *American Renaissance* (London & New York, 1941), Willard Thorp, *Herman Melville: Representative Selections* (New York, 1938), and Harry Levin, *The Power of Blackness* (New York, 1958). See also D. H. Lawrence, *Studies in Classic American Literature* (Garden City, 1923), Milton R. Stern's Introduction to *Typee and Billy Budd* (New York, 1958), and R. W. B. Lewis's discussion of *Billy Budd* in *The American Adam* (Chicago, 1955).

6. George Paston, *At John Murray's: Records of a Literary Circle, 1813–1892* (London, 1932), pp. 39n, 51.

7. *Log*, p. 278.

8. The added chapters are XX, XXI, and XXVII; "There are also . . . additions relating chiefly to the Taboo, the cause of Missions, and the religious belief of the Marquesans. . . ." *Log*, pp. 200–201. Leyda refers to "large additions to XXIV, XXVI, and XXX" (*The Portable Melville*, p. 9).

9. Paston, p. 52.

10. *Log*, p. 196.

11. Appleton and Melvill are identified by Leyda in *Log*, p. 300.

12. Charles Roberts Anderson, *Melville in the South Seas* (New York, 1939), p. 119. Anderson quotes *Typee*, pp. 170–171, to illustrate Melville's dismissal of travel accounts. Melville was doubtless also an avid reader of sea fiction. Thomas Philbrick suggests that Melville learned much about the fictional use of symbolism from Joseph C. Hart's *Miriam Coffin* (1834) and the later novels of Cooper, especially *Afloat and Ashore* (1844) and *The Sea Lions* (1849). See *James Fenimore Cooper and the Development of American Sea Fiction* (Cambridge, Mass., 1961), pp. 42–84, 94–100, 144, 264–266.

13. "Hawthorne and his Mosses, by a Virginian Spending July in Vermont" (*The Portable Melville*, pp. 417–418).

14. P. 68. When trace of the boy and girl is first noted, storyteller Tommo injects, "The plot was now thickening."

15. Three instances, each reported by Tommo with no allusion to its implications: After witnessing a religious ceremony Tommo remarks, "The whole of these proceedings were like those of a parcel of children playing with dolls and baby houses" (176). "There are no wild animals of any kind on the island, unless it be decided that the natives themselves are such" (212). Watching the Typees trying to work, "one is reminded of an infinity of black ants clustering about and dragging away to some hole the leg of a deceased fly" (159).

16. Melville's desire to stress his point led him to tattoo a chief whose real counterpart "is of very high blood & not tatooed [*sic*] at all." See portion of the *Journal of A. G. Jones, 1854–55*, ed. by Mabel Weeks with the title "Long Ago and 'Faraway,' " *Bulletin of the New York Public Library* (July, 1948), p. 7. Watching one native being tattooed, Tommo refers to his eyes as "the windows of his soul" (218). And he sees "four or five hideous old wretches, on whose decrepit forms time and tattooing seemed to have obliterated every trace of humanity." The wholly tattooed Typee ages to a green hue strongly reminiscent of the unromantic green so repulsive to Tommo aboard ship (92).

17. Similarly, Kory-Kory lectures Tommo on the richness of life in Typee: "He continued his harangue . . . enlarging, probably, upon the moral reflections it suggested; and proceeded in such a strain of unintelligible and stunning gibberish, that he actually gave me the headache for the rest of the day" (103).

18. "Gradually I lost all knowledge of the regular recurrence of the days of the week, and sunk insensibly into that kind of apathy which ensues after some violent outbreak of despair. My limb suddenly healed, the swelling went down, the pain subsided, and I had every reason to suppose I should soon completely recover from the affliction that had so long tormented me" (123). A few pages later, after almost identical remarks, Tommo adds: "Freed from apprehensions on this point . . . I flung myself anew into all the social pleasures of the valley, and sought to bury all regrets, and all remembrances of my previous existence, in the wild enjoyments it afforded" (144). Tommo is now prepared to praise Typean culture: "In [this] altered frame of mind . . . every object that presented itself to my notice in the valley struck me in a new light, and the opportunities I now enjoyed of observing the manners of its inmates tended to strengthen my favorable impressions" (126). See also the unsuccessful efforts of the Typees to cure Tommo's leg (80); "Their mild applications, though they soothed the pain, did not remove the disorder . . ." (98). Anderson identifies the ineffectual doctor as "one of the highest priests of the valley" (169). Note also that as the leg does heal, Tommo is no longer afforded special transport on Kory-Kory's back; he returns to the ground and becomes part of the native community.

19. P. 56. My emphasis.

20. *The Portable Melville*, pp. 378–379.

Typee: The Quixotic Pattern

John Seelye*

Though *Typee* was presumably based on Melville's adventures on Nukuheva, the form is the romantic quest, with the familiar devices of an illusory basis, action inspired by boredom and a promise of paradise, a consequent penetration into a mystery, subsequent disillusionment, and an eventual retreat to the "real" world. If the "Fragment" mirrors *Alastor*, *Typee* takes its pattern from Scott's Waverley Novels. Ultimately inspired by Cervantes, this quixotic pattern is one of intellectual stripping and reeducation, of introducing a romance-fed youth into the realities of life as it is found. Romantic in atmosphere, it is anti-romance in purpose, with an ironic emphasis on countering dreams with hard fact.

Tommo is typically quixotic, a wandering Waverley who knows nothing about the South Seas except what he has heard and read, a guidebook and tall-tale miscellany of attractions and frights. Native girls are "houris" culled from the *Arabian Nights*, and the islands are generalized "groves," "blue waters," and "savage woodlands" (*T*, p. 5).[1] But the islands of the South Seas turn out not to be the arcadia of low-lying country that he has imagined from his reading. He soon discovers them to be steep and mountainous, a wilderness of forests and towering cliffs. Furthermore, he finds little enough of paradise—at least on first encounter—for civilization has come to the South Seas, and the idealized natives of his dreams have been hopelessly corrupted by their contact with commerce. The pilot who guides the *Dolly* into the bay is a drunken English derelict, and the sailors' first sight of the islanders is a tangled confusion of merchant canoes vying with each other in an attempt to reach the American ship. A group of swimming native girls is first mistaken by Tommo for a school of fish, then, when he realizes his mistake, likened to mermaids. Clinging to the *Dolly*, "sparkling with savage vivacity, laughing gaily at one another, and chattering away with infinite glee," they seem the very type of primitive innocence, but once aboard the ship, the girls undergo a final metamorphosis. "Not the

*Reprinted from John Seelye, *Melville: The Ironic Diagram* (Evanston: Northwestern Univ. Press, 1970), pp. 14–24, by permission of John Seelye.

feeblest barrier was interposed between the unholy passions of the crew and their unlimited gratification" (pp. 14–15).

Undiscouraged by what he has witnessed, untutored by the demonstration of illusoriness, Tommo continues to be inspired by the accounts he has read of the islands. On the *Dolly*, all is known—life is sterile, routine, fixed. The island beyond the bay stands for all that is unknown, its emerald foliage mocking the flat green color with which the ship's bulwarks are painted. Although they reverse the imagery of the first chapter of *Moby-Dick*, the passages describing Tommo's discontent are motivated by the same idea. There, the inhabitants of the island city, Manhattan, yearn for the open sea; here, even the beams and planks of the ship seem to yearn for the shore. The whaler, in *Moby-Dick* a vessel of adventure, aimed for the voyage out, is here an ark of boredom, a contrast to the lure of the mysterious island beyond.

Tommo jumps ship with Toby, a daredevil youth ideally suited to an adventurous quest after a hidden valley and the first of several "companions" who appear in Melville's novels. An elaboration upon the "squire" figure in romances and the picaresque novel, like Queequeg he serves as an usher into the unknown, "one of those class of rovers you sometimes meet at sea, who never reveal their origin, never allude to home, and go rambling over the world as if pursued by some mysterious fate they cannot possibly elude." Byronic Toby seems an abstraction of the romantic spirit, dark complexioned, with "jetty locks" and "large black eyes," and a temperament to match: "He was a strange wayward being, moody, fitful, and melancholy—at times almost morose" (p. 32). He is an intense version of Tommo's own impulsiveness.

The deserting sailors are hardly ashore before they discover the folly of their plan. Instead of "broad and capacious valleys" beyond the first ridge, they find only mountains and ravines, and the breadfruit trees which were to supply them with food are nowhere in sight. Following what promises to be a native path, they are led by nightfall into a cul-de-sac, a dark chasm dripping with spray from a waterfall. Forced to sleep in this miserable hole, they are reduced from romantic expectations to a "dismal sense of our forlorn condition," and Tommo is nearly "unmanned" by his wretchedness (p. 46). Soaked to the skin, shivering and half-starved, the runaways cross over the dark territory through which the voyager must pass before he can gain the enchanted terrain beyond. The next morning, still undaunted by nature's inhospitality, the sailors catch their first sight of the interior valley, a vision of immaculate repose compared by Tommo to "the enchanted gardens in the fairy tale" (p. 49).

But, like the forbidding mountains which surround it, the beautiful valley is ironic ground. Tommo is soon to discover cryptic monuments which the natives cannot explain—natives who are silent about the ultimate fate of their cherished guest and whose spokesman is the mute Mehevi, grim equivalent of the mysterious monuments. And yet much delight awaits him as well, in the form of Fayaway and her happy friends. Surrounded by mystery and beauty, Tommo often feels "transported to some fairy region, so unreal did everything appear" (p. 134). And like the prisoner of fairies, he is never quite sure whether he is in paradise or hell. At times, indeed, he feels like an ass.

The moment he has caught his first "glimpse of the gardens of Paradise," Tommo begins to feel the torments of the damned. In Melville's mythology, penetration into nature's mysteries is often rewarded by a mutilating shock, and Tommo's first peep into the Typee valley is accompanied by the painful swelling of his leg which will cripple him throughout the remainder of his stay on the island. Significantly, he attributes the injury to the bite of a snake, "the congenial inhabitant of the chasm" where he and Toby spent the night. For the chasm and the valley are two halves of a whole, representative of the duality of the natural world which the wandering sailors have invaded.

As the island contains both the dark chasm and the sunny valley, so the valley contains spheres of love and fear. Though captivated by the simple life and physical beauty of the inhabitants, Tommo can never completely relax for long among them, and Toby's mysterious disappearance, along with his discovery of the grisly banquet in the warriors' hall, eventually overrules any delight he may have experienced with Fayaway. In time it is the paradisiacal green land which must be abandoned, while the open sea stands for freedom: "Oh glorious sight and sound of ocean! with what rapture did I hail you as familiar friends!" (p. 248). With Tommo's return to the sea his linear invasion of mystery becomes a circle, the dominant dimension of Melville's ironic diagram.

The movement of the narrative up to Tommo's entrance into the Typee valley is relatively straightforward and rapid. The quest here is simple and the obstacles obvious. But once Tommo is among the Typees, the movement of the story becomes serpentine and slow, defined both by his inability to decipher many of the mysterious events he encounters and by his wavering between acceptance of the savages' happy-go-lucky existence and his fear of their cannibalism and treachery. Instead of moving across mountains and ravines, he wanders haphazardly about the village and valley, making a series of discoveries—both pleasant and fearsome— which lead up to his eventual uncovering of the human remains in the banquet hall. At that point, the tensions of the preceding episodes are resolved, and the narrative line becomes once again simple and uncomplicated by uncertainties. Having received a positive answer to the question of the Typees' cannibalism, Tommo is glad to flee their paradise.

This section of the book, in which the quest pattern is at once complex and muted, looks forward to Melville's later writings—in particular his short stories, where the wanderings of the quester are limited and where the ironic landscape is restricted to a law office, a New England mountainside, or the decks of a Mississippi steamboat. The situation in the Typee

Valley, moreover, is an anticipatory echo of "Benito Cereno," where we have once again a white man moving at great risk among savages, another white man held prisoner by the same savages, and an apparent valet who is actually a jailer. Like Tommo, Captain Delano vacillates between assurance and fear, and whereas the later story is made more complex by misdirecting the captain's suspicions towards the Spaniards, the real threat in both stories is concealed by the purposefully ambiguous demeanor of the savages. In both stories, too, we have a static pattern of action whose tension is caused by suspense and an atmosphere of threat, tension which ultimately explodes in violent, revelatory movement.

Because of the hidden "truth" of the situation in "Benito Cereno," the innocent, optimistic Captain Delano is often the unwitting victim of irony. What he sees as loving, dutiful kindness on the part of Babo, Cereno's former slave but now his master, is in reality a species of slow torture. The lock and key with which the Spaniard holds the giant mutineer, Atufal, "prisoner" is actually an emblem of his own captivity. The obedient attentiveness with which the "slaves" aid the Spaniards in carrying out menial tasks is actually the means by which a close watch is kept on the white prisoners. Certain contradictions to normal order and routine arouse Delano's suspicions, but because of his obtuseness he is unable to discover the truth.

Similar ironies appear in *Typee*. It is some time before Tommo discovers that Kory-Kory's attentiveness is a means of keeping watch on him, and in the interval he continues to marvel at the excellent care given him by the savages, particularly their insistence that he eat at every opportunity. Especially sardonic in this regard are Tommo's enthusiastic descriptions of the banquets in the Ti, for it is here that he eventually discovers the evidence which qualifies his earlier assertion, "it did my heart, as well as my body, good to visit it" (pp. 151–52). Amplifying this irony are a series of pig-man ambiguities, commencing with Toby's gloomy suspicion that the first dish of meat they are served is "baked baby" when it is actually a "juvenile porker" and ending with Tommo's discovery of what Kory-Kory hastens to explain away as "puarkee." To the natives, humans are known familiarly as "long pig," and Tommo's description of the hog butchery which precedes the "Feast of the Calabashes" is grimly (albeit innocently) suggestive: "Again and again he missed his writhing and struggling victim, but though puffing and panting with his exertions, he still continued them; and after striking a sufficient number of blows to have demolished an entire drove of oxen, with one crashing stroke he laid him dead at his feet" (p. 158). By omitting the word "pig" throughout the episode, Melville creates an ambiguity which Tommo does not grasp.

Equivocal devices like these keep the reader reminded of the possibility that the Typees are cannibals and that Tommo is intended for some ritual feast. At the same time, we are not sure until the final revelation that they *are* cannibals, and we never do find out whether Tommo is really being fattened for the kill or is merely the happy victim of the savages' proverbial hospitality. As in "Benito Cereno," moreover, the ambiguity seems to have a purpose beyond the creation of suspense. In the later story, Delano is kept from the truth by his stereotyped attitude towards Negroes, whom he regards as docile and unaspiring servants, and Spaniards, whom he associates with pirates and treachery. In *Typee*, Melville addresses himself to the tendency of his contemporaries either to regard the South Sea islanders as unregenerate cannibals all or to dismiss the idea of their cannibalism as perfectly ridiculous. Up until Tommo's final discovery, the Typees' cannibalism is merely a rumor, and the runaway sailor balances his fears by rhapsodic descriptions of their idyllic life. "Truth," declares Tommo, "loves to be centrally located, [and] is again found between the two extremes; for cannibalism to a certain moderate extent is practised among several of the primitive tribes in the Pacific, but it is upon the bodies of slain enemies alone; and horrible and fearful as the custom is, immeasurably as it is to be abhorred and condemned, still I assert that those who indulge in it are in other respects humane and virtuous" (p. 205). Since Melville is trying to establish this median "Truth," it is necessary that his narrator witness the remains of a cannibal banquet enjoyed by savages who are "in other respects humane and virtuous."

Tommo, as an instrument of Truth, may be considered a balancewheel of opinion, vacillating between the extreme positions maintained by society until his discovery of the cannibal banquet provides him with definitive knowledge of the savages' best and worst faults. At times he is Rousseauistic in his admiration of the Typees' nobility and peace of mind, their perpetual hilarity and joyous good nature; at others, he trembles with fear over the savages' well-known propensity for sudden treachery. As long as his attention is on the fair aspects of the natives, Tommo is able to maintain a Delano-like composure, but once he recalls the proverbial fickleness of primitive man, fearful apprehensions seize him. It is this vacillation between extreme attitudes which produces in *Typee* an equivalent of the symposium-circle found in Melville's later works—a wholeness of opposite viewpoints. In effect, *Typee* is an anatomy of savagery, a savagery which is shown to be humane and treacherous, virtuous and cruel.

Each character in the cast of primitive types that Tommo encounters in the Typee Valley represents one aspect of "natural" man, often corresponding to the various ideas of savagery held by Melville's contemporaries. Mehevi, chief of the Typees, corresponds to Rousseau's Noble Savage, a "splendid islander" with an apollonian physique. Tommo calls him "Nature's nobleman" and, while standing in awe of him, praises his hospitality. But Mehevi has other characteristics as well, an "inflexible rigidity of expression" made even more terrible by his habitual silence (p. 119). It is Mehevi's stern silence, especially, which dampens Tommo's enjoyment of the "mirth, fun, and high good humor" reigning in the valley. Whenever Mehevi appears, Tommo's "elasticity of mind which [had] placed me beyond the reach of . . . dismal forebodings" snaps back to "frightful apprehensions with regard to my own fate" (pp. 123, 140).

Grim and silent, a Greek god in appearance, hospitable and gracious, Mehevi is central to the mystery of the Typees. Ranged about him are the other savage types: Mow-Mow, the brutal, scarred, "ignoble" savage; Fayaway, who seems a cross between Atala and Undine, an idealized Belle Sauvage; and the kindly Kory-Kory, Tommo's man Friday and jailer. Domestic life is represented by Marheyo, a fatherly type who is the sailor's commiserating host, and his wife, Tinor, a model of primitive housewifery. The valley is a microcosmic arrangement of alternatives, providing a circular diagram of contrasts and designed to demonstrate that primitive man is not one, easily categorized, type. Moreover, this variety of savage types suggests yet another implication. As natural men, the natives serve as correlatives of nature's plenitude, their character types and range of moods an index to the "all" that was for Melville a blank canvas of possibilities.

Kory-Kory is covered with tattoos, "representations of birds and fishes, and a variety of most unaccountable-looking creatures, suggesting to me the idea of a pictorial museum of natural history" (p. 83). He is a savage Everyman and a correlative of the natural world into which Tommo has crept and crawled, and as the fact of his tattooing is a token of his savagery (Tommo shrinks with disgust from the idea of having his own civilized hide marked up), so the images presented on his body suggest his oneness with nature. Similarly, the noble Mehevi is tattooed with a triangle, a "sort of freemason's badge" which suggests to Tommo his "exalted rank" as one of "Nature's noblemen" (pp. 228, 78), and the ignoble Mow-Mow is decorated with an ugly scar, token of his warlike nature.

It is Mow-Mow, not Mehevi, who attempts to kill Tommo during his pell-mell escape from the valley, for, like Babo in "Benito Cereno," he represents the dark malignity of natural savagery. When the furiously swimming Mohawk-Marquesan closes on his whaleboat, Tommo thrusts a boat hook at him, and then—shocked by the "ferocious expression" on the savage's face—faints dead away. The action anticipates the scene in "Benito Cereno" where the "lividly vindictive" features of Babo, as he writhes "snakishly" in an attempt to stab his former master, cause the Spaniard to fall back in a dead faint. In both instances we are given a glimpse of naked nature, embodied in the pure malevolence of which natural man is capable, a human coefficient of Moby Dick's "two long crooked rows of white, glistening teeth, floating up from the undiscoverable bottom . . . his vast, shadowed bulk still half blending with the blue of the sea" (p. 540).

The symbolic intimation of this disembodied grin—the merging of the Whale with the natural element—is undeniable, and symbolic too is Babo's "snakish writhing." But Mow-Mow's attack is symbolic only to the extent that it represents the ferocity of which natural man is capable. He is as symbolic as one of Cooper's Indians, but no more. He is *of* nature, but is not Nature, for the episode lacks the associational machinery of Melville's later works, the imagery by which the Whale becomes personified natural malevolence, or Babo the human counterpart of a poisonous reptile.

By means of diagram and half-realized symbol, Melville seems to be suggesting that the Typees, like Moby Dick, are animated nature—a phenomenological whole that baffles inquiry. But these patterns of intimation can be detected only by comparing them to the later works. The materials of symbolism and irony are present, and the young author seems to be hinting at their full significance, but nothing comes of it. The patterns of appearance and reality, sea and shore, enchantment and silence, delight and fear, all have symbolic counterparts in Melville's later work but are in themselves without the power of symbols. The microcosmic village, the relativistic range of savage types, the identification of primitive man with the natural world—all have their equivalents in the later work, but in *Typee* they remain latent, unrealized as symbolic potential.

When a contemporary of Melville's described *Typee* as "*Rasselas* rewritten by Irving," he wrote more wisely than he knew. For despite the book's ebullient, happy-go-lucky tone, its structure implies an underlying pessimism. Like *Rasselas*, *Typee* is a futile quest. The Irvingesque style might be compared to an ironic mask, like laughing Ishmael, whose jolliness is mockery, but if it was conceived as such, it plainly does not work. Perhaps the problem resulted from a conflict in purpose, for Melville seems to have been divided between a desire to report how things "really" were in the Islands and an equally strong desire to create a fiction, a planned series of clues, indirections, and climaxes, ironically conceived and executed. The "uses" of the hero-narrator are consequently at odds. At one moment we are to credit him with exposing civilized abuses against the hapless natives, at another we are to regard him as an unsuspecting dupe of cannibal tricks.

However it may have been, the voice which Melville chose for *Typee* is an insufficient instrument. It is the discursive voice of exposition, a fashionable manner that is fine for a travel book but too inflexible for the presentation of romantic ironies. Moreover, the first-person voice, dictated in his early works by autobiographical necessity (and the market), was often to give Melville trouble. Because of the frequent tension between his private artistic and philosophical aims and the need to satisfy his readers, who wished for more scenery and less skepticism, the first-person voice often betrayed him, leading him from the popular dimension towards the private sector of philosophic speculation. "I" is never in Melville's novels a consistently ironic mask, whether it be the "I" of Ishmael or Ahab.

It is notable, then, that in a number of his short stories Melville was able to establish a surprisingly consistent persona. Perhaps because of the very shortness of the form, he was able to keep his materials under better control than in his longer fiction, those risky voyages where he was apt to be caught by "a blast resistless" and blown far off course. Certainly the best of his short stories in this regard is "Bartleby," but the short sketch which served as an introduction to a volume of his collected stories, *Piazza Tales*, perhaps better suits the present purpose. Not only is the narrator a quester after mystery, but the imagery and situation recall both the "Fragment" and *Typee*. By examining it, we can see materials which appear in the early work integrated into an example of Melville's mature craft.

Notes

1. Pagination, indicated in parentheses, refers to the Northwestern University Press and the Newberry Library edition of *Typee* (Evanston and Chicago, 1968).

Typee and *Omoo*: Herman Melville and the Ungraspable Phantom of Identity

Robert E. Abrams*

In Book XXI of *Pierre*, Melville envisages the artist who has gained the "ultimate element" in his quest for esthetic maturity as someone "fairly afloat in himself." In contrast to those securely committed to a fixed interpretation of experience and to a well-defined self-image, the great creator lacks a settled moral, intellectual, and psychological identity; he does not need one, for he can "float over all bottomlessnesses with a jeering impunity."[1] Certainly such a vision of the artist as a man "afloat" is applicable to Melville himself, for like so many writers—like Shakespeare whom he so much admired, like Keats, Joyce, and Gide—Melville appears to have written not out of a firmly established identity, but, rather, out of a capacity to enter sympathetically into and to temporarily inhabit multiple speaking voices, philosophical postures, and states of mind. As Richard Poirier has written, it is hard to make out "some imaginable psychological shape called the author"[2] behind Melville's conflicting perspectives and styles. "What we have," according to Charles Feidelson, Jr., "is not a portrait of the man who lived in Pittsfield and New York, but a kind of presence—hardly a portrait—of the artist."[3] As "the artist," Melville is unencumbered by a finite, self-compromising identity. Certainly it is the elastic, infinitely available "artist" in him and not the finite public "man"—the public man's "reputation," so goes the famous letter to Hawthorne, being "horrible,"[4] who prefers speaking through a multitude of fictional personae rather than in his own proper person, who writes in mockery of closed systems and beliefs rather than out of them, who declares in a letter to Hawthorne in the autumn of 1851: "This is a long letter . . . . Possibly, if you . . . answer it, and direct it to Herman Melville, you will missend it—for the very fingers that now guide this pen are not precisely the same that just took it up and put it on this paper. Lord, when shall we be done changing? (17[?] November 1851, p. 143). Like Keats, Melville could well have written: "As to the poetical Character itself, (I mean that sort of which, if I am any thing, I am a

*Reprinted from *Arizona Quarterly*, 31 (Spring, 1975), 33–50, by permission of *Arizona Quarterly*. This selection is taken from pp. 33–45.

Member; . . .) it is not itself—it has no self—it is every thing and nothing. . . ."[5]

To be sure, Melville hardly began writing books as a man "afloat in himself." The lad who returned home from the South Seas to delight his sisters with tales of the cannibals had no doubt been morally and intellectually stretched by his travels, but he remained enough the upright grandson of General Peter Gansevoort to consent to a shave in order to "make himself presentable . . . to his mother."[6] Soon, however, he retired to his study to write *Typee* (1846) and *Omoo* (1847)—books which, I hope to show, began revealing to him the unsuspected "bottomlessnesses" of his being. As in the case of the artist Crispin in Wallace Stevens's "The Comedian as the Letter C," the young novelist's tidy little "mythology of self"—formed and reinforced in the genteel drawing rooms of Pearl Street, Bleecker Street, and lower Broadway, New York City—was "blotched out beyond unblotching"[7] as he poured himself into the evolving narrative "I" of these tales.

Traditional readings of *Typee* and *Omoo* have failed to make this sufficiently clear. Over the years critics have approached the two books in a variety of ways—as "breezy memoirs of travel," as explorations of the "problem of authority," as a "defense of the Noble Savage and a eulogy of his happy life," as a reluctant acknowledgment that man belongs in the harsh and insecure world of experience in spite of his nostalgia for a lost Eden, and as an introduction to the "Melvillian rover, the man destined for an endless voyage."[8] I would argue, however, that what is most important about these early tales—at least from the standpoint of Melville's artistic development—is that they record his growing awareness of the fundamental elasticity and mutability of his so-called "identity." Certainly Melville acknowledges that he has experienced the liberating loss of a static "mythology of self" through the act of writing his early novels in his widely quoted letter to Hawthorne: "Until I was twenty-five [when Melville began *Typee*], I had no development at all. From my twenty-fifth year I date my life. Three weeks have scarcely passed, at any time between then and now, that I have not unfolded within myself" (1[?] June 1851, p. 130).

It is significant that Melville's first two works show him entering his protean literary existence through the doorway of anthropology, becoming aware of what Ruth Benedict has termed the fundamental "plasticity" of the self through an enlightening peep out of the provincial West into other cultures. According to Benedict, the central tenet of modern anthropology is that a man never perceives reality "with pristine eyes"; rather, he sees self and world largely as "edited" by the "customs and institutions and ways of thinking" of his society.[9] Such a revelation is anticipated by Melville in his early novels as he stumbles upon the jolting discovery that his identity has been by and large invented for him by his culture—a deceptively permanent impress upon inherently fluid and ductile material. In the clash of Western and Polynesian images of man, his voyaging fictional surrogate begins to suspect that there is no fixed human essence, no static, graspable pattern behind such varied and contradictory forms. Above all, he becomes skeptical of and thus liberated from all closed definitions of himself.

It should be stressed that the loss of a self-defining "mythology," which, however inhibiting and delusive, provides Melville's narrating alter ego with an "I" out of which he can speak, a self he can offer confidently to the world, occurs slowly, reluctantly, painfully. *Typee*, Melville's first South Sea romance, by and large stresses the horror of such a loss. D. H. Lawrence writes in his classic study of this strange tale of captivity in a cannibal valley: "Try to go back to the savages, and you feel as if your very soul was decomposing inside you." Lawrence emphasizes that this is "what really happens." If one stays too long among the savages, one gradually goes "to pieces."[10] It is precisely the "decomposing" of his white, western self, the fear of his going utterly "to pieces" in the cannibal valley, which so appalls Tom in "Paradise." The moment Melville's fictional delegate enters the land of the Typees, it becomes apparent that he has wandered into a world where the old, familiar terms through which he has hitherto conceived of his identity are no longer valid, no longer understood:

> I . . . intimated that I was known as "Tom." But . . . the chief could not master it: "Tommo," "Tomma," "Tommee," every thing but plain "Tom." As he persisted in garnishing the word with an additional syllable, I compromised the matter with him at the word "Tommo;" and by that name I went during my entire stay in the valley. (p. 72)

The tone of the passage indicates that the experience of being unrecognized as "plain 'Tom' " is not entirely unwelcome to Melville's hero. He emerges in early chapters as something of the voyaging incognito that Hazlitt so alluringly depicts himself as in "On Going on a Journey"— the man who takes to the open road in order to lose a reputation and a name and to become freely anonymous among strangers. Like Toby, his one close companion aboard the *Dolly*, Melville's wanderer has "moved in a different sphere of life" (p. 32) but is now in voluntary exile from it, never alluding to his specific origin and roots. Indeed, Paul Witherington notes that a close reading of the episode in which the young renegade introduces himself to the Typee chief reveals that his name is not even definitely "Tom," never mind the "Tommo" that the Typees recast it into: "I . . . intimated that I was known as 'Tom.' But I could not have made a worse selection."[11] Even before his entry into the Typee valley, then, "Tom" has become a runaway incognito, untethered from his past and evidently in the habit of "selecting" his name at will. But among the cannibals he becomes too invisible and nameless to himself, and he begins trying desperately to close up the yawning hole in his identity he in large measure has opened.

In some ways anticipating Pip, that later, more unfortunate Melvillian castaway who loses his identity to the sea because it fails utterly to acknowledge him, to reflect him back to himself, Tom becomes exasperated and then fearful as he fails to find confirming reflections of his white, western self in the land of the Typees. To this insular tribe of cannibals, he exists abstracted from all historical contexts and commitments. "I have no doubt," he writes of his entrance along with Toby into the Typee valley, "that we were the first white men who ever penetrated thus far into their territories" (p. 74). To the cannibals Tom is largely an invisible man, his country and his traditions, his language, religion, and dress, all beyond their comprehension. Such invisibility becomes especially frightening to him after Toby's disappearance. Then the insidious (if utterly guileless) nullification of his white, western self Tom experiences among the Typees—their tendency to speak to him in their own language as if he "could understand every word" (p. 81), their assumption that he will regard the tatooing of his face as "beautifying" (p. 219)—reaches critical proportions. In large measure the savages simply *do not see* Tom, and the implication of *Typee*, indeed, the implication of so much of Melville's fiction, is that our fragile identities must in some way be externalized, objectified, tangibly reflected back to us, in order to exist. Locked up and invisible inside himself, on the threshold of psychological annihilation, Tom becomes frantic to surface and to elicit a confirming external response: "There was no one with whom I could freely converse; no one to whom I could communicate my thoughts; no one who could sympathise [sic] with my sufferings. A thousand times I thought how much more endurable would have been my lot had Toby still been with me. But I was left alone, and the thought was terrible to me" (p. 231).

Although invisible to the cannibals in his white, western identity, the intruder does become perceived by and accepted among them as "Tommo"—their own image of him largely based on their provincial assumptions of what constitutes self. In the same way that they cannot conceive of his name without a final vowel, so do they automatically assume that he will desire to have his face tatooed, that he will want to walk around naked to the waist, that he will be sufficiently challenged by their daily round of bland, easy tasks. They see not the actual white intruder but, to refer again to Ruth Benedict's metaphor, a culturally "edited" version of him. It is to Tom "edited" and Typeeanized that they persist in addressing themselves—offering him poee-poee, for example, and assuming that he will know how to eat it, and continually chastising him for breaking their taboos as if he knew better. His queer, unaccountable lapses from Type decorum and logic never fail to amaze them. His objection to the tatooing of his face, for example, "surpassed his majesty's comprehension," for how could a "sober-minded and sensible individual" (p. 219) not desire the operation? Again and again the Typees reopen the subject. They evidently are incapable of grasping Tom's motives for refusal.

The Typees, then, are not maliciously insensitive to the habits and mores of their guest; they act out of innocence. Yet innocence—as *Billy Budd*, decades after *Typee*, makes so disturbingly clear—has its aggressive underside; it seeks above all else to preserve itself, shying away from discomforting revelations when possible, striking out when put too uncompromisingly on the spot. At the root of the savages' failure to acknowledge the white man in Tom no doubt lurks their subconscious recognition that in him they have come upon a truly odd bird threatening to undermine their most elemental notions regarding universe and self. So threatened, they are anxious to dress the stranger in tappa cloth, to put their Typee markings on his queer western face—in short, to negate the alien intruder by gobbling him up. Identity being precarious in the world of *Typee*, it is either gobble up or be gobbled. Certainly the image early in the book of the cannibal king dressed by the French "in a magnificent military uniform, stiff with gold lace" (p. 7), suggests that the swallowing up of other identities in defense of one's own is a universal trait among threateningly varied forms of men.

That one can in large measure be swallowed up and transformed is demonstrated by an increasingly fatalistic Tom as he begins to "bury . . . all remembrances" of his "previous existence" (p. 144) and to yield to Typee ways. The cannibalization of his identity is not merely a matter of superficial alterations—the tappa cloth at first "modified" to suit his "views of propriety" (p. 121) but later worn naked to the waist, or his learning to eat, even to "relish" (p. 209), raw fish. Among the Typees the white renegade's very consciousness of reality starts to give way as well. "In the altered frame of mind to which I have referred," Tom writes, "every object . . . struck me in a new light" (p. 126). His old, western assumptions regarding money, status, competition, and fine dress are steadily undermined. So is his western sense of time. Losing "all knowledge of the regular recurrence of the days of the week" (p. 123) in the lazy, languorous valley, Melville's renegade begins to experience time as it exists for the Typees—less pressing, less hurried, less meticulously and anxiously measured. More and more the captive accommodates himself to Typee habits and learns to see reality through Typee eyes. His metamorphosis into a savage, however, ends abruptly when the cannibals threaten to tatoo his face: "This incident opened my eyes . . . and I now felt convinced that in some luckless hour I should be disfigured in such a manner as never more to have the *face* to return to my countrymen" (p. 219). "When at Rome do as the Romans do" (p. 209) may become the motto of a progressively more Typeeanized Tom, but he balks at the requested surrender of his very face, a true point of no return. After this episode his life becomes "one of absolute wretchedness" (p. 231) and he searches frantically for ways to flee the cannibal Typees.

Melville's first novel, then, certainly *verges* on the recognition, so strongly developed in such later works as *The Confidence-Man*, that a man's identity is ultimately flimsy, mutable, subject to startling transformations. Among the savages Tom's dress, his eating habits, his very sense of reality begin to alter. His metamorphosis, to be sure, is aborted in horror. At the time of the tale's writing, Melville's hero has managed to escape the cannibal valley and to return to the "bustle and stir" of a "busy city" (p. 244); there, presumably, he has reclaimed his old name, resumed his old forms; he is one of us come home. But the question persists: Who, *ultimately*, is he? Having returned to Mother and Home, he no doubt behaves quite sincerely like a "quiet, sober-minded, modest young man" (p. 152)—the picture he offers of himself in all earnestness in Chapter 20. But surely in jumping ship with Toby, in chuckling at the cannibal queen's exposure of her "sweet form" (p. 8), above all, in flouting "the ridiculous affectations of gentility" (p. 127) among palm trees and bare-chested Typee girls, he has assumed a far different character than the one alloted him in the drawing room. Ultimately, his identity remains as problematic and open as the inscrutable "hieroglyphics" discovered on Polynesian queen and American sailor alike under their costumes in Chapter 1.

Nonetheless, it is important to stress that in self-consciously writing up his South Sea adventures for home consumption, Tom the former renegade, now an aspiring celebrity and novelist, tries to project a far more stable, socially acceptable self than is actually warranted by his tale. So very much the genteel youth, at times, is Tom the reminiscing narrator, so attentive to the drawing-room proprieties, that Richard Ruland regards him as an intensely audience-conscious storyteller squirming under the eye of "the vast public for informative, uplifting . . . writing."[12] Reaching outward to that "vast public"—to the subscribers of Murray's Home and Colonial Library, to the reviewers of the stodgy London *Athenaeum*, to Judge Lemuel Shaw of Boston to whom the English edition of the book is "affectionately" dedicated—the narrator-hero of *Typee* (barely distinguishable to readers of the novel from twenty-five-year-old Herman Melville himself) seems anxious not to shock or to offend. The self he *consciously* projects thus tends to be a publicly authorized one obligingly pictured according to approved models. Certainly such an obligingly pictured Tom emerges in his narration of his first encounter with Typee girls:

> These lively young ladies were . . . wonderfully polite and humane; fanning aside the insects that occasionally lighted on our brows; presenting us with food; and compassionately regarding me in the midst of my afflic-

tions. But in spite of all their blandishments, my feelings of propriety were exceedingly shocked, for I could not but consider them as having over-stepped the due limits of female decorum. (p. 77)

Even in the much discussed Chapter 26, full of criticisms of the mis-sionaries and Rousseauistic celebrations of savage simplicity and grace, an essentially genteel Tom is careful not to overstep "the due limits." His polite, decorous voice reveals an ultimate deference to the standards of the parlor. By and large he sounds like an earnest Victorian schoolboy criticizing his elders only because he has taken their teachings and ad-monitions to heart. "Let the savages be civilized," he agrees, "but civilize them with benefits, and not with evils; and let heathenism be destroyed, but not by destroying the heathen" (p. 195). Tom is Rousseau made safe for the middle-class fireside. He ends his little lecture on cannibals and missionaries with the conciliatory admission that his "reflections . . . may not be free from error. If such be the case, I claim no further indulgence than should be conceded to every man whose object is to do good" (p. 199).

Typee, then, is narrated by an intensely audience-conscious Tom, a Tom afraid of going too far, of violating too flagrantly prescribed usages and forms. His South Sea escapades often prove irksomely embarrassing to him and one gets the impression that he has swept much under the rug. No doubt such a narrating "I" is in part attributable to revisions of the novel made by Gansevoort Melville and John Murray (or his reader) before its London publication. Since the original manuscript is lost, it is impossible in many instances to tell where, specifically, the book has been altered, but it is clear that Tom is Melville edited, Melville somewhat redone "on the score of taste."[13] It is highly doubtful, however, that Tom as edited by Murray represents a radical departure from Melville's own personality and voice. Certainly in his letters to family and to friends—to his sister Catherine, to Duyckinck his New York editor, to the eminently respectable Judge Shaw—the young author of *Typee* sounds very much like his decorous narrator. "What a charming name is yours," he writes with a flourish to his sister,"—the most engaging I think in our whole family circle.—I dont' [sic] know how it is precisely, but I have always been very partial to this particular appellative & can not avoid investing the person who bears it, with certain quite captivating attributes" (20 Jan. 1845, pp. 21–22). More than a year later, Melville is assuring the august Judge Shaw that he will "not soon forget that agreeable visit to Boston"—a visit during which, presumably, he has assiduously obeyed "the due limits of . . . decorum" with "Miss Elizabeth" (19 March 1846, p. 24). Such letters reveal a Melville still very much under the sway of the parlor, too dedicated to "our whole family circle," its sentiments, aspira-tions, and forms, to allow himself—even in imagination—to betray too markedly the mid-nineteenth-century ideal of the modest young man.

Nonetheless, the semi-autobiographical *Typee* is a strange and unorthodox book. Memories of the South Seas obviously tug at Melville's narrating alter ego Tom, threatening to undermine the safe, respectable, middle-class persona he is trying to sustain. The decision to jump ship proves especially difficult for him to smooth over. "To use the concise, point-blank phrase of the sailors," he begins, wincing at being forced to abandon the euphemisms of the parlor, "I had made up my mind to 'run away.' " Quickly, however, he retreats from such a vulgar, "point-blank" characterization of himself: "Now as a meaning is generally attached to these two words in no way flattering to the individual to whom they are applied, it behoves me, for the sake of my own character, to offer some explanation of my conduct." Tom's verbal control over his "character" is finally reestablished in the schoolboy defense of self which follows: "In all contracts, if one party fail to perform his share of the compact, is not the other virtually absolved from his liability? Who is there who will not answer in the affirmative?" (p. 20).

Passages such as this call into question Paul Witherington's recent reading of *Typee* as "an experimental novel" which "openly searches for forms with which to convey the increasing complexity of its ideas."[14] Tom the retrospective narrator, Melville's literary ambassador to the world at large, is simply too anxious to preserve what he terms "my own character" to abandon too baldly authorized attitudes, stances, and tones. Concerned from beginning to end with the moral figure he is striking, he ends up offering a generally safe, censored vision of experience expressed through stilted and euphemistic prose. Fascinating (but morally objectionable) scenes are obligingly expunged: "The varied dances of the Marquesan girls are beautiful in the extreme, but there is an abandoned voluptuousness in their character which I dare not attempt to describe" (p. 15). Off-color events which the decorous Tom does "dare to describe" tend to elicit his clucking disapproval: "Not the feeblest barrier was interposed between the unholy passions of the crew and their unlimited gratification. The grossest licentiousness and the most shameful inebriety prevailed" (p. 15). Tom's narrative is flawed by his anxiety to relate his wild adventures through a voice that will be morally and esthetically acceptable to his audience. For the only publicly authorized voice available to him is that of the drawing room, the public school essay, the "sentimental" novel—a voice patently unequal to his South Sea adventures, distorting them by reducing them to its own genteel terms: "To the gratification of my palate . . . [the cannibals] paid the most unwearied attention. They continually invited me to partake of food, and when after eating . . . I declined the viands they continued to offer me, they seemed to think that my appetite stood in need of some piquant stimulant to excite its activity" (p. 113).

To be sure, not all scenes in *Typee* are so stiltedly rendered. The cannibal queen's unforgettable exposure of her "hieroglyphics" is hardly standard fare for readers of the Home and Colonial Library, and during one loose moment, Tom does "dare" to describe the Marquesan dancing girls: "The Marquesan girls dance all over . . . . In good sooth, they . . . sway their floating forms, arch their necks, toss aloft their naked arms, and glide, and swim, and whirl" (p. 152). Tom is no doubt fond of the Typees; he is "fain to confess" that in many ways the savages enjoy "an infinitely happier . . . existence" (p. 124) than is possible in Victorian drawing rooms. But when all is said and done, they are "nothing better than a set of cannibals" (p. 118), and if "Miss Fayaway" is selected for special attention, it is because, like all good heroines of sentimental novels, she has "blue eyes" (p. 86) and features as "perfectly formed as the heart . . . of man could desire" (p. 85) and, above all, a "mind . . . swayed by gentle impulses hardly to be anticipated from one in her condition" (p. 108). Such statements help validate Tom's credentials as a gentleman of the parlor even as he narrates his strange sojourn among the cannibals. But the whole experience (as he remarks specifically of the Marquesan girls' dances) "was almost too much for a quiet, sober-minded, modest young man like myself" (p. 152).

Notes

1. Throughout this article, citations to *Typee, Omoo, Mardi,* and *Pierre*—here to pp. 283–84 of *Pierre*—are to the Northwestern-Newberry Edition of *The Writings of Herman Melville* (Vols. I, II, III, and VII), ed. Harrison Hayford, Hershel Parker, and G. Thomas Tanselle (Evanston and Chicago: Northwestern University Press and The Newberry Library, 1968–1971). Subsequent citations to these novels will appear in the text.

2. *The Performing Self: Compositions and Decompositions in the Languages of Contemporary Life* (New York: Oxford University Press, 1971), p. 8.

3. *Symbolism and American Literature* (Chicago: The University of Chicago Press, 1953), p. 163.

4. Dated 1(?) June 1851, as printed in *The Letters of Herman Melville,* ed. Merrell R. Davis and William H. Gilman (New Haven: Yale University Press, 1960), p. 130. Subsequent citations to Melville's letters are to this edition and will appear in the text.

5. Letter to Richard Woodhouse, dated 27 October 1818, as printed in *The Letters of John Keats,* ed. Hyder Edward Rollins (Cambridge: Harvard University Press, 1958), I, 386–87.

6. Letter from Gansevoort Melville to his brother Allan, mid-October (?) 1844, as paraphrased in *The Melville Log,* ed. Jay Leyda (New York: Harcourt, Brace and World, 1951), I, 187.

7. *The Collected Poems of Wallace Stevens* (New York: Alfred A. Knopf, 1965), p. 28.

8. For the discussions referred to, see Harry Levin, *The Power of Blackness* (New York: Alfred A. Knopf, 1958); Nicholas Canaday, Jr., *Melville and Authority,* University of Florida Monographs, Humanities, No. 28 (Gainesville: University of Florida Press, 1968); Charles Roberts Anderson, *Melville in the South Seas* (New York: Columbia University Press, 1939); William B. Dillingham, *An Artist in the Rigging: The Early Work of Herman Melville* (Athens: University of Georgia Press, 1972); and Feidelson, *Symbolism.* Probably the two best pieces of criticism on the early novels are D. H. Lawrence's chapter on them in *Studies in Classic American Literature* (New York: Thomas Seltzer, 1923), pp. 193–213, and Edwin M.

Eigner's "The Romantic Unity of Melville's *Omoo*," *Philological Quarterly*, 46 (January 1967), 96–108. Both critics address themselves to what Lawrence terms the potential psychological "decomposing" of a white man in the "non-moral tropics."

9. *Patterns of Culture* (Boston: Houghton Mifflin Company, 1934), pp. 1–20.

10. *Studies*, pp. 203–04.

11. The passage quoted in my text (p. 72 of *Typee*) is referred to by Witherington in "The Art of Melville's *Typee*," *Arizona Quarterly*, 26 (Summer 1970), 144.

12. "Melville and the Fortunate Fall: Typee as Eden," *Nineteenth-Century Fiction*, 23 (December 1968), 318.

13. For this and other information of the circumstances surrounding the publication of *Typee*, see the Historical Note by Leon Howard in the Northwestern-Newberry Edition of the novel, pp. 277–302.

14. "Art of Melville's *Typee*," p. 139.

Melville's *Typee*: Fact, Fiction, and Esthetics

Michael Clark*

A balanced analysis of Herman Melville's *Typee* cannot lightly accept a simple judgment of the book, for its critical history is riddled with contradictory assertions and opinions. It has been classified as fiction, autobiography, and travel literature, with certitude on all sides, but without general agreement. We do know that the events in *Typee* have their basis in Melville's life, that Melville affirmed to his publisher, John Murray, the book to be factual, that the book was first published in Murray's series of travel literature, and that Richard Tobias Greene turned up after *Typee* was published and confirmed as true those events he had personally witnessed.[1] Furthermore, recent critics have given carefully considered analyses of *Typee* which stress its factual nature. F. O. Matthiessen, for example, has called the book a "record of experience"[2] and, recently, Charles R. Anderson has pointed out the book's technical flaws and chosen to call it a "loose fictional chronicle" rather than a novel.[3] In addition, Anderson's original study of *Typee, Melville in the South Seas*, reveals to what extent Melville's first book is rooted in the author's experience in the Pacific.[4] And it is the facts, apparently, which have relegated *Typee* to the travel and autobiographical sections of the library shelves.

But *Typee* is much more than a factual account of Melville's sojourn in the South Seas. John Murray, with a publisher's sixth sense, detected the "taint of fiction"[5] and Irving, hearing portions of the work read, deemed the book "exquisite" and the style "graphic."[6] And although an early reviewer objected to the liberties both in morals and in facts that *Typee* presented, he nevertheless judged the book to be "not without literary merit."[7] This initial approbation of the book's "readability" has continued with modern critics such as Richard Ruland[8] and Paul Witherington,[9] who have attempted to account for the book's final effect on the reader by examining artistic techniques such as symbolism, imagery, and structure. Granting the validity of some of their insights and, with some reservations, of their classification of *Typee* as belles-lettres, certain problems remain.

*Reprinted from *Arizona Quarterly*, 34 (1978), 351–70, by permission of *Arizona Quarterly*.

211

What is the relationship between literal fact and symbol? Where does fact shade into imaginary event? And at what point does imaginary reconstruction of an event become fiction? These questions have plagued critics of *Typee* since it was first published. And these questions have been raised, I think, largely because Melville has managed in his first book to do so much with the given facts. Although any report of a South Seas adventure might have had an inherent interest to the receptive, curious audience of mid-nineteenth-century America, Melville manages to transcend the bland reportage that, we might imagine, characterized the average travel book of the period, the majority of which have long since been forgotten. But whether Melville reconstituted his personal experiences with the conscious artistry that some critics have asserted is a question that will not be easily resolved. The problem has come to revolve around the question of "conscious intention." The critic often assumes that he can ascertain what exactly Melville "designed" in writing *Typee*. Yet this emphasis seems to be misplaced, for nothing we know of Melville's writing habits suggests a "design," except in the most rudimentary sense.

I believe that any attempt to bring to bear conventional concepts of genre to the study of Melville's writings, especially of *Typee*, invites an examination of the discrepancies between the convention and Melville's work, his "botches."[10] Perhaps, then, what is needed is not the usual prescriptive analysis but a descriptive approach to Melville's work. Instead of reading *Typee* and expecting the book to measure up to preconceived notions of genre, perhaps it is more useful to ask oneself how, in fact, the book manages to entertain. What makes the facts come alive? The emphasis in such an approach is on expression rather than on form (in the normal conception of novelistic form). For no matter how much we can argue about Melville's artistry, conscious or otherwise, there is no doubt that when he wrote *Typee*, the author possessed an acutely sensitive esthetic sensibility and that the results of that mind working on interesting personal experiences would necessarily produce a book that was both complex and expressive of the author's rich emotional life.

The major concern of this article, then, will not be on "the novel *Typee*," but rather on the character who calls himself Tommo, who creates a work of prose from that complex, essentially unanalyzable organ, the mind. The emphasis on the narrator telling the reader about his perceptions of the world allows us to reevaluate *Typee* by the esthetic assumptions that the narrator himself, either knowingly or unknowingly, possesses. Therefore, for our purposes, the narrator is not important as a character, at least not in the normal sense of the word. As Charles Feidelson, Jr., has noted, Tommo is less a character than "a capacity for perception."[11] Furthermore, the *way* he sees is of central concern to us here. The product of his perception is not the finely conceived architectonics of the conventional fictional mode, as some critics, notably Charles

R. Anderson (noted above), have cogently argued. Nevertheless, it would be incorrect to say that Melville is not concerned with form. What is obvious in *Typee*, whether the author intended it or not, is an intensely concentrated effort by Melville to find the formal components of expression which fit most closely his perceptions: the two are essentially related and are fundamentally esthetic in nature. This paper will analyze the nature of the narrator's perception by examining the basic artistic principles which Melville—like all artists, in whatever medium—uses to achieve his goal of expressing his impressions of the world: harmony, balance, centrality, and development (or progression). These elements are what esthetician Dilman Gotshalk identifies as the "chief formal principles used by the imagination of artists for the purification and enhancement of existential structure in works of art."[12] And as I hope to show, these principles, though Melville had no reason to be conscious of them, constituted his sensibilities even at the young age of twenty-five and determined that he was much more than a writer of travel literature, in *Typee* as well as in later works.

Before examining *Typee* specifically, it will be useful both to define our terms and to justify this unusual approach. It is especially necessary to explain our terminology since some critics have examined Melville's fiction from an esthetic approach. For example, of the four commonly accepted esthetic principles, balance has often been linked with Melville's art. But rather than being examined strictly as an esthetic principle, balance is usually considered as a quality of Melville's work that has its roots in the democratic experience, which is peculiar to American writers. Matthiessen suggests this connection when he states that Melville always retained "a firm hold on the conception of a balanced society, on the desirable relation of man to man."[13] More recently, Beongcheon Yu also associates political equality with this esthetic principle in *Moby-Dick*.[14]

Without denying the pertinence of the political influence, one might be more justified in saying that the relationship between politics and esthetic qualities is more complex. First, it seems that balance is not important to the writer for the same reasons that it is important to the politician or to the political ethos of the people. Thus the principle of balance, I think, has not a direct but an indirect link to the American political experience. The reasons for this are complex, but they lie in the fact that the condition of democracy makes severe demands on the writer; it separates him from traditional values but gives him nothing in return. This fact has been admirably summarized by Loren Baritz, who notes the effect on the writer of the democracy that the American Revolution produced:

> Theology was dead, politics exhausted, and philosophy inaccessible because of a relative lack of facilities and training. Creative Americans were largely forced back on their own individual resources in the antebellum period by virtue of their being Americans.[15]

But the effects of the new democracy on American writers were more far-reaching than the post-revolutionary-war period. As late as 1916, John Dos Passos felt the unusual demands placed on the writer in America. Because the American past was predicated on the dissolution of the Old World ties, Dos Passos notes, the American artist is cut off from useful traditions and must rely on his own "glowing life within."[16] And this "glowing life" of the American artist constitutes the basic components of man's perceptive abilities, which include not only a devotion to "balance" but also, as I hope to show, to the other form-giving qualities—harmony, centrality, and progression. These four elements need not to have been learned by Melville, for all men possess them, though artists, to be sure, are gifted with these qualities to an unusually refined degree.

This introduction will permit us to see, then, that what Melville needed to begin a writing career was not a knowledge of the developing novel genre; he needed only a mind which was open to the esthetic possibilities that life had to offer. A theory of fiction is not as necessary as is a mind which is open to experience and which can extract from experience elements which reveal the author's own unique vision of life. It is this quality, I think, which prompts Warner Berthoff to describe Melville's narrators as possessing a "reserved freedom of response" which manifests itself in the "rhythm of their absorption and detachment."[17] Melville's narrators have minds which seem naked of the dress of affiliations. They perceive reality directly, without any link with a political or religious ethos. This quality is much like what Melville in *Clarel* ascribed to Nathan, who, like Melville himself, did not find religious acceptance easy:

> Alone, and at Doubt's freezing pole
> He wrestled with the pristine forms
> Like the first man. By inner storms
> Held in solution, so his soul
> Ripened for hour of such control
> As shapes, concretes.[18]

These brilliant lines, in which imagery beautifully amplifies the ideas, can be fruitfully applied to Melville's own quest for expression. The man alone confronts the chaotic experiences of his life and struggles to find the suitable "shapes" to express adequately the emotional content of those experiences.

How does one begin to analyze this person Tommo who tells us his story? Perhaps the best starting point is to identify the unusual qualities that the mind of this narrator evinces in the most trying of circumstances, cannibal captivity. For the predominant quality of the narrator's consciousness is its impressionability, whether for fear, for the unusual, or for the beautiful. His mind actively seeks to measure itself against significant experience, and his concern with beauty in general illustrates his strong esthetic bent. As we shall see, Tommo reveals a pervasive attraction for purely esthetic qualities. Thus it is tempting to accept at face value the later evaluation Melville made in *Clarel* of his younger self. Like Tommo, the young Melville was both adventurer and sensitive observer; he

> . . . supplemented Plato's theme
> With daedal life in boats and tents,
> A messmate of the elements;
> And yet, more bronzed in face than mind,
> Sensitive still and frankly kind.[19]

How susceptible he is to the pleasing impression is manifest throughout *Typee*. A good example of this is the first sight Tommo gets of Typee valley. The vision so overwhelms him, Tommo says, that "had a glimpse of the gardens of Paradise been revealed to me I could scarcely have been more ravished with the sight" (p. 49). And we are led to believe that the exquisite charm of this vision plays no small part in overcoming his scruples about descending into the valley and, therefore, risking a possible encounter with cannibals. And we are told that once among the natives, his inclination to escape is effectively subverted one time by the "soothing influence" on his mind of the "beauty of the scene" (p. 110). Another example of his sensibilities is his description of the natives' beauty to be comparable to that of a "sculptor's model" (p. 180).

A more striking and sustained example of the narrator's concern with esthetic experience is manifested in his reaction to the mundane domestic activity of making tappa. A less likely example of esthetic appreciation would be difficult to find. But this practical activity is transmuted by Tommo into an enjoyable experience. After a long description of the tappa-making process, Tommo notes that the result is a cloth of "dazzling whiteness" (p. 148). And though the Typees prefer the relatively staid "natural tint," that does not stop the narrator from describing the esthetic possibilities of the simple cloth, to which he has at other times been exposed. "The notable wife of Kammahammaha," he notes, "used to pride herself in the skill she displayed in dyeing her tappa with contrasting colors disposed in regular figures" (p. 148). And then, as if to stress that he is open to every possibility of appreciation, Tommo notes that he

> was often attracted by the noise of the mallet, which, when employed in the manufacture of the cloth, produces at every stroke of its hard, heavy wood, a clear, ringing, and musical sound, capable of being heard at a great distance. When several of these implements happen to be in operation at the same time, and near one another, the effect upon the ear of a person, at a little distance, is really charming. (p. 148)

If making tappa is a useful art for the Typees, for Tommo it is an experience which can only be called esthetic. Surely, he is a walking art appreciation course, whose object is not a gallery of oils, but life itself.

It is obvious, then, that this finely tuned sensibility is more than receptive to esthetic experiences, even under the trying circumstances of captivity. His descriptions of his own passive susceptibility to the "beautiful" and "charming" tell us much about the esthetic nature of his consciousness. But as we have seen, the re-creation of his experiences, their transmutation into prose, reveals that his perceptions are of equal importance to the "facts" themselves. It is this shift of emphasis from object to perceiver, I think, which makes *Typee* so "readable," whereas other contemporary travel accounts did not receive the initial plaudits that *Typee* did, nor did they, for the most part, outlive their initial reception. Thus in *Typee* Melville manages to achieve what Susanne Langer calls "the illusion of life directly lived."[20] And this "illusion" is not contingent on the use—or on the nonuse—of "facts," for as Langer, again, notes, "a slavish transcript of actual life is dim beside the word-created experiences of virtual life, as a plaster mask made directly from a living subject is a dead counterfeit compared to even the most 'conservative' portrait sculpture."[21] In *Typee* Melville has for the most part effectively subordinated the facts to his own unique way of seeing, and he has done this by using what has been mentioned as the four formal elements of esthetic perception: centrality, development, harmony, and balance. His use of these four principles will now be examined in detail.

The first formal esthetic principle to be examined is centrality. Gotshalk defines this as the "confluence of perceptual interest to, or dominance of perceptual interest at, a point."[22] In fiction, this center of interest is often a first-person narrator, and even if the story is about someone else (say, a Bartleby or a Gatsby), then more often than not the narrator is still the object of interest, though in a much more subtle way. With omniscient or first-person narrators, the character of central interest is usually well defined. Yet whatever complications and ambiguities that may accumulate around this concept, it is clear that in *Typee* centrality can refer only to Tommo, the narrator.

Tommo not only invites our interest, but by his rhetorical manipulation of the fictive world, he demands it. It is clear from the beginning of the book that the reader's options for "choosing sides" are woefully one-sided. The *Dolly's* captain, for example, is "tyrannical" (p. 21), and "with a very few exceptions," Tommo notes, his crew "was composed of a parcel of dastardly and mean-spirited wretches, divided among themselves, and only united in enduring without resistance the unmitigated tyranny of the captain" (p. 21). Likewise, with certain qualifications, David Williams's article on *Typee* is correct in pointing out that even Toby suffers by contrast to Tommo because of the latter's "self-aggrandizement and self-congratulation."[23] But rather than criticize Tommo's delineation of the uniqueness of his own character, it seems more useful to appreciate his unceasing efforts to define his world, which is, whether in regard to self or to environment, characteristic of Melville's fiction.

Tommo is, then, a character who is intensely aware of his individuality. Indeed, his impulse to jump ship derives from the insoluble conflict of his individuality with the world. What he lacks on board ship, of course, is free expression, but, unknown to him, repression also awaits him in the Typee valley. For example, although gratification of bodily desires is never a problem in the valley, he is nevertheless restrained from free bodily movement. Note, for instance, the language he employs to describe the hindrance to his going to meet Toby, who had been rumored (falsely) to have returned: the chief who stops Tommo had an "inflexible rigidity of expression," put "his hand upon my shoulder," assumed "a tone of authority," issued an "unexpected command," made "efforts to restrain me," and "reiterated his commands still more sternly" (p. 119). The quick succession of inhibiting gestures and words gives an urgency to Tommo's desires for freedom. Consequently, it seems that the isolation he had felt on shipboard is not necessarily the result of "self-aggrandizement" as Williams would have us believe. Rather, it is a sign of the tragic isolation that all men participate in. And thus his shipboard alienation is mirrored in his similarly oppressed condition in Typee: "There was no one with whom I could freely converse; no one to whom I could communicate my thoughts; no one who could sympathise with my sufferings" (p. 231). It is this insight into a man's isolated condition on which the story's telling is predicated. Centrality, then, has to do less with egomania than with a realization that life is by nature a tragic affair.

The second esthetic principle of form that we shall examine is development. In the novel, this is the progression of the story, the plot. Generally, plot suggests a series of related actions which develop momentum because of complication. But for Melville this rather sophisticated technique was not to be discovered until *Mardi*, where it is imperfectly realized. And it would not be used with effectiveness until he came to write *Moby-Dick*. But in *Typee* the mainsprings of action are weak. The source of action, of progression, in the story lies in a more fundamental realm than action. It lies in the consciousness of existence, which devolves from the narrator's sense of tragic isolation and is given expression in the metaphor of "seeing," which is suggested in the book's subtitle: "A *Peep* at Polynesian Life" (my italics). For the motivation for movement lies in the tension between a consciousness of a "lack" and a vision of fulfillment.

As I suggested, the word "peep" seems to have rich connotations for Melville. He seems to have associated the act of seeing with the discovery of the forbidden, of the unknown, and of the desirous, not just of physical things but also of the moral. For example, at the sexually suggestive dance scene in *Omoo* (which was cut from *Typee* because it was too risque) the narrator tells us that he and Long Ghost "had a peep at the dancers."[24] And in a later book, Pierre's fateful encounter with Isabel (which is of momentous consequence) is preceded by Mrs. Glendinning's seemingly innocuous remark that she wants to "peep in" at the girls in the Llanyllyns's sewing circle.[25] The act of "looking," then, has implications of moral discovery and either results from or is the cause of "curiosity," from which action becomes inevitable.

The sense of progression in Melville's fictive worlds has been ad-

mirably schematized by Charles Feidelson, Jr. For both Melville and
Emerson, Feidelson says, "life was a transition from one sphere to
another, each potentially including the former."[26] And for Melville, the
transition was activated by a literal and metaphoric vision. Thus
Tommo's intolerable state of existence aboard the *Dolly* makes the narrator daydream of a better state, which in his mind is potentially
achievable: "I straightway fell to picturing myself seated beneath a cocoa-
nut tree on the brow of the mountain, with a cluster of plantains within
easy reach" (p. 31). It matters little here that Tommo is unrealistic. His
vision of a condition better than his present one (on ship as well as in
Typee valley) plays no small role in his decisions to act. Likewise, his first
view of Typee valley reveals "a glimpse of the gardens of Paradise" (p. 49)
and, after some reservations, actuates Toby and Tommo to descend to the
floor of the valley. Yet the vision is belied by the presence of cannibals and
also by their first actual encounter with this Eden: when they attempt to
feed themselves, they find the fruit "much decayed" (p. 67). The innate
drive to penetrate to the core of existence, no matter how decayed it must
inevitably prove to be, is further illustrated by the final terrifying discovery in Typee valley. At the pi-pi, Tommo's attention is captured by a
vessel of wood: "prompted by a curiosity I could not repress . . . I raised
one end of the cover." What he discovers in looking, of course, is evidence
of cannibalism, "the last horrid revelation" (p. 238). But this is not the
last such discovery in the Melville canon, for the endless search is the in-
electuable condition of the Melvillean man, and the search is pro-
grammed to fail because the expectation which is engendered by the initial "peep" is always an ideal and as such cannot be realized.[27]

A third principle of esthetic form that Gotshalk defines is harmony,
which is qualified as possessing either complete similarity or partial
similarity. Gotshalk gives an example of harmony in literature as "the
repetition at a later stage of an earlier action in a drama."[28] Another
critic, De Witt Parker, calls this principle "thematic variation" in which a
theme is "elaborated and embroidered" in order to make it "echo and
reëcho in our minds."[29] In any case, this principle is most difficult of the
four to clearly define in fiction, though perhaps its closest parallel in the
literary critic's nomenclature is symbolism. Yet to avoid the problem of
determining whether Melville was consciously working in the symbolic
mode, it is enough to say that the incidents which concern us are important not for the clearly defined possibilities that they open up as much as
for their "resonance," their ability to create an ambience which is il-
lustrative of other, parallel situations. Gotshalk's distinction of "complete" and "partial" harmonies will be useful to our examination of
Typee.

An element which illustrates the principle of partial harmony is a
descriptive passage at the beginning of *Typee*. While I do not think that
this scene rises to the level of symbol, it does represent a rich field of allu-

sion, innuendo, and connotation that creates an ambience particularly helpful in understanding Tommo's situation.

> There is but one solitary tenant in the chicken coop, once a gay and dapper young cock, bearing him so bravely among the coy hens. But look at him now; there he stands, moping all the day long on that everlasting one leg of his. He turns with disgust from the mouldy corn before him, and the brackish water in his little trough. He mourns no doubt his lost companions, literally snatched from him one by one and never seen again. But his days of mourning will be few; for Mungo, our black cook, told me yesterday that the word had at last gone forth, and poor Pedro's fate was sealed. His attenuated body will be laid out upon the captain's table next Sunday, and long before night will be buried with all the usual ceremonies beneath that worthy individual's vest. Who would believe that there could be any one so cruel as to long for the decapitation of the luckless Pedro; yet the sailors pray every minute, selfish fellows, that the miserable fowl may be brought to his end. (p. 4)

Pedro is surely one to be pitied. And it is certainly helpful to the story that a theme of helplessness is introduced early to set the tone for Tommo's own misfortunes.

Yet a closer examination of the details of this tableau is rewarding, for there are many obvious parallels that can be drawn between Pedro and Tommo. The fact that Pedro is a "solitary tenant" does suggest the perpetual condition of Tommo (e.g., his alienation from his crewmates and his isolation in Typee valley). And like Pedro, Tommo has the use of only one good leg for much of the story. But the most striking feature of this story is the personification of the bird and, with that, the transmutation of a chicken dinner into a cannibal feast. The humor of the passage tends to disarm the reader and to distance the event from the obviously serious implication it carries for the rest of *Typee*. In particular, the passage casts the captain as a cannibal, and it implies that to Tommo, all experience (not just with savages) partakes of a life-threatening quality against which the narrator must continually battle. Thus the captain is a cannibal to Tommo, too, for he is "tyrannical" and gives a "scanty allowance" (p. 21) of substandard food (which again reminds us of Pedro). With only the least bit of displacement (for, after all, the cock does not escape the cannibal), the story of Pedro serves to amplify Tommo's own predicament.

"Complete harmony" is best illustrated in *Typee* by the relationship of Tommo to the character of Marnoo. This character is important to the plot of Melville's first book because by fortuitously appearing when he does, he reawakens Tommo's latent desire to escape from captivity. But Marnoo's actual role in Tommo's escape is largely second-hand and fails to justify Tommo's extended, flattering description of him. Therefore, although it is clear that Marnoo represents some sort of ideality, it is dif-

ficult to ascertain exactly what that ideality is. And Melville, as if to stress
the importance of this character, gives him for a moment the central position in the narrative. Tommo tells us, "When I observed the striking devotion of the natives to him [Marnoo], and their temporary withdrawal of
all attention from myself, I felt not a little piqued" (p. 137). The temporary displacement of primary interest, as we shall see, is justified by
thematic as well as by plot considerations.

The fact that Marnoo replaces Tommo for a short while as the center
of interest in the narrative suggests the thematic identification between
the two. The parallel can be seen most clearly in their respective assimilation of the artist's role. For example, there can be little doubt from the
way the native is described that Melville means Marnoo's ideality to be
suggestive of art and the art process. He has "natural eloquence," a
"grace" in his attitudes, "striking gestures," and the changing accents of
"the most accomplished orator" (p. 137). Furthermore, as Paul Witherington has suggested, Marnoo's tattoo of an "artu" tree may be a symbol
for art.[30] Also, the description of the native's tattooed back is clearly suggestive of an organic conception of art: "Upon his breast, arms, and legs,
were exhibited an infinite variety of figures; every one of which, however,
appeared to have reference to the general effect sought to be produced"
(p. 136). Thus Marnoo not only represents the free state that Tommo in
captivity longs for, but also the native seems to be "an exemplar of art" (as
Witherington notes), whom Tommo wishes to approximate in his narrative, both in eloquence and in the result of organic form.

But Marnoo's ideality demands further examination. Marnoo is the
one character in *Typee* who comes closest to fully integrating the totality
of experience. Not only is he a noble savage, a condition which Tommo
obviously admires, but also he is not restricted (as the other natives in
Typee valley are) by the deadening subconsciousness of the savage state.
Marnoo, like Tommo, possesses superiority over the natives because of his
exposure to civilization. Tommo describes it thus: "The natural quickness
of the savage had been wonderfully improved by his intercourse with the
white men, and his partial knowledge of a foreign language gave him a
great ascendancy over his less accomplished countrymen" (p. 140). He is
even given a position of honor in Typee valley, and the ease with which he
moves between such disparate cultures as the savage state and civilization
makes Marnoo an enviable model for Tommo. It is of no little concern,
then, that the "natural eloquence" and "striking gestures" that the native
employs in mastering the Typees are mirrored by Tommo in his escape
from the valley, when he importunes Mow-Mow with "an eloquence of
gesture" (p. 247). And most improbably, the savage chief is "unable to
resist" these gestures, a fact which suggests that Tommo has carefully
learned his lesson from the master. Of course, Tommo's escape has none
of Marnoo's grace, for Tommo can never return to Typee at will—it is a
one-way trip. Yet the escape permits him to attain a position where boun-

daries can be crossed and recrossed at will: not in the physical world but in the imaginative process of writing. Tommo's frequent, effective comparisons and contrasts between the two disparate societies are ample proof that he has attained "non-compartmentalization."[31] So if Marnoo is a symbol for art, Tommo becomes an incarnation of that symbol in his own narration of *Typee*.

The final esthetic principle which Gotshalk notes is balance, which like harmony is actually a complex concept. On the one hand, balance is achieved by "symmetry," by the balance of similars. But it can also be achieved by "asymmetry," by the use of contrast. Obviously, the narrator of *Typee* makes much use of both types of balance. Symmetrical balance, for example, can be seen in the narrator's obvious reluctance to accept experience at face value. In fact, events often become less significant than the act of interpretation, in this case, of pairing of similars that helps us to understand not so much the event, as the narrator's attitude toward the event. An illustration of this is Tommo's comments on the "lovely damsels" with whom he shares Marheyo's household. These girls, he tells us, "instead of thrumming pianos and reading novels, like more enlightened young ladies, substituted for these employments the manufacture of a fine species of tappa." Tommo also notes that these same girls spend the majority of their time "gadding and gossipping with their acquaintances" (p. 85). Thus he interprets the unfamiliar activity he confronts by making references to a somewhat parallel event from a known culture. And it is this very quality of balance which attracts Tommo to praise what exists "to a certain degree"—the "equality of condition" of the general population of Typee (p. 185). At the same time, this concern for balance causes him to criticize the Typees: "I could not understand why a woman should not have as much right to enter a canoe as a man" (p. 133).

In a similar manner, asymmetrical balance, or contrast, is an important element in Tommo's perception of life. For example, after noting that the spear in Typee is doubled as an oar (p. 78), he observes that Kolory's spear "instead of terminating in a paddle at the lower end, after the general fashion of these weapons, was curved into a heathenish-looking little image" (p. 174). Whether this description is modeled on an actual artifact of Typee valley or whether it is a product of Melville's fertile imagination is less important, I think, than the characteristic interpretation that the narrator gives to it. The spear is, Tommo says, "emblematic" of Kolory's "double functions" of soldier-priest: "With one end in carnal combat he transfixed the enemies of his tribe; and with the other as a pastoral crook he kept in order his spiritual flock" (p. 174). Melville is not as subtle here as he is later in *Moby-Dick* where he describes Queequeg's hatchet-pipe, which has a similar dual purpose; yet the same rich imagination is present which takes joy in the yoking of dissimilar objects and in the irony created thereby.

Contrast, of course, is used by Melville in many other situations. It is perhaps the most noticeable principle in *Typee*, if not in all of Melville's work. He notes, for example, the incongruous nature of the peaceful and beautiful Nukuheva Bay and the "black hulls" of the French ships, whose "bristling broadsides proclaimed their warlike character" (p. 12). Another time, Tommo describes Admiral Du Petit Thouars standing next to a savage chief: "they stood side by side, these two extremes of the social scale" (p. 29). At times, the contrast between civilized and savage is to the obvious flattery of the uncivilized state (for example, the raising of children, p. 112); at other times, the scale is weighted in favor of civilization (implied, for example, in the description of one of Typee's roads, p. 90). The list could be extended well past the limits of interesting analysis. Suffice it to say that in any contrast, Melville was painfully aware that "Truth" resided in the never-never land, "centrally located . . . between the two extremes" (p. 205). The implication of this fundamental fact of life is disturbing. For every thesis, one can find an antithesis, and Melville was painfully aware that it was a moral duty not to accept either (or any) extreme. The question of how this principle applies to a relative judgment of civilization and savage life is, perhaps, the central problem in determining the implications of the esthetic consciousness of *Typee*'s narrator.

From the foregoing examples of Melville's perception, one can see the pervasive influence of the essentially esthetic form-giving qualities, all of which depend not on conscious intention but on the well developed esthetic temperament. But, finally, one must ask what this essentially esthetic vision of life means. The narrator of *Typee* is an individual sensitive enough to appreciate the innate value of the uncivilized state—and the experience there permitted him to justly evaluate the shortcomings of civilization. But whereas the state of nature offered no permanent value to the civilized mind, the civilized state he returned to was obviously too brutal for this man who felt so deeply the sources of his humanity. Therefore, after being once again a crew member of a man-of-war, he loses his faith in mankind (p. 203). In essence, he enjoyed both worlds and was happy in neither. And it is for that reason that he created a third, made partly from his experiences, partly from his unique way of perceiving life, and partly from his imagination. The result, however, was wholly expressive of his self, of his own response to life.

But is *Typee* primarily a book which is a condemnation of civilization? The cultural criticism does seem to support the critics who argue that this work is basically factual or a travel account. And the evidence that such critics as Dryden marshal makes it difficult to deny that a large part of *Typee* is devoted to criticism of Western civilization.[32] Yet *Typee* manages to be much more. It is true that Tommo on innumerable occasions compares the state of nature favorably to civilization. For example, he likes the dress code of the Typee women better than that of civilized women (p. 161). Yet overall the comparisons are not necessarily one-sided. For example (besides one or two already mentioned), a crowd of natives reminds Tommo "of a group of idlers gathered about the door of a village tavern" (p. 89). Thus critics who argue that Melville is praising savage life to the detriment of civilization or vice versa, do so, too often, at the expense of the abundant contradictory evidence. Melville, through Tommo, exalts neither savagery nor civilization, except incidentally. His central concern, rather, is his own free imaginative life in its ability to draw parallels in the least likely of circumstances. The emphasis is on expression. What we have in *Typee* is a mind that refuses to be quiescent, but which like the traveler Marnoo crosses boundaries at will. But in Tommo's case, the boundaries are both of time and space and are conquered by his far-reaching imaginative vision.

It is this fact, the central role of the process of perception, that makes it less important whether to call *Typee* fact or fiction. Instead of a narrow contrast or comparison, the range of Tommo's perceptions includes all time, all space, and the emphasis falls on the act of seeing rather than on the objective world. So Tommo sees two men in the distance and they look like "Hebrew spies" (p. 107); Tommo's native dress is similar to a toga of "a senator of Rome" (p. 121); Marheyo looks like a "valiant Templar arrayed in a new and costly suit of armor" (p. 122); and Tommo feels at one time "transported to some fairy region" (p. 134). These reflections, which only Tommo can make, reveal as much, if not more, about him as they do about either Typee valley or civilization. And these observations should remind us that if we want to go to Melville's Typee, a steamer or an airplane won't do.

Notes

1. This modest summary of *Typee's* history is based on what must be the fullest single treatment of the subject, Leon Howard's "Historical Note" to the Northwestern-Newberry edition. For further information, the reader is referred to Herman Melville, *Typee: A Peep at Polynesian Life*, ed. Harrison Hayford, Hershel Parker, and G. Thomas Tanselle (Evanston, Ill.: Northwestern University Press, 1968), pp. 277–302. Subsequent references to *Typee* will refer to this edition and will be cited in the text.

2. F. O. Matthiessen, *American Renaissance: Art and Expression in the Age of Emerson and Whitman* (New York: Oxford University Press, 1941), p. 371.

3. Charles R. Anderson, "Melville's South Sea Romance," *Eigo Seinen* [*The Rising Generation*], 115 (1969), 565.

4. Charles R. Anderson, *Melville in the South Seas* (New York: Columbia University Press, 1939). See especially Chapters 5–8.

5. Quoted in Jay Leyda, *The Melville Log: A Documentary Life of Herman Melville, 1819–1891* (New York: Harcourt, Brace and Company, 1951), I, 200.

6. Leyda, I, 202.

7. Anonymous review of *Typee*, *The New Englander*, 4 (1846), 449–50. Reprinted in *The Recognition of Herman Melville: Selected Criticism Since 1846*, ed. Hershel Parker (Ann Arbor: The University of Michigan Press, 1967), p. 5.

8. Richard Ruland, "Melville and the Fortunate Fall: Typee as Eden," *Nineteenth Century Fiction*, 23 (1968), 312–23.

9. Paul Witherington, "The Art of Melville's *Typee*," *Arizona Quarterly*, 26 (1970), 136–50.

10. The term is Melville's evaluation of his work, which he used in a letter to Hawthorne, and it reveals the author's awareness that his books were amenable neither to conventional concepts of the novel nor to his own standards of writing. This suggests that neither genre criticism nor Melville's own theorizing posit adequate critical frameworks by which to evaluate his work. His books are sui generis and evolve their own esthetic assumptions. See Letter of 1(?) June 1851 in *The Letters of Herman Melville*, ed. Merrell R. Davis and William H. Gilman (New Haven: Yale University Press, 1960), p. 128.

11. Charles Feidelson, Jr., *Symbolism and American Literature* (Chicago: University of Chicago Press, 1953), p. 165.

12. D. W. Gotshalk, *Art and the Social Order* (Chicago: University of Chicago Press, 1947), p. 114. The four principles mentioned above are generally accepted formal principles—though some critics include more elements, some note fewer, and often other terms are employed for these concepts. Nevertheless, critics generally agree that these four elements constitute the fundamental esthetic principles by which the mind perceives and orders existence.

13. Matthiessen, p. 442.

14. Beongcheon Yu, "Ishmael's Equal Eye: The Source of Balance in *Moby-Dick*," *ELH*, 32 (1965), 110–25.

15. Loren Baritz, *City on a Hill: A History of Ideas and Myths in America* (New York: John Wiley & Sons, Inc., 1964), pp. 206–07.

16. John Dos Passos, "Against American Literature," *The New Republic*, 8 (1916), 270.

17. Warner Berthoff, *The Example of Melville* (Princeton: Princeton University Press, 1962), p. 121.

18. *Clarel, A Poem and Pilgrimage in the Holy Land*, ed. Walter E. Bezanson (New York: Hendricks House, Inc., 1960), I.xvii.194–99.

19. *Clarel*, I.xxxi. 19–23.

20. Susanne K. Langer, *Feeling and Form: A Theory of Art* (New York: Charles Scribner's Sons, 1953), p. 297.

21. Langer, p. 292.

22. Gotshalk, p. 113.

23. David Williams, "Peeping Tommo: Typee as Satire," *The Canadian Review of American Studies*, 6 (Spring 1975), 42.

24. *Omoo: A Narrative of Adventures in the South Seas*, ed. Harrison Hayford, Hershel Parker, and G. Thomas Tanselle (Evanston, Ill.: Northwestern University Press, 1968), p. 240.

25. *Pierre; or The Ambiguities*, ed. Harrison Hayford, Hershel Parker, and G. Thomas Tanselle (Evanston, Ill.: Northwestern University Press, 1971), p. 44.

26. Feidelson, p. 165.

27. The motif of the disappointed search for ideality can be found even in Melville's earliest published writing, "Fragments from a Writing Desk, No. 2."

28. Gotshalk, p. 110.

29. DeWitt H. Parker, *The Analysis of Art* (New Haven: Yale University Press, 1926), p. 37.

30. Witherington, p. 146.

31. Witherington uses the term "non-compartmentalized" to describe Marnoo's ability to move freely from culture to culture.

32. Edgar A. Dryden, *Melville's Thematics of Form: The Great Art of Telling the Truth* (Baltimore: The Johns Hopkins Press, 1968), pp. 45–46.

Tragedy in the State of Nature: Melville's *Typee*

Thomas J. Scorza*

There is no external evidence that Herman Melville possessed or read a copy of Aristotle's *Poetics* before the last two or three years of his life.[1] Yet Melville clearly had come to agree much earlier with the thrust of Aristotle's statement in the *Poetics* that "poetry is . . . of graver import than history, since its statements are of the nature rather of universals, whereas those of history are singulars."[2] Indeed, there is no better indication of Melville's long-held view that poetry is superior to history than his first novel, *Typee*, published in 1846 and begun less than two years earlier, when he was just 25 years old. Melville wrote *Typee* after the most exciting episode of his life, his abandonment of an American whaling vessel in the Marquesas Islands in 1842 and his subsequent one-month residence among the Typees, a tribe of cannibals on Nukuheva Island. But while Melville thus had fallen into a perfect source of materials for a *singular* "true adventure" story, he chose instead to write a novel which presented a narrative dealing with *universals*. Indeed, the great irony of *Typee* is that it was published and generally accepted as a remarkable but historically true account of the adventures of a "common sailor" in the South Seas, while Melville himself had intended his work to speak principally of an uncommon truth beyond mere history. In the guise of a narrative of "true adventure," Melville had presented a critique of some of the most fundamental tenets of Western civilization, and even his more suspicious early readers and reviewers did not fully appreciate the real character of the transhistorical "unvarnished truth" the author had promised in his Preface to *Typee*.[3]

1. TO THE STATE OF NATURE

The narrator of *Typee* is a crewman on a ship which has been "six months out of sight of land." The long and unrelieved encounter with "the sky above, the sea around, and nothing else!" has severed the connection between the society constituted by the ship and that society's roots in

*Reprinted from *Interpretation*, 8, no. 1 (January, 1979), 103–20, by permission of *Interpretation*.

the land. The ship's society has been separated from the source of its life, and in every decisive respect, the ship and its society are adrift: the ship is simply being "tossed on the billows of the wide-rolling Pacific." When the narrator asks, "Is there nothing fresh around us? Is there no green thing to be seen?" he sounds the plaintive note of a member of a society which has lost its lifegiving sense of purpose, its "rootedness." Thus, the fact that "weeks ago" the ship's "fresh provisions were all exhausted" is important only because it points to the more crucial fact that the ship's society has exhausted its *moral* stores in its cruise "beneath the scorching sun of the Line" (p. 3). In all, the narrator's ship, the *Dolly*, is representative of a culture in the midst of a fundamental crisis of identity. The *Dolly* is the modern West in a condition of moral disorder.

Given this state of affairs, it is no wonder that the narrator is exhilirated by the announcement that his ship has been put on a course to the Marquesas. The very name of those Islands conjures up "strange visions," including visions of *"heathenish rites and human sacrifices"* (p. 5). Such visions are in keeping with the fact that, unlike the ship's society (and its parent society), the Marquesas Islands have not been introduced to Christianity. The Christian missionaries "had abandoned" the Marquesans to their "idols of wood and stone," and while a Protestant Mission had been established at nearby Tahiti, the missionaries had despaired of ever reclaiming the Marquesans themselves from "heathenism" (pp. 5, 6). Ironically, the narrator anticipates redemption from his predicament by means of a visit to a place which has not received the message of the Redeemer.

Indeed, the narrator's deliverance seems to require the actual destruction of all vestiges of the ship's attachment to Christianity. Thus, with a subtlety befitting Melville's concern for the sensitivities of his Christian readers,[4] the narrator inserts a comic tale about the welcomed upcoming demise of a "passenger" with a noted Christian name:

> There is but one solitary tenant in the chicken-coop, once a gay and dapper young cock. . . . But look at him now; there he stands, moping all the day long on that everlasting one leg of his. . . . He mourns no doubt his lost companions, literally snatched from him one by one, and never seen again. But his days of mourning will be few; for Mungo, our black cook, told me yesterday that the word had at last gone forth, and poor Pedro's fate was sealed. His attenuated body will be laid out upon the captain's table next Sunday, and long before night will be buried with all the usual ceremonies beneath that worthy individual's vest. . . . They say the captain will never point the ship for the land so long as he has in anticipation a mess of fresh meat. This unhappy bird can alone furnish it; and when he is once devoured, the captain will come to his senses. I wish thee no harm, Peter; but as thou art doomed, sooner or later, to meet the fate of all thy race; and if putting a period to thy existence is to be the signal for our deliverance, why—truth to speak—I wish thy throat cut this very moment; for oh! how I wish to see the living earth again! (p. 4)

The ironic biblical language of the narrator's tale only emphasizes the implications for Christianity of the captain's "last supper" before harboring the *Dolly*. The "word" has gone forth that the captain shall prevail against "Peter," and the narrator can hardly wait for his "deliverance."[5]

However, the Marquesas Islands are not only devoid of the *Christian* elements of the ship's immediate and parent Western society: in fact, the Islands have been untouched by the whole of the civilization embodied in the *Dolly*. Thus, the inhabitants of Nukuheva Island, "the most important" of the Marquesas, and especially the "hostile clans" like the Typees, "retain their original primitive character, remaining very nearly in the same state of nature in which they were first beheld by white men" (p. 11). The narrator's joy at the prospect of sailing towards the Marquesas hence is premised upon his understanding that such a course represents a return to the state of nature, and his joy implies that it is precisely such a return which may promise relief from the societal malaise in which he finds himself. The narrator implies, that is, that his society has erred in its departure from the moral standards of the state of nature and that its return to health requires a renewal of its adherence to those natural standards. As the very timbers of the *Dolly* yearn for the shore (p. 4), so does the narrator seek a return to the place of origin and birth.

This last implication is confirmed as the narrator explains why he has decided to "run away" from the *Dolly*. In an argument which closely parallels *The Declaration of Independence*, the narrator declares the causes which have impelled him to separate himself from the ship's society, and he indicates his enlightened understanding that the *Dolly*'s society was created by a social contract and founded upon natural rights philosophy:

> When I entered on board the Dolly, I signed as a matter of course the ship's articles, thereby voluntarily engaging and legally binding myself to serve in a certain capacity for the period of the voyage; and, special considerations apart, I was of course bound to fulfill the agreement. But in all contracts, if one party fails to perform his share of the compact, is not the other virtually absolved from his liability? Who is there who will not answer in the affirmative?
>
> Having settled the principle, then, let me apply it to the particular case in question. In numberless instances had not only the implied but the specified conditions of the articles been violated on the part of the ship in which I served. The usage on board of her was tyrannical. . . . The captain was the author of these abuses; it was in vain to think that he would either remedy them, or alter his conduct, which was arbitrary and violent in the extreme. . . .
>
> But, after all, these things could have been endured awhile, had we entertained the hope of being speedily delivered from them by the due completion of the term of our servitude. But what a dismal prospect awaited us in this quarter! The longevity of Cape Horn whaling voyages is

proverbial, frequently extending over a period of four or five years. (pp. 20–21)

According to the narrator, thus, the captain of the *Dolly* derived his authority only from the voluntary consent of the crew; the captain's tyrannical violation of his compact with the crew may justly lead to their exercise of the natural right of rebellion; and while the captain's abuses may have been endured awhile, the prospect of a continued "long train of abuses" absolves the crew of any need to continue suffering. The narrator, for one, is prepared "to dissolve the political bands which have connected" him to the *Dolly*.[6]

The failure of the ship's captain to respect the natural rights of the crew duplicates the failure of the parent Western society to honor "the rights of humanity" in the larger world. The tyrannical actions of the conquering French, who "have ever plumed themselves upon being the most humane and polished of nations," especially demonstrate the hypocrisy of the West. While professing a belief in the rights of man, the French perpetrate "outrages and massacres" at Tahiti, "the queen of the South Seas" (pp. 17, 18). Worse still, the actions of the Western conquerors also show the hypocrisy of their Christian faith, which, the narrator implies, *should* give revelatory support to the secular notion of equal human rights. With biting irony, the narrator thus concludes an account of an earlier American "unprovoked" atrocity against the Typees by describing how the "invaders" set "fire to every house and temple in their route; . . . defaced the once-smiling bosom of the valley, and proclaimed to its pagan inhabitants the spirit that reigned in the breasts of Christian soldiers" (p. 26). In all, the narrator's account reveals the moral bankruptcy of a society which professes natural rights and brotherly love and yet acts with the most self-serving ruthlessness. Whatever may be the narrator's own relation to the other teachings of the Christian faith, he certainly believes that one sees the true character of men when one sees the fruits of their actions.

The end result of Western society's severance of its roots in the "Laws of Nature and of Nature's God" is that the society has become simply conventional or artificial. The inside of the bulwarks of the *Dolly* is "painted green . . . a vile and sickly hue" (p. 4), while Nukuheva Island is indented by "broad and verdant valleys" of indescribable natural beauty (p. 24). Whereas the conquering French admiral wears "a richly decorated admiral's frockcoat, a laced chapeau bras, and upon his breast . . . a variety of ribbons and orders," the "patriarch-sovereign" of the shoreline natives of Nukuheva appears "in all the nakedness of nature" (p. 29). And in the context of these and other contrasts between the conventional and the natural, the narrator dares to wonder whether the imposing battlements and sophistication of the former really do evidence a superiority to the latter. Looking upon the meeting of the French admiral and the native patriarch, the narrator concludes with these "philosophical reflections":

> At what an immeasurable distance, thought I, are these two beings removed from each other. In the one is shown the result of long centuries of progressive civilization and refinement, which have gradually converted the mere creature into the semblance of all that is elevated and grand; while the other, after the lapse of the same period, has not advanced one step in the career of improvement. "Yet, after all," quoth I to myself, "insensible as he is to a thousand wants, and removed from harassing cares, may not the savage be the happier man of the two?" (p. 29).

As the novel opens, then, the narrator appears as an enlightened believer both in the "rights of humanity" and in at least that version of Christianity which is consistent with natural rights philosophy. His own society, supposedly founded on these beliefs, has abandoned them in deed and has forfeited any claim to natural justice. So radical has the narrator's disenchantment become that he has begun to wonder whether conventional civilization can ever retain its roots in nature: "Thrice happy are they who, inhabiting some yet undiscovered island in the midst of the ocean, have never been brought into contaminating contact with the white man. . . . and were civilization itself to be estimated by some of its results, it would seem perhaps better for what we call the barbarous part of the world to remain unchanged" (pp. 15, 17). The narrator's disenchantment with Western civilization, that is, makes a romantic return to the pre-Christian and uncivilized state of nature a very inviting prospect. He apparently hopes to experience there a renewal of his attachment to those fundamental enlightened truths which his society has abandoned.

II. INTO THE STATE OF NATURE

Entrance into the state of nature apparently requires a rite of purification, a rite whereby the civilized are cleansed of civilization's system and its norms. Collectively, the crew of the *Dolly* is offered this rite in the harbor of Nukuheva, where the ship is boarded by a swarm of naked young girls who cause a purgative orgy marked by "every species of riot and debauchery" (p. 15). Individually, the narrator experiences the rite when he journeys briefly in the ship's boat to the "glen of Tior," where he plunges into the cool waters of a grove and feels as if he were "floating in some new element" (p. 28). Unlike the rest of the crew, the narrator wants to take full advantage of his rite of purification, and he thus commits himself to abandoning civilization altogether. This commitment, however, immediately raises a major problem: having cast off the bonds of civilization, the narrator will enter an uncivilized world. Or, more precisely, the narrator will enter a world which he believes may have many potential perils, not the least of which is "the possibility of falling in with a foraging party of . . . bloody-minded Typees" (p. 31). In an effort to provide for such possible dangers, then, the narrator enlists a companion, Toby, who will accompany him on his escape into the Island. But the quickly arranged "engagement" (p. 33) between the two is merely an attempt to deal with their fear of the possible perils of the state of nature, and their fate will still be dependent upon the actual character of that state.

The initial experience of the two runaways does not bode well. After climbing a steep shoreline mountain, they do not find sweeping valleys on the opposite side, but rather an elevated plateau of "ridges and inter-vales," with no fruit trees in sight (p. 41). Their meager provisions will obviously soon be exhausted, and they are able to make very little progress among the chasms in finding their way to the inhabited valleys. More-over, while shielding himself from a heavy rain, the narrator begins to feel the symptoms of a mysterious malady: one of his legs swells "to such a degree" and pains him "so acutely" that he "half" suspects that he "had been bitten by some venomous reptile" (p. 48). Subsequently, the nar-rator learns that there are no snakes on the islands of Polynesia, so his suspicion about the source of his malady turns out to be ill-founded. The added mystery, for the reader, is that the narrator had previously de-scribed Toby and himself as "a couple of serpents" as they climbed the in-itial ridge on the island (p. 39). In any case, unexpectedly, in the midst of his feverish sensations, the narrator pushes aside a branch and finds himself looking upon a beautiful, inhabited valley. He compares the sight to "a glimpse of the gardens of Paradise" (p. 49)—their prior wandering over and into the ridges of the plateau, one ravine of which contained a pool "which seemed to penetrate into the very bowels of the earth" (p. 45), has ended in apparent salvation.

But upon which valley do the runaways look? Is it the valley of the peaceful Happars, or the valley of the cannibal Typees? The mere possi-bility that the valley might be inhabited by the "cruel" (p. 51) Typees in-duces the narrator to persuade Toby that they ought to seek out another valley, a possibly uninhabited one which might be on the other side of the far ridge which borders the valley they have discovered. However, the way to this ridge turns out to be blocked by chasm after chasm, and the narrator continues to suffer great pain in his leg. Starving and disheart-ened to the point of renouncing their escape from the *Dolly*, they decide to face whatever awaits them in the inhabited valley they first discovered. There they will encounter the state of nature, whether it be the peaceful Paradise promised by its aspect, or the hell implied by the various deep "circles" formed by the ridges upon the plateau above the valley. The mere possibility that it may indeed be a hell suggests to the reader that the actual experience of the narrator and Toby in the valley is meant to reveal an unbiased view of the true character of the state of nature. Without de-nying any of the relevant possibilities, Melville will use their "singular" adventure to present his poetic vision of "the unvarnished truth," and the reader may well be expected to assume that the truth is as potentially dangerous and as difficult to attain as the destination of Melville's characters.[7]

III. THE TRUE CHARACTER OF THE STATE OF NATURE

As it turns out, the runaways have wandered into the valley of the dreaded Typees, so the picture of the state of nature to follow is one which actually anticipates the worst possibilities. However, when the narrator and Toby come upon the Typees, they are received with great enthusiasm and concern, perhaps because when asked, the narrator allies himself with the right tribe, although he does not know "by what impulse" he chooses to say that "Typee" rather than "Happar" is "mortarkee," or "good."[8] In any case, the Typee natives are delighted by his good judgment, and one of them identifies himself as "Mehevi," asking the narrator for *his* name in return. Fearing that the natives may have difficulty pronouncing his "real name," the narrator gives his name as "Tom" and is called thenceforth "Tommo" (p. 72). Melville's playfulness with his narrator's name places him at the proper authorial distance from his narrator's enlightened judgments and the "true adventure" which now continues.

The Typees are not merely receptive: they turn out to be positively compassionate, giving special attention to Tommo's painful leg and assigning "Kory-Kory" to administer to his every need. The two runaways are lodged in the hut of Kory-Kory's family, where not the least added attraction is the beautiful Fayaway, a young "child of nature" who happily "for the most part clung to the primitive and summer garb of Eden" (pp. 86, 87). The presence of Fayaway, the officiousness of Kory-Kory, and the regimen of the Typean "philosophy" of "eat plenty, ah! sleep very good" (p. 88), soon begins to return Tommo to health and good spirits, a process punctuated, however, by lingering doubts about "the fickle passions which sway the bosom of a savage" (p. 76). Tommo finally persuades the Typees to allow Toby to return over the mountains to Nukuheva harbor to obtain medicine for his painful leg, but Toby is turned back and wounded by the enemy Happars. Tommo is despondent over this event and gives up "all hopes of recovery" (p. 104). His resulting melancholy continues for some time, and he finally falls "a victim to despair" (p. 109) when Toby manages to escape to some trading boats offshore and does not return to the valley.

The even kinder treatment by the natives, following Toby's departure, is astounding. Tommo is carried about by Kory-Kory, annointed daily by the girls of the house, and generally allowed to have his full of the beauty, erotic delights, and abundance of the Typee valley. Nevertheless, Tommo observes, "I can scarcely understand how it was that, in the midst of so many consolatory circumstances, my mind should still have been consumed by the most dismal forebodings, and have remained a prey to the profoundest melancholy" (p. 118). The continuing pain in his leg and a variety of actions which clearly reveal that the Typees have no intention of allowing him to escape force Tommo finally to give himself over to the moment. This surrender, has, however, one positive effect:

> Day after day wore on, and still there was no perceptible change in the conduct of the islanders towards me. Gradually I lost all knowledge of the regular recurrence of the days of the week, and sunk insensibly into that kind of apathy which ensues after some violent outbreak of despair. My limb suddenly healed, the swelling went down, the pain subsided, and I had every reason to suppose I should soon completely recover from the affliction that had so long tormented me (p. 123).

Now the peaceful and joyful life of the Typees which absorbs Tommo clearly indicates that Hobbes erred when he claimed that in the state of nature "*there is always war of every one against every one.*"[9] According to Tommo, the Typees "seemed to be governed by that sort of tacit common-sense law which, say what they will of the inborn lawlessness of the human race, has its precepts graven on every breast" (p. 201). Nor was Locke correct when he claimed that the state of nature was not a state of war because it was governed by a "Law of Nature," or "Reason."[10] The Typees do not reason: their "perception of what is *just* and *noble*" is due to their "indwelling" (p. 201) intuitive and apparently pre-rational sense, something akin to natural compassion. And while Locke's notion that private property is a natural institution is affirmed by the example of the Typees' personal property, Tommo discovers that the Typees completely lack Lockean industriousness and acquisitiveness.[11] In all, the Typean state of nature is both peaceful and unsophisticated, and it is marked by none of civilized life's "harassing cares." The Typees are as heartful, innocent, spontaneous, natural, and simple as civilized men are heartless, sophisticated, scheming, artificial, and complex.

In depicting a simple life for the Typees, Melville could draw upon a Western tradition which reaches back at least as far as Socrates' description of the "first city" in Book Two of the *Republic*, or the historical analysis of the origin of cities in Book Three of Plato's *Laws*.[12] As a source for the hints about the apparent sexual freedom which reigns among the Typees, Melville possibly drew, perhaps indirectly, upon such a modern work as Diderot's *Supplement to Bougainville's Voyage*.[13] However, the three most generally relevant background sources for *Typee* are Montaigne's essay, "Of Cannibals" (1577–78), Gonzalo's utopian plan in Shakespeare's *The Tempest* (1611), and Rousseau's *First and Second Discourses* (1750, 1755).

While there is a good deal of irony apparent in Montaigne's essay, he presents a superficially laudatory view of life among cannibals in Brazil, ostensibly based on an eye-witness account. Montaigne claims that the life of innocence described to him far surpasses the notions of perfection advanced by either Lycurgus or Plato. According to Montaigne, the cannibals constitute "a nation wherein there is no manner of traffic, no knowledge of letters, no science of numbers, no name of magistrate or of political superiority; no use of servitude, riches or poverty; no contracts, no successions, no dividing of properties, no employments, except those of leisure; no respect of kindred, except for the common bond; no clothing, no agriculture, no metal, no use of wheat or wine. The very words that signify lying, treachery, dissimulation, avarice, envy, detraction, and pardon were never heard of." Further, Montaigne's cannibals are rarely sick; they live in the shadow of shoreline mountains; they believe in the immortality of the soul; their men have several wives; they fight bloody wars with enemies who live beyond the mountains; and they eat the bodies of their dead enemies out of revenge. Montaigne even defends their cannibalism by arguing that Western criminal punishment and religious tortures are far more barbarous. Finally, Montaigne pointedly argues that the cannibals do not adhere to their simple life merely out of bondage to custom "without reasoning or judgment," and in fact, he ends his essay with examples of their mental "capacity," as evidenced in their poetry and the egalitarian political opinions of three cannibals who were brought to France.[14]

Montaigne's cannibal utopia was the apparent model for Gonzalo's speeches in Act II of *The Tempest*:

> I' th' commonwealth I would by contraries Execute all things. For no kind of traffic Would I admit; no name of magistrate; Letters should not be known; riches, poverty, And use of service, none; contract, succession, Bourn, bound of land, tilth, vineyard, none; No use of metal, corn, or wine, or oil; No occupation; all men idle, all; And women too, but innocent and pure; No sovereignty. . . . All things in common nature should produce Without sweat or endeavor. Treason, felony, Sword, pike, knife, gun, or need of any engine Would I not have; but nature should bring forth. Of it own kind, all foison, all abundance. To feed my innocent people. . . . I would with such perfection govern, sir, T' excel the Golden Age.[15]

While Gonzalo of course makes no reference to cannibalism, and while his own picture of perfection differs in some important particulars from Montaigne's (especially in his apparent retention of families and clothing, possibly concessions to the sensibilities of *Shakespeare*'s Christian audience), his general depiction of pristine innocence is clearly of a piece with "Of Cannibals."

Tommo's experience with the Typees is generally consistent with a combination of Montaigne's and Gonzalo's descriptions. Among the Typees, there is no commerce, no letters or philosophy, apparently no mathematics, no economic inequality, no business transactions, no clearly private real estate, almost no work, very little clothing, no agriculture or technology, no sickness, and no viciousness. And among the Typees there is natural abundance, innocence, a belief in an after-life, and polygamy (but with a plurality of husbands). Apparently like Gonzalo's utopians, the Typees retain a family structure, although the family is greatly extended by the practice of polygamy. And like Montaigne's cannibals, the Typees have wars, but they are "marked by no very sanguinary traits."[16]

While much of the substance, the language, and even some of the lesser anecdotes of *Typee* thus may derive from Montaigne's essay and/or Gonzalo's speeches, it is *Rousseau* who is directly cited in Tommo's narrative. In describing the "perpetual hilarity" among the Typees, Tommo says that their "continual happiness . . . sprung principally from that all-pervading sensation which Rousseau has told us he at one time experienced, the mere buoyant sense of a healthful physical existence." Tommo then goes on immediately to say that "sickness was almost unknown" among the "healthful" Typees (pp. 126, 127). While the allusion to Rousseau's celebration of the "sentiment of one's existence" is a reference to a notion which appears variously in a number of his works, Tommo's immediate mention of the Typees' natural health appears to suggest the *Second Discourse* as the most relevant reference, perhaps at second hand; in that work, Rousseau had argued both that there was no illness in the state of nature and that savage man's soul was "given over to the sole sentiment of its present existence."[17] Moreover, the direct reference to Rousseau occurs amid many either obvious or subtle points which are as consistent with Rousseau's description of the state of nature in the *Second Discourse* as they are with Montaigne's and Gonzalo's utopias.[18]

However, the strongest connections between *Typee* and Rousseau's works occur in two particular aspects of *Typee*'s presentation of the state of nature and in *Typee*'s generally negative attitude towards enlightenment. First, the Typees' natural compassion is a perfect reflection of the "principle" of pity which Rousseau found in natural man. This principle "anterior to reason" is a salient element of the states of nature in both *Typee* and the *Second Discourse*, but it is either absent or very subdued in Montaigne's and Gonzalo's innocent regimes.[19] Secondly, while both Montaigne and Gonzalo indicated that there is no philosophy in their primitive utopias, Montaigne apparently asserted that his cannibals *could* reason, and Gonzalo was not assertive in his deprecation of reason itself. *Typee*, however, follows the *Second Discourse* in its insistence that natural man's "thoughtless happiness" indicates the unnaturalness of reason: while the Typees speak, in their natural unanimity they neither reason nor dispute, and they thus could not, for instance, "support a debating society for a single night."[20] Finally, Tommo's narrative explicitly raises many profound questions about the value of enlightened civilization, questions which appear to have been based on some familiarity with Rousseau's *First Discourse*. Indeed, at times, Tommo's language is Rousseau's: Tommo's French admiral had been converted by progress into "the semblance of all that is elevated and grand," and Rousseau's civilized people are marked by "the semblance of all the virtues without the possession of any."[21] In all, thus, Tommo's direct reference to Rousseau is merely the most obvious signal of the extent to which the state of nature in *Typee* is consistent with Rousseauean principles.

However, the similarities between *Typee* and Rousseau's *Discourses* are the more remarkable when the reader notices that parts of Melville's novel seem calculated to correct certain notions commonly associated with Rousseau. While both Montaigne and Gonzalo had clearly described utopian *communities*, Rousseau had pictured natural man as a solitary creature, at least at the earliest stage of the state of nature. The Typees, however, live in a tightly organized community, one in which the communal organization far exceeds the level of regimentation achieved even in the latest stage of Rousseau's state of nature.[22] In their own state of nature, the Typees seem to embody almost all the innocence of Rousseau's earliest savages, even though their society is decisively a political or civil one. Tommo learns, in fact, that the notion that there is no positive or civil law among the Typees would be based on a totally superficial observation of their conduct. The Typees appear to be governed by no law precisely because their law, in the form of "the thrice mysterious taboo" (p. 177), operates so efficiently that its hand has become invisible. Tommo thus says that the "savage . . . lives in the continual observance of [the taboo's] dictates, which guide and control every action of his being" (p. 221). Oddly enough, the merely apparent lawlessness of the Typees is exactly like the merely apparent lawlessness of Lycurgus' Spartans: they appear to be lawless because their unwritten law completely dominates their souls. Rousseau's notion that men are by nature "born free" is flatly contradicted by the operation of the Typees' apparently natural "yoke," their taboo.[23]

Along with their reflection of the politically and legally restrained character of the state of nature, the Typees also give evidence that human inequality is a natural phenomenon, another point which contradicts the common understanding of Rousseau. In contrast to Rousseau's notion that inequality is "almost null in the state of nature," Tommo finds that King Mehevi is a chief "highest in rank" and that his official distinction is conferred by *Nature* itself. Mehevi is a truly "*noble* savage," and he "might certainly have been regarded as one of *Nature's* noblemen." Tommo discovers, that is, that the state of nature evidences what is called "natural regality" in *Billy Budd*.[24] While Mehevi's regal office certainly contradicts both Montaigne and Gonzalo—who had excluded magistrates, political superiority, and sovereignty from their utopias—his "regal character" (p. 187) contradicts Rousseau, who apparently had argued for a natural human equality which far exceeded the political and economic equality advanced by Montaigne and Gonzalo.

In all, the Typean state of nature is political, hierarchical, and restrained by law. Melville's poetic visit to the state of nature shows that in certain decisive respects Montaigne, Gonzalo, and especially Rousseau had erred in describing the natural state of man. Along with his three predecessors, Melville sees original Nature as both abundant and beneficent, but he claims that Nature authorizes a political hierarchy among men, and to the simple life of Montaigne's cannibals, Gonzalo's utopians, and Rousseau's savages, Melville adds a political and legal structure worthy of Lycurgus' Sparta.[25] The effective natural hierarchy among the naturally compassionate and simple Typees seems to indicate that the best political community can exist not only without Lycurgus' harsh clothing, but also without Plato's philosopher-kings. The Typees, who are "wholly unchanged from their original primitive condition" (p. 170), have surpassed the perfection achieved by either statesmanship or philosophy.

IV. TRAGEDY AMONG THE TYPEES

However strongly Tommo had desired to return to the state of nature, he had always anticipated leaving whenever a "favorable opportunity" offered itself (p. 33). Even though he is treated so well by the Typees, Tommo remains apprehensive about their potential savagery and cannibalism, and he is willing even to risk trying to use "Marnoo," a visiting native dignitary, to persuade the Typees to release him. When this attempt fails, Tommo gives himself over wholly to the "wild enjoyments" of the Typee valley (p. 144). However, when the Typees indicate, some three months into Tommo's visit, that they want to tatoo and therefore "to make a convert of" him, Tommo's painful malady returns, and he is reduced to the state of a captive in "misery" (pp. 220, 231–32). His desire to escape is then heightened to the point of desperation when he discovers physical evidence of the Typees' cannibalism (pp. 238–39). But his first attempt to escape, made in conjunction with a return visit by Marnoo, is completely cut off by the Typees. Finally, Tommo takes advantage of an unexpected visit by a whale-boat to the Typees' shore to make a headlong dash back to civilization. Only an apparent division among the Typees over whether they could continue to hold Tommo against his will allows him to go to the beach and to get into the waiting boat. But some of the natives try to swim out and intercept the fleeing boat, and Tommo's final act in the state of nature is then a tragic one:

> After a few breathless moments I discerned Mow-Mow. The athletic islander, with his tomahawk between his teeth, was dashing the water before him till it foamed again. He was the nearest to us, and in another instant he would have seized one of the oars. Even at the moment I felt horror at the act I was about to commit; but it was no time for pity or compunction, and with a true aim, and exerting all my strength, I dashed the boat-hook at him. It struck him just below the throat, and forced him downwards. I had no time to repeat my blow, but I saw him rise to the

surface in the wake of the boat, and never shall I forget the ferocious expression of his countenance (p. 252).

This tragic and pitiless end to Tommo's adventure in the state of
nature makes it difficult to read *Typee* simply as a romantic paean to
natural innocence.[26] Moreover, the observations above about the important *differences* between the Typean and the Rousseauean-romantic states
of nature would seem to indicate that Melville intended to correct rather
than to praise the conceptions of man's natural condition espoused by
romanticism and its "Father." Thus, it is far more *plausible* to argue, as
some critics have done, that Tommo's "blow" upon Mow-Mow, or his
disgust at the "man-devouring horror" of cannibalism, or his debilitating
leg injury are symbolic constructs which show Melville's outright rejection
of primitive utopianism, a rejection which led him either to embrace conscious civilization once again or to engage in a quasi-existentialist struggle
between primitive innocence and civilized corruption.[27] Such a plausible
argument would involve the contention that Typean life itself is radically
defective in that it does not satisfy the needs of Tommo's self-consciousness, his spirit, or his intellectual strivings; such an argument would also
have to maintain that, for all its flaws, civilization or contact with
civilization is nevertheless the precondition for fulfilling man's more
spiritual and less physical needs. However, beyond all else, this plausible
argument would have to maintain that Tommo's "longing" for the things
of the spirit or the mind is seen by Melville as a *natural* longing in man,
one not addressed by Typean life. And it is here that the plausible argument becomes problematic.

For one thing, the "wholly . . . primitive" Typees certainly do not
support the notion that serious religiosity or other forms of spirituality are
parts of man's nature. Tommo pointedly describes the "very low ebb" of
"religious affairs" among the "thoughtless" Typees (p. 174), and he
characterizes the primitive and natural Typees as people "sunk in
religious sloth" (p. 179). More pointedly, although *Tommo* speaks of the
inherent "yearning after the unknown future" by man's "immortal spirit"
(p. 173), the Typees themselves show no evidence of such a yearning.
Thus, when Tommo and Kory-Kory visit "the mausoleum of a deceased
warrior chief," and *Tommo* becomes interested in having Kory-Kory
speak of "the Polynesian heaven," Kory-Kory is simply uninterested. As
far as Tommo can understand it, Kory-Kory's response to his question
about the heavenly state of the deceased warrior translates as "A bird in
the hand is worth two in the bush" (pp. 171–73). For the natural Typees,
there is no immortal yearning because there is no reason to yearn, just as
there is no intellectual longing because there is no reason to think.
Whatever may be said of the value of faith and thought, the natural
Typees do not seem to testify to Melville's affirmation of the natural occurrence of these phenomena.

The difficulty of the above plausible interpretation points to the possibility of a more radical interpretation of Melville's lesson in *Typee*. Having "corrected" the romantic utopia, did Melville seek to reject his corrected picture of the state of nature, or did he seek instead to show that his own state of nature was in fact the place of human happiness, even *if* the modern Western alien would not accept it? Is the tragedy of *Typee* due to flaws in Melville's corrected state of nature, or to flaws in Tommo, his narrator? Does the tragic and pitiless ending of Tommo's visit to the Typees point to their or to his defects?

Now, Tommo is clearly revolted by the Typees' cannibalism, although he repeats Montaigne's defense of the practice in comparison to Western "civilized barbarity."[28] And it is true that the "last horrid revelation" (p. 238) about the Typees' continuing practice of cannibalism is a major ingredient in Tommo's resolution to attempt his escape at all cost. However, Tommo is revolted by cannibalism precisely because *he* sees the practice as "*man*-eating." The Typees, however, do not eat *men*: indeed, they do not know *men*. The Typees eat only Happars and other enemy "strangers and aliens" (p. 205), and they do not recognize the common "humanity" (p. 17) perceived by Tommo. That is to say, Tommo's attitude towards the Typees' cannibalism is dependent upon his "spiritualized" cosmopolitan and rationalistic abstraction from the differences among men. The radically and naturally parochial Typees "pass away their days" in such a "little space" that it seems "almost incredible" to Tommo (p. 27). His horror at the practice of cannibalism thus points to his own radical distance from natural ethnocentricity. Having learned to reason and to abstract, Tommo has been cut off from the natural. His own fundamentally egalitarian conception of "man" is at variance with the natural character of the distinctions which exist between tribes, just as his own enlightened egalitarianism was at variance with the natural distinctions within the Typee tribe.

Tommo's leg pain, which is so often mentioned, may also point to his rationalistic or "spiritualized" flaw. The pain occurs as Tommo just begins his entry into the state of nature (p. 48) and plagues him until he gives himself over to the Typean life (p. 123). The pain returns only when the prospect of being tatooed makes Tommo conscious once again of his supposed predicament in paradise (pp. 231–32). Rather than showing the problems inherent in Typean physical life, the pain indicates a force which calls Tommo away from that life. When Tommo lives the life of the Typees, the pain abates and, in fact, disappears: the life of "thoughtless happiness" (p. 204) is a life without suffering and without the consciousness of loss or want. The pain in Tommo's leg, rather than pointing to the problem of physicality, points in fact to Tommo's inability to embrace physicality, an inability which flows from his having been infected by Western consciousness, reason, and intellectuality. It is Tommo's "*mind*" which, despite the "many consolatory circumstances" of the valley, is "consumed by . . . forebodings . . . and . . . melancholy" (p. 118, italics added). Tommo bears heavily the absence of anyone "to whom [he] could communicate [his] *thoughts*" (p. 231, italics added). Tommo is surprised that the Typees, who are total strangers to modern science and technology, almost never seek to avail themselves of his "superior information" (p. 120). In all, Tommo is kept from embracing the state of nature because that state denies any place to mind, "spirit," and the very love of wisdom. The fact that Tommo's attraction towards these things is symbolized by a painful infection should be sufficient evidence of Melville's judgment of their ultimate worth.

It is no wonder, then, that Tommo had described Toby and himself as "a couple of serpents" climbing the "lofty elevation" of the Island (p. 39). Nor is it any longer surprising that Tommo "half suspected" that his leg "had been bitten by some venomous reptile" (p. 48). Nor, finally, is it surprising that a native doctor had tried to expel the "demon located in the calf of [his] leg" (p. 80). It is clear now that Tommo is flawed precisely because he represents the influence of *Billy Budd*'s "urbane Serpent," the purveyor of "the questionable apple of knowledge."[29]

In the end, whatever may be the differences between *Typee* and Rousseau's *Second Discourse*, the novel appears to follow in his attack on reason and enlightenment. Or, perhaps more correctly, Typee amounts to another episode in the "old quarrel between philosophy and poetry."[30] Melville's poetic imitation of a perfectly happy and perfectly un-sophisticated state of nature amounts to a claim that the pursuit of knowledge and philosophy are destructive of the good city. Just as Tom-mo's erotic desire for Fayaway once led him to break the taboo against taking women in canoes (pp. 132–33), philosophic *eros* destroys and subverts the order of the good city. For Melville, the modern West was corrupted to the same extent that it was decisively scientific, philosophic, and rational, and he thus contradicted the point of Socrates' allegory of the cave by showing Western society drifting aimlessly directly "beneath the scorching sun of the Line" (p. 3); the ultimate tragedy of *Typee* is then Tommo's inability to cleanse himself of the effects of the "bite of the ser-pent" of which Alcibiades had complained in Plato's *Symposium*.[31]

While Tommo had intended to find in the state of nature standards which would renew the health of his modern Western civilization, he found instead, but he rejected, a living refutation of the worth of the very love of wisdom celebrated by both the ancient and the modern West. *Typee* is thus, in all, an appropriate poetic statement in behalf of the posi-tion Melville had presented in a letter to Nathaniel Hawthorne:

> It is a frightful poetical creed that the cultivation of the brain eats out the heart. But it's my *prose* opinion that in most cases, in those men who have fine brains and work them well, the heart extends down to hams. And though you smoke them with the fire of tribulation, yet, like veritable

hams, the head only gives the richer and the better flavor. I stand for the heart. To the dogs with the head! I had rather be a fool with a heart, than Jupiter Olympus with his head.[32]

Notes

An earlier version of this paper was presented on 8 December 1975 to the Chicago chapter of the Conference for the Study of Political Thought. I wish to thank Professor Richard S. Hartigan of Loyola University of Chicago for making the necessary arrangements for that presentation.

1. See Merton M. Sealts, Jr., *Melville's Reading* (Madison: Univ. of Wisconsin Press, 1966), pp. 36–37, entry 14b; and p. 134, n. 108. Leon Howard, in *Herman Melville: A Biography* (Berkeley: Univ. of California Press, 1967), p. 116, sees evidence of Melville's "perhaps secondhand" familiarity with Aristotle as early as *Mardi*, written in 1847–48.

2. *Poetics* 1451b 5–8. One corollary of the argument of this paper is, however, that Melville, unlike Aristotle, regarded poetry as superior also to philosophy.

3. Herman Melville, Preface, in *Typee: A Peep at Polynesian Life*, ed. Harrison Hayford, Hershel Parker, and G. Thomas Tanselle (Evanston, Ill.: Northwestern Univ. Press, 1968), p. xiv. On the contemporary acceptance of the "authenticity" of *Typee*, see Leon Howard's Historical Note in this edition, pp. 279–80, 286–88, and 293. (Unless accompanied by additional footnote material, subsequent references to this edition of *Typee* will appear in parentheses in the text.)

4. Melville anticipated problems with his Christian readers in *Typee*'s Preface, p. xiv. See Daniel Aaron, "Melville and the Missionaries," *NEQ*, 8 (1935), 404–08, for a brief account of the antagonism which *Typee* actually provoked among certain Christians. The antagonism suggests that *Typee* strikes deeper than a simple critique of *some* of the practices of *some* Christian missionaries would have struck.

5. The suggested interpretation of this passage will perhaps seem more plausible when one notes also the narrator's apparent amusement as he tells a story in which a Christian "goddess," the wife of a missionary, is symbolically raped in the Marquesas, pp. 6–7.

6. Milton R. Stern, in *The Fine Hammered Steel of Herman Melville* (Urbana, Ill.: Univ. of Illinois Press, 1957), p. 36, considers the narrator's "legalistic argument" a mere "rationalization which will justify his actions." It is argued here, however, that the narrator, like Jefferson in the *Declaration*, presents a rational argument which shows *why* his principle of natural justice authorizes a "revolution" in the case at hand.

7. In a letter to Evert A. Duyckinck on 3 March 1849—*The Letters of Herman Melville*, ed. Merrell R. Davis and William H. Gilman (New Haven: Yale Univ. Press, 1960), p. 80—Melville wrote, "For I hold it a verity, that even Shakespeare [sic], was not a frank man to the uttermost. And, indeed, who in this intolerant Universe is, or can be?" This is only one of many instances in which Melville implied that his own insights were both clearly rare and dangerously unpalatable. (See also Melville's letters to Lemuel Shaw, 6 October 1849, and to Duyckinck, 14 December 1849, pp. 91–92, and 95–96.)

8. The narrator's impulsive response adds to the mystery surrounding the Typees' friendly reception of the runaways. Note also that the narrator's inexplicable response actually occurs *after* two young Typees had given the two white men the impression that they were among the friendly Happars (pp. 69–71).

9. Thomas Hobbes, *Leviathan*, ed. Michael Oakeshott (London: Collier-Macmillan, 1962), p. 100. Cf. *Typee*, p. 128, where Tommo finds that even a battle between the Typees and the Happars can be compared to "the exhibition of a genteel comedy."

10. John Locke, "The Second Treatise of Government," in *Two Treatises of Government*, ed. Peter Laslett (New York: The New American Library, 1965), p. 311.

11. Cf. Locke, "Second Treatise," pp. 327–44 and *Typee*, pp. 150, 195, and 201–02.

12. *Republic* 369b–372e; *Laws* 676a–683b.

13. Melville borrowed an English translation of Bougainville's *Voyage* (1772) itself from the New York Society Library early in 1848—Sealts, *Melville's Reading*, p. 43, entry 85. The possibility of Melville's earlier acquaintance with notions derived from Diderot's Supplement (1796) is left open in Charles Roberts Anderson's study of Melville's early reading—*Melville in the South Seas*, Columbia University Studies in English and Comparative Literature, No. 138 (New York: Columbia Univ. Press, 1949), pp. 189–91.

14. Montaigne, "Of Cannibals," in *Selected Essays*, ed. Blanchard Bates, trans. Charles Cotton and W. Hazlitt (New York: Modern Library, 1949), pp. 74–89. Cf. especially *Typee*, p. 126.

15. William Shakespeare, *The Tempest*, ed. Robert Langbaum, The Signet Classic Shakespeare (New York: The New American Library, 1963), pp. 67–68, II.i.152–61, 164–69, 172. Again, cf. especially *Typee*, p. 126.

16. Cf. especially Montaigne, "Of Cannibals," p. 79, Gonzalo's first speech, II.i. 152–61, and *Typee*, pp. 126–30.

17. Jean-Jacques Rousseau, "Discourse on the Origin and Foundations of Inequality Among Men," in *The First and Second Discourses*, ed. Roger D. Masters, trans. Roger D. and Judith R. Masters (New York: St. Martin's Press, 1964), pp. 109–11, and 117.
The direct reference to Rousseau in *Typee* illustrates the superiority of internal to external evidence of Melville's reading. Sealts, in *Melville's Reading*, p. 89, entry 429, locates Melville's only externally confirmed possession of any of Rousseau's works, a "much desired copy" of the *Confessions*, in late 1849, about five years after Melville began writing *Typee*. Anderson, in *Melville in the South Seas*, p. 130, suggests a likely second hand source of the Rousseauean elements in *Typee*, but he goes on to suggest that the young Melville actually had read Rousseau directly and carefully (p. 178).

18. Cf., for instance, "Discourse on Inequality," p. 107 and *Typee*, p. 149 on the uniformity of life in the state of nature. Similar comparisons can be made concerning the robustness of savage children, natural man's love of sleep, and the absence of any fear of death in the state of nature. See "Discourse on Inequality," pp. 106, 112, and 116, and cf. *Typee*, pp. 215, 88, and 173, respectively.

19. Cf. "Discourse on Inequality," pp. 95, 130 and *Typee*, pp. 200–01.

20. Cf. *Typee*, pp. 203–04 and "Discourse on Inequality," pp. 94–96, 117–19, and 131–33.

21. Cf. *Typee*, p. 29 and "Discourse on the Sciences and Arts," in *The First and Second Discourses*, p. 36. For other examples of Rousseauean questioning of the value of advanced civilization, see *Typee*, pp. 15, 17, 26, 112, 124, 195, 198, and 202. Also, see the startling similarity between Rousseau's and Tommo's claims that the appearance of a natural man clearly shows the character of his soul—"Discourse on the Sciences and Arts" p. 37 and *Typee*, p. 142.

22. Cf., for instance, *Typee*, pp. 221–24 and "Discourse on Inequality," pp. 148–51.

23. See Jean Jacques Rousseau, *The Social Contract*, trans. Willmoore Kendall (Chicago: Henry Regnery Co., 1954), p. 2.

24. Cf. Rousseau, "Discourse on Inequality," p. 180; *Typee*, p. 71, 90 (italics added), and 78 (italics added); and Herman Melville, *Billy Budd, Sailor*, ed. Harrison Hayford and Merton M. Sealts, Jr. (Chicago: Univ. of Chicago Press, 1962), p. 43.

25. See *Typee*, p. 215, where Tommo makes an explicit comparison between the Typees and the "Lacedemonians."

26. For example, Anderson argues, in *Melville in the South Seas*, p. 178, that "*Typee* . . . is a wholehearted defense of the Noble Savage and a eulogy of his happy life. . . . Virtually the whole book is written in the romantic literary tradition inaugurated by Rousseau a century before."

27. James L. Babin, in "Melville and the Deformation of Being: From Typee to Leviathan," *Southern Review*, NS 7 (1971), 89–114, argues that Melville rejects Typean life because it cannot meet the needs of Tommo's self-consciousness or spirit.

Milton R. Stern, in both *The Fine Hammered Steel*, pp. 29–65 and his "Introduction," in *Typee* and *Billy Budd* (New York: E. P. Dutton, 1958), pp. vi–xxv, argues that Typean life is radically limited and that Melville's intended lesson in *Typee* is that man must struggle in the world outside Eden to earn his truly human nobility.

The arguments of Babin and Stern represent the most thoughtful and serious treatments of *Typee* which I have encountered.

28. Cf. *Typee*, p. 125 and Montaigne, "Of Cannibals," pp. 82–83.

29. See *Billy Budd, Sailor*, p. 52.

30. Plato, *Republic* 607b. On this "old quarrel," see especially Leo Strauss, *Socrates and Aristophanes* (New York: Basic Books, 1966).

31. *Symposium* 218a.

32. Letter to Nathaniel Hawthorne, 1? June 1851, in *The Letters of Herman Melville*, p. 129.

Typee and Omoo: Of "Civilized" War on "Savage" Peace

Joyce Sparer Adler*

> Towards noon we drew abreast the entrance to the harbor, and at last we
> slowly swept by the intervening promontory, and entered the bay of
> Nukuheva. No description can do justice to its beauty; but that beauty
> was lost to me then, and I saw nothing but the tri-colored flag of France
> trailing over the stern of six vessels, whose black hulls and bristling broad-
> sides proclaimed their warlike character. There they were, floating in
> that lovely bay, the green eminences of the shore looking down so tran-
> quilly upon them, as if rebuking the sternness of their aspect. *To my eye
> nothing could be more out of keeping than the presence of these vessels*;
> but we soon learnt what brought them there. The whole group of islands
> had just been taken possession of by Rear-Admiral Du Petit Thouars, in
> the name of the invincible French nation. (*Typee*, ii, 12)[1]

The war-or-peace theme in Melville's work that makes its first appearance in the passage quoted becomes the underlying theme of *Typee*
(1846) and *Omoo* (1847). In them the opposition and choice take this
more concrete form: "civilized" wars of colonialist domination or the
fulfillment of the inherent human desire for peaceful relations among
men, as evidenced in the daily life of "savage" groups not yet corrupted by
modern civilization. Beneath the adventure story in *Typee* and its sequel,
beneath the geographical and anthropological descriptions—often, even,
beneath the humor—is Melville's interpretation of what occurred in the
South Pacific from the early 1800s to the time when he, a twenty-three-
year-old sailor, glimpsed warships in the midst of tropical beauty and
tranquillity. The early spectacle influenced his perspective on all he
would see in Polynesia and became an essential part of his vision of the
nineteenth-century world. It brought to consciousness what would be the
feeling of a lifetime, that nothing could be more out of keeping with good
and beauty than what the warships signified; war, as the footnote to
Omoo's Chapter xxix defines it, is the "greatest of evils."[2] The picture of
the frigates in the harbor of Nukuheva, if well executed by a graphic artist, could serve as a frontispiece for Melville's first two books printed
as one.

*Reprinted by permission of the New York University Press from *War in Melville's Imagina-
tion* by Joyce Sparer Adler. Copyright © 1981 by New York University.

Together, *Typee* and *Omoo* present the three stages of Polynesian history as Melville interpreted them, all of which he could observe side by side as he moved from island to island and from shore to interior. The first is life in a "state of nature," as in the everyday life of the people of the remote Typee valley. The second is the stage of widening encroachment by "civilization," whose purpose it is to exploit the islands and the islanders. The third is the period of complete occupation rule, resulting in the dying out of Polynesians, so fully and movingly described in *Omoo*. Each work reverberates the other's special theme, and both merge into the one they share. *Typee* predicts the extermination of the Typees because of what civilization soon will bring; *Omoo* looks back on the peace and happiness the Tahitians enjoyed before the coming of the white Christian invaders. Both books show civilization and Christianity in the South Seas as the opposite, in effect, of what they pretend to be. Civilization, presumably the ameliorator of life, brings death; Christianity, presumably the bearer of light, puts out the sun—the culture—which the Polynesians need in order to live. Melville's history of the war the nineteenth-century colonialists waged on the people of the South Pacific is the real, though not the external story of *Typee/Omoo*. Its implications, however, are not for that area of the world alone.

The implied theme of *Typee* is: Who are the real cannibals, the Typees who practice a ritual of eating the flesh of their dead attackers or the aggressor nations who have come to devour the islands? The answer, offered implicitly by the book as a whole, is also offered explicitly: "The fiend-like skill we display in the invention of all manner of death-dealing engines, the vindictiveness with which we carry on our wars, and the misery and desolation that follow in their train, are enough of themselves to distinguish the white civilized man as the most ferocious animal on the face of the earth" (xvii, 125).

Typee's subtitle, *A Peep at Polynesian Life*, half shows, half hides, Melville's intention. The bulk of the work—twenty-two out of thirty-four chapters—concerns the life of the Typees, in which absence of class distinctions or rigid family divisions, the practice of cooperation, and equal sharing of food and land typify the general spirit and organization of life. But Melville is no primitivist: modern civilization is from first to last, in all his work, his main concern. His account of the Typees' customs, crafts, traditions, pleasures, and rituals is the basis for a comparative study: the peaceful day-to-day life of the Typees is a vantage point from which to see more clearly the destructive aspects of nineteenth-century Christian civilization. *Typee* could just as easily be subtitled *A Peep at Civilization by Means of a Peep at Polynesian Life*.

At the beginning of *Typee* it appears that France alone is to be the target of Melville's condemnation of the war in the South Seas. He recounts her takeover of the Marquesas, unmasking her pretenses at humanity, Christianity, refinement, fairness, truth, and valor. Her occupation of the islands is "iniquitous" and "a signal infraction of the rights of humanity." He tells how she set up a puppet ruler and then sent warships to defend him; he anticipates other subterfuges the French will commit "to defend whatever cruelties they may hereafter think fit to commit in bringing the Marquesan natives into subjection"; and he explains that it was under cover of a similar pretense that the French "perpetrated" their "outrages and massacres at Tahiti the beautiful" (iii, 17–18). The Nukuhevans detest those who have made this "cavalier appropriation" of their shores and want to defend their land, but they are helpless in the face of the military might of the French. Thus, early in *Typee*, Melville begins to develop his idea that brute Force alone makes possible human enslavement and its accompanying ills: in his vision of the world, war is not only the greatest of evils; it is the original one.

But it becomes apparent that France, whose annexation of the Marquesas Melville happened to witness, is representative of all the nations that have come to "prey like bears," as *Mardi* will soon say. Other than French atrocities are narrated, the first and most outstanding among them being those committed by Capt. David Porter and his men from the U.S. frigate *Essex* who some years earlier attempted unsuccessfully to subjugate the Typees. Forced to retreat and abandon their "design of conquest," these "invaders, on their march back to the sea, consoled themselves for their repulse by setting fire to every house and temple in their route; and a long line of smoking ruins defaced . . . the valley, and proclaimed to its pagan inhabitants the spirit that reigned in the breasts of Christian soldiers." Melville generalizes:

> How often is the term "savages" incorrectly applied! None really deserving of it were ever yet discovered by voyagers or by travellers. They have discovered heathens and barbarians, whom by horrible cruelties they have exasperated into savages. It may be asserted without fear of contradiction, that in all the cases of outrages committed by Polynesians, Europeans have at some time or other been the aggressors, and that the cruel and bloodthirsty disposition of some of the islanders is mainly to be ascribed to the influence of such examples. (iv, 27)

The Typees in their remote valley have not yet been influenced by these examples. Melville wonders at their humaneness, and a conception that will at his most despairing be absent from his work but that will achieve great imaginative expression in *Moby-Dick* and *Billy Budd* appears in expository form in *Typee*. He voices his belief in humanity's latent original virtue in response to the question of how to explain the enigma that among the heathen Typees all went on with a harmony "unparalleled . . . in the most select, refined, and pious associations of mortals in Christendom." It must have been the result of an "inherent principle of honesty and charity" that is "graven on every breast" but that can be "distorted by arbitrary codes." It is to this "indwelling, this universally diffused perception of what is *just* and *noble*, that the integrity of the Marquesans in their intercourse with each other is to be attributed" (xxvii, 200–201).

The Typees are fortunate that they have not yet had the religion proclaimed by the imperialist nations forced upon them, for the imposition of Christianity upon "pagan" peoples is a death-dealing process as Melville describes it (xxvi, 195–96). The Anglo-Saxons "have extirpated Paganism from the greater part of the North American continent; but with it they have likewise extirpated the greater portion of the Red race." Similarly, the result of attempts that were presumably to "ameliorate the spiritual condition of the Polynesians . . . has almost invariably been to accomplish their temporal destruction!" The islander who still lives "finds himself an interloper in the country of his fathers." The fruits of the earth where he was born are "remorselessly seized upon and appropriated by the stranger, are devoured before the eyes of the starving inhabitants, or sent on board the numerous vessels which now touch at their shores." The Polynesian is told to work for next to nothing; the only alternative he has is to starve. "Not until I visited Honolulu was I aware of the fact that the small remnant of the natives had been civilized into draught horses, and evangelized into beasts of burden." The destruction of peoples has become worldwide: "Civilization is gradually sweeping from the earth the lingering vestiges of Paganism, and at the same time the shrinking forms of its unhappy worshippers." Melville is troubled to think of the dread fate the Typees face when in a few years Christian civilization inevitably "shall have driven all peace and happiness from the valley."

This fate, as illustrated in Tahiti and confirmed in Hawaii and other Polynesian islands, is the main subject of *Omoo*, which, grasped as a whole, is nothing less than a charge of genocide. Melville calls the process "depopulation" and attributes it to the starvation brought by civilization; to the corruption and demoralization caused by the invaders; and to the destruction of Polynesian culture, a process he terms *denationalization*.

Melville's "Preface" to *Omoo* shows his main purpose to be social enlightenment, not entertainment: "As a roving sailor, the author spent about three months in various parts of the islands of Tahiti and Imeeo . . . under circumstances most favorable for correct observations on the social condition of the natives" (p. xiv).[3] His letter submitting *Omoo* to John Murray, his British publisher, indicates that he intended the theme of the book to be Polynesian life "as affected by intercourse with the whites" ("Historical Note," p. 330).

In Tahiti, as in the Marquesas, the aggressor nation in 1842 is France. But once again that country is not Melville's sole target. The cession of Tahiti to the French, just concluded when the narrator arrives, is acceded to by Britain, for "mighty interests" of her own, despite her repeated past assurances to the island that she would guarantee its independence (xxxii, 124). The United States, too, plays a war-promoting role: the French warship, the *Reine Blanche,* is "one of the heavy sixty-gun frigates now in vogue all over the world . . . which we Yankees were the first to introduce. In action, these are the most murderous vessels ever launched" (xxix, 109). The genocidal effects of economic and cultural domination are well advanced by the time the French arrive. The "most distressing consequence of civilization" in places like Tahiti—lack of food, previously unknown—is now "ever present," because "the demands of the shipping exhaust the uncultivated resources of the island" (xxxiv, 131–32). Christian missionaries have been the allies of the exploiters. There have been religious wars. In a valley of the island of Imeeo, Melville sees that rich with trees as it is, few are useful to the natives, and he wonders why none is a coconut or breadfruit tree. The scene from the past, described to him as the answer, symbolizes the intentional destruction of life brought about by Christian crusaders from Tahiti: "In the sanguinary religious hostilities which ensued upon the conversion to Christianity of the first Pomaree, a war party from Tahiti destroyed (by 'girdling' the bark) entire groves of these invaluable trees. For some time afterward, they stood stark and leafless in the sun; sad monuments of the fate which befell the inhabitants of the valley" (lv, 214).

Deprived of an adequate supply of food, the Tahitians have been wasting away. But what Melville stresses especially is that the attacks on their culture, the "denationalizing" process (xlvii, 183) supervised by the missionaries and enforced by the religious police, has destroyed the Polynesians' will to live. Innocent sports and pastimes—wrestling, foot racing, throwing the javelin, archery, dancing, tossing the football, kite flying, flute playing, and singing traditional songs—have been made punishable offenses. Necklaces and garlands of flowers, tattooing, and national costumes, modest enough to Melville, are forbidden. The breadfruit harvest festival has been suppressed. Old beliefs, arts, and traditions are made to seem evil or valueless. Privacy is invaded by the religious constabulary. Personal names disapproved of by the missionaries are changed to biblical names meaningless to those renamed and hence ridiculous to Melville (lxxiii, 277). The abolition of their culture has not been "willingly acquiesced in" by the Tahitians (xlvii, 183). Conformity has been achieved by terror. Melville relates how under Pomaree II "by force of arms, was Christianity finally triumphant"; there was "great slaughter" in these "religious wars" (lxxx, 302).

Demoralized, idle, or indulging in sensualities not known to them before the advent of the white man, the Polynesians, it seems to Melville, cannot long exist (xlix, 190–92). According to Captain Cook, in 1777 the population of Tahiti was about two hundred thousand; "By a regular census taken some four or five years ago, it was found to be only nine thousand." The evils causing the Tahitians' extinction are "solely of foreign origin," as is the venereal disease "which now taints the blood of at least two thirds of the common people of the island." In the context of race extinction in which Melville describes the sufferings brought by it in *Omoo*, the "poison" of syphilis comes close to being a symbol of all the corrupting and death-bringing influences of "intercourse with the whites"; indeed, what the composite canvas of *Typee* and *Omoo* depicts is the rape of Polynesia—its conquest and occupation by brute Force.

Melville's response to the war whose nature, methods, masks, and results he saw in the South Seas is the source of virtually all in *Typee* and *Omoo* that foretells the workings of his mature poetic imagination: alertness to scenes and figures capable of communicating fundamental realities of human life in his time; sensitivity to ironies and inner contradictions indicative of the nature of the distorting codes of nineteenth-century civilization that are inimical to peaceful human relations; and a deep sense of what is beautiful in people, nature, and life in contrast to what is ugly or grotesque.

The young Melville wanted worldly success. Yet, exotic as are many of the experiences he included in his first two books, much as he spiced his accounts with dangers and dancing girls, and amenable as he was to making some changes to meet the wishes of his publishers, he still placed his great emphasis on the destructive effects of the imperialist and religious wars of conquest in the South Pacific, a theme that could not fail to alienate a large part of his potential public, as the following passage in *Typee* demonstrates he well knew: "As wise a man as Shakespeare has said, that the bearer of evil tidings hath but a losing office; and so I suppose will it prove with me" (xxvi, 198). We must be impressed by how strong a motive force, then as afterward, was his compulsion to voice through his art his abhorrence of the wars of "white civilized man."

Notes

1. *Typee* (Evanston, Ill: Northwestern Univ. Press and the Newberry Library, 1968). All references in the text will be to this edition. The emphasis in this quotation is mine. In subsequent references to this and other works of Melville in the text, the book form "(ii, 12)," or a slightly modified version of it, will be used to cite chapter and page numbers.

2. *Omoo* (Evanston, Ill.: Northwestern Univ. Press and the Newberry Library, 1968).

3. Van Wyck Brooks considered *Omoo* "a book of pure adventure" written in a "morning mood." Gordon Roper's "Historical Note" in the Northwestern edition of *Omoo* quotes other critics whose readings of *Omoo* are similar.

Melville's *Typee*:
A Tale of Two Worlds

John Wenke*

I

With the rudiments of *Typee*'s plot, primarily a tale of escape/capture/escape, Melville gives initial form to the story of man's attempt to reconcile the opposing forces of freedom and necessity, a preoccupation which persists throughout his career.[1] When Tommo escapes from the *Dolly,* he tries to evade the restrictive contingencies of his life as a sailor and discover an existence which conforms to his naive expectations of good food, good drink, rest, recuperation, and the leisure to choose his next ship. Tommo and Toby desert the ship not so much out of desire to explore the island, however alluring it may seem, but to escape a captain who is violating their rights.[2] At the outset of the book, the ship fails to provide sustenance for the crew. They are virtually out of food. There is no green to offset the monotonous effects of the ocean's all-encompassing blue. The "painted green" on board is a "vile and sickly hue."[3]

Tommo's desertion constitutes a minimal act of self-assertion, a defeat of oppressive circumstances. But in lacking a full comprehension of the complexities of the world into which he flees, he encounters more problematic confinements. The farther he travels from the ship, the more delusive and ephemeral his freedoms become. As Tommo comes eventually to recognize, merely escaping one form of subjugation does not lead to self-determination. What is needed, Melville suggests, is some form of self-transformation, which permits one to overcome difficulties without blundering into more threatening ones, essentially an ability to *know* the extent of one's freedom and the degree to which it is circumscribed by limitations. Thus the possibilities of freedom in *Typee* relate integrally to the achievement of self-knowledge and knowledge of the ambiguous world of experience.

Milton R. Stern has identified *Typee* as Melville's first exploration of the "conduct of wrongly informed vision."[4] Throughout Tommo's and Toby's progress into the unknown, their perceptions are persistently

*This essay was written specifically for this volume and is published here for the first time by permission of the author.

proved wrong.[5] For example, Tommo believes that there will be plenty to eat in the mountains, that they will be able to see the bay without being seen, that their elevated vantage point will allow them to descend at will into the supposedly friendly Happar valley. In the absence of knowledge, the travelers stumble into one trap after another. Their expected freedom becomes imprisonment: the reeds are like steel bars and their great height and density greatly impede the travelers' ability to pass: "When we arrived within a short distance of the ridge, we were stopped by a mass of tall yellow reeds, growing together as thickly as they could stand, and as tough and stubborn as so many rods of steel. . . . [T]heir great height completely shut us out from the view of surrounding objects, and we were not certain but that we might have been going all the time in a wrong direction" (pp. 37–38).

Tommo's many mistakes emphasize Melville's concern in *Typee* with the primacy of the subjective. Freedom and necessity in Melville's world tend not to be absolute conditions, but have meaning in relation to an individual's private capacity either to assert self-control and overcome difficulty, or to submit to the control of forces beyond the will. At one point, Tommo gives up and sinks down "with a sort of dogged apathy." Toby, on the contrary, arouses him with "a plan to free us from the net in which we had become entangled" (p. 38). As the mind asserts control over the blank world of experience, so one brings to consciousness the possibility for self-determined responses to the impingements of necessity. One exercises freedom through the ability to overcome restricting circumstances. But, as we shall see, Tommo's overcoming of the confinements in the jungle and the mountains leads to an essentially childlike state of dependence, and the sense of liberation is then shown to be self-deluding.

In passing from the ship into the Typee valley, Tommo travels from the Western world of mind and history into the primitive world of unconsciousness and prehistory.[6] What was initially a simple act of escape has been transformed into a complicated rite of passage, which brings Tommo (and Melville) to examine the conflicting demands of both worlds. The Western and primitive worlds offer antithetical possibilities for the development of identity. Tommo is Melville's first character who encounters cultural relativism. Indeed, much of *Typee* explores the effects of pre-conscious experience on a western mind. Throughout the narrative, Tommo must constantly reevaluate his relation to experience. As he moves physically and psychologically away from the world of the ship and the context of history, Tommo has great difficulty understanding his status in the valley. He continually wonders about the extent of his freedom within the valley and the implications of his apparent imprisonment. Tommo's uncertainty increases with his lack of communication, his separation from Toby, and the mysterious leg ailment which flares up whenever he thinks about trying to leave the valley. Life with the Typees, in fact, confronts Tommo with the most paradoxical condition of all: the valley's indolent freedoms may actually mask the reality of lifelong immurement; benign appearances may conceal cannibalistic intentions. "Might it not be," Tommo ponders, "that beneath these fair appearances the islanders covered some perfidious design, and that their friendly reception of us might only precede some horrible catastrophe" (p. 76)?

II

As a man standing between two worlds, Tommo must decide whether he wishes to retain his identity as a Western man, and thus become a prisoner, or be incorporated into the Typee tribe, and thus enjoy the childlike, nonrational freedoms of primitive life.[7] In *Typee*, Melville dramatizes the way in which primitivistic freedoms cannot coexist with the demands for acquisition, self-determination, and technological domination which characterize Western man. In fact, Tommo's private story within the valley gives focus to the story of cultural genocide taking place throughout the Pacific.[8] While Tommo explores the possibility of balancing Western and primitive possibilities of selfhood on an individual level, the rampant colonialism and the impinging malignity of perverse authoritarianism embody the force of historical necessity which carries on the destruction of the natural liberties of primitive man. The imposition of Western will over the Polynesian natives violates Melville's sense of a balanced freedom which seeks to reconcile the poles of license and subjugation. Indeed, colonialism in *Typee* represents the first appearance in Melville's canon of the dangers of the unrestricted will. Such absolutistic license anticipates on a political and anthropological level the metaphysical absolutism of Taji and Ahab. In usurping the freedoms of the primitive tribes in the Pacific, the Western powers annihilate the identity of primitive man.

Melville's condemnation of willful license is animated early in the narrative by the contrast between the natural freedom of the Polynesian women and the depraved licentiousness of the sailors aboard the *Dolly*. In describing the women, Tommo remarks, "Their appearance perfectly amazed me; their extreme youth, the light clear brown of their complexions, their delicate features, and inexpressibly graceful figures, their softly moulded limbs, and free unstudied action, seemed as strange as beautiful" (p. 15). The beauties of the primitive oppose the debaucheries of civilization. While Tommo humorously suggests that the *Dolly* "was fairly captured," the inverse is actually true. The women fall prey to the "unholy passions" and "grossest licentiousness" of the crew (p. 15). The actions of the sailors introduce the way in which the Western world overwhelms the savages, the extension of which is manifest in the French who use "[f]our heavy, double-banked frigates and three corvettes to frighten a parcel of naked heathen into subjection" (p. 16)! By extending sovereignty over the natives, the French pervert the exercise of authority. Unlike Tommo who can temporarily escape from the repressive authority of the ship, the islanders have nowhere to go once the Europeans arrive. They are victims of the invaders.

But because of the difficult terrain and their relative inaccessibility, the Typees remain isolated from civilization, thereby maintaining their own natural, primitive freedoms. In the center of the island, the Typees are limited to a "little space." Paradoxically, this restricted area allows them to retain their way of life for a time. In discussing the placement of the glen of Tior, Tommo offers an early instance of Melville's preoccupation with walls. Here, the mountain walls—"stupendous barriers"—are not signs of sterility, barrennness, or nothingness, as walls later are in "Bartleby the Scrivener." Instead they are the means whereby the Typees manage to remain in happy seclusion: "Hemmed in by these stupendous barriers, the valley would be altogether shut out from the rest of the world, were it not that it is accessible from the sea at one end, and by a narrow defile at the other" (p. 28). As Melville constantly reiterates, the geographical isolation of the Typees provides only a temporary evasion of Western domination. The destruction of the Typee world is only a matter of time.

Melville uses the light "yoke of servitude" which the Typees enjoy under Mehevi, their chief, to draw a contrast with the depravity that afflicts the Tahitians and the Hawaiians who have adopted nominal Christianity. What most enrages Melville is the way Western civilization enslaves the primitives by destroying their inherited state of felicity. A native becomes "an interloper in the country of his fathers. . . . The spontaneous fruits of the earth, which God in his wisdom had ordained for the support of the indolent natives [are] remorselessly seized upon and appropriated by the stranger" (pp. 195–96). In the process of being stripped of identity, the natives lose the possibility of freedom, which entirely depends upon the ability to retain a natural relation to their world. By dragging the Polynesians into the Western world, the colonialists, in Melville's view, enslave the natives. In Honolulu, for example, the natives are "civilized into draught horses, and evangelized into beasts of burden. But so it is. They have been literally broken into the traces, and are harnessed to the vehicles of their spiritual instructors like so many dumb brutes" (p. 196)! By transforming the natives into "*draught* bipeds," the reforming missionaries are blinded by the ideal of a higher good and fail to see the havoc they cause (p. 196). The denationalized natives are reduced to a state of abject servility. As Melville dramatizes in *Omoo*, nominal Christianity leads to the unhealthy absence of constructive activity. The prospect of gaining a balanced freedom by overcoming difficulties in the world of work, as Redburn and White-Jacket do, seems an utter impossibility for the Polynesians. The freedoms of one world cannot easily be assumed by a member of the other world. When such a thing is tried, one encounters the problem of losing the self and risking lifelong captivity.

III

Regarding Tommo's personal story within the valley, Melville insistently dramatizes the inability of Western man to become fully committed to the freedoms of the primitive life without risking a radical transformation of identity. Throughout his stay in the valley, Tommo's sense of self oscillates between the consciousness of imprisonment and the temporary sense of liberation. Essentially, Tommo's search for freedom concerns an exploration of antithetical possibilities for consciousness and identity. Alternately, Tommo lives in two states of mind. He admires and fears the Typees. On the one hand, they lack the vicissitudes of life which afflict Western man.[9] On the other, the inscrutable elements of Typee life threaten to consume him forever. Tommo's appreciation for the Typees' numerous freedoms conflicts with perplexing doubts regarding their ultimate intentions. Thus cannibalism becomes the narrative's central metaphor for the primitive's threat to consume Tommo's contemporary identity.

Luther Stearns Mansfield argues incorrectly that Tommo "represented essentially free man. . . . With ingenuity and perhaps a little luck—and only a few minor complications—Tommo could do what he wished, and in Melville's context it would be foolish to think of him as anything but free."[10] Tommo does have freedom in the valley, but it is not so simple. In order to enjoy himself, Tommo makes mental adjustments which create the context for freedom. When he denies, or forgets, his life as a Western man, he can immerse himself wholeheartedly in the valley's sensual pleasures. He becomes miserable and acutely aware of being a prisoner when he recalls his past life in the West or projects himself into the future.[11] When he resigns himself to remaining within the narrow limits of the Typee valley, he convinces himself that it is a "Happy Valley." He then appreciates the beauties of the world and his leg ailment disappears. His moments of freedom occur because he has an "elasticity of mind which placed me beyond the reach of those dismal forebodings to which I had so lately been a prey" (p. 123). It is with such an "altered frame of mind" that Tommo possesses his greatest freedom within the limitations imposed by the valley:

> I thought that for a sojourn among cannibals, no man could have well made a more agreeable one.
> To be sure there were limits set to my wanderings. Toward the sea my progress was barred by an express prohibition of the savages; and after having made two or three ineffectual attempts to reach it, as much to gratify my curiosity as anything else, I gave up the idea. (pp. 123–24)

At one point, Tommo explicitly indicates how his freedom in the valley entails a rejection of memory and an embrace of sensual pleasure: "I was free from pain and able to take exercise. In short, I had every reason to anticipate a perfect recovery. Freed from apprehensions on this point, and resolved to regard the future without flinching, I flung myself anew into all the social pleasures of the valley, and sought to bury all regrets, and all remembrances of my previous existence, in the wild enjoyments it afforded" (p. 144). The key words here, "flung" and "wild," suggest Tommo's antirational, hedonistic immersion into primitive unconscious pleasures, which are, from the point of view of the West, incompatible with the demand for communal order.

The freedoms of the valley are short-lived and insidiously self-destructive. In making a total commitment to these ephemeral freedoms, by extending the unanchored or ahistorical life through time, Tommo would eventually destroy his identity as a Western man. When Tommo's memory reasserts itself, his enjoyment of the valley ends, and he lapses into a state of frustrated anticipation. Tommo alternately enjoys two distinct kinds of freedoms—the primitive and the Western. The virtues and allurements of each world predominate at different times, and his sense of freedom or imprisonment depends on whether he lives in the moment or in consciousness of past or future. In essence and here is the reason why Tommo must flee the Typees—the powers of mind and judgment which allow him to appreciate the virtues of both worlds, the powers of mind which allow him to assimilate another cultural standpoint, are precisely those attributes which militate against making a total commitment to the primitive world and its absence of historical consciousness. Tommo's need to retain his identity as a Western man suggests that any freedom worth keeping, any capacity for self-determination which will permit him to retain his "face," must be discovered in the context of historical necessity, the world epitomized by the man-of-war. Neither the hedonism of the valley nor the sloth of the rover's life in *Omoo* provides a satisfactory conclusion to Tommo's search for selfhood. This is why the object of Tommo's original quest—to find a well-governed ship—concludes his narrative in *Omoo*.[12]

As Ishmael is later to discover, freedom must be circumscribed by a complex intermingling of necessity and chance. Like Ishmael, Tommo is indeed a "Loose-Fish and a Fast-Fish, too," and he manifests his greatest capacity for self-knowledge when he recognizes the virtues and failures of each world.[13] Knowledge of self and the world can never be meaningfully divorced in Melville's view. Tommo never completely repudiates the natural beauties of the Typees and he never completely rejects his civilized past. He attacks the perversions of colonialism, but he does so from the point of view of a Western, rather than a primitive, man. At times, Tommo expresses the capacity to remain between two worlds. He enjoys the pleasures of the valley, while still retaining a racial identity distinct from the natives. In fact, his final resolution to escape is precipitated by the Typee's desire to assimilate him completely into their way of life. To allow himself to be tattooed would destroy his mediate position—that is, the freedom to roam within and enjoy the physical and psychological freedoms of the valley, while still retaining such links to the outside world as memory, his ability to perform a sailor's work, and the desire to return to the ship. The tattoo represents an irrevocable sign of an inward transformation of identity. With the literal loss of his face, Tommo would lose his options. The temporary freedoms of the valley are lures toward assimilation and mask the insidious threat, if extended through time, of consuming him forever. Ironically, Mehevi offers Tommo "a choice of patterns" and earnestly assures him that his "choice was wholly unrestricted" (p. 220). Since self-determination cannot coexist with the authority ruling the valley, Tommo escapes imprisonment and continues his search for the good ship. The "Happy Valley" is now a "narrow valley," and the sea looms as the means of escape, just as the island had earlier.

Some critics have a hard time accepting Tommo's dramatic escape during which he stabs Mow-Mow in the neck, possibly killing him. Sedgwick finds that the "narrative climax is deeply at odds with the rest of the book." Edward S. Grejda argues that the atmosphere of sinister darkness which suddenly characterizes the Typees emerges from Melville's desire to end the book stunningly. John Bernstein makes the untenable claim that Tommo goes off to become a rebel: "Tommo quits the Happy Valley of the Typees in order that he may lead the life of a rebel and fight against the forces of injustice."[14] One need not impose the role of either Prometheus or Thomas Jefferson on Tommo to see that he flees the valley in order to retain his identity. His allegiance to mind and self informs his escape. In seeking to assimilate Tommo, the Typees impel him to return to the world of history and civilization where he can seek a livable balance between personal autonomy and communal balance.

IV

Tommo's failure to find an idealized, noncontingent state of existence introduces Melville's exploration of the interrelation of freedom and necessity. As developed through Tommo, Redburn, and White-Jacket, and culminating in Ishmael, the achievement of freedom largely entails the ability to transfer the locus of control from forces outside the self to a conscious exercise of choice. The Melville hero tries to establish an identity balanced between unimpeded, absolutistic expressions of will and total subjugation to necessity. In seeking this balance, the Ishmael persona creates the possibility for a social order founded upon democratic brotherhood rather than fiat, an order which can reflect the coexistence of private mind and public society. During his adventures, Tommo encounters the enticements of primitive unconsciousness in *Typee* and the indolence of roving in *Omoo*, while White-Jacket must confront the man-of-war world which seeks to reduce "the people" to an undifferentiated, subjugated mass. For Melville, the societal expression of a balanced freedom must exist within the encompassing framework of historical time and include a respect for the natural rights of all men. The Melville hero knows that there are limitations to his capacity for self-determination; he understands the way in which necessity must sometimes impinge upon volition; he comprehends the degree to which he is a "fast-fish" and a "loose-fish" at the same time. As we have seen in Melville's presentation of Tommo's tale of two worlds, the meaning of freedom cannot even be considered without a careful and highly self-conscious regard for those forces within one's being, in nature, society, and the universe which circumscribe and redefine the exercise of will.

Notes

1. See the following accounts for important discussions of *Typee* as an embryonic presentation of Melville's imagination: William Ellery Sedgwick, *Herman Melville: The Tragedy of Mind* (Cambridge, Mass., 1944; rpt. New York: Russell and Russell, 1972), pp. 19–36; Leon Howard, *Herman Melville* (1951; rpt. Berkeley: Univ. of California Press, 1967), pp. 92–100; Milton R. Stern, *The Fine Hammered Steel of Herman Melville* (Urbana: Univ. of Illinois Press, 1957), pp. 29–65; Edgar A. Dryden, *Melville's Thematics of Form* (Baltimore: Johns Hopkins Press, 1968), pp. 37–46; John Seelye, *Melville: The Ironic Diagram* (Evanston: Northwestern Univ. Press, 1970), pp. 11–28; A. Carl Bredahl, Jr., *Melville's Angle of Vision*, Univ. of Florida Monographs, Humanities, No. 37 (Gainesville: Univ. of Florida Press, 1972), pp. 7–16. Stern best sums up the way in which *Typee* presents a seminal voyage "into the sea of relationships between the western world, the primitive world, the quester, and the lure. The apparent vehicle for those relationships is the occasional treatment of the contact between Christianity and the Marquesans. The more important and less apparent vehicle is an opposition between mind and body, mind and heart, communication and the lack of communication" (p. 31).

2. Nicholas Canaday, Jr., in *Melville and Authority*, Univ. of Florida Monographs, Humanities, No. 28 (Gainesville: Univ. of Florida Press, 1968), argues that "the fictional pattern of the dissatisfied sailor who deserts his ship to escape a tyrannical captain—a pattern that reappears throughout Melville's writing—is established early in *Typee*" (p. 2).

3. *Typee*, ed. Harrison Hayford et al. (Evanston: Northwestern Univ. Press and the Newberry Library, 1968), p. 4. All citations are from this text and will be identified by page number within parentheses following the quotation.

4. Stern, p. 25.

5. Bredahl argues, "*Typee* emphasizes the boundaries to both physical and psychological perspective. The view from the *Dolly*, Nukuheva, the mountains, and the Typee valley are all limited by such physical realities as land and distance. Similarly, any choice or judgment is in large part limited by location or background as is stressed on the trip across the mountains, where physical boundaries are placed on freedom of choice and movement" (p. 14).

6. There is a varied and extensive heritage concerning the relationship between primitive and western worlds in *Typee* as involving an exploration of Edenic possibility. Charles Robert Anderson, in *Melville in the South Seas*, Columbia Univ. Studies in English and Comparative Literature, No. 38 (New York: Columbia Univ. Press, 1939), establishes many facts of Melville's life in the south seas. Anderson sees *Typee* "chiefly as a defense of unspoiled primitivism" (p. 238); Newton Arvin, in *Herman Melville*, American Men of Letters Series (New York: Sloane, 1950), discusses Melville's psychological kinship with primitive man. See also Stern, pp. 34–47; James E. Miller, Jr., "*Typee* and *Omoo*: The Quest for the

Garden," in *A Reader's Guide to Herman Melville* (New York: Noonday, 1962), pp. 18–37; Faith Pullin, "Melville's *Typee*: The Failure of Eden," in *New Perspectives on Melville*, ed. Faith Pullin (Kent, Ohio: Kent State Univ. Press, 1978), pp. 1–28.

7. Thomas J. Scorza, in "Tragedy in the State of Nature: Melville's *Typee*," *Interpretation*, 8 (1979), 103–20, argues that the "Typees are as heartful, innocent, spontaneous, natural, and simple as civilized men are heartless, sophisticated, scheming, artificial, and complex" (p. 110).

8. See Scorza's discussion of "the conquering French," (p. 106).

9. See Anderson, pp. 138–40, for his discussion of the pleasures Melville found in the primitive valley and the valley's contrast to civilization.

10. Luther Stearns Mansfield, "Some Patterns from Melville's 'Loom of Time,' " in *Essays on Determinism in American Literature*, Kent Studies in English, No. 1, ed. Sydney J. Krause (Kent, Ohio: Kent State Univ. Press, 1964), p. 21.

11. Dryden argues that Tommo's leg gives him trouble when he thinks about leaving. Although this point has been addressed frequently, Dryden is the first to relate the swollen leg to Tommo's sense of time (pp. 41–42).

12. See Steven E. Kemper, "*Omoo*: Germinal Melville," *Studies in the Novel*, 10 (1978), 101–13.

13. *Moby-Dick*, ed. Hershel Parker (New York: Norton, 1967), p. 334.

14. Sedgwick, p. 20; Edward S. Grejda, *The Common Continent of Men* (Port Washington, N.Y.: Kennikat, 1974), p. 21; John Bernstein, *Pacificism and Rebellion in the Writings of Herman Melville*, Studies in American Literature, No. 1 (The Hague: Mouton, 1964), p. 23.

An Annotated Bibliography of
Typee Studies

Joseph Wenke*

The purpose of this bibliography is to provide an accurate list of all the presently known English language materials that have contributed to the history of the critical reputation of *Typee*. Because the production of scholarly and critical writings quickly and markedly increased after World War II, I have used 1945 as a date determining policies of inclusion: in compiling this bibliography, I have included all known discussions and mentions of *Typee* from 1846 to 1945 with the exception of unexpanded references to Melville as the author of *Typee*, unexpanded mentions of *Typee* in booksellers' announcements and advertisements, unevaluative notices of editions, printed extracts, and booklists, and reviews of Melville's books after *Mardi*. I have also generally excluded undeveloped references to *Typee* in notices and reviews of Melville's lectures and reviews of books on Melville. I have explained the few exceptions to these two rules in the notes that accompany the items.

I have included evaluative references to *Typee* in reviews of *Omoo* and *Mardi* primarily because these books are often examined in relation to *Typee*. Indeed, in many cases these reviews continue the discussion of issues originally raised in reviews of Melville's first book. As a result, such reviews of *Omoo* and *Mardi* form an important part of the contemporary critical response to *Typee*.

I have included biographical sketches and obituaries that contain summaries of Melville's adventures in the South Seas and, in some instances, brief comments on *Typee*. However, I have included only until 1921 items that merely refer to the biographical background of *Typee*, for it was in that year that Raymond M. Weaver published *Herman Melville: Mariner and Mystic*, the first book-length biography. Consequently, the development of what was commonly known about Melville can be traced through this bibliography by anyone interested in the development of Melville's reputation.

In compiling the list of *Typee* studies since 1945, I have excluded mere references to *Typee* in reviews of editions and reviews of books on

*This bibliography was compiled specifically for this volume and is published here for the first time by permission of the author.

Melville. I have included articles and books that contain brief mentions of *Typee* only if the references are of scholarly interest. Otherwise I have required that items include at least a briefly sustained discussion or interpretive reference to *Typee*. I should also state that because of the obvious limitations imposed by publishing schedules, I have made no attempt to make the bibliography comprehensive beyond 1979. As a result, the listings for 1980–81 undoubtedly are incomplete.

Whenever possible, I have personally checked the accuracy of items listed in previously published Melville bibliographies. When I have been unable to do so, I have relied upon the information provided in Brian Higgins's *Herman Melville: An Annotated Bibliography, Vol. 1: 1846–1930* (Boston: G. K. Hall, 1979) and Steve Mailloux and Hershel Parker, *Checklist of Melville Reviews* (The Melville Society, 1975). Whenever I have not been able to check the authenticity of an item beyond its scholarly source, I have listed that source along with the item.

I have not attempted to compile a fully annotated bibliography. The notes are intended primarily to list reprintings and to identify items that may be of only limited interest to many students and scholars. All untitled, unannotated items on the periodicals list throughout 1846 and 1847 are reviews or notices of *Typee*. Reviews of *Omoo* and *Mardi* that include evaluative references to *Typee* are identified respectively by the notations "*Omoo / Typee*" and "*Mardi / Typee*." In most cases I have silently corrected mistakes in previous bibliographies, including those of Higgins and of Mailloux and Parker. In a few instances, however, corrective comments do accompany items. Page numbers appearing within brackets indicate specific page numbers of references to *Typee* within articles or sections of books.

I have divided the bibliography into two separately numbered sections, periodicals and books (which includes pamphlets). In referring to items in the bibliography, I have used the prefix "P" for periodical and "B" for book together with the number of the item being cross-referenced. I have listed chronologically all items by year prior to 1920 and by decade after that year. Because the most familiar names in Melville scholarship begin to appear in the 1920s, I have used a system of decades as an aid to the Melville scholar: often one knows that a particular scholar wrote a piece *around* such or such a year, but does not recall the exact year. The alphabetical listings within decades are designed to facilitate memory and the use of this bibliography. For those interested in precise chronological development of criticism, it is easy enough to shift about the items listed within each decade for a year-by-year approach. I have attempted to facilitate the location of references while still preserving in the bibliography a clear sense of chronology. Such an arrangement will, I believe, enhance the value of this bibliography as a practical reference tool for students and scholars interested in understanding and, perhaps through their own work, redefining the critical reputation of *Typee*.

PERIODICALS

1846–1919

1. *Athenaeum* (London), No. 956 (21 Feb. 1846), pp. 189–91. Reprinted in P39 and P45.

2. *Athenaeum* (London), No. 957 (28 Feb. 1846), pp. 218–20. Reprinted in P45 and P46.

3. *Spectator* (London), 19 (28 Feb. 1846), 209–10. Reprinted in P45; reprinted in part in P420, p. 28 and B295, pp. 53–55.

4. *Critic* (London), NS 3 (7 March 1846), 219–22. Reprinted in part in B295, pp. 56–57.

5. *Examiner* (London), 7 March 1846, pp. 147–48. Reprinted in B295, pp. 60–64.

6. *John Bull* (London), 7 March 1846, p. 156. Reprinted in part in P420, p. 29; reprinted in B295, 64–65.

7. *Mirror* (London), 47 (7 March 1846), 154–57.

8. *Critic* (London), NS 3 (14 March 1846), 251–54. Reprinted in part in B295, pp. 57–59.

9. *New York Evening Mirror*, 17 March 1846. Cited in Steve Mailloux and Hershel Parker's *Checklist of Melville Reviews*, p. 1.

10. *New York Morning News*, 18 March 1846. Reprinted in P15; reprinted in part in P497, p. 2.

11. *Atlas* (London), 21 March 1846, pp. 185–86.

12. [New York] *Anglo American*, 6 (21 March 1846), 523.

13. *New York Morning News*, 21 March 1846. Extracts followed by comments on the missionaries and a brief comment on *Typee*. Reprinted in P25.

14. [New York] *Spirit of the Times*, 16 (21 March 1846), 48. Reprinted in P467, pp. 58–59 and P488.

15. *New York Weekly News*, 21 March 1846. Reprint of P10; reprinted in part in P484, pp. 568–69.

16. *Boston Daily Advertiser*, 23 March 1846, p. 2.

17. *New Bedford Daily Mercury*, 23 March 1846, p. 1. Reprinted in P21, P100, and B295, p. 66.

18. *Philadelphia Dollar Newspaper*, 25 March 1846. Reprinted in P527, p. 56.

19. [Hawthorne, Nathaniel]. *Salem Advertiser*, 25 March 1846. Reprinted in P433; B287; B316; B321, p. 13; and B295, pp. 67–68.

20. *Albany Argus*, 26 March 1846.

21. *New Bedford Mercury*, 27 March 1846. Reprint of P17.

22. "American Poetry." *New York Morning News*, 27 March 1846. Prints humorous poem, "To Toby, Victimised to the appetite of certain individuals inhabiting an island in the Pacific Ocean." Reprinted in part in P497, pp. 2–3.

23. *Atlas* (London), 28 March 1846, pp. 202–03.

24. *Critic* (London), NS 3 (28 March 1846), 315–20. Reprinted in part in B295, pp. 59–60.

25. *New York Weekly News*, 28 March 1846. Reprint of P13; reprinted in part in P484, pp. 569–70.

26. *Sun* (London), No. 16700 (30 March 1846), p. 3. Reprinted in P533, p. 9.

27. *New York Gazette and Times*, 30 March 1846, pp. 1–2. Reprinted in B295, pp. 68–70.

28. *Tait's Edinburgh Magazine*, NS 13 (Apr. 1846), 268.

29. *Douglas Jerrold's Shilling Magazine* (London), 3 (Apr. 1846), 380–83. Reprinted in B295, pp. 70–73.

30. *Eclectic Review* (London), NS 19 (Apr. 1846), 448–59. Reprinted in part in P420, pp. 24–25, and B225, p. 212.

31. *Simmonds' Colonial Magazine and Foreign Miscellany* (London), 7 (Apr. 1846), 499–501.

32. [New York] *American Review: A Whig Journal*, 3 (Apr. 1846), 415–24. Reprinted in part in B225, p. 212.

33. [New York] *Illustrated Magazine*, 1 (Apr. 1846), 380.

34. [Richmond] *Southern Literary Messenger*, 12 (Apr. 1846), 256.

35. [New York] *National Anti-Slavery Standard*, 6 (2 Apr. 1846), 175.

36. *Cincinnati Morning Herald*, 3 Apr. 1846.

37. *Cincinnati Morning Herald*, 4 Apr. 1846. Cited in B260, p. 34.

38. [New York] *Albion*, NS 5 (4 Apr. 1846), 168.

39. "Adventures in the Marquesas Islands." [New York] *Anglo American*, 6 (4 Apr. 1846), 555–57. Reprint of P1.

40. *New York Daily Tribune*, 4 Apr. 1846. Reprinted in B282, p. 3 and B295, pp. 77–78.

41. *New York Evening Mirror*, 3 (4 Apr. 1846), 416. Cited in P419, p. 11 and B225, p. 210.

42. [West Roxbury (Mass.)] *Harbinger*, 2 (4 Apr. 1846), 263–66. Reprinted in part in B295, pp. 74–77.

43. *Times* (London), 6 Apr. 1846, p. 3. Reprinted in part in B295, pp. 78–80.

44. C., H. *New York Evangelist*, 9 Apr. 1846. Reprinted in B295, p. 81.

45. "Herman Melville's Residence in the Marquesas." [Boston] *Littell's Living Age*, 9 (11 Apr. 1846), 82–93. Reprint of P3, P1, and P2.

46. "Adventures in the Marquesas Islands." [New York] *Anglo American*, 6 (11 Apr. 1846), 580–82. Reprint of P2.

47. [New York] *Golden Rule and Odd-Fellows' Family Companion*, 4 (11 Apr. 1846), 246. Reprinted in P527, p. 67.

48. *New York National Press: A Home Journal*, 11 Apr. 1846. Brief introduction to an extract. Cited in P527, p. 59.

49. *Brooklyn Eagle*, 15 Apr. 1846.

50. *John Bull* (London), 17 Apr. 1846. Cited in B215, p. 16.

51. *Morning Courier and New-York Enquirer*, 17 Apr. 1846. Reprinted in P442, pp. 204–05; reprinted in part in B225, p. 211.

52. "Herman Melville's Book." *Albany Argus*, 21 Apr. 1846. Reprinted in P53.

53. "Herman Melville's Book." *Albany Argus*, 24 Apr. 1846. Reprint of P52.

54. *Charleston* (S.C.) *Southern Patriot*, 25 Apr. 1846.

55. "Adventure of Herman Melville." *Chambers's Edinburgh Journal*, NS 5 (25 Apr. 1846), 265–69. Summary. Reprinted in P66 and P198.

56. [New York] *Knickerbocker*, 27 (May 1846), 450. Reprinted in part in B225, p. 216.

57. [New York] *Merchants' Magazine and Commercial Review*, 14 (May 1846), 491.

58. [New York] *National Magazine and Industrial Record*, 2 (May 1846), 1172. Reprinted in P527, pp. 58–59.

59. [New York] *United States Magazine and Democratic Review*, NS 18 (May 1846), 399. Reprinted in P419, p. 17 and B295, p. 83.

60. [Philadelphia] *Godey's Magazine and Lady's Book*, 32 (May 1846), 238.

61. [Philadelphia] *Graham's Magazine*, 28 (May 1846), 240. Reprinted in B295, p. 82.

62. "The Marquesas and the Marquesans." *Chambers's Edinburgh Journal*, NS 5 (2 May 1846), 282–84. Description of the islands published as a "sequel to the Adventure of Herman Melville, which appeared in our last number."

63. *New York Evangelist*, 9 May 1846. Cited in B260, p. 44.

64. "Typee, a Veritable Narrative." *New York Evening Mirror*, 9 May 1846. Reprinted in P65.

65. *New York Morning News*, 19 May 1846. Reprint of P64.

66. "Adventure of Herman Melville." [Boston] *Illustrated Family Magazine*, 3 (June 1846), 277–83. Reprint of P55. Incorrectly dated May 1846 in Steve Mailloux and Hershel Parker's *Checklist of Melville Reviews*, p. 5.

67. "Alleged Forgery." *Almanack of the Month* (London), 1 (June 1846), 368–69. Reprinted in P70; P420, pp. 37–38; and B295, p. 84; reprinted in part in B225, p. 220.

68. *New York Herald*, 4[?] June 1846. Obituary of Gansevoort Melville. Mention of *Typee*. Quoted in P69.

69. *Albany Argus*, 5 June 1846. Obituary of Gansevoort Melville which includes a reference to *Typee* in a quotation from P68.

70. "Ingenious Notice of 'Typee.'" *New York Morning News*, 29 June 1846. Introduction and reprint of P67.

71. [Boston] *Universalist Quarterly and General Review*, 3 (July 1846), 326–27. Reprinted in part in P462, p. 127.

72. *Gentleman's Magazine* (London), NS 26 (July 1846), 66.

73. [New Haven] *New Englander*, 4 (July 1846), 449–50. Reprinted in B282, pp. 4–5.

74. "*Typee*: The Traducers of Missions." [New York] *Christian Parlor Magazine*, 3 (July 1846), 74–83. Reprinted in part in P462, pp. 120–22; B225, p. 224; and B295, pp. 85–89.

75. "How strangely things turn up!" *Buffalo Commercial Advertiser*, 1 July 1846. Introduction and letter from "Toby." Reprinted in P76, P78, and B155, pp. 16–19; reprinted in part in P83; P93; P442, p. 207; and B225, p. 220.

76. "Toby Identified!" *Albany Evening Journal*, 3 July 1846. Introduction and reprint of P75; reprinted in part in P80.

77. Greene, Richard T. *Albany Argus*, 3 July 1846. Reprint of part of P75. Cited in B225, p. 221.

78. "A Veritable Witness." *Albany Argus*, 4 July 1846. Introduction and reprint of P75; reprinted in P82.

79. *Albany Evening Journal*, 6 July 1846. No longer doubts the authenticity of *Typee*. Reprinted in P82 and P442, p. 207.

80. "Toby." *Buffalo Commercial Advertiser*, 6 July 1846. Reprint of part of P76; reprinted in part in P83.

81. *Albany Argus*, 7 July 1846. Quotes from Melville's note which assures the editor that Richard Tobias Greene is "Toby." Reprinted in P83.

82. *Morning Courier and New-York Enquirer*, 9 July 1846. Reprints P78 and P79 and retracts former statement of doubt about the authenticity of *Typee*.

83. *New York Morning News*, 9 July 1846. Reprint of part of P75 and P80; reprint of P81; reprinted in P90.

84. Greene, Richard T. "Toby's Own Story." *Buffalo Commercial Advertiser*, 11 July 1846. Cited in B225, p. 221. Reprinted in P86 and P87.

85. *Boston Recorder*, 12 July 1846. Cited in B260, p. 44.

86. Greene, Richard T. "Toby's Own Story." *Albany Evening Journal*, 13 July 1846. Reprint of P84. Cited in B225, p. 222.

87. Greene, Richard T. "Toby's Own Story." *New York Morning News*, 15 July 1846. Reprint of P84. Cited in P497, p. 4.

88. "Typee: The Traducers of Missions." *New York Evangelist*, 16 July 1846, p. 114.

89. *New York Weekly News*, 18 July 1846. Reprint of "Toby's Own Story." Cited in P484, p. 571.

90. "Singular Development / Typee—Mr. Melville—Toby." *New York: National Press: A Home Journal*, 25 July 1846. Reprint of P83.

91. "Adventures in the Pacific—Dr. Coulter and Herman Melville." *Dublin University Magazine*, 28 (Aug. 1846), 127–39.

92. *New York Evening Mirror*, 1 Aug. 1846. Reprint of P75. Cited in P419, p. 11.

93. *Athenaeum* (London), No. 980 (8 Aug. 1846), p. 819. Comments on "Toby's" reappearance and reprints in part P75.

94. *New York Morning News*, 10 Aug. 1846. Notice of the publication of the revised edition of *Typee* followed by an extract from the Sequel. Cited in P497, p. 4.

95. [New York] *Christian Parlor Magazine*, 3 (Sept. 1846), 160. Review of the revised edition of *Typee*.

96. *New Quarterly Review* (London), 8 (Oct. 1846), 18–35.

97. "Ladies, Attention!" *Honolulu Polynesian*, 3 Oct. 1846.

98. *Athenaeum* (London), No. 988 (3 Oct. 1846), pp. 1014–15.

99. [Honolulu] *Friend*, 4 (15 Oct. 1846), 157. Comment on *Typee*.

100. *Honolulu Polynesian*, 17 Oct. 1846. Introduction and reprint of P17; reprinted in P104 and P105.

101. "The Story of Toby; a Sequel to *Typee*." *Guardian* (London), No. 28 (4 Nov. 1846), pp. 445–47. Review of "The Story of Toby." Reprinted in P532, pp. 3–4.

102. *Literary Gazette* (London), No. 1560 (12 Dec. 1846), p. 1042.

103. "Beauty and Deformity." [Cincinnati] *Herald of Truth*, 1 (Jan. 1847), 23–25. Mainly extracts.

104. "A Residence on the Marquesas." [Monterey] *Californian*, 1 (2 Jan. 1847), 1. Reprint of P100.

105. "A Residency on the Marquesas." [Monterey] *Californian*, 1 (9 Jan. 1847), 1. Continues reprint of P100.

106. "The Library of Choice Reading." [New York] *United States Magazine and Democratic Review*, 20 (March 1847), 239. Mention.

107. Griswold, Rufus W. Review of *The Prose Writers of America*. [New York] *Literary World*, No. 7 (20 March 1847), p. 151. Mention.

108. "Herman Melville's Omoo." *Spectator* (London), 20 (10 Apr. 1847), 351–52. *Omoo / Typee*. Reprinted in P135; reprinted in part in B295, pp. 91–92.

109. *Bell's Weekly Messenger* (London), 12 Apr. 1847. *Omoo / Typee*.

110. *John Bull* (London), 17 Apr. 1847, p. 248. *Omoo / Typee*. Reprinted in B295, p. 93.

111. *People's Journal* (London), 17 Apr. 1847, pp. 223–24. *Omoo / Typee*. Reprinted in part in B295, pp. 94–95.

112. "The New Work by the Author of Typee." [New York] *Spirit of the Times*, 17 (24 Apr. 1847), 99. Announcement of the publication of *Omoo*. Comment on *Typee*.

113. *Sun* (London), No. 17036 (26 Apr. 1847), p. 3. *Omoo / Typee*. Reprinted in P533, pp. 9–10.

114. [Boston] *Christian Observatory*, 1 (May 1847), 230–34. Reprinted in part in P462, pp. 123–24.

115. "Mr. Melville's New Work." *Albany Evening Journal*, 1 May 1847. *Omoo / Typee*.

116. *New York Evening Mirror*, 1 May 1847. *Omoo / Typee*.

117. *New York Atlas*, 2 May 1847. *Omoo / Typee*.

118. *Albany Evening Journal*, 3 May 1847, p. 2. *Omoo / Typee*.

119. *New York Evening Mirror*, 3 May 1847. *Omoo / Typee*.

120. *Boston Daily Advertiser*, 4 May 1847. *Omoo / Typee*.

121. *Boston Daily Bee*, 5 May 1847. *Omoo / Typee*.

122. *Boston Post*, 5 May 1847. *Omoo / Typee*. Reprinted in B295, p. 96.

123. *New York Evening Post*, 5 May 1847. *Omoo / Typee*.

124. [New York] *Albion*, NS 6 (8 May 1847), 228. *Omoo / Typee*. Reprinted in B295, p. 97.

125. [New York] *Anglo American*, 9 (8 May 1847), 69. *Omoo/ Typee*. Reprinted in P419, p. 13.

126. [New York] *Literary World*, No. 14 (8 May 1847), pp. 319–21. *Omoo / Typee*. Reprinted in part in B295, pp. 97–99.

127. Review of *A Summer in the Wilderness* by Charles Lanman. *New York Evening Mirror*, 12 May 1847. Comparison with *Typee*. Cited in B225, p. 244.

128. [Schenectady (N.Y.)] *Parthenon*, NS 1 (15 May 1847), 31. *Omoo / Typee*.

129. "Polynesian Life.—'Typee' and 'Omoo.' By Herman Melville." *New York Evening Mirror*, 21 May 1847. Joint review of *Typee* and *Omoo*. Reprinted in P131 and B295, pp. 99–104; reprinted in part in B225, pp. 244–45.

130. "Literary Gossip." *American Literary Gazette and New York Weekly Mirror*, NS 6 (22 May 1847), 11. *Omoo / Typee*.

131. "Polynesian Life.—'Typee' and 'Omoo.' By Herman Melville." *American Literary Gazette and New York Weekly Mirror*, NS 6 (22 May 1847). Reprint of P129.

132. *Washington National Era*, 27 May 1847. *Omoo / Typee*.

133. *Washington National Intelligencer*, 27 May 1847. Joint review of *Typee* and *Omoo*. Reprinted in B295, pp. 105–111. Dated 26 May 1847.

134. B. [New York] *National Anti-Slavery Standard*, 7 (27 May 1847), 207. *Omoo / Typee*. Reprinted in B295, pp. 112–13.

135. "Herman Melville's Omoo." [Boston] *Littell's Living Age*, No. 159 (29 May 1847), pp. 426–27. Reprint of P108.

136. *Literary Gazette* (London), No. 1584 (29 May 1847), pp. 396–97. *Omoo / Typee*.

137. "Pacific Rovings." *Blackwood's Edinburgh Magazine*, 61 (June 1847), 754–67. *Omoo / Typee*. Reprinted in P146 and P150; reprinted in part in P420, pp. 33–34 and B295, pp. 114–19.

138. [New Orleans] *Commercial Review of the South and West*, 3 (June 1847), 586. *Omoo / Typee*.

139. [New York] *Columbian Magazine*, 7 (June 1847), 283. *Omoo / Typee*. Reprinted in part in B321, pp. 14–15.

140. [New York] *Knickerbocker*, 29 (June 1847), 562. *Omoo / Typee*. Reprinted in B295, pp. 119–20.

141. [Honolulu] *Friend*, 5 (1 June 1847), 86. Review of the revised edition of *Typee*. Reprinted in part in B225, p. 246.

142. Review of *The Monk's Revenge*, by Samuel Spring. [New York] *Literary World*, No. 19 (12 June 1847), p. 441.

143. *Guardian* (London), No. 74 (16 June 1847), pp. 380–81. *Omoo / Typee*. Reprinted in P532, pp. 4–5.

144. "Blackwood's Review of 'Omoo.' " *Albany Evening Journal*, 25 June 1847. *Omoo / Typee*.

145. G[reeley], H[orace]. "Editorial Correspondence." *New York Weekly Tribune*, 26 June 1847. *Omoo / Typee*. Reprinted in P449, pp. 94–95 and B295, pp. 121–22. Dated 23 June 1847; reprinted in part in B225, p. 248.

146. "Pacific Rovings." [New York] *Eclectic Magazine*, 11 (July 1847), 408–19. Reprint of P137.

147. P[eck], G[eorge] W[ashington]. "Omoo." [New York] *American Review: A Whig Journal*, 6 (July 1847), 36–46. *Omoo / Typee*. Reprinted in part in B295, pp. 123–32.

148. Review of *Adventures on the Western Coast of South America and the Interior of California* by John Coulter. *Examiner* (London), 10 July 1847, pp. 435–36. Comparison with *Typee*.

149. *Morning Courier and New-York Enquirer*, 14 July 1847. *Omoo / Typee*.

150. "Pacific Rovings." [Boston] *Littell's Living Age*, 14 (24 July 1847), 145–53. Reprint of P137.

151. "Breach of Promise Suit Expected." *New York Daily Tribune*, 7 Aug. 1847. Mention of Fayaway. Cited in B225, p. 256.

152. "Omoo—By the Author of Typee." *Times* (London), 24 Sept. 1847, p. 7. *Omoo / Typee*. Reprinted in part in B295, pp. 134–38.

153. "Typee." [New York] *Robert Merry's Museum*, 14 (Oct. 1847), 109–14. Summary.

154. "Ik Marvel" [Mitchell, Donald G.]. "Reverie of a Bachelor." [Richmond (Va.)] *Southern Literary Messenger*, Oct. 1847. Cited in B225, p. 264.

155. "Grace Greenwood" [Lippincott, Sarah Jane]. "Letter from the Author of 'Typee.' " [Philadelphia] *Saturday Evening Post*, 9 Oct. 1847. Reprinted in B5 and P435, pp. 456–57.

156. "Protestant Missions in the Sandwich Islands." [Baltimore] *United States Catholic Magazine and Monthly Review*, 6 (Nov. 1847), 569, 580–83. Reprinted in P419, pp. 16–17.

157. "Typee." [New York] *Robert Merry's Museum*, 14 (Nov. 1847), 135–39. Continues summary.

158. *Dublin Review* (London), 23 (Dec. 1847), 341–63. *Omoo / Typee*.

159. "Typee." [New York] *Robert Merry's Museum*, 14 (Dec. 1847), 173–78. Concludes summary.

160. "Protestantism in the Society Islands." [Baltimore] *United States Catholic Magazine and Monthly Review*, 7 (Jan. 1848), 1–10. Joint review of *Typee* and *Omoo*.

161. "Missionary Operations in Polynesia." [New Haven] *New Englander*, 6 (Jan. 1848), 41–58 [44]. *Omoo / Typee*.

162. Warren, John Esaias. Extract from *Para; or Scenes and Adventures on the Banks of the Amazon*. *Bentley's Miscellany* (London), 23 (Jan. 1848), 18. Allusion to Fayaway. Reprinted in B10.

163. Duyckinck, Evert A. "Wrinkles." [New York] *Union Magazine*, 2 (Feb. 1848), 58. Mention.

164. "Polynesia." *English Review* (London), 9 (March 1848), 51–84 [52, 59–61, 64–73]. Joint review of *Typee* and *Omoo*.

165. "Breach of Promise." *Honolulu Polynesian*, 18 March 1848, p. 174. Mention of Fayaway. Reprinted in P417, p. 407.

166. "Typee and Omoo." *Honolulu Polynesian*, 18 March 1848, p. 174. Reprinted in part in P417, p. 407.

167. *Honolulu Sandwich Islands News*, 23 March 1848. Cited in B225, p. 274.

168. "Missions Commercially Considered." [Honolulu] *Friend*, 6 (1 Apr. 1848), 27–28. Mention. Reprinted in P417, p. 408.

169. H., E. B. "Catholic and Protestant Missions." [Boston] *Christian Examiner and Religious Miscellany*, 44 (May 1848), 417, 437–38. Reprinted in part in P462, pp. 125–26.

170. "Tempting Titles." *Puppet-Show* (London), 1 (2 Sept. 1848), 201. *Omoo / Typee*.

171. *Globe* (London), No. 14818 (19 March 1849), p. 3. Announcement of the publication of *Mardi*. Mention of *Typee*. Reprinted in P172.

172. "The Literary Season." *Sun* (London), No. 17622 (19 March 1849), p. 3. Reprint of P171. Reprinted in P533, p. 8.

173. *Athenaeum* (London), No. 1117 (24 March 1849), pp. 296–98. *Mardi / Typee*. Reprinted in B295, pp. 139–41.

174. *Examiner* (London), 31 March 1849, pp. 195–96. *Mardi / Typee*. Reprinted in B295, pp. 143–46.

175. *Weekly Chronicle* (London), 1 Apr. 1849. *Mardi / Typee*. Reprinted in P525, pp. 585–86.

176. "Melville's New Book—Mardi." [New York] *Literary World*, No. 114 (7 Apr. 1849), pp. 309–10. *Mardi / Typee*. Reprinted in P185 and P186.

177. [New York] *Literary World*, No. 115 (14 Apr. 1849), pp. 333–36. *Mardi / Typee*. Reprinted in part in B282, pp. 9–11 and B295, pp. 150–52.

178. *New York Sunday Times and Noah's Weekly Messenger*, 15 Apr. 1849. *Mardi / Typee*.

179. *Boston Post*, 18 Apr. 1849, p. 1. *Mardi / Typee.* Reprinted in B282, pp. 14–15 and B295, pp. 155–56.

180. *Philadelphia Dollar Newspaper*, 18 Apr. 1849. *Mardi / Typee.* Reprinted in P527, p. 56.

181. *Springfield* (Mass.) *Republican*, 20 Apr. 1849. *Mardi / Typee.*

182. [New York] *Albion*, NS 8 (21 Apr. 1849), 189. *Mardi / Typee.* Reprinted in B295, pp. 157–58.

183. "Melville's Mardi." *New York Home Journal*, 21 Apr. 1849. *Mardi / Typee.*

184. [Syracuse] *Literary Union*, 1 (21 Apr. 1849), 42. *Mardi / Typee.* Reprinted in P527, pp. 62–64.

185. *Washington National Intelligencer*, 26 Apr. 1849. Reprint of P176.

186. "Melville's New Book—Mardi." [Boston] *Littell's Living Age*, 21 (28 Apr. 1849), 184–86. Reprint of P176.

187. [New York] *Literary American*, 2 (28 Apr. 1849), 402. *Mardi / Typee.*

188. [New York] *Merchants' Magazine and Commercial Review*, 20 (May 1849), 572. *Mardi / Typee.*

189. "Letters from New-York." [Richmond (Va.)] *Southern Literary Messenger*, 15 (May 1849), 309. *Mardi / Typee.* Reprinted in part in B225, p. 305.

190. *New York Home Journal*, 5 May 1849. *Mardi / Typee.* Reprinted in part in B225, p. 302.

191. *New York Daily Tribune*, 10 May 1849, p. 1. *Mardi / Typee.* Reprinted in part in B225, p. 303; reprinted in B282, pp. 16–17 and B295, pp. 161–63.

192. *Sun* (London), No. 17683 (29 May 1849), p. 3. *Mardi / Typee.* Reprinted in P533, pp. 10–12.

193. Review of *Adventures in Borneo. Gentleman's Magazine* (London), NS 31 (June 1849), 625–26. Mention. Reprinted in P531, p. 6.

194. [New York] *Holden's Dollar Magazine*, 3 (June 1849), 370–73. *Mardi / Typee.*

195. [Philadelphia] *Godey's Magazine and Lady's Book*, 38 (June 1849), 436. *Mardi / Typee.*

196. [Philadelphia] *Graham's Magazine*, 34 (June 1849), 385. *Mardi / Typee.* Reprinted in B321, p. 16.

197. [Philadelphia] *Peterson's Magazine*, 15 (June 1849), 219. *Mardi / Typee.* Reprinted in P527, p. 66.

198. *Adelaide* (South Australia) *Miscellany of Useful and Entertaining Knowledge*, 9 June 1849, pp. 295–302. Reprint of P55.

199. Chasles, Philarète. "Herman Melville's Voyages." *Boston Daily Advertiser*, 15 June 1849, p. 2. Translation of part of "Voyages réals et fantastiques d'Hermann Melville" by Philarète Chasles, which appeared

in the Paris *Revue des deux mondes,* 2 (15 May 1849), 541–70. Reprinted in P200 and P202.

200. Chasles, Philarète. "Herman Melville's Voyages." *Albany Argus,* 18 June 1849. Reprint of P199.

201. Review of *Kaloolah* by W. S. Mayo. [New York] *Literary World,* No. 125 (23 June 1849), p. 533. Mention.

202. Chasles, Philarète. "Herman Melville's Voyages." *Albany Weekly Argus,* 23 June 1849. Reprint of P199.

203. *Philadelphia Dollar Newspaper,* 27 June 1849. Review of the 1849 edition of *Typee.* Reprinted in P527, p. 57.

204. [New York] *Spirit of the Times,* 19 (30 June 1849), 228. Review of the 1849 edition of *Typee.*

205. "Melville's Mardi." [New York] *United States Magazine and Democratic Review,* 25 (July 1849), 44–50. *Mardi / Typee.* Reprinted in part in B282, pp. 18–19; reprinted in B295, pp. 177–83.

206. *New York Evangelist,* 5 July 1849, p. 4. Review of the 1849 edition of *Typee.*

207. [New York] *Literary American,* 3 (7 July 1849), 15. Review of the 1849 edition of *Typee.* Reprinted in part in P528, p. 7.

208. *Springfield* (Mass.) *Republican,* 7 July 1849. Review of the 1849 edition of *Typee.*

209. "What is Talked About." [New York] *Literary World,* No. 128 (14 July 1849), p. 32. Mention.

210. *New York Independent,* 19 July 1849, p. 132. Review of the 1849 edition of *Typee.* Reprinted in P521, p. 435.

211. Chasles, Philarète. "The Actual and Fantastic Voyages of Herman Melville." [New York] *Literary World,* No. 131 (4 Aug. 1849), 89–90. Translation of part of "Voyages réals et fantastiques d'Hermann Melville" by Philarète Chasles, which appeared in the Paris *Revue des deux mondes,* 2 (15 May 1849), 541–70. Survey of Melville's first three works. Reprinted in part in B321, pp. 17–18 and B295, pp. 164–69.

212. *New York Literary World,* No. 132 (11 Aug. 1849), 101–03. Continues translation and adds corrective comments. Reprinted in part in B321, pp. 18–21 and B295, pp. 169–77.

213. [New York] *American Review: A Whig Journal,* NS 4 (Sept. 1849), 329. *Mardi / Typee.*

214. Review of *Four Years in the Pacific* by Lieut. the Hon. Fred Walpole, R.N. *Examiner* (London), before 22 Sept. 1849. Mention. Quoted in P215.

215. "Scenes in the Pacific." [New York] *Literary World,* No. 138 (22 Sept. 1849), pp. 248–49. Review of *Four Years in the Pacific,* by Lieut. the Hon. Fred Walpole, R.N. Comparison with *Typee.* Quotes P214.

216. [Andover (Maine)] *Biblical Repository and Classical Review,*

3rd ser., 5 (Oct. 1849), 754. Review of the 1849 edition of *Typee*. Reprinted in P462, pp. 124–25.

217. [Charleston (S.C.)] *Southern Quarterly Review*, 16 (Oct. 1849), 260–61. *Mardi / Typee*.

218. [New York] *Methodist Quarterly Review*, 4th ser., 1 (Oct. 1849), 679. Review of the 1849 edition of *Typee*.

219. [Willis, N. P.]. Review of *Los Gringos* by Lieut. Henry A. Wise. *New York Home Journal*, 13 Oct. 1849. Mention. Cited in P419, p. 25.

220. Review of *Los Gringos* by Lieut. Henry A. Wise. [New York] *Literary World*, No. 143 (27 Oct. 1849), pp. 355–56. Quotes Wise's allusion to Fayaway.

221. [New Orleans] *De Bow's Commercial Review of the South and West*, 7 (Nov. 1849), 465. Review of the 1849 edition of *Typee*.

222. [Philadelphia] *Sartain's Union Magazine*, 5 (Nov. 1849), 320. Review of the 1849 edition of *Typee*.

223. Review of *Los Gringos* by Lieut. Henry A. Wise. *New York Evangelist*, 8 Nov. 1849. Mention.

224. Review of *Los Gringos* by Lieut. Henry A. Wise. [Philadelphia] *Godey's Magazine and Lady's Book*, 40 (Jan. 1850), 78. Comparison with *Typee*.

225. Review of *The Whale and His Captors* by Henry T. Cheever. *New York National Anti-Slavery Standard*, 3 Jan. 1850. Comparison with *Typee*.

226. Review of *Wandering Sketches of People and Things in South America, Polynesia, California and Other Places* by William Maxwell Wood. [New York] *Literary World*, No. 153 (5 Jan. 1850), p. 7. Mention.

227. Hawkins, H. R. *Lansingburgh* (N.Y.) *Gazette*, 14 March 1850. Mention in letter. Cited in P439 and B225, p. 368.

228. "Marine Intelligence." [Honolulu] *Friend*, 8 (1 Apr. 1850), 28. Mention.

229. "Twilight Musings." [Honolulu] *Friend*, 8 (1 Apr. 1850), 29. Mention. Reprinted in P417, p. 408.

230. [Mitchell, Donald G.]. "Authors and Authorlings." *New York Lorgnette*, 24 Apr. 1850. Mentions. Reprinted in B7; Reprinted in part in B225, p. 372.

231. "Publishers' Circular." [New York] *Literary World*, No. 169 (27 Apr. 1850), p. 427. Mention.

232. "The Earl of Carlisle's View of America." [New York] *Literary World*, No. 207 (18 Jan. 1851), p. 41. Mention.

233. Review of *Para* by John Esaias Warren. [New York] *Literary World*, No. 231 (5 July 1851), p. 5. Mention.

234. "Howadji" [Curtis, George William]. "Summer Notes of a Howadji." [New York] *Daily Tribune*, 10 (Sept. 1851), p. 3. Reprinted with some alterations in B13.

235. "Retrospective Survey of American Literature." *Westminster Review* (London), NS 1 (1 Jan. 1852), 304. Mention.

236. Review of *The Book of Ballads*, ed. Bon Gualtier. [New York] *Literary World*, No. 257 (3 Jan. 1852), p. 7. Mention.

237. Francis, John Wakefield. "Personal and Historical Reminiscences. From an Address before the Typographical Society." [New York] *Literary World*, No. 261 (31 Jan. 1852), pp. 91–93. Mention. Reprinted in P238.

238. Francis, John Wakefield. "Reminiscences of Printers, Authors, and Booksellers in New York." [New York] *International Magazine*, 5 (Feb. 1852), 265. Reprint of P237.

239. Review of *Recollections of a Journey through Tartary* by E. R. Huc. [New York] *Literary World*, No. 271 (10 Apr. 1852), p. 261.

240. Review of *The Men of the Time*. [New York] *Literary World*, No. 289 (14 Aug. 1852), pp. 99–101 [100]. Reprints B11.

241. "Taconic." "Literary Correspondence. Homes of Literary Men in Berkshire, Mass." [New York] *Norton's Literary Gazette and Publishers' Circular*, 2 (15 Sept. 1852), 167–68. Mention.

242. [O'Brien, Fitz-James]. "Our Young Authors." [New York] *Putnam's Monthly*, 1 (Feb. 1853), 155–64. Survey of Melville's works from *Typee* to *Pierre*. Reprinted in part in B282, pp. 62–68 and B295, pp. 323–29.

243. "A Missionary Wanted for Marquesas." [Honolulu] *Friend*, 10 [NS 2] (1 Apr. 1853), 28. Mention. Reprinted in part in P417, p. 408.

244. Review of *The Captive in Patagonia* by Benjamin Franklin Bourne. [Cincinnati] *Pen and Pencil*, 1 (23 Apr. 1853), 539. Mention.

245. "Literature, Books of the Week, Etc." [New York] *Literary World*, No. 326 (30 Apr. 1853), p. 356. Mention.

246. "Sir Nathaniel." "American Authorship. No. IV—Herman Melville." *New Monthly Magazine* (London), 98 (July 1853), 300–08. Survey of Melville's works from *Typee* to *Pierre*. Reprinted in P247, P248, and P249; reprinted in part in B282, pp. 69–71 and B295, pp. 330–36.

247. "Sir Nathaniel." "American Authorship—Herman Melville." [Boston] *Littell's Living Age*, 38 (20 Aug. 1853), 481–86. Reprint of P246.

248. "Sir Nathaniel." "Herman Melville." [New York] *Eclectic Magazine*, 30 (Sept. 1853), 46–52. Reprint of P246.

249. "Sir Nathaniel." "American Authorship. No. IV—Herman Melville." [Augusta (Ga.)] *Southern Eclectic Magazine*, 1 (Nov. 1853), 181–86. Reprint of P246.

250. "The Missions of Polynesia." *Quarterly Review* (London), 94 (Dec. 1853), 80–122 [107]. Mention of *Typee* and allusion to Fayaway.

251. Review of *Na Motu: or, Reef-Rovings in the Pacific* by Edward T. Perkins. *Athenaeum* (London), No. 1411 (11 Nov. 1854), pp. 1360–61. Mention.

252. *Ohio State Journal.* 2 Dec. 1854. Mention. Quoted in P254. Cited in P441, p. 54.

253. "A Visit to the Scene of the Typee." [New Bedford] *Whalemen's Shipping List,* 12 (5 Dec. 1854), 306. Mention.

254. Greene, Richard Tobias. *Sandusky* (Ohio) *Mirror,* 7 Dec. 1854. Mention. Quotes P252. Reprinted in P441, p. 54.

255. "A Trio of American Sailor-Authors." *Dublin University Magazine,* 47 (Jan. 1856), 47–54. Article on Cooper, Dana, and Melville. Includes comments on *Typee* in a survey of Melville's works. Reprinted in P257; reprinted in part in P260; P420, pp. 35–36; B282, pp. 73–81; and B295, pp. 349–53.

256. [New York] *Life Illustrated,* 9 Feb. 1856. Editorial reference to *Typee.* Cited in B225, p. 512.

257. "A Trio of American Sailor-Authors." [Boston] *Littell's Living Age,* 48 (1 March 1856), 560–66. Reprint of P255.

258. X., G. R. S. "Dottings about Island Coasts." [New York] *Spirit of the Times,* 26 (24 May 1856), 170–71. Many comments. Reprinted in part in P463.

259. "Christian Missions: Their Principle and Practice." *London Westminster and Foreign Quarterly Review,* NS 10 (1 July 1856), 1–51 [passim]. Many mentions.

260. "Herman Melville." *Pittsfield* (Mass.) *Berkshire County Eagle,* 8 Aug. 1856, p. 1. Reprint of part of P255, with an additional editorial postscript comparing *The Piazza Tales* with *Typee* and *Omoo.*

261. "American Authors—Melville." *New York Christian Intelligencer,* 22 Jan. 1857. Mention in critical survey. Reprinted in P263; reprinted in part in B315, pp. 100–101.

262. [O'Brien, Fitz-James]. "Our Authors and Authorship. Melville and Curtis." [New York] *Putnam's Monthly,* 9 (Apr. 1857), 384–93. Reprinted in part in B282, pp. 84–93 and B295, pp. 361–68.

263. "American Authors—Melville." *Ilion* (N.Y.) *Independent,* 16 Apr. 1857. Reprint of P261.

264. "The Sandwich Islands. Their History." *Chicago Magazine,* 1 (15 May 1857), 226–27. Mention.

265. [Greene, Richard Tobias]. [New York] *Putnam's Monthly,* 10 (July 1857), 140. Letter to the Editor. Reprinted in B225, p. 581.

266. "Lectures." *Witness* (Montreal), 19 Dec. 1857. Included in this list because of its denunciation of the Mercantile Library Association of Montreal for inviting Melville, the "enemy of Christian Missions," to lecture. Reprinted in P267 and B233, p. 25.

267. "The Mercantile Library Association and the 'Montreal Witness.' " *True Witness and Catholic Chronicle* (Montreal), 25 Dec. 1857. Reprints P266 and responds, defending Melville and his criticism of the "Methodist missions." Reprinted in P507, pp. 134–36.

268. "Foreign Intelligence. France." *Times* (London), 29 Dec. 1857, p. 2. Mention. Reprinted in P541.

269. *Witness* (Montreal), 23 Jan. 1858. Reprints from the *American Presbyterian* a news item on the cannibals in the "celebrated valley of Typee" and comments ironically on Melville's characterization of "those paradisical innocents." Reprinted in P507, p. 136.

270. T[uckerman], H. T. "Authors at Home: Authors in Berkshire." [Philadelphia] *American Literary Gazette and Publishers' Circular*, 2 (16 Nov. 1863), 40. Mention. Reprinted in P271; B225, p. 664; B315, p. 103; and B295, pp. 386–87.

271. [Tuckerman, H. T.]. "Authors in Berkshire." *Pittsfield* (Mass.) *Berkshire County Eagle*, 10 Dec. 1863, p. 1. Reprint of P270.

272. Review of *Wild Life Among the Pacific Islanders* by E. H. Lamont. *Athenaeum* (London), No. 2061 (27 Apr. 1867), p. 542. Mention.

273. Coan, Titus. "The First Missionary Trip of the New 'Morning Star.' " [Honolulu] *Supplement to the Friend*, NS 18 (1 July 1867), 58. Comments on the topography of Nukuheva. Reprinted in revised form in B35, pp. 199–200.

274. S., R. "Marquesas Islands—Melville's 'Typee.' " *Athenaeum* (London), No. 2113 (25 Apr. 1868), pp. 595–96. Comments on Melville's errors in topography. Reprinted in P426, pp. 527–31.

275. "Literary Invalids." [Richmond (Va.)] *Southern Opinion*, 4 July 1868. Mention. Reprinted in B311, pp. 58–59.

276. Review of *Kaloolah* by W. S. Mayo. [San Francisco] *Overland Monthly*, 10 (Jan. 1873), 103–04. Mention.

277. Gordon, Clarence. "Mr. DeForest's Novels." [Boston] *Atlantic Monthly*, 32 (Nov. 1873), 611–21 [611]. Mention.

278. Review of *South-Sea Idyls* by Charles Warren Stoddard. *New York Independent*, 18 Dec. 1873, p. 1577. Mention.

279. "B. V" [Thomson, James]. "Walt Whitman." London *National Reformer*, NS 24 (30 Aug. 1874), 135. Comparative comment. Reprinted in B108.

280. Russell, W. Clark. "Sea Stories." *Contemporary Review* (London), 46 (Sept. 1884), 343–63. Mentions. Reprinted in part in B225, pp. 785–86; B282, pp. 117–20; B315, pp. 104–05; and B295, pp. 409–11.

281. *London Daily Telegraph*, 16 Jan. 1885. Mention. Reprinted in B225, p. 788.

282. Buchanan, Robert. "Socrates in Camden, With a Look Round." *Academy and Literature* (London), 28, No. 693 (15 Aug. 1885), 102–03. Mention in poem. Reprinted with some alterations in B47; reprinted in B170, pp. 349–50; B225, p. 792; and B282, p. 121.

283. "The South Sea." *Brooklyn Eagle*, 14 Sept. 1885. Reprint of P281. Cited in B225, p. 793.

284. Hawthorne, Julian. "Man-Books." [Chicago] *America: A Jour-*

nal of To-day, 1 (27 Sept. 1888), 11–12. Mention. Reprinted in part in B225, p. 810 and B315, pp. 106–08.

285. Salt, Henry S. "Herman Melville." *The Scottish Art Review* (London), 2 (Nov. 1889), 186–90. Reprinted in part in B282, pp. 122–30; B315, pp. 109–10; and B295, pp. 413–17.

286. Bok, Edward William. "Notes on Authors." [New York] *Publishers' Weekly*, 38 (15 Nov. 1890), 705. Mention. Reprinted in P287; B225, p. 827; and B295, pp. 417–18.

287. [Bok, Edward William]. [Boston] *Literary World*, 21 (6 Dec. 1890), 469. Reprint of P286.

288. [New York] *Critic*, NS 14 (13 Dec. 1890), 310. Mention.

289. Stevenson, Robert Louis. "The South Seas: A Record of Three Cruises." *Black and White* (London), 1 (28 Feb. 1891), 114. Mention. Reprinted in B66.

290. "Recent Deaths." *Boston Evening Transcript*, 29 Sept. 1891.

291. *New York Daily Tribune*, 29 Sept. 1891. Obituary.

292. "Death of a Once Popular Author." *New York Press*, 29 Sept. 1891.

293. "Death of Herman Melville. Author of Several Volumes of Poems and Romances." *New York World*, 29 Sept. 1891, p. 4.

294. *Boston Morning Journal*, 30 Sept. 1891. Obituary.

295. Ellis, A. B. "On Polyandry." [New York] *Popular Science Monthly*, 39 (Oct. 1891), 801–09. Mention.

296. "Herman Melville." *New York Town Topics*, 1 Oct. 1891, p. 3. Obituary. Reprinted in P320.

297. [Stedman, Arthur]. "Herman Melville's Funeral." *New York Daily Tribune*, 1 Oct. 1891, p. 14. Reprinted in P309 and B324, pp. 99–101; reprinted in part in P317 and B225, p. 837.

298. "Herman Melville." *New York Times*, 2 Oct. 1891. Obituary. Reprinted in part in P313; reprinted in B295, pp. 418–20.

299. 'Tavener.' "Here in Boston." *Boston Post*, 2 Oct. 1891. Mention in brief article occasioned by Melville's death.

300. [New York] *Critic*, NS 16 (3 Oct. 1891). Obituary. Brief comment and reprint of B46.

301. *Boston Sunday Herald*, 4 Oct. 1891, p. 14. Obituary.

302. "The Literary Wayside." *Springfield* (Mass.) *Sunday Republican*, 4 Oct. 1891, p. 6. Obituary. Reprinted in part in B295, pp. 420–23.

303. H[illiard], O. G. "The Late Hiram Melville. A Tribute to His Memory from One Who Knew Him." *New York Times*, 6 Oct. 1891, p. 9. Letter to the Editor. Mention. Reprinted in P313.

304. Schonberg, James. *New York Home Journal*, 7 Oct. 1891. Obituary. Cited in P453, p. 329.

305. "Old and New." *St. Johnsbury* (Vt.) *Republican*, 8 Oct. 1891. Obituary.

306. Stoddard, Richard H. "Herman Melville." *New York Mail and Express*, 8 Oct. 1891, p. 5. Obituary and reprint of Melville's letter to Hawthorne, 1 [?] June 1851. Reprinted in part in P319 and B295, pp. 423–25.

307. [Boston] *Literary World*, 22 (10 Oct. 1891), 366. Notes Melville's death and reprints B46.

308. "Herman Melville." [New York] *Harper's Weekly Magazine*, 35 (10 Oct. 1891), 782. Obituary.

309. [Stedman, Arthur]. "Herman Melville." [New York] *Critic*, NS 16 (10 Oct. 1891), 190. Reprint of P297.

310. Stedman, Arthur. "Marquesan Melville. A South Sea Prospero who Lived and Died in New York." *New York World*, 11 Oct. 1891, p. 26. Reprinted in part in P314; reprinted in B324, pp. 101–10.

311. "Literary Gossip." *Athenaeum* (London), No. 3338 (17 Oct. 1891), p. 519. Obituary.

312. "Obituary." *Saturday Review* (London), 72 (17 Oct. 1891), 434.

313. [New York] *Critic*, NS 16 (17 Oct. 1891). Reprints in part P298. Reprints and notes errors in P303.

314. Stedman, Arthur. "Herman Melville." [New York] *Critic*, NS 16 (24 Oct. 1891), 222–23. Reprint of part of P310.

315. Smith, J. E. A. "Herman Melville: A Great Pittsfield Author—Brief Biographical Sketch." *Pittsfield* (Mass.) *Evening Journal*, 27 Oct. 1891, p. 4. Mention. Reprinted in B324, pp. 120–22; reprinted with some alterations in B71.

316. ———. "Herman Melville: A Great Pittsfield Author—Brief Biographical Sketches." *Pittsfield* (Mass.) *Evening Journal*, 29 Oct. 1891, p. 4. Mention. Reprinted in B324, pp. 123–26; reprinted with some alterations in B71.

317. Stedman, Arthur. [New York] *Current Literature*, 8 (Nov. 1891), 339–40. Reprint of part of P297.

318. ———. "Melville of Marquesas." [New York] *Review of Reviews*, 4 (Nov. 1891), 428–30. Biographical sketch. Reprinted in B324, pp. 110–15.

319. "Mr. Stoddard on Herman Melville." [New York] *Critic*, NS 16 (14 Nov. 1891), 272–73. Introduction and reprint of part of P306. Incorrectly dated 4 Nov. 1891 in Beatrice Ricks and Joseph D. Adams' *Herman Melville: A Reference Bibliography, 1900–1972*, p. 351.

320. "Herman Melville." *Pittsfield* (Mass.) *Evening Journal*, 21 Nov. 1891, p. 8. Reprint of P296.

321. Smith, J. E. A. "Herman Melville: A Great Pittsfield Author— Brief Biographical Sketch." *Pittsfield* (Mass.) *Evening Journal*, 21 Nov. 1891, p. 4. Reprinted in B324, pp. 126–29; reprinted with some alterations in B71.

322. ———. "Herman Melville: A Great Pittsfield Author—Brief

Biographical Sketches." *Pittsfield* (Mass.) *Evening Journal*, 16 Dec. 1891, p. 2. Mention. Reprinted in B324, pp. 129–32.

323. Coan, Titus Munson. "Herman Melville." [Boston] *Literary World*, 22 (19 Dec. 1891), 492–93. Biographical sketch. Reprinted in B324, pp. 116–19.

324. Salt, Henry S. "Marquesan Melville." *Gentleman's Magazine* (London), 272 (March 1892), 248–57. Reprinted in P325; reprinted in part with some alterations in B55 and B56; reprinted in part in B315, pp. 112–14 and B295, pp. 430–33.

325. ———. "Marquesan Melville." [New York] *Eclectic Magazine*, NS 55 (Apr. 1892), 517–23. Reprint of P324.

326. Stedman, Arthur, ed. "Poems by Herman Melville." [New York] *Century Magazine*, 44 [NS 22] (May 1892), 104–05. Mention.

327. "Travels, Far and Near." [New York] *Book Buyer*, 9 (Oct. 1892), 386. Review of the Stedman (United States Book Co.) edition of *Typee*. Reprinted in P522, p. 13.

328. "The Romances of Herman Melville." [Boston] *Literary World*, 23 (8 Oct. 1892), 352–53. Review of the Stedman (United States Book Co.) editions of *Typee* and *Omoo*.

329. Payne, William Morton. "Pictures from the Pacific." [Chicago] *Dial*, 13 (16 Oct. 1892), 244–46. Review of the Stedman (United States Book Co.) editions of *Typee* and *Omoo*.

330. "A New Edition of Herman Melville." [New York] *Literary News*, 13 (Nov. 1892), 338. Review of the Stedman (United States Book Co.) edition of Melville's works.

331. "Survey of Current Literature." [New York] *Literary News*, 13 (Nov. 1892), 344. Review of the Stedman (United States Book Co.) editions of *Typee* and *Omoo*.

332. "Herman Melville's Romances." [New York] *Critic*, NS 18 (3 Dec. 1892), 308–09. Review of the Stedman (United States Book Co.) edition of *Typee*. Reprinted in B295, pp. 434–35.

333. [Strachey, J. St. L.]. "Herman Melville." *Spectator* (London), 70 (24 June 1893), 858–59. Review of the Stedman (Putnam) edition of Melville's works. Reprinted in part in B282, pp. 136–37.

334. Cutler, James Tucker. "The Literary Associations of Berkshire." [Boston] *New England Magazine*, NS 9 (Sept. 1893), 8–9. Mention.

335. "Arts and Letters." *Hartford Daily Courant*, 2 June 1896, p. 8. Notice of the Stedman (American Publishers Corp.) edition of *Typee*. Reprinted in P517, p. 8.

336. "Cheap Editions of Novels." *Hartford Daily Times*, 26 June 1896, p. 11. Notice of the Stedman (American Publishers Corp.) edition of *Typee*. Reprinted in P517, p. 8.

337. [Boston] *National Magazine*, 4 (July 1896), 304–05. Review of

the Stedman (American Publishers Corp.) edition of *Typee*. Reprinted in P522, p. 14.

338. *Omaha Daily Bee*, 6 July 1896, p. 5. Notice of the Stedman (American Publishers Corp.) edition of *Typee*. Reprinted in P517, p. 8.

339. "Men, Women and Books." *New York Recorder*, 23 Aug. 1896, p. 32. Notice of the Stedman (American Publishers Corp.) edition of *Typee*. Reprinted in P517, p. 8.

340. [Boston] *National Magazine*, 5 (Oct. 1896), 112. Review of the Stedman (American Publishers Corp.) edition of *Omoo*. Mention. Reprinted in P518, p. 535.

341. [New York] *Bookman*, 4 (Oct. 1896), 171–72. Review of the Stedman (American Publishers Corp.) edition of Melville's works. Reprinted in P522, p. 13.

342. "Herman Melville." [New York] *Literary News*, 17 (Oct. 1896), 304–05. Biographical and critical mentions. Reprinted in P518, pp. 533–34.

343. J., G. C. "Books and Their Makers." *Buffalo Commercial Advertiser*, 26 Oct. 1896, p. 9. Mentions that the Stedman (American Publishers Corp.) edition of Melville's works is selling well. Reprinted in P517, p. 8.

344. [New York] *Book Reviews*, 4 (Nov. 1896), 212–13. Reprint of P345. Reprinted in P518, p. 535.

345. [New York] *Current Literature*, 20 (Nov. 1896), 472. Notice of the Stedman (American Publishers Corp.) edition of Melville's works. Reprinted in P344.

346. Bright, Edward. "Fly Leaves." [New York] *Illustrated American*, 22 (14 Aug. 1897), 218. Mention. Reprinted in P519.

347. "Literary Chat." [New York] *Munsey's Magazine*, 18 (Feb. 1898), 791. Mention. Reprinted in P517, p. 9.

348. F., T. B. "Book News in London." *New York Times Saturday Review of Books and Art*, 22 July 1899, p. 489. Mention.

349. MacMechan, Archibald. "The Best Sea Story Ever Written." *Kingston* (Ontario) *Queen's Quarterly*, 7 (Oct. 1899), 120–30. Mention in reevaluation of Melville's reputation centering on the merits of *Moby-Dick*. Reprinted in P356, B119, and B288; reprinted in part in B282, pp. 137–45.

350. Toft, Peter. "In Praise of Herman Melville." *New York Times Saturday Review of Books and Art*, 17 March 1900, p. 176. Mention in Letter to the Editor. Reprinted in P516, pp. 71–72.

351. Sacque, Havre. "Condensed Life of Herman Melville." [Boston] *National Magazine*, 12 (Apr. 1900), 804. Biographical sketch. Reprinted in P518, p. 536.

352. "The Best Books of Herman Melville." *Cleveland Plain Dealer*, 18 Nov. 1900, Sec. 3, p. 3. Review of the Stedman (Dana Estes & Co.) edition of Melville's works. Reprinted in P517, p. 10.

353. R., R. "Herman Melville's Novels." *Chicago Inter Ocean*, 26 Nov. 1900, p. 12. Review of the Stedman (Dana Estes & Co.) edition of Melville's works. Reprinted in P520, pp. 7–8.

354. [Boston] *Literary World*, 31 (1 Dec. 1900), 260. Review of the Stedman (Dana Estes & Co.) edition of Melville's works. Reprinted in P517, pp. 10–11.

355. Ferris, Mary L. D. "Herman Melville." [New York] *Bulletin of the Society of American Authors*, 6 (Sept. 1901), 289–93. Biographical sketch. Reprinted in P512, pp. 2–3.

356. MacMechan, Archibald. "Herman Melville." *Humane Review* (London), 7 (Oct. 1901), 242–52. Reprint of P349.

357. 'The Bookworm.' "Bibliographical." *Academy and Literature* (London), 66, No. 1659 (20 Feb. 1904), 187. Notes the forthcoming John Lane edition of *Typee*. Mentions the publication of previous editions. Reprinted in P520, p. 8.

358. Alden, William Livingston. "John Lane's Pocket Library." *New York Times Saturday Review of Books and Art*, 5 March 1904, p. 150. Notes the forthcoming John Lane edition of *Typee* and *Omoo*.

359. ———. "Mr. Alden's Views." *New York Times Review of Books and Art*, 12 March 1904, p. 172. Mention. Reprinted in P516, pp. 73–74.

360. O., E. G. "Egomet." *Academy and Literature* (London), 66, No. 1666 (9 Apr. 1904), 406. Mention. Reprinted in P520, p. 8.

361. S., F. T. "Reprints and New Editions." *Academy and Literature* (London), 66, No. 1666 (9 Apr. 1904), 404. Review of the John Lane edition of *Typee*.

362. Alden, William Livingston. "Mr. Alden's Views." *New York Times Saturday Review of Books and Art*, 30 Apr. 1904, p. 294. Mention in reply to P360. Reprinted in P516, p. 74.

363. Jerrold, Walter. "Bibliographical." *Academy and Literature* (London), 67, No. 1691 (1 Oct. 1904), 253. Mention. Reprinted in P520, p. 8.

364. G., W. W. "Herman Melville." *New York Times Saturday Review of Books and Art*, 29 July 1905, p. 502. Mention in Letter to the Editor. Reprinted in P516, pp. 76–77.

365. 'Marquesas.' "Herman Melville." *New York Times Saturday Review of Books and Art*, 12 Aug. 1905, p. 535. Mention in Letter to the Editor. Reprinted in P516, pp. 77–78.

366. Cook, Albert S. "Miscellaneous Notes." *Modern Language Notes*, 22 (Nov. 1907), 207. Mention.

367. London, Jack. "Typee." [Portland (Ore.)] *Pacific Monthly*, March 1910, pp. 267–81. Reprinted in B111.

368. Quiller-Couch, A. "Of Boys' Books." *Times Literary Supplement* (London), No. 847 (11 Apr. 1918), pp. 1–2. Mention.

369. "A New Yorker's Centenary." *New York Times Book Review*, 20 July 1919, p. 376. Mention in survey.

370. "Herman Melville." *New York Times*, 27 July 1919, Sec. 3, p. 1. Mention.

371. Jackson, Holbrook. "Herman Melville." *Anglo-French Review* (London), 2 (Aug. 1919), 59–64. Mentions.

372. Owlett, F. C. "Herman Melville (1819–1891): A Centenary Tribute." London *Bookman*, 56 (Aug. 1919), 164–67. Mention in a biographical and critical survey.

373. Hale, Philip. "As the World Wags." *Boston Herald*, 1 Aug. 1919. Mention.

374. "An American Romancer: Centenary of Herman Melville, Writer of Sea Tales." *New York Evening Post*, 2 Aug. 1919, pp. 1, 6. Mention.

375. "Melville and Our Sea Literature." *New York Evening Post*, 2 Aug. 1919.

376. Weaver, Raymond M. "The Centennial of Herman Melville." [New York] *Nation*, 109 (2 Aug. 1919), 145–46. Mention in a biographical and critical survey. Reprinted in B289.

377. Mather, Frank Jewett, Jr. "Herman Melville." [New York] *Review*, 1 (9 Aug. 1919), 276–78. Mentions in a biographical and critical survey. Reprinted in part in B282, pp. 155–60.

378. ————. "Herman Melville." [New York] *Review*, 1 (16 Aug. 1919), 298–301. Continues P377. Mention. Reprinted in B282, pp. 160–69; reprinted in part in B315, pp. 127–30.

379. "Another Significant American Centenary." [New York] *Current Opinion*, 67 (Sept. 1919), 184–85. Mention.

380. Church, John W. "A Vanishing People of the South Seas." [Washington] *National Geographic Magazine*, 36 (Oct. 1919), 285.

The 1920s

381. "Barrie's Magic Island." *Times* (London), 27 May 1922, p. 13. Mention in report of a speech given by J. M. Barrie.

382. "The Men That Found the South Seas." [New York] *Mentor*, 10 (Feb. 1922), 18–31 [18–19].

383. "The Mystery of Herman Melville." [New York] *Current Opinion*, 71 (Oct. 1921), 502–03.

384. Birrell, Augustine. "The Great White Whale: A Rhapsody." *Athenaeum* (London), No. 4735 (28 Jan. 1921), pp. 99–100. Mention in article on *Moby-Dick* occasioned by the publication of B154. Reprinted in P385; B134; and B315, pp. 137–40.

385. ————. "The Immortal White Whale." [Boston] *Living Age*, 308 (12 March 1921), 659–61. Reprint of P384.

386. Boynton, Percy H. "Pessimism and Criticism." [New York] *Literary Review*, 3 (10 Feb. 1923), 446. Mention. Reprinted in B136.

387. [Brooks, Van Wyck]. "A Reviewer's Notebook." [New York]

Freeman, 7 (9 May 1923), 214–15. Mention in notice of the Constable edition of Melville's works. Reprinted with some alterations in B138, pp. 171–79.

388. Canby, Henry Seidel. "Conrad and Melville." [New York] *Literary Review*, 2 (4 Feb. 1922), 393–94. Reprinted in B139 and B140.

389. De Voto, Bernard. "Editions of 'Typee.' " [New York] *Saturday Review of Literature*, 5 (24 Nov. 1928), 406. Letter to the Editor.

390. Hale, Philip. "As the World Wags." *Boston Herald*, 22 June 1921. Mention.

391. Hudson, Hoyt H. "The Mystery of Herman Melville." [New York] *Freeman*, 3 (27 Apr. 1921), 156–57. Mentions in article occasioned by the publication of B152 and B154.

392. Josephson, Matthew. "The Transfiguration of Herman Melville." [New York] *Outlook*, 150 (19 Sept. 1928), 809–11, 832, 836.

393. Lovett, Robert Morss. "The South Sea Style." [New York] *Asia*, 21 (Apr. 1921), 316–20, 366, 368. Mentions.

394. Lucas, F. L. "Herman Melville." *New Statesman* (London), 18 (1 Apr. 1922), 730–31. Mention. Reprinted in B153.

395. Marshall, H. P. "Herman Melville." *Mercury* (London), 11 (Nov. 1924), 56–70. Mentions in survey.

396. Metcalf, Eleanor Melville. "A Pilgrim by Land and Sea." [Boston] *Horn Book*, 3, No. 1 (Feb. 1927), 3–11. Brief references to *Typee* in an article written for children.

397. Meynell, Viola. "A Great Story Teller: Herman Melville." [Boston] *Living Age*, 304 (20 March 1920), 715–20. Reprint of P398.

398. ———. "Herman Melville." *Dublin Review* (London), 166 (Jan.–March 1920), 96–105. Closing reference to *Typee* in article on *Moby-Dick*. Reprinted in P397.

399. Mumford, Lewis. "The Significance of Herman Melville." [New York] *New Republic*, 56 (10 Oct. 1928), 212–14. "Epilogue" of B158 with minor differences. Includes brief references to *Typee*.

400. ———. "The Young Olympian." [New York] *Saturday Review of Literature*, 5 (15 Dec. 1928), 514–15. Somewhat shorter version of the first four sections of B158.

401. Nash, J. V. "Herman Melville, 'Ishmael' of American Literature." [Chicago] *Open Court*, 40 (Dec. 1926), 734–42.

402. Palsits, Victor Hugo, ed. "Family Correspondence of Herman Melville, 1830–1904. In the Gansevoort-Lansing Collection." *Bulletin of The New York Public Library*, 33 (July 1929), 507–25 [513–14]. Reprinted in B160.

403. ———. "Family Correspondence of Herman Melville, 1830–1904." *Bulletin of The New York Public Library*, 33 (Aug. 1929), 575–625 [619]. Continues P402. Reprinted in B160.

404. Pattee, Fred Lewis. "Herman Melville." [New York] *American Mercury*, 10 (Jan. 1927), 33–43. Reprinted with some alterations in B183.

405. Sadleir, Michael. "Letters to the Editor. The Works of Herman Melville." *Nation and Athenaeum* (London), 29 (11 June 1921), 396. Mentions.

406. Salt, Henry S. "Herman Melville." *Literary Guide* (London), NS 311 (May 1922), 70. Mention in survey.

407. Strachey, J. St. Loe. "Herman Melville: Mariner and Mystic." *Spectator* (London), 128 (6 May 1922), 559–60. Review of B170. Included in this list because of Strachey's recollection of "a lady of letters" who in 1893 said "I can't tell you how enthusiastic we all were, young and old, at the end of the 'forties and beginning of the 'fifties, over *Typee, Omoo,* and *Moby-Dick.* There was quite a furore over Melville in those days. All the young people worshipped him." Reprinted in part in B258, pp. 628–29 and B282, p. 174.

408. Tomlinson, H. M. "A Clue to Moby Dick." [New York] *Literary Review,* 2 (5 Nov. 1921), 141–42. Mentions in survey. Reprinted in P409.

409. ———. "The Greatest Story of the Sea. The 'Moby Dick' Mystery." *Review of Reviews* (London), 64 (Dec. 1921), 432–36. Reprint of P408.

410. T[omlinson], H. M. "The World of Books." *Nation and Athenaeum* (London), 29 (4 June 1921), 363. Mentions. Reprinted in B315, pp. 142–43.

411. T[omlinson], H. M. "The World of Books." *Nation and Athenaeum* (London), 33 (7 Apr. 1923), 17. Mention. Reprinted in B315, pp. 151–53.

412. Van Doren, Carl. "Melville before the Mast." [New York] *Century Magazine,* 108 (June 1924), 272–77. Reprint of B166.

413. Van Vechten, Carl. "The Later Works of Herman Melville." [New Orleans] *Double Dealer,* 3 (Jan. 1922), 9–20. Mentions in survey. Reprinted with some alterations in B169.

414. Weaver, Raymond M. "Herman Melville." [New York] *Bookman,* 54 (Dec. 1921), 318–26. Most of chapter 1 of B170.

415. Woolf, Leonard. "Herman Melville." *Nation and Athenaeum* (London), 33 (1 Sept. 1923), 688. Mention in notice of the Jonathan Cape edition of Melville's works. Reprinted in part in B258, pp. 629–31.

The 1930s

416. Aaron, Daniel. "An English Enemy of Melville." *New England Quarterly,* 8 (Dec. 1935), 561–69. Reprints B9.

417. ———. "Melville and the Missionaries." *New England Quarterly,* 8 (Sept. 1935), 404–08. Reprints P165, P168, and P229; reprints in part P166 and P243.

418. Adkins, Nelson F. "A Note on Herman Melville's *Typee.*" *New England Quarterly,* 5 (Apr. 1932), 348–51. Reprints B23.

419. Anderson, Charles Roberts. "Contemporary American Opin-

ions of *Typee* and *Omoo.*" *American Literature,* 9 (March 1937), 1–25. Reprints P59, P125, P156; reprints in part B7.

420. ———. "Melville's English Debut." *American Literature,* 11 (March 1939), 23–28. Reprints in part P3, P6, P30, P137, and P255; reprints P67.

421. ———. "The Romance of Scholarship: Tracking Melville in the South Seas." *Colophon,* NS 3 (1938), 259–79.

422. Birss, John Howard. "Melville's Marquesas." [New York] *Saturday Review of Literature,* 7 (2 Jan. 1932), 429. Reprints B4.

423. Blackmur, R. P. "The Craft of Herman Melville." *Virginia Quarterly Review,* 14 (Spring 1938), 266–82. Mention. Reprinted in part in B315, pp. 179–80.

424. Braswell, William. "A Note on the Anatomy of Melville's Fame." *American Literature,* 5 (Jan. 1934), 360–64.

425. Forsythe, R. S. "Herman Melville in the Marquesas." *Philological Quarterly,* 15 (Jan. 1936), 1–15.

426. Gohdes, Clarence. "Gossip about Melville in the South Seas." *New England Quarterly,* 10 (Sept. 1937), 526–31. Reprints P274.

427. Homans, George C. "The Dark Angel: The Tragedy of Herman Melville." *New England Quarterly,* 5 (Oct. 1932), 699–730 [707, 709, 710].

428. Menard, Wilmon. "A Forgotten South Sea Paradise." [New York] *Asia,* 33 (Sept.–Oct. 1933), 457–63, 510–11 [459].

429. Morris, Lloyd. "Melville: Promethean." [Chicago] *Open Court,* 45 (Sept. 1931), 513–26.

430. ———. "Melville: Promethean (II)." [Chicago] *Open Court,* 45 (Oct. 1931), 621–35.

431. Riegel, O. W. "The Anatomy of Melville's Fame." *American Literature,* 3 (May 1931), 195–203.

432. Ritchie, Mary C. "Herman Melville." *Kingston* (Ontario) *Queen's Quarterly,* 37 (Winter 1930), 36–61.

433. Stewart, Randall. "Hawthorne's Contributions to *The Salem Advertiser.*" *American Literature,* 5 (Jan. 1934), 327–41 [328–29]. Reprints P19.

434. Thomas, Russell. "Yarn for Melville's *Typee.*" *Philological Quarterly,* 15 (Jan. 1936), 16–29. Abstracted in B294, p. 72.

435. Thorp, Willard. " 'Grace Greenwood' Parodies *Typee.*" *American Literature,* 9 (Jan. 1938), 455–57. Reprints P155.

The 1940s

436. Birss, John Howard. "The Story of Toby, A Sequel to *Typee.*" *Harvard Library Bulletin,* 1 (Winter 1947), 118–19.

437. Charvat, William. "Melville's Income." *American Literature,* 15 (May 1943), 251–61 [passim]. Reprinted in B245.

438. Chase, Richard. "An Approach to Melville." [New York] *Partisan Review*, 14 (May–June 1947), 285–94.

439. Gilman, William H. "A Note on Herman Melville in Honolulu." *American Literature*, 19 (May 1947), 169. Reprints P227.

440. Gohdes, Clarence. "British Interest in American Literature . . . Mudie's Select Library." *American Literature*, 13 (Jan. 1942), 356–62.

441. ——. "Melville's Friend Toby." *Modern Language Notes*, 59 (Jan. 1944), 52–55. Reprints P254.

442. Haraszti, Zoltán. "Melville Defends *Typee*." *More Books, Bulletin of the Boston Public Library*, 22 (June 1947), 203–08. Reprints P51 and P79; reprints in part P75.

443. Howard, Leon. "Melville's Struggle with the Angel." *Modern Language Quarterly*, 1 (June 1940), 195–206. Reprinted in B282, pp. 223–37.

444. Opitz, Edmund A. "Herman Melville: An American Seer." *Contemporary Review* (London), 170 (Dec. 1946), 348–53.

444a. Pommer, Henry F. "Melville as Critic of Christianity." *Friends' Intelligencer*, 102 (1945), 121–23.

445. Scudder, H. H. "Hawthorne's Use of *Typee*." *Notes and Queries*, 187 (21 Oct. 1944), 184–86.

446. Watters, R. E. "Melville's Metaphysics of Evil." *University of Toronto Quarterly*, 9 (Jan. 1940), 170–82.

447. ——. "Melville's 'Sociality.'" *American Literature*, 17 (March 1945), 33–49.

448. Weaks, Mabel. "Long Ago and 'Faraway': Traces of Melville in the Marquesas in the Journals of A. G. Jones, 1854–1855." *Bulletin of The New York Public Library*, 52 (July 1948), 362–69.

449. Williams, Mentor L. "Horace Greeley Reviews *Omoo*." *Philological Quarterly*, 27 (Jan. 1948), 94–96. Reprints P145.

The 1950s

450. Beatty, Lillian. "Typee and Blithedale: Rejected Ideal Communities." *The Personalist*, 37 (Autumn 1956), 367–78.

451. Charvat, William. "Melville and the Common Reader." *Studies in Bibliography*, 12 (1959), 41–57. Reprinted in B245.

452. Firebaugh, Joseph J. "Humorist as Rebel: The Melville of *Typee*." *Nineteenth-Century Fiction*, 9 (Sept. 1954), 108–20. Abstracted in B294, pp. 72–73; reprinted in part in B321, pp. 55–61.

453. Hetherington, Hugh W. "A Tribute to the Late Hiram Melville." *Modern Language Quarterly*, 16 (Dec. 1955), 325–31.

454. Jones, Bartlett C. "American Frontier Humor in Melville's *Typee*." *New York Folklore Quarterly*, 15 (Winter 1959), 283–88. Abstracted in B294, p. 74.

455. Leyda, Jay. "Another Friendly Critic for Melville." *New England Quarterly*, 27 (June 1954), 243–49.

456. Miller, James E., Jr. "Melville's Search for Form." *Bucknell Review*, 8 (Dec. 1959), 260–76.

457. ———. "The Complex Figure in Melville's Carpet." *Arizona Quarterly*, 15 (Autumn 1959), 197–210.

458. Petrullo, Helen B. "The Neurotic Hero of *Typee*." *The American Imago*, 12 (Winter 1955), 317–23. Abstracted in B294, p. 73.

459. Rosenberry, Edward H. "Queequeg's Coffin-Canoe: Made in *Typee*." *American Literature*, 30 (Jan. 1959), 529–30.

460. Sale, Arthur. "The Glass Ship: A Recurrent Image in Melville." *Modern Language Quarterly*, 17 (June 1956), 118–27.

461. Stanton, Robert. "*Typee* and Milton: Paradise Well Lost." *Modern Language Notes*, 74 (May 1959), 407–11.

462. Williams, Mentor L. "Some Notices and Reviews of Melville's Name in American Religious Periodicals, 1846–1849." *American Literature*, 22 (May 1950), 119–27. Reprints in part P74, P114, P169, and P71; reprints P216.

463. Yates, Norris. "A Traveller's Comments on Melville's *Typee*." *Modern Language Notes*, 69 (Dec. 1954), 581–83. Reprints in part P258.

The 1960s

464. Anderson, Charles Roberts. "Melville's South Sea Romance." *Eigo Seinen (The Rising Generation)* (Japan), 115 (1969), 478–82, 564–68.

465. Canaday, Nicholas, Jr. "The Theme of Authority in Melville's *Typee* and *Omoo*." *Forum* (Houston), 4 (1963), 38–41. Reprinted in B244, pp. 1–8.

466. Creeger, George R. "The Symbolism of Whiteness in Melville's Prose Fiction." *Jahrbuch Fur Amerikastudien*, 5 (1960), 147–63 [148–49].

467. Flanagan, John T. "*The Spirit of the Times* Reviews Melville." *Journal of English and Germanic Philology*, 64 (1965), 57–64. Reprints P14.

468. Fletcher, Richard M. "Melville's Use of Marquesan." *American Speech*, 39 (May 1964), 135–38.

469. Gross, Theodore. "Herman Melville: The Nature of Authority." *Colorado Quarterly*, 16 (Spring 1968), 397–412.

470. Guttman, Allen. "From *Typee* to *Moby-Dick*: Melville's Allusive Art." *Modern Language Quarterly*, 24 (Sept. 1963), 237–44.

471. Hall, Joan Joffe. "Melville's Use of Interpolations." *University Review* (University of Missouri at Kansas City), 33 (Autumn 1966), 51–59.

472. Hamada, Masajiro. "Two Utopian Types of American

Literature: *Typee* and *The Crater.*" *Studies in English Literature* (Japan), 40 (March 1964), 199–214.

473. Houghton, Donald E. "The Incredible Ending of Melville's *Typee.*" *Emerson Society Quarterly*, No. 22 (1st Quarter 1961), pp. 28–31.

474. Ishag, Saada. "Herman Melville as an Existentialist: An Analysis of *Typee, Mardi, Moby Dick*, and *The Confidence Man.*" *Emporia State Research Studies*, 14 (Dec. 1965), 5–41, 60–62.

475. Ives, Sidney. "A Melville Ghost." *Papers of the Bibliographical Society of America*, 59 (3rd Quarter 1965), 318.

476. Mize, George E. "Evert Duyckinck: Critic to His Times." *ESQ*, No. 55 (2nd Quarter 1969), pp. 89–95.

477. Myers, Andrew B. "Washington Irving in London in 1846." *Bulletin of The New York Public Library*, 70 (Jan. 1966), 34–35.

478. Parker, Hershel, ed. "Gansevoort Melville's 1846 London Journal, Part I." *Bulletin of The New York Public Library*, 69 (Dec. 1965), 633–54. Reprinted in B281.

479. ———. "Gansevoort Melville's 1846 London Journal, Part II." *Bulletin of The New York Public Library*, 70 (Jan. 1966), 36–49. Reprinted in B281.

480. ———. "Gansevoort Melville's 1846 London Journal, Part III (Conclusion)." *Bulletin of The New York Public Library*, 70 (Feb. 1966), 113–31. Reprinted in B281.

481. Pavese, Cesare. "The Literary Whaler (1932)." Trans. Barbara Melchiori Arnett. *Sewanee Review*, 68 (July–Sept. 1960), 407–18. Reprinted in B282, pp. 194–203.

482. Ruland, Richard. "Melville and the Fortunate Fall: *Typee* as Eden." *Nineteenth-Century Fiction*, 23 (Dec. 1968), 312–23. Abstracted in B294, pp. 74–75.

483. Simpson, Eleanor E. "Melville and the Negro: From *Typee* to 'Benito Cereno.' " *American Literature*, 41 (March 1969), 19–38.

484. Tanselle, G. Thomas. "The First Review of *Typee.*" *American Literature*, 34 (Jan. 1963), 567–71. Reprints in part P15 and P25.

485. ———. "The Sales of Melville's Books." *Harvard Library Bulletin*, 17 (April. 1969), 195–203.

486. ———. " 'Typee' and De Voto Once More." *Papers of the Bibliographical Society of America*, 62 (4th Quarter 1968), 601–04.

487. Travis, Mildren K. "Mardi: Melville's Allegory of Love." *Emerson Society Quarterly*, No. 43 (2nd Quarter 1966), pp. 88–94.

488. Walser, Richard. "Another Early Review of *Typee.*" *American Literature*, 36 (Jan. 1965), 515–16. Reprints P14.

489. Weathers, Winston. "Melville and the Comedy of Communications." *Etc., A Review of General Semantics*, 20 (Dec. 1963), 411–20.

The 1970s

490. Abrams, Robert E. "*Typee* and *Omoo*: Herman Melville and the Ungraspable Phantom of Identity." *Arizona Quarterly*, 31 (Spring 1975), 33–50.

491. Adler, Joyce Sparer. "Melville's *Typee* and *Omoo*: Of 'Civilized' War on 'Savage' Peace." *Minnesota Review*, NS No. 10 (Spring 1978), pp. 95–102.

492. ———. "The Imagination and Melville's Endless Probe for Relation." *American Transcendental Quarterly*, No. 19 (1973), pp. 37–42.

493. Babin, James L. "Melville and the Deformation of Being: From Typee to Leviathan." *Southern Review*, 7, No. 1 (Winter 1971), 89–114.

494. Baird, James. "*Typee* as Paradigm: Prefigurations of Melville's Later Work." *Extracts*, No. 15 (1973), p. 2.

495. Barry, Elaine. "Herman Melville: The Changing Face of Comedy." *American Studies International*, 16, No. 4 (Summer 1978), 19–33.

496. Baym, Nina. "Melville's Quarrel with Fiction." *PMLA*, 94 (Oct. 1979), 909–923.

497. Bergmann, Johannes D. "The New York *Morning News* and *Typee*." *Extracts*, No. 31 (1977), pp. 1–4. Reprints in part P10 and P22.

498. Clark, Michael. "Melville's *Typee*: Fact, Fiction, and Aesthetics." *Arizona Quarterly*, 34 (Winter 1978), 351–70.

499. Cohen, Hennig. "The 'Famous Tales' Anthologies: Recognition of Melville, 1899." *The Papers of the Bibliographical Society of America*, 68 (2nd Quarter 1974), 179–80.

500. Cook, Richard M. "Evolving the Inscrutable: The Grotesque in Melville's Fiction." *American Literature*, 49 (Jan. 1978), 544–59.

501. Curran, Ronald T. "Insular Typees: Puritanism and Primitivism in *Mourning Becomes Electra*." *Revue des Langues Vivantes*, 41 (1975), 371–77.

502. Frederick, Joan. "Feet of Clay: Authority Figures in Melville's Early Novels." *James Madison Journal*, 37 (1979), 50–58.

503. Gollin, Rita K. "The Forbidden Fruit of *Typee*." *Modern Language Studies*, 5, No. 2 (1975), 31–34.

504. Huntress, Keith. "Melville, Henry Cheever, and 'The Lee Shore.'" *New England Quarterly*, 44 (Sept. 1971), 468–75.

505. Joswick, Thomas P. "'Typee': The Quest for Origin." *Criticism*, 17 (Fall 1975), 335–54.

506. Kemper, Steven. "*Omoo*: Germinal Melville." *Studies in the Novel*, 10 (Winter 1978), 420–31.

507. Kennedy, Frederick James. "Herman Melville's Lecture in

Montreal." *New England Quarterly*, 50 (March 1977), 125–37. Reprints P267 and P269.

508. Ketterer, David. "Censorship and Symbolism in *Typee.*" *Melville Society Extracts*, No. 34 (1978), p. 8.

509. Key, James A. "*Typee:* A Bird's-Eye View." *Publications of the Arkansas Philological Association*, 1, No. 2 (1975), 28–36.

510. McCarthy, Paul. "Melville's Families: Facts, Figures, and Fates." *South Dakota Review*, 15, No. 1 (Spring 1977), 73–93.

511. ———. "Melville's Rascals on Land, Sea, and in the Air." *Southern Quarterly*, 16 (July 1978), 311–36.

512. McNeilly, Dorothy V. B. D. R. "The Melvilles and Mrs. Ferris." *Extracts*, No. 28 (1976), pp. 1–9. Reprints P355.

513. Madison, Mary K. "Fanny Trollope's Nephew Edits *Typee.*" *Melville Society Extracts*, No. 39 (1979), p. 15.

514. Milder, Robert. "Melville Criticism in the 1970s; or, Who's Afraid of Wellek and Warren?" *Melville Society Extracts*, No. 43 (1979), pp. 4–7.

515. Monteiro, George. "A Half Hour with Melville, 1887." *Papers of the Bibliographical Society of America*, 69 (3rd Quarter 1975), 406–07. Reprints B39.

516. ———. " 'Far and Away the Most Original Genius That America Has Produced': Notations on the New York *Independent* and Melville's Reputation at the Turn of the Century." *Resources for American Literary Study*, 5 (Spring 1975), 69–80. Reprints P350, P359, P362, P364, and P365.

517. ———. "Fugitive References to Melville, 1851–1900." *Melville Society Extracts*, No. 39 (1979), pp. 7–11. Reprints P335, P336, P338, P339, P343, P347, P352, and P354.

518. ———. "Herman Melville in the 1890's." *Papers of the Bibliographical Society of America*, 70 (4th Quarter 1976), 530–36. Reprints P340, P342, P344, and P351.

519. ———. "Melville: A Reference in 1897." *Extracts*, No. 26 (June 1976), p. 13. Reprints P346.

520. ———. "Melville in the Chicago *Inter Ocean* and the London *Academy.*" *Melville Society Extracts*, No. 38 (1979), pp. 7–9. Reprints P353, P357, P360, and P363.

521. ———. "Melville Reviews in *The Independent.*" *Papers of the Bibliographical Society of America*, 68 (4th Quarter 1974), 434–39. Reprints P210.

522. ———. "More on Herman Melville in the 1890's." *Extracts*, No. 30 (1977), pp. 12–14. Reprints P327, P337, and P341.

523. Parker, Hershel. "Evidences for 'Late Insertions' in Melville's Works." *Studies in the Novel*, 7 (Fall 1975), 407–24.

524. ———. "Melville and the Concept of Author's Final Intentions." *Proof*, 1 (1971), 156–68.

525. ———. "Three Melville Reviews in the London *Weekly Chronicle.*" *American Literature,* 41 (Jan. 1970), 584–89. Reprints P175.

526. Polk, James. "Melville and the Idea of the City." *University of Toronto Quarterly,* 41 (Summer 1972), 277–92.

527. Pollin, Burton R. "Additional Unrecorded Reviews of Melville's Books." *Journal of American Studies,* 9 (Apr. 1975), 55–68. Reprints P18, P47, P58, P180, P184, P197, and P203.

528. ———. "Unreported American Reviews of Melville, 1849–1855." *Extracts,* No. 23 (1975), pp. 7–8. Reprints in part P207.

529. Rosenthal, Bernard. "Elegy for Jack Chase." *Studies in Romanticism,* 10 (Summer 1971), 213–29.

530. Scorza, Thomas J. "Tragedy in the State of Nature: Melville's *Typee.*" *Interpretation,* 8, No. 1 (Jan. 1979), 103–20.

531. Smith, Nelson C. "Eight British Reviews and Notices of Melville, 1846–1891." *Extracts,* No. 23 (1975), pp. 6–7. Reprints P193.

532. ———. "Four New London Reviews." *Melville Society Extracts,* No. 40 (1979), pp. 3–6. Reprints P101 and P143.

533. ———. "Melville Reviews in the London *Sun.*" *Melville Society Extracts,* No. 36 (1978), pp. 8–12. Reprints P26, P113, P172, and P192.

533a. Subramani. "The Mythical Quest: Literary Responses to the South Seas." *Literary Half-Yearly,* 18, No. 1 (1977), 165–86.

534. Sweeney, Gerald M. "Melville's Smoky Humor: Fire-Lighting in *Typee.*" *Arizona Quarterly,* 34 (Winter 1978), 371–76.

535. Tanselle, G. Thomas. "Bibliographical Problems in Melville." *Studies in American Fiction,* 2 (1974), 57–74.

536. ———. "Textual Study and Literary Judgment." *Papers of the Bibliographical Society of America,* 65 (2nd Quarter 1971), 109–22.

537. ———. "Typee and De Voto: A Footnote." *Papers of the Bibliographical Society of America,* 64 (2nd Quarter 1970), 207–09.

538. Waite, Robert. "Melville's Memento Mori." *Studies in American Fiction,* 5 (1977), 187–97.

539. Williams, David. "Peeping Tommo: *Typee* as Satire." *Canadian Review of American Studies,* 6, No. 1 (Spring 1975), 36–49.

540. Witherington, Paul. "The Art of Melville's *Typee.*" *Arizona Quarterly,* 26 (Summer 1970), 136–50.

541. Woodson, Thomas. "More from *The Times* of London." *Melville Society Extracts,* No. 44 (1979), p. 13. Reprints P268.

1980

542. Dauber, Kenneth. "American Culture as Genre." *Criticism,* 22 (Spring 1980), 101–15.

543. Giltrow, Janet. "Speaking Out: Travel and Structures in Herman Melville's Early Narratives." *American Literature,* 52 (March 1980), 18–32.

544. Sattelmeyer, Robert. "Thoreau and Melville's *Typee.*" *American Literature*, 52 (Nov. 1980), 462–74.

BOOKS

1847–1919

1. Bingham, Hiram. *A Residence of Twenty-One Years in the Sandwich Islands*. Hartford, Ct.: H. Huntington, 1847; New York: Sherman Converse, 1847, p. 466n. Mention. Incorrectly cited as p. 446 in P417.

2. Channing, William Ellery. "The Island Nukuheva," in *Poems, Second Series*. Boston: James Munroe and Co., 1847, pp. 144–52; rpt. in *The Collected Poems of William Ellery Channing the Younger, 1817–1901*. Ed. Walter Harding. Gainesville, Fla.: Scholars' Facsimiles & Reprints, 1967, pp. 302–10.

3. Sanders, Mrs. Elizabeth (Elkins). *Remarks on the "Tour Around Hawaii" by The Missionaries, Messrs. Ellis, Thurston, Bishop, and Goodrich*. Salem, Mass.: 1848, pp. 34, 36. Mentions.

4. Wise, Lieut. [Henry A.]. *Los Gringos: or, An Inside View of Mexico and California, with Wanderings in Peru, Chili, and Polynesia*. New York: Baker and Scribner, 1849, pp. 398–99. Reprinted in P422.

5. "Grace Greenwood" [Lippincott, Sarah Jane]. "Letter from the Author of 'Typee,' " in *Greenwood Leaves: A Collection of Sketches and Letters*. Boston: Ticknor, Reed, and Fields, 1850, pp. 294–96. Reprints P155.

6. "Ik Marvel" [Mitchell, Donald G.]. *Reveries of a Bachelor: or A Book of the Heart*. New York: Baker and Scribner, 1850, p. 21. Mentions.

7. [Mitchell, Donald G.]. *The Lorgnette: or, Studies of the Town. By an Opera Goer*. New York: Stringer and Townsend, 1850, I, 277, 279. Reprints P230; reprinted in part in P419, p. 22.

8. Warter, John Wood, ed. *Southey's Common-Place Book*. Third Series. London: Longman, Brown, Green, and Longmans, 1850, p. 585. Mention in editorial footnote.

9. Lucett, Edward. *Rovings in the Pacific, from 1837 to 1849; with a Glance at California*. London: Longman, Brown, Green, and Longmans, 1851, I, 293–97. Reprinted in P416, pp. 562–66; reprinted in part in B175.

10. Warren, John Esaias. *Para; or, Scenes and Adventures on the Banks of the Amazon*. New York: G. P. Putnam, 1851, p. 31. Allusion to Fayaway. Reprints P162.

11. "Melville, Herman," in *The Men of the Time*. New York: Redfield, 1852, pp. 350–51. Biographical sketch. Reprinted in P240 and B324, pp. 89–90; also published with various revisions in the following editions: London: David Bogue, 1853, pp. 310–11; London: David Bogue, 1856, p. 547. Cited in B324, p. 16; London: W. Kent & Co., 1857,

pp. 310–11; New York and London: Routledge, Warne, and Routledge, 1862, pp. 543–44; London: George Routledge and Sons, 1865, p. 586; London: George Routledge and Sons, 1868, p. 575; London: George Routledge and Sons, 1872, p. 674; London: George Routledge and Sons, 1875, pp. 718–19. For a brief discussion of the successive revisions of this biographical sketch see B324, p. 16.

12. Chasles, Philarète. *Anglo-American Literature and Manners.* Trans. Donald MacLeod. New York: Charles Scribner, 1852; microfiche. Louisville, Ky.: Lost Cause Press, 1973, pp. 118–27.

13. Curtis, George William. *Lotus-Eating: A Summer Book.* New York: Harper & Brothers, 1852, p. 132. Reprints P234 with some alterations.

14. "Godfrey Greylock" [Smith, J. E. A.]. *Taghconic; or Letters and Legends about Our Summer Home.* Boston: Redding and Co., 1852, p. 16. Mention. Reprinted in B324, pp. 194–95.

15. Parker, E. M. Wills. *The Sandwich Islands As They Are, Not As They Should Be.* San Francisco: Burgess, Gilbert & Still, 1852, p. 7. Mention.

16. Gerstaecker, F. *Narrative of a Journey Round the World.* London: Hurst and Blackett, 1853, II, 209. Mention.

17. Hunt, T. Dwight. *The Past and Present of the Sandwich Islands.* San Francisco: Whitton, Towne & Co., 1853, pp. 28–29. Mention.

18. Duyckinck, Evert A. and George L. "Herman Melville," in *Cyclopaedia of American Literature.* New York: Charles Scribner, 1855, II, 672–76. Biographical sketch. Reprinted in B324, pp. 91–95; reprinted in part in B295, pp. 345–48; rpt. in revised form. Ed. M. Laird Simons. Philadelphia: William Rutter & Co., 1875, II, 636–69; rpt. Detroit: Gale Research Co., 1965, II, 636–39.

19. [Gostwick, Joseph]. *Hand-Book of American Literature, Historical, Biographical, and Critical.* Philadelphia: J. B. Lippincott & Co., 1855 [?], p. 189. Mention. Reprinted in B315, p. 97.

20. Botta, Anne C. Lynch. *Handbook of Universal Literature.* Boston: Ticknor and Fields, 1860, p. 538. Mention.

21. "Melville, Herman," in *A Dictionary of Contemporary Biography: A Handbook of the Peerage of Rank, Worth and Intellect.* London and Glasgow: Richard Griffin and Co., 1861, p. 272. Mention.

22. "Melville, Herman," in *The New American Cyclopaedia: A Popular Dictionary of General Knowledge.* Eds. George Ripley and Charles A. Dana. New York and London: D. Appleton and Co., 1861, XI, 370–71. Biographical sketch.

23. Nichols, Thomas Low. *Forty Years of American Life.* London: John Maxwell and Co., 1864, II, 344–46. Reprinted in P418, pp. 349–51; rpt. with some alterations, 2nd ed. London: Longmans, Green & Co., 1874, pp. 227–28; rpt. New York: Stackpole Sons, 1937, pp. 212–13.

24. "Melville, Herman," in *Chambers's Encyclopaedia: A Diction-*

ary of Universal Knowledge for the People. London: W. & R. Chambers, 1868, VI, 397. Biographical sketch. Cited in B324, pp. 208–09; also published with various revisions in the following editions: Philadelphia: J. B. Lippincott Co., 1875, VI, 397; New York: Collier, 1886, V, 321. Reprinted with some alterations in B49 and B50; Philadelphia: J. B. Lippincott Co., 1891, VII, 129; London: W. & R. Chambers, 1891, VII, 129.

25. "Melville, Herman," in *Beeton's Dictionary of Universal Biography.* London: Ward, Lock and Co., 1869, p. 708. Biographical sketch.

26. Dillingham, John H. "Herman Melville," in supplement to *The Prose Writers of America.* Ed. Rufus W. Griswold. Philadelphia: Porter and Coates, 1870; microprint. Louisville, Ky.: Lost Cause Press, 1956, pp. 665–66. Biographical headnote to extracts from *Typee.* Conclusion taken from P255.

27. Allibone, S. Austin. "Melville, Herman," in *A Critical Dictionary of English Literature and British and American Authors.* II. Philadelphia: J. B. Lippincott & Co., 1871; rpt. Detroit: Gale Research Co., 1264–65. Biographical sketch, documentation of critical response to Melville's books from *Typee* to *The Confidence-Man.*

28. Drake, Francis S. "Melville, Herman," in *Dictionary of American Biography, Including Men of the Time.* Boston: James R. Osgood and Co., 1872, p. 615. Biographical sketch.

29. Hart, John S. *A Manual of American Literature: A Text-Book for Schools and Colleges.* Philadelphia: Eldredge & Bro., 1872; New York: Johnson Reprint Corp., 1969, p. 486. Mention. Reprinted in B282, p. 103.

30. Underwood, Francis H. "Herman Melville," in *A Hand-Book of English Literature. Intended for the Use of High Schools.* Boston: Lee & Shepard, 1872; New York: Lee, Shepard & Dillingham, 1872, II, 458. Headnote to an extract from *Typee.* Reprinted in B282, pp. 103–04; reprinted with some alterations in B57.

31. "Melville, Herman." *The Best Reading.* New York: G. P. Putnam's Sons, 1873, p. 98. *Typee* listed with its price.

32. Stoddard, Charles Warren. *South-Sea Idyls.* Boston: James R. Osgood and Co., 1873, p. 314; also published as *Summer Cruising in the South Seas.* London: Chatto and Windus, 1874, p. 279. Mention.

33. Johnson, Rossiter. *Little Classics. Authors.* Boston: James R. Osgood and Co., 1875, pp. 172–73. Biographical sketch.

34. Colange, L. "Melville, Herman," in *Zell's Popular Encyclopedia.* Philadelphia: T. Ellwood Zell & Co., 1878, II, 1621. Biographical sketch.

35. Coan, Titus. *Life in Hawaii: An Autobiographical Sketch of Mission Life and Labors (1835–1881).* New York: Anson D. F. Randolph & Co., 1882, pp. 190, 199–200. Mention and revised version of P273.

36. Adams, Oscar Fay. "Melville, Herman," in *A Brief Handbook of*

American Authors. Boston: Houghton Mifflin Co., 1884; rpt. Boston: Milford House, 1973, p. 113. Mention.

37. Hawthorne, Julian. *Nathaniel Hawthorne and His Wife*. Boston and New York: Houghton Mifflin Co., 1884, I; London: Chatto and Windus, 1885, I; rpt. Hamden, Ct.: Archon Books, 1968, I, passim.

38. Longfellow, Henry Wadsworth. *Life of Henry Wadsworth Longfellow*. Ed. Samuel Longfellow. Boston: Ticknor and Co., 1886; London: Kegan Paul, Trench & Co., 1886, II, 52, 301. Mentions.

39. Morris, Charles. "H. Melville," in *Half-Hours with the Best American Authors*. Philadelphia: J. B. Lippincott Co., 1887. Mention. Reprinted in P515, p. 406.

40. Sonnenschein, William Swan. *The Best Books: A Reader's Guide to the Choice of the Best Available Books*. London: Swan Sonnenschein Lowry & Co., 1887, p. 215. *Typee* listed in Geography of Australasia: Polynesia Bibliography.

41. Whipple, Edwin Percy. *American Literature and Other Papers*. Boston: Ticknor and Co., 1887; rpt. New York: Johnson Reprint Corp., 1969, p. 125. Mention.

42. "Melville, Herman," in *Appleton's Cyclopaedia of American Biography*. Ed. James Grant Wilson and John Fiske. New York: D. Appleton and Co., 1888, IV, 293–94. Biographical sketch. Reprinted in B324, pp. 95–97; rpt. with some additions, New York: D. Appleton and Co., 1898, IV, 293.

43. "Melville, Herman," in *Alden's Cyclopedia of Universal Literature*. New York: John B. Alden, 1889, p. 407. Biographical sketch.

44. Clayden, P. W. *Rogers and His Contemporaries*. London: Smith, Elder & Co., 1889, pp. 343–44. Mention.

45. Richardson, Charles F. "The Lesser Novelists," in *American Literature, 1607–1885*. New York and London: G. P. Putnam's Sons, 1889, II, 403–04. Mention. Reprinted in B225, p. 812 and B315, pp. 108–09.

46. Stedman, Arthur. "Melville, Herman," in *A Library of American Literature from the Earliest Settlement to the Present Time*. Ed. Edmund Clarence Stedman and Ellen Mackay Hutchinson. New York: Charles L. Webster & Co., 1890; rpt. St. Clair Shores, Mich.: Scholarly Press, 1971, XI, 554. Biographical sketch. Reprinted in P300, P307, and B324, p. 98.

47. Buchanan, Robert. "Canto II. The First Haven. (Natura Naturens)," in *The Outcast*. London: Chatto and Windus, 1891, pp. 76–78. Reprints P282 with some alterations.

48. "Herman Melville," in *Appleton's Annual Cyclopaedia and Register of Important Events of the Year 1891*. NS 16 New York: D. Appleton and Co., 1892, 503–05. Biographical essay. Reprinted in B324, pp. 149–54.

49. "Melville, Herman," in *The Columbia Cyclopedia*. XIX. New

York: Garretson, Cox & Co., 1892, n. pag. Reprints B24 with some alterations. New York: Collier, 1886, V, 321.

50. "Melville, Herman," in *The International Cyclopaedia*. Ed. H. T. Peck. New York: Dodd, Mead & Co., 1892, IX, 684–85. Reprints B24 with some alterations. New York: Collier, 1886, V, 321.

51. Hawthorne, Julian and Leonard Lemmon. "Herman Melville, An Early Sea-Novelist," in *American Literature; A Text-Book for The Use of Schools and Colleges*. Boston: D. C. Heath, 1892, pp. 208–09. Mentions. Reprinted in B282, pp. 131–32.

52. Stedman, Arthur, ed. "Introduction," in *Typee*. New York: United States Book Co., 1892; London: G. P. Putnam's Sons, 1892; rpt. New York: American Publishers Corp., 1896; rpt. Boston: Dana Estes & Co., 1900; rpt. Boston: L. C. Page Co., 1920, pp. xv–xxxvi. Reprinted in B324, pp. 155–66.

53. Blackburn, Charles F. "Herman Melville," in *Rambles in Books*. London: Sampson Low Marston & Co., 1893, p. 82. Mention.

54. Godwin, Parke. *George William Curtis: A Commemorative Address Delivered Before the Century Association, New York, December 17, 1892*. New York: Harper & Brothers, 1893, p. 17n. Mention. Reprinted in B61.

55. Salt, Henry S. "Memoir of Herman Melville," in *Omoo*. London: John Murray, 1893, pp. xi–xxi. Reprints part of P324 with some alterations.

56. Salt, Henry S. "Memoir of Herman Melville," in *Typee*. London: John Murray, 1893, pp. xi–xxi. Reprints part of P324 with some alterations.

57. Underwood, Francis H. *The Builders of American Literature; Biographical Sketches of American Authors Born Previous to 1826*. First Series. Boston: Lee and Shepard, 1893, pp. 233–34. Reprints B30 with some alterations. Comments on the Stedman (United States Book Co.) edition.

58. "Melville, Herman," in *The Century Cyclopaedia of Names*. Ed. Benjamin E. Smith. New York: Century Co., 1894, p. 674. Biographical sketch.

59. Lowell, James Russell. *Letters of James Russell Lowell*. Ed. Charles Eliot Norton. New York: Harper & Brothers, 1894, I, 141. Mention.

60. Watkins, Mildred Cabell. *American Literature*. New York: American Book Co., 1894, pp. 47–48. Mention.

61. Godwin, Parke. *Commemorative Addresses by Parke Godwin*. New York: Harper & Brothers, 1895, pp. 18–19. Reprints B54.

62. Smith, J. E. A. *The Poet Among the Hills: Oliver Wendell Holmes in Berkshire*. Pittsfield, Mass.: George Blatchford, 1895, pp. 28, 32. Mentions. Reprinted in B324, pp. 199–201.

63. Sonnenschein, William Swan. *A Reader's Guide to Contem-

porary Literature, Being the First Supplement to the Best Books. London: Swan Sonnenschein & Co., 1895, pp. 293, 583. Briefly annotated listing in Polynesia bibliography; listing in bibliography of "Minor American Topical Novels."

64. Matthews, Brander. "Other Writers," in *An Introduction to the Study of American Literature.* New York: American Book Co., 1896, pp. 225–26. Mention.

65. Pattee, Fred Lewis. *A History of American Literature.* Boston and New York: Silver, Burdett & Co., 1896, pp. 152–53. Biographical sketch.

66. Stevenson, Robert Louis. *In the South Seas.* New York: Charles Scribner's Sons, 1896, p. 26. Reprints P289.

67. "Herman Melville (1819–1891)," in *A Library of the World's Best Literature, Ancient and Modern.* Ed. Charles Dudley Warner. New York: The International Society, 1897, XXV, 9867–69; New York: R. S. Peale and J. A. Hill, 1897, XVII, 9867–69. Biographical headnote to extracts from *Typee.*

68. "Melville, Herman," in *The National Cyclopaedia of American Biography.* New York: James T. White & Co., 1897, IV, 59. Biographical Sketch.

69. Bates, Katharine Lee. "National Era: Prose Fiction," in *American Literature.* New York: Macmillan Co.; London: Macmillan and Co., 1897, p. 276. Mention.

70. Becke, Louis. *Wild Life in Southern Seas.* London: T. F. Unwin, 1897, p. 292. Mention.

71. Smith, J. E. A. *Biographical Sketch of Herman Melville. 1891.* n.p., 1897; rpt. Worcester, Mass., 1934; Princeton, N.J., 1936. Reprints with some alterations P315, P316, and P321.

72. Noble, Charles. "Period of the Later Nineteenth Century, 1850–1880," in *American Literature: A Text-Book for Academies and High Schools.* New York: Macmillan Co., 1898; London: Macmillan & Co., 1898, pp. 287–88; rev. ed. New York: The Macmillan Co., 1907, pp. 293–94. Mention.

73. Mitchell, Donald G. *Leather-Stocking to Poe's "Raven."* vol. 2 of *American Lands and Letters.* New York: Charles Scribner's Sons, 1899, p. 235. Mention. Reprinted in part in B315, pp. 114–15.

74. Peck, Harry Thurston. "Herman Melville," in *Masterpieces of the World's Literature, Ancient and Modern.* Ed. Harry Thurston Peck. New York: American Literary Society, 1899, XV, 7853. Biographical headnote to an extract from *Typee.*

75. Stevenson, Robert Louis. *The Letters of Robert Louis Stevenson.* Ed. Sidney Colvin. London: Methuen and Co., 1899, II; New York: Charles Scribner's Sons, 1899, II; Ann Arbor, Mich.: University Microfilms, 1969, II, 115, 182. Mentions.

76. Bronson, Walter C. "Other Writers," in *A Short History of*

American Literature. Boston: D. C. Heath & Co., 1900, pp. 148–49. Mention.

77. Stedman, Edmund Clarence. "Biographical Notes," in *An American Anthology,* 1787–1900. Ed. Edmund Clarence Stedman. Boston: Houghton Mifflin Co., 1900, p. 809. Mention.

78. Stodart-Walker, Archibald. *Robert Buchanan, the Poet of Modern Revolt: An Introduction to His Poetry.* London: Grant Richards, 1900, p. 262. Mention.

79. Wendell, Barrett. *A Literary History of America.* New York: Charles Scribner's Sons, 1900; London: T. Fisher Unwin, 1901; rpt. Detroit: Gale Research Co., 1968, p. 229. Mention. Reprinted in B282, p. 146.

80. Newcomer, Alphonso G. *American Literature.* Chicago: Scott, Foresman and Co., 1901, p. 128. Mention. Reprinted in B315, p. 119.

81. Abernethy, Julian W. "Present Schools and Tendencies," in *American Literature.* New York: Maynard, Merrill & Co., 1902, pp. 456–57. Reprinted in B282, pp. 146–47.

82. Carpenter, Edward, ed. *Iolaus: An Anthology of Friendship.* London: Swan Sonnenschein & Co., 1902; Manchester: The Author, 1902; Boston: Charles E. Goodspeed, 1902, p. 8. Introduction to extracts from *Omoo* and *Typee.*

83. Mallary, R. De Witt. *Lenox and the Berkshire Highlands.* New York and London: G. P. Putnam's Sons, 1902, p. 62. Mention.

84. Payne, William Morton. "A Century of American Fiction," in *Editorial Echoes.* Chicago: A. C. McClurg & Co., 1902, p. 109. Mention.

85. R[ichardson], C[harles] F. "Melville, Herman," in *Encyclopaedia Britannica.* 10th ed. London and Edinburgh: Adam and Charles Black, 1902; New York: The Encyclopaedia Britannica Co., 1902, VI, 631. Biographical sketch. Reprinted in part in B315, pp. 120–21; rpt. in abbreviated form in B112.

86. Trent, William Peterfield, ed. "Introduction," in *Typee.* Boston: D. C. Heath & Co., 1902, pp. iii–v.

87. "Melville, Herman," in *Lamb's Biographical Dictionary of the United States.* Ed. John Howard Brown. V. Boston: James H. Lamb Co., 1903, n. pag. Biographical sketch. Reprinted in B95.

88. "Melville, Herman," in *The New International Encyclopaedia.* Ed. Daniel Coit Gilman, H. T. Peck, and Frank Moore Colby. New York: Dodd, Mead and Co., 1903, XII, 93–94. Biographical sketch.

89. Baker, Ernest A. *A Descriptive Guide to the Best Fiction, British and American.* London: Swan Sonnenschein and Co., 1903; New York: Macmillan Co., 1903; p. 262. Listing, brief comment. Reprinted in B115.

90. Hawthorne, Julian. *Hawthorne and His Circle.* New York and London: Harper & Brothers, 1903; rpt. Hamden, Ct.: Archon Books, 1968, p. 32. Mention.

91. Payne, John. "Herman Melville," in *Vigil and Vision. New Son-*

nets. London: Villon Society, 1903; rpt. New York: AMS Press, 1970, p. 62. Reprinted in B282, p. 148.

92. Stevenson, Mrs. M. I. *From Saranac to the Marquesas and Beyond.* London: Methuen & Co., 1903, pp. 107–08. Mention in letter, 13 Aug. 1888.

93. Trent, William Peterfield. *A History of American Literature, 1607–1865.* New York: D. Appleton and Co., 1903; London: William Heinemann, 1903; rpt. Norwood, Pa.: Norwood Editions, 1978, passim.

94. "Melville, Herman," in *The Bibliophile Library of Literature, Art, and Rare Manuscripts.* Comp. Nathan Haskell Dole, Forrest Morgan, and Caroline Ticknor. New York and London: International Bibliophile Society, 1904, XXX, 10226. Biographical sketch.

95. "Melville, Herman," in *The Twentieth Century Biographical Dictionary of Notable Americans.* Ed. Rossiter Johnson. Boston: Biographical Society, 1904, VII; rpt. Detroit: Gale Research Co., 1968, n. pag. Reprints B87.

96. Balfour, Marie Clothilde. "Melville and the Marquesas: A Few Notes Upon His Facts and General Information," in *Typee.* Ed. W. Clark Russell. London and New York: John Lane, 1904; London: G. Routledge, 1910, pp. 429–51. "Editor's Preface," pp. v–x. Reprinted in part in B258, pp. 624–25 and B315, p. 122.

97. ———. "Tahiti in 1842: as Melville Saw It," in *Omoo.* Ed. W. Clark Russell. London and New York: John Lane, 1904, pp. 445–62. Mention.

98. Trent, William Peterfield. *A Brief History of American Literature.* New York: D. Appleton and Co., 1904, passim.

99. Moulton, Charles Wells, ed. "Herman Melville," in *The Library of Literary Criticism of English and American Authors.* Buffalo: Moulton Pub. Co., 1905, VIII, 62–64. Mentions in entry composed of quotes from various commentaries on Melville.

100. "Melville, Herman," in *Nelson's Encyclopaedia: Everybody's Book of Reference.* Ed. Frank Moore Colby and George Sandeman. New York: Thomas Nelson & Sons, 1906, VIII, 77. Biographical sketch.

101. "Melville, Herman," in *The Americana: A Universal Reference Library.* Ed. Frederick Converse Beach. New York: Scientific American Compiling Dep't, 1907, n. pag. Mention.

102. Rhys, Ernest. "Editor's Introduction," in *Typee.* New York: E. P. Dutton & Co., 1907; London: J. M. Dent & Co., 1907, pp. vii–x.

103. ———. "Editor's Note," in *Omoo.* New York: E. P. Dutton & Co., 1908; London: J. M. Dent & Co., 1908, p. vii. Biographical sketch.

104. Cooper, Lane. "The Poets," in *A Manual of American Literature.* Ed. Theodore Stanton. New York and London: G. P. Putnam's Sons, 1909, p. 263. Mention.

105. Miller, Marion Mills. *Manual of Ready Reference to The Authors' Digest Containing Brief Analyses of the World's Great Stories.*

New York: Authors Press, 1909, p. 86. *Typee* listed, summarized in one sentence.

106. Simonds, William Edward. *A Student's History of American Literature*. Boston and New York: Houghton Mifflin Co., 1909, p. 304. Mention. Reprinted in B282, p. 149.

107. Christian F. W. *Eastern Pacific Lands: Tahiti and the Marquesas Islands*. London: Robert Scott, 1910, p. 155. Mention.

108. Thomas, James ('B–V'). *Walt Whitman; The Man and The Poet*. London: The Editor, 1910; rpt. Folcroft, Pa.: Folcroft Library Editions, 1976, p. 32. Reprints P279.

109. Halleck, Reuben Post. "Supplementary List of Authors and Their Chief Works: Eastern Authors," in *History of American Literature*. New York: American Book Co., 1911, p. 407. *Typee* listed, brief comment.

110. Jackson Holbrook. "Southward Ho!" in *Romance and Reality: Essays and Studies*. London: Grant Richards, 1911; New York: Mitchell Kennerly, 1912, pp. 26–37 [27–31 et passim]. Reprinted in B114.

111. London, Jack. "Typee," in *The Cruise of the Snark*. New York: The Macmillan Co., 1911; rpt. London: Seafarer Books, 1971, pp. 154–77. Reprints P367.

112. [Richardson, Charles F.]. "Melville, Herman," in *Encyclopaedia Britannica*. 11th ed. Cambridge, England: The University Press, 1911; New York: Encyclopaedia Britannica Co., 1911, XVIII, 102–03. Abbreviated version of B85.

113. Cavins, William B. *A History of American Literature*. New York: Oxford University Press, 1912, p. 369.

114. Jackson, Holbrook. "Southward Ho!" in *Southward Ho! and Other Essays*. New York: E. P. Dutton & Co., 1912; London: J. M. Dent & Sons Ltd., 1912; rpt. Freeport, N.Y.: Books for Libraries Press, 1968, pp. 6–9, 12, 16. Reprints B110.

115. Baker, Ernest A. *A Guide to the Best Fiction in English*. London: George Routledge & Sons, 1913, p. 392. Reprints *Typee* reference in B89.

116. Frazer, Sir James George. *The Belief in Immortality and the Worship of the Dead*. London: Macmillan and Co., 1913; rpt. London: Dawsons, 1968, II, passim.

117. Johnson, Martin. "In the Marquesas," in *Through the South Seas with Jack London*. London: T. Werner Laurie, 1913; New York: Dodd, Mead and Co., 1913; rpt. Cedar Springs, Mich.: Wolf House Books, 1972, pp. 161–63.

118. Long, William J. *American Literature: A Study of the Men and the Books that in the Earlier and Later Times Reflect the American Spirit*. Boston: Ginn and Co., 1913, p. 247. Mention. Reprinted in B258, p. 625.

119. MacMechan, Archibald. "The Best Sea Story Ever Written," in

The Life of a Little College and Other Papers. Boston: Houghton Mifflin Co., 1914, pp. 181–97. Reprints P349.

120. Metcalf, John Calvin. *American Literature.* Richmond, Va.: B. F. Johnson Pub. Co., 1914, pp. 389–91. Mention.

121. Kellner, Leon. *American Literature.* Trans. Julia Franklin. Garden City, N.Y.: Doubleday Page & Co., 1915, passim.

122. London, Charmian Kittredge. *The Log of the Snark.* New York: Macmillan Co., 1915, passim.

123. Newcomer, Alphonso G., Alice E. Andrews, and Howard Judson Hall, eds. "Herman Melville," in *Three Centuries of American Poetry and Prose.* Chicago: Scott, Foresman and Co., 1917, p. 774; rpt. with some alterations, 1929, p. 635. Biographical headnote to an extract from *Typee.*

124. Van Doren, Carl. "Contemporaries of Cooper," in *The Cambridge History of American Literature.* Ed. William Peterfield Trent et al. New York: G. P. Putnam's Sons, 1917; Cambridge, England: The University Press, 1917, I, 320–23. Reprinted with some alterations in B167 and B168.

125. Chase, Frederic Hathaway. *Lemuel Shaw: Chief Justice of the Supreme Judicial Court of Massachusetts, 1830–1860.* Boston: Houghton Mifflin Co., 1918, passim.

126. Bronson, Walter C. *A Short History of American Literature.* Revised and Enlarged. Boston: D. C. Heath and Co., 1919, p. 460. Mention.

127. O'Brien, Frederick. *White Shadows in the South Seas.* New York: Century Co., 1919, pp. 301–02. Mention.

128. Pattee, Fred Lewis. "Herman Melville (1819–1891)," in *Century Readings for a Course in American Literature.* New York: Century Co., 1919, p. 407. Biographical headnote to extracts from *Typee* and *Moby-Dick.*

The 1920s

129. Anderson, Johannes C. *Myths & Legends of the Polynesians.* London: George G. Harrap & Co., 1928, p. 458. Mention.

130. "Introduction," in *Moby-Dick.* Philadelphia: Macrae Smith Co., 1925; rpt. New York: Library Publications, 1930 [?], pp. 3–4. Mention.

131. "Preface," in *Romances of Herman Melville.* New York: Pickwick Publishers, 1928, pp. v–vi.

132. Beebe, William. *Galapagos: World's End.* New York and London: G. P. Putnam's Sons, 1924, passim.

133. Bennett, Arnold. *The Savour of Life: Essays in Gusto.* London:

Cassell, 1928, pp. 248–49; Garden City, N.Y.: Doubleday, Doran & Co., 1928, pp. 305–07. Mention. Reprinted in B282, p. 187.

134. Birrell, Augustine. "The Immortal White Whale," in *Fact, Fancy and Opinion*. Ed. Robert M. Gay. Boston: Atlantic Monthly Press, 1923, pp. 47–51. Reprints P384.

135. Boynton, Percy H. "Herman Melville," in *More Contemporary Americans*. Chicago: University of Chicago Press, 1927; rpt. Freeport, N.Y.: Books for Libraries Press, 1967, pp. 29–50. [31–35 et passim].

136. ———. *Some Contemporary Americans: The Personal Equation in Literature*. Chicago: University of Chicago Press, 1924; rpt. New York: Biblo and Tannen, 1966, p. 275. Reprints P386.

137. Braddy, Nella. "Melville, Herman," in *The Guide to Literature*. Vol. 25 of *The University Library*. Ed. John Finley. Garden City, N.Y.: Doubleday, Page & Co., 1926, p. 142. Mention.

138. Brooks, Van Wyck. "Notes on Herman Melville," in *Emerson and Others*. New York: E. P. Dutton and Co., 1927; rpt. New York: Octagon Books, 1973, pp. 171–205 [passim]. Reprints P387 with some alterations.

139. Canby, Henry Seidel. "Conrad and Melville," in *Definitions: Essays in Contemporary Criticism*. First Series. New York: Harcourt, Brace and Co., 1922; rpt. Port Washington, N.Y.: Kennikat Press, 1967, pp. 257–68 [262–63]. Reprints P388.

140. ———. "Conrad and Melville," in *Modern Essays*. Second Series. Ed. Christopher Morley. New York: Harcourt, Brace and Co., 1924, pp. 201–14. Reprints P388.

141. Cournos, John. "Herman Melville—The Seeker," in *A Modern Plutarch*. Indianapolis: Bobbs-Merrill Co., 1928, pp. 78–95 [passim]; London: T. Butterworth, 1928, pp. 77–89 [passim].

142. Dellenbaugh, Frederick S. "Travellers and Explorers, 1846–1900," in *The Cambridge History of American Literature*. Ed. William Peterfield Trent et al. New York: G. P. Putnam's Sons, 1921; Cambridge, England: The University Press, 1921, III, 156. Mention.

143. Early, Preston Hussey. "Introduction," in *Mardi*. Boston: The St. Botolph Society, 1923, pp. vii–xi. Mention.

144. Freeman, John. *Herman Melville*. New York: Macmillan Co., 1926; London: Macmillan and Co., 1926; Ann Arbor, Mich.: University Microfilms, 1965; rpt. Norwood, Pa.: Norwood Editions, 1976, pp. 25–27, 42–43, 74–80, 171–72, et passim.

145. Gosse, Sir Edmund. "Herman Melville," in *Silhouettes*. London: William Heinemann, Ltd., 1925; New York: Charles Scribner's Sons, 1925; rpt. Folcroft, Pa.: Folcroft Library Editions, 1972, pp. 355–62 [passim].

146. Handy, E. S. Craighill. *The Native Culture in the Marquesas*. Honolulu: Bernice P. Bishop Museum, Bulletin 9, pub. 9, 1923; rpt. New York: Kraus Reprint Co., 1971, passim.

147. Handy, Willowdean Chatterson. *Tattooing in the Marquesas*. Honolulu: Bernice P. Bishop Museum, Bulletin 1, pub. 3, 1922; rpt. New York: Kraus Reprint Co., 1971, passim.

148. Hind, C. Lewis. "Herman Melville," in *More Authors and I*. New York: Dodd, Mead and Co., 1922; London: John Lane, 1922; rpt. Freeport, N.Y.: Books for Libraries Press, 1969, pp. 223–28 [passim].

149. Keller, Helen Rex. *The Reader's Digest of Books*. New York: Macmillan Co., 1922, passim.

150. Lawrence, D. H. "Herman Melville's 'Typee' and 'Omoo,' " in *Studies in Classic American Literature*. New York: Thomas Seltzer, 1923, pp. 193–213; London: Martin Secker, 1924, pp. 132–44; rpt. Harmondsworth and New York: Penguin Books, 1977, pp. 139–52. Reprinted in B247, pp. 11–20; reprinted with some alterations in B269; reprinted in part in B321, p. 39.

151. Leisy, Ernest. "Herman Melville," in *American Literature: An Interpretative Survey*. New York: Thomas Y. Crowell Co., 1929, pp. 102–05 [passim].

152. Leonard, Sterling Andrus. "Introduction" and "Biographical Note," in *Typee*. New York: Harcourt, Brace and Howe, 1920, pp. v–viii.

153. Lucas, F. L. "Herman Melville," in *Authors Dead & Living*. London: Chatto and Windus, 1926; New York: Macmillan Co., 1926; rpt. Freeport, N.Y.: Books for Libraries Press, 1968, pp. 105–15. Reprints P394.

154. Meynell, Viola. "Introduction," in *Moby-Dick; or The Whale*. London: Oxford University Press, 1920, pp. v–viii. Mention.

155. Minnigerode, Meade. *Some Personal Letters of Herman Melville and a Bibliography*. New York and New Haven: E. B. Hackett, Brick Row Book Shop, 1922; rpt. Freeport, N.Y.: Books for Libraries Press, 1969, pp. 10–28, 101–24, et passim. Reprints P75.

156. ———. *The Fabulous Forties, 1840–1850: A Presentation of Private Life*. New York: G. P. Putnam's Sons, 1924, pp. 113–14. Mention.

157. Morris, Lloyd. *The Rebellious Puritan: Portrait of Mr. Hawthorne*. New York: Harcourt, Brace and Co., 1927; London: Constable and Co., 1928; rpt. Port Washington, N.Y. and London: Kennikat Press, 1969, pp. 243–51 [243, 246]. Mentions.

158. Mumford, Lewis. *Herman Melville: A Study of His Life and Vision*. London: J. Cape, Ltd., 1929; New York: Harcourt, Brace & Co., 1929; New York: The Literary Guild of America, 1929, pp. 67–78 et passim; rev. ed. London: Secker & Warburg, 1963; New York: Harcourt, Brace & World, 1963, pp. 42–49 et passim.

159. Overton, Grant, *The Answerer*. New York: Harcourt, Brace and Co., 1921, p. 277. Mention.

160. Paltsits, Victor Hugo, ed. *Family Correspondence of Herman Melville, 1830–1904. In the Gansevoort-Lansing Collection*. New York: New York Public Library, 1929; rpt. Norwood, Pa.: Norwood Editions,

1977, passim. Reprint of P402 and P403.

161. Parrington, Vernon. "Herman Melville—Pessimist," in *The Romantic Revolution in America, 1880–1860*. Vol. 2 of *Main Currents in American Thought: An Interpretation of American Literature from the Beginnings to 1920*. New York: Harcourt, Brace and Co., 1927, pp. 258–67 [261–62].

162. Richardson, William L. and Jesse M. Owen. *Literature of the World: An Introductory Study*. Boston: Ginn & Co., 1922, p. 484. Mention.

163. Sadleir, Michael. "Herman Melville, 1819–1891," in *Excursions in Victorian Bibliography*. London: Chaundy & Cox, 1922; rpt. Norwood, Pa.: Norwood Editions, 1975, pp. 217–34 [passim].

164. Salt, Henry S. *Seventy Years Among Savages*. New York: Thomas Seltzer, 1921; London: Allen and Unwin, 1921, pp. 69, 110, 112. Mentions.

165. Sullivan, J. W. N. "Herman Melville," in *Aspects of Science*. Second Series. New York: Alfred A. Knopf, 1926, pp. 190–205 [passim].

166. Van Doren, Carl. "Introduction," in *White Jacket*. London: Oxford University Press, 1924, pp. v–xiv. Mention. Reprinted in P412.

167. ———. "Melville," in *A Short History of American Literature*. Ed. William Peterfield Trent et al. New York: G. P. Putnam's Sons, 1922; Cambridge, England: The University Press, 1922, pp. 198–201. Reprints B124 with some alterations.

168. ———. *The American Novel*. New York: Macmillan Co., 1921, pp. 68–76; rev. ed., 1940, pp. 84–192. Reprints B124 with some alterations.

169. Van Vechten, Carl. "The Later Works of Herman Melville," in *Excavations: A Book of Advocacies*. New York: Alfred A. Knopf, 1926, pp. 65–88. Reprints P413 with some alterations.

170. Weaver, Raymond M. *Herman Melville: Mariner and Mystic*. New York: George H. Doran Co., 1921; rpt. New York: Pageant Books, 1961; rpt. New York: Cooper Square Publishers, 1968; pp. 205–14, 252–56, et passim. Reprints P282.

171. ———. "Introduction," in *Shorter Novels of Herman Melville*. New York: Liveright Publishing Corp., 1928, pp. vii–xlvii [passim].

172. Williamson, Robert W. *The Social and Political Systems of Central Polynesia*. Cambridge, England: The University Press, 1924, I, 318. Mention.

The 1930s

173. Adams, Henry. *Letters of Henry Adams (1858–91)*. Ed. Worthington Chauncy Ford. I. Boston: Houghton Mifflin Co., 1930; rpt. New York: Kraus Reprint Co., 1969, I, 483. Mention in letter, 3 May 1891.

174. Alcott, A. Bronson. *The Journals of Bronson Alcott*. Ed. Odell

Shepard. Boston: Little, Brown and Co., 1938, p. 185. Mention in journal entry for 9 Dec. 1846.

175. Anderson, Charles Roberts. *Melville in the South Seas*. New York: Columbia University Press, 1939; rev. ed. New York: Dover, 1966; London: Constable and Co., Ltd., 1966, pp. 117–95 et passim. Reprints in part B9, pp. 233–35.

176. Blankenship, Russell. "Herman Melville (1819–1891)," in *American Literature as an Expression of the National Mind*. New York: Henry Holt and Co., 1931, pp. 377–87; rev. ed. New York: Henry Holt and Co., 1949; rpt. New York: Cooper Square Publishers, 1973, pp. 377–88.

177. Boynton, Percy H. *Literature and American Life*. Boston and New York: Ginn and Co., 1936, pp. 461–77 et passim.

178. Calverton, V. F. *The Liberation of American Literature*. New York: Charles Scribner's Sons, 1932; Ann Arbor, Mich.: University Microfilms, 1967; rpt. New York: Octagon Books, 1973, p. 272.

179. Canby, Henry Seidel. "Hawthorne and Melville," in *Classic Americans: A Study of Eminent American Writers from Irving to Whitman*. New York: Harcourt, Brace and Co., 1931; rpt. New York: Russell & Russell, 1959, pp. 226–65 [250–51].

180. Fletcher, John Gould. *The Two Frontiers: A Study in Historical Psychology*. New York: Coward-McCann, 1930, pp. 258–59.

181. "George Paston." [Symonds, Emily Morse]. *At John Murray's: Records of a Literary Circle, 1843–1892*. London and New York: John Murray, 1932, pp. 51–54. Account of the publication of *Typee*.

182. Josephson, Matthew. "Libertarians and Others," in *Portrait of the Artist as American*. New York: Harcourt, Brace and Co., 1930; rpt. New York: Octagon Books, 1964, pp. 3–43 [28–30].

183. Pattee, Fred Lewis, "Revaluations," in *The New American Literature, 1890–1930*. New York and London: Century Co., 1930; rpt. New York: Cooper Square Publishers, 1968, pp. 359–84 [365–72]. Reprints P404 with some alterations.

184. Quinn, Arthur Hobson. "Herman Melville and the Exotic Romance," in *American Fiction: An Historical and Critical Survey*. New York and London: D. Appleton-Century Co., 1936, pp. 149–58 [150–51 et passim].

185. Rourke, Constance. *American Humor: A Study of the National Character*. Garden City, N.Y.: Doubleday, 1931, pp. 154–60 [passim]; New York: Harcourt, Brace and Co., 1931, pp. 191–200 [passim].

186. Shurcliff, Sidney Nichols. *Jungle Islands: The "Illyria" in the South Seas*. New York and London: G. P. Putnam's Sons, 1930, p. 114. Mention.

187. Thorp, Willard, ed. "Introduction," in *Herman Melville: Representative Selections*. New York: American Book Co., 1938, pp. xi–cxxix, cxli, cxlvii.

188. Untermeyer, Louis. "Herman Melville," in *American Poetry from the Beginning to Whitman*. New York: Harcourt, Brace and Co., 1931; also published as *American Poetry from the Beginning to Walt Whitman*. London: J. Cape, 1932, pp. 547–55 [passim].

189. Weaver, Raymond M. "Introduction," in *Typee*. New York: Limited Editions Club, 1935; rpt. New York: Heritage Press, 1963, pp. iii–xxii.

190. ———. "Melville," in *American Writers on American Literature*. Ed. John Macy. New York: Tudor Pub. Co., 1931; New York: H. Liveright, 1931, pp. 190–206.

191. Williams, Stanley T. *American Literature*. Philadelphia and London: J. B. Lippincott Co., 1933; rpt. Norwood, Pa.: Norwood Editions, 1975, pp. 91, 92. Mentions.

192. Winters, Yvor. "Herman Melville and the Problems of Moral Navigation," in *Maule's Curse: Seven Studies in the History of American Obscurantism*. Norfolk, Ct.: New Directions, 1938, pp. 53–89 [passim]. Reprinted in B207.

The 1940s

193. Braswell, William. *Melville's Religious Thought: An Essay in Interpretation*. Durham, N.C.: Duke University Press, 1943; rpt. New York: Pageant Books, 1959; rpt. New York: Octagon Books, 1973, passim.

194. Brooks, Van Wyck. *The Times of Melville and Whitman*. New York: E. P. Dutton and Co., 1947, pp. 155–56 et passim; rev. ed., 1953, pp. 158–59 et passim.

195. Calhoun, Dorothy C. "Typee: A Fifteen-Minute Radio Play," in *One Hundred Non-Royalty One-Act Plays*. Ed. William Kozlenko. New York: Greenberg, 1940; New York: Grosset & Dunlap, 1940, pp. 794–802.

196. Chase, Richard. *Herman Melville: A Critical Study*. New York: Macmillan Co., 1949; rpt. New York: Folkroft Press, 1970; rpt. New York: Hafner Pub. Co., 1971, pp. 9–15 et passim.

197. Cowie, Alexander. "Herman Melville (1819–1891)," in *The Rise of the American Novel*. New York: American Book Co., 1948, pp. 363–411 [368–72 et passim].

198. Gohdes, Clarence. *American Literature in Nineteenth-Century England*. New York: Columbia University Press, 1944; rpt. Carbondale: Southern Illinois University Press, 1963, p. 34. Mention.

199. Matthiessen, F. O. *American Renaissance: Art and Expression in the Age of Emerson and Whitman*. New York and London: Oxford University Press, 1941, passim.

200. Paltsits, Victor Hugo. "Herman Melville's Background and New Light on the Publication of *Typee*," in *Bookmen's Holiday*. New

York: New York Public Library, 1943, pp. 243–68. Also published by the New York Public Library in 1943 as a separate pamphlet.

201. Pattee, Fred Lewis. "Melville and Whitman," in *The Feminine Fifties*. New York and London: D. Appleton-Century Co., 1940; rpt. Port Washington, N.Y.: Kennikat Press, 1966, pp. 28–49 [29–30, 34–35, et passim].

202. Pollock, Thomas Clark. *The Nature of Literature: Its Relation to Science, Language and Human Experience*. Princeton: Princeton University Press, 1942; rpt. New York: Gordian Press, 1965, pp. 138 et passim.

203. Sedgwick, William Ellery. *Herman Melville: The Tragedy of Mind*. Cambridge, Mass.: Harvard University Press, 1944; London: Humphrey Milford, Oxford University Press, 1944; rpt. New York: Russell & Russell, 1962, pp. 19–35 et passim.

204. Stone, Geoffrey. *Melville*. New York: Sheed & Ward, 1949; rpt. New York: Octagon Books, 1976, pp. 54–65 et passim.

205. Thorp, Willard. "Herman Melville," in *Literary History of the United States*. Ed. Robert E. Spiller et al. New York: Macmillan Co., 1948; rev. ed. 1953, pp. 441–71 [444–45 et passim].

206. Vincent, Howard P. *The Trying-Out of Moby-Dick*. Boston: Houghton Mifflin, 1949; rpt. Carbondale: Southern Illinois University Press, 1965, pp. 13–14.

207. Winters, Yvor. "Herman Melville and the Problems of Moral Navigation," in *In Defense of Reason*. New York: Swallow Press & W. Morrow and Co., 1947; rpt. London: Routledge & Kegan Paul, 1960, pp. 200–33 [passim]. Reprints B192.

208. Wright, Nathalia. *Melville's Use of the Bible*. Durham, N.C.: Duke University Press, 1949; rpt. with a new appendix. New York: Octagon Books, 1969, passim.

The 1950s

209. Arvin, Newton. *Herman Melville*. New York: William Sloane Associates, 1950; London: Methuen, 1950; rpt. Westport, Ct.: Greenwood Press, 1972, pp. 3–6, 78–89, et passim.

210. Babcock, C. Merton. "Introduction," in *Typee*. New York: Harper and Brothers, 1959, pp. vii–xiv.

211. Baird, James. *Ishmael: A Study of the Symbolic Mode in Primitivism*. Baltimore: Johns Hopkins Press, 1956; rpt. New York: Harper and Brothers, 1960, pp. 100–21, 208–13, 252–55, 274–75, 287–91, 294–95, et passim.

212. Bode, Carl. *The Anatomy of American Popular Culture*. Berkeley: University of California Press, 1959, pp. 225–27, 271.

213. Clark, Harry Hayden. "Changing Attitudes in Early American

Literary Criticism: 1800–1840," in *The Development of American Literary Criticism*. Ed. Floyd Stovall. Chapel Hill: University of North Carolina Press, 1955; rpt. New Haven, Ct.: College and University Press, 1964, pp. 15–73 [38–39].

214. Cunliffe, Marcus. "Melville and Whitman," in *The Literature of the United States*. Harmondsworth and Baltimore: Penguin Books, 1954; rev. ed., 1961, pp. 105–19; 3rd ed., 1967, pp. 113–28.

215. Davis, Merrell R. *Melville's Mardi: A Chartless Voyage*. New Haven: Yale University Press, 1952; London: Geoffrey Cumberlege, Oxford University Press, 1952; rpt. Hamden, Ct.: Archon Books, 1967, pp. 5–28, 201–07, 218–21, et passim.

216. Fadiman, Clifton. "Introduction," in *Typee*. New York: Bantam Books, 1958, pp. xv–xxi.

217. Feidelson, Charles, Jr. "The Fool of Truth," in *Symbolism and American Literature*. Chicago: University of Chicago Press, 1953, pp. 162–212 [164–66, 169–70].

218. Gibbings, Robert. "Introduction," in *Typee*. London: The Folio Society, 1950, n. pag.

219. Gilman, William H. *Melville's Early Life and Redburn*. New York: New York University Press, 1951; London: Geoffrey Cumberlege, Oxford University Press, 1951; rpt. New York: Russell and Russell, 1972, pp. 161–63 et passim.

220. Honig, Edwin. *Dark Conceit: The Making of Allegory*. Evanston, Ill.: Northwestern University Press, 1959; London: Faber & Faber, 1960; rpt. Providence, R.I.: Brown University Press, 1972, pp. 138–39.

221. Howard, Leon. *Herman Melville: A Biography*. Berkeley: University of California Press, 1951, pp. 92–100, 105–07, 117–19, et passim.

222. James C. L. R. *Mariners, Renegades and Castaways: The Story of Herman Melville and the World We Live In*. New York: C. L. R. James, 1953, pp. 82–83, et passim.

223. Levin, Harry. *The Power of Blackness: Hawthorne, Poe, Melville*. New York: Alfred A. Knopf, 1958; rpt. New York: Vintage Books, 1960, pp. 172–73 et passim.

224. Lewis, R. W. B. "Melville: The Apotheosis of Adam," in *The American Adam: Innocence, Tragedy, and Tradition in the Nineteenth Century*. Chicago: University of Chicago Press, 1955, pp. 127–55 [135, 136]. Reprinted in B270.

225. Leyda, Jay, ed. *The Melville Log: A Documentary Life of Herman Melville, 1819–1891*. 2 vols. New York: Harcourt, Brace and Co., 1951; rpt., with a new supplement. New York: Gordian Press, 1969. Many references. Reprints many reviews of *Typee*.

226. ———. *The Portable Melville*. New York: Viking Press, 1952, pp. 342–45 et passim.

227. Mason, Ronald Charles. *The Spirit Above the Dust: A Study of Herman Melville.* London: John Lehmann, 1951; Ann Arbor, Mich.: University Microfilms, 1965; 2nd ed. Mamaroneck, N.J.: Paul P. Appel, 1972, pp. 21–39 et passim.

228. Metcalf, Eleanor Melville. *Herman Melville: Cycle and Epicycle.* Cambridge, Mass.: Harvard University Press, 1953; rpt. Westport, Ct.: Greenwood Press, 1970, passim.

229. Miller, Perry. *The Raven and The Whale: The War of Words and Wits in the Era of Poe and Melville.* New York: Harcourt, Brace and Co., 1956; rpt. Westport, Ct.: Greenwood Press, 1973, passim.

230. Pommer, Henry F. *Milton and Melville.* Pittsburgh: University of Pittsburgh Press, 1950; rpt. New York: Cooper Square Publishers, 1970, passim.

231. Quinn, Arthur Hobson, ed. "The Romance of History and the Frontier," in *The Literature of the American People: An Historical and Critical Survey.* New York: Appleton-Century-Crofts, 1951, pp. 226–47 [244–45].

232. Rosenberry, Edward H. *Melville and the Comic Spirit.* Cambridge, Mass.: Harvard University Press, 1955; rpt. New York: Octagon Books, 1969, passim.

233. Sealts, Merton M., Jr. *Melville as Lecturer.* Cambridge, Mass.: Harvard University Press, 1957; London: Oxford University Press, 1957; rpt. Folcroft, Pa.: Folcroft Press, 1970, passim. Reprints P266.

234. Simms, William Gilmore. *The Letters of William Gilmore Simms.* Eds. Mary C. Oliphant, Alfred Taylor Odell, and T. C. Duncan Eaves. Columbia: University of South Carolina Press, 1953, II, 158n.

235. Stern, Milton R., ed. "Introduction" and "A Note about the Text of *Typee*," in *Typee and Billy Budd.* New York: E. P. Dutton & Co., 1958, pp. vi–xxvi. Reprinted London: J. M. Dent and Heron Books, 1968.

236. ———. *The Fine Hammered Steel of Herman Melville.* Urbana: University of Illinois Press, 1957, pp. 29–65 et passim.

237. Thompson, Lawrance. *Melville's Quarrel with God.* Princeton: Princeton University Press, 1952; London: Geoffrey Cumberlege, Oxford University Press, 1952, pp. 42–55 et passim.

238. Wykes, Alan. *A Concise Survey of American Literature.* New York: Library Publishers, 1955; London and Edinburgh: Morrison and Gibb Ltd., 1955, pp. 67–68.

The 1960s

239. Abel, Darrel. *A Simplified Approach to Melville.* Great Neck, New York: Barron's Educational Series, 1964, pp. 7–12.

240. Baritz, Loren. "The Demonic: Herman Melville," in *A City on a Hill: A History of Ideas and Myths in America.* New York and London: John Wiley & Sons, 1964, pp. 271–332 [273–77 et passim].

241. Bernstein, John. *Pacifism and Rebellion in the Writings of Herman Melville.* The Hague: Mouton & Co., 1964; rpt. Darby, Pa.: Arden Library, 1978, pp. 15–24 et passim.

242. Berthoff, Warner. *The Example of Melville.* Princeton: Princeton University Press, 1962; rpt. New York: W. W. Norton & Co., 1972, passim.

243. Bowen, Merlin. *The Long Encounter: Self and Experience in the Writings of Herman Melville.* Chicago: University of Chicago Press, 1960; London; Cambridge University Press, 1960, pp. 51–55 et passim.

244. Canaday, Nicholas, Jr. *Melville and Authority.* Gainesville: University of Florida Press, 1968, pp. 1–8 et passim. Reprints P465.

245. Charvat, William. "Melville's Income," "Melville," and "Melville and the Common Reader," in *The Profession of Authorship in America, 1800–1870.* Ed. Matthew J. Bruccoli. Columbus: Ohio State University Press, 1968, pp. 190–203 [passim], 204–61, 262–82. Reprints P437 and P451.

246. Chase, Richard, ed. "Herman Melville," in *Major Writers of America.* Gen. Ed. Perry Miller. New York: Harcourt, Brace & World, 1962, I, 877–91 [882, 884, et passim]. Also reprints Melville's letter to Hawthorne, 1 [?] June 1851, pp. 900–02.

247. ———. "Introduction," in *Melville: A Collection of Critical Essays.* Englewood Cliffs, N.J.: Prentice-Hall, 1962, pp. 1–10 [3, 7–8]. Reprints B150.

248. Davis, Merrell R., and William H. Gilman, eds. *The Letters of Herman Melville.* New Haven: Yale University Press, 1960, pp. 24–27, 35–47, 292–95, et passim.

249. Doughty, Howard. *Francis Parkman.* New York: Macmillan Co., 1962, pp. 158–59 et passim.

250. Dryden, Edgar A. *Melville's Thematics of Form: The Great Art of Telling the Truth.* Baltimore: Johns Hopkins University Press, 1968, pp. 33–46 et passim.

251. Ellsberg, Edward. "Foreword," in *Melville: The Best of Moby Dick and Typee; also Billy Budd Complete.* New York: Platt & Munk, 1964, pp. 9–13.

252. Finkelstein, Dorothee Metlitsky. *Melville's Orienda.* New Haven and London: Yale University Press, 1961; rpt. New York: Octagon Books, 1971, pp. 122–25, 180–81, et passim.

253. Franklin, H. Bruce. *The Wake of the Gods: Melville's Mythology.* Stanford, Calif: Stanford University Press, 1963, pp. 9–16 et passim.

254. Frost, O. W. *Joaquin Miller.* New York: Twayne Publishers, 1967; New Haven: College and University Press, 1967, p. 72. Comparison of *Typee* and *Life Amongst the Modocs.*

255. Fussell, Edwin. "Herman Melville," in *Frontier: American*

Literature and the American West. Princeton: Princeton University Press, 1965, pp. 232–326 [234–38 et passim].

256. Gale, Robert L. *Plots and Characters in the Fiction and Narrative Poetry of Herman Melville*. Hamden, Ct.: Archon Books, 1969; Cambridge, Mass.: MIT Press, 1972, pp. 123–30 et passim.

257. Geismar, Maxwell. "Introduction," in *Billy Budd and Typee*. New York: Washington Square Press, 1962, pp. xiii–xxvi.

258. Hayford, Harrison and Hershel Parker, eds. *Moby-Dick*. New York: W. W. Norton & Co., 1967. Reprints Melville's letter to Hawthorne, 1 [?] June 1851, pp. 556–60. Also reprints in part B96, P407, and P415. Reprints B118.

259. Hayford, Harrison, ed. "A Note on the Text" and "Afterword," in *Typee*. New York: The New American Library, 1964, pp. 303–17.

260. Hetherington, Hugh W. *Melville's Reviewers, British and American, 1846–1891*. Chapel Hill: University of North Carolina Press, 1961; rpt. New York: Russell & Russell, 1975, pp. 20–65 et passim.

261. Hillway, Tyrus. *Herman Melville*. New York: Twayne Publishers, 1963; New Haven: College and University Press, 1963, pp. 67–69 et passim.

262. Hough, Henry Beetle. *Melville in the South Pacific*. Boston: Houghton Mifflin Co., 1960; Cambridge, Mass.: Riverside Press, 1960, pp. 11–102.

263. Howard, Leon. *Herman Melville*. University of Minnesota Pamphlets on American Writers, No. 13, Minneapolis: University of Minnesota Press, 1961, pp. 8–10 et passim. Reprinted in B264; rev. ed., 1971, pp. 8–10 et passim.

264. ———. "Herman Melville," in *Six American Novelists of the Nineteenth Century: An Introduction*. Ed. Richard Foster. Minneapolis: University of Minnesota Press, 1968, pp. 82–117 [84–86 et passim]. Reprints B263.

265. ———. "Historical Note," in *Typee*. Eds. Harrison Hayford, Hershel Parker, and G. Thomas Tanselle. Vol. I of *The Writings of Herman Melville*. Gen. Ed. Harrison Hayford. Evanston and Chicago: Northwestern University Press and the Newberry Library, 1968, pp. 277–302; "Note on the Text" by the editors, pp. 303–25.

266. ———. "The Time of Tension," in *Literature and the American Tradition*, Garden City, N.Y.: Doubleday & Co., 1960, pp. 167–96 [169, 170].

267. Humphreys, A. R. *Herman Melville*. New York: Barnes & Noble, 1962; New York: Grove Press, 1962; Edinburgh: Oliver and Boyd, 1962, pp. 10–16.

268. Kaul, A. N. "Herman Melville: The New-World Voyageur," in *The American Vision: Actual and Ideal Society in Nineteenth-Century Fiction*. New Haven: Yale University Press, 1963, pp. 214–79 [222–35 et passim].

269. Lawrence, D. H. "Herman Melville's 'Typee' and 'Omoo,' " in *The Symbolic Meaning: The Uncollected Versions of Studies in Classic American Literature*. Ed. Armin Arnold. Fontwell, Arundel, England: Centaur Press Ltd., 1962, pp. 217–29; New York: Viking Press, 1964, pp. 197–209. Reprints B150 with some alterations.

270. Lewis, R. W. B. "Melville: The Apotheosis of Adam," in *The Modern Critical Spectrum*. Ed. Gerald Jay Goldberg and Nancy Marmer Goldberg. Englewood Cliffs, N.J.: Prentice-Hall, 1962, pp. 321–41 [327, 328]. Reprints B224.

271. London, Jack. *Letters from Jack London: Containing an Unpublished Correspondence Between London and Sinclair Lewis*. Ed. King Hendricks and Irving Shepard. New York: Odyssey Press, 1965; London: MacGibbon & Kee, 1966, p. 256. Mention in letter, 16 Jan. 1908.

272. Mansfield, Luther Stearns. "Some Patterns from Melville's 'Loom of Time,' " in *Essays on Determinism in American Literature*. Ed. Sydney J. Krause. Kent, Ohio: Kent State University Press, 1964, pp. 19–35 [21–23].

273. Marx, Leo. *The Machine in the Garden: Technology and the Pastoral Ideal in America*. New York: Oxford University Press, 1964, pp. 281–85 et passim.

274. Mayoux, Jean-Jacques. *Melville*. Trans. John Ashbery. New York: Grove Press, 1960; London: Evergreen Books, Ltd., 1960, pp. 26–30, 35–45, et passim.

275. Miller, Edwin Haviland. " 'Singing the Phallus,' " in *Walt Whitman's Poetry: A Psychological Journey*. Boston: Houghton Mifflin Co., 1968; New York: New York University Press, 1969, pp. 115–39 [123].

276. Miller, F. De Wolfe. "Another Chapter in the History of the Great White Whale," in *Melville and Hawthorne in the Berkshires: A Symposium*. Ed. Howard P. Vincent. Kent, Ohio: Kent State University Press, 1968, pp. 109–17 [111].

277. Miller, James E., Jr. *A Reader's Guide to Herman Melville*. New York: Farrar, Straus and Cudahy, 1962; New York: Noonday Press, 1962; London: Thames and Hudson, 1962; rpt. New York: Octagon Books, 1973, pp. 18–35 et passim.

278. ———. "Melville's Quest in Life and Art," in *Quests Surd and Absurd: Essays in American Literature*. Chicago and London: University of Chicago Press, 1967, pp. 161–85 [172–73 et passim].

279. Miller, Perry. *Nature's Nation*. Cambridge, Mass.: Harvard University Press (Belknap), 1967, passim.

280. Murray, Henry A. "Dead to the World: The Passions of Herman Melville," in *Essays in Self-Destruction*. Ed. Edwin S. Shneidman. New York: Science House, 1967, pp. 7–29 [passim].

281. Parker, Hershel, ed. *Gansevoort Melville's 1846 London Journal and Letters from England, 1845*. New York: New York Public Library, 1966. Reprints P478, P479, and P480.

282. ———. "Preface," in *The Recognition of Herman Melville: Selected Criticism since 1846.* Ann Arbor: The University of Michigan Press, 1967, pp. v–xii [passim]. Reprints reviews, critical surveys, scholarly articles, and sections of books that discuss or at least mention *Typee.*

283. Roper, Gordon. "Historical Note," in *Omoo.* Eds. Harrison Hayford, Hershel Parker, and G. Thomas Tanselle. Vol. II of *The Writings of Herman Melville.* Gen. Ed. Harrison Hayford. Evanston and Chicago: Northwestern University Press and the Newberry Library, 1968, pp. 319–44 [passim].

284. Sealts, Merton M., Jr. "The Records of Melville's Reading," in *Melville's Reading: A Check-List of Books Owned and Borrowed.* Madison, Milwaukee, and London: University of Wisconsin Press, 1966, pp. 3–26, 121–34 [passim].

285. Shneidman, Edwin S. "The Deaths of Herman Melville," in *Melville and Hawthorne in the Berkshires: A Symposium.* Ed. Howard P. Vincent. Kent, Ohio: Kent State University Press, 1968, pp. 118–43 [passim].

286. Thomas, Clara. "Introduction," in *Typee.* New York: Airmont Pub. Co., 1965.

287. Thorp, Willard, ed. *Great Short Works of the American Renaissance.* New York: Harper & Row, 1968, p. 721. Reprints P19.

288. Vincent, Howard P. *The Merrill Studies in Moby-Dick.* Columbus, Ohio: Charles E. Merrill Pub. Co., 1969, pp. 22–31. Reprints P349.

289. Weaver, Raymond. "The Centennial of Herman Melville," in *One Hundred Years of the Nation: A Centennial Anthology.* Ed. Henry M. Christman and Abraham Feldman. New York: Macmillan Co., 1965, pp. 113–18 [114–15]. Reprints P376.

290. Young, Philip. "Introduction," in *Typee.* Ed. Herbert Van Thal. London: Cassell, 1967, pp. vii–xvii.

The 1970s

291. Allen, Gay Wilson. *Melville and His World.* New York: Viking Press, 1971; London: Thames and Hudson, 1971, pp. 59–65, 86–87, et passim.

292. Barnett, Louise K. "Melville and the Universal Paradigm of White Domination," in *The Ignoble Savage: American Literary Racism, 1790–1890.* Westport, Ct. and London: Greenwood Press, 1975, pp. 166–84 [167–70, 173–75].

293. Bixby, William. *Rebel Genius: The Life of Herman Melville.* New York: David McKay Co., 1970, pp. 50–63, 86–91, et passim.

294. Bowen, James K. and Richard Van Der Beets. *A Critical Guide to Herman Melville, Abstracts of Forty Years of Criticism.* Glenview, Ill. and London: Scott, Foresman and Co., 1971. Prints abstracts of several articles on *Typee.*

295. Branch, Watson G., ed. "Introduction," in *Melville: The Critical Heritage*. London and Boston: Routledge & Kegan Paul, 1974, pp. 1–49 [3–13 et passim]. Reprints many reviews of *Typee*, reviews of *Omoo* and *Mardi* which also mention *Typee*, and general estimates of Melville's reputation which comment on *Typee*.

296. Bredahl, A. Carl, Jr. *Melville's Angles of Vision*. Gainesville: University of Florida Press, 1972, pp. 7–15 et passim.

297. Brooks, Cleanth, R. W. B. Lewis, and Robert Penn Warren, eds. "Herman Melville (1819–1891)," in *American Literature: The Makers and the Making*. New York: St. Martin's Press, 1973, I, 809–34 [816–17 et passim].

298. Browne, Ray B. *Melville's Drive to Humanism*. Lafayette, Ind.: Purdue University Studies, 1971, pp. 10–16 et passim.

299. Day, A. Grove. *Melville's South Seas: An Anthology*. New York: Hawthorn Books, 1970, pp. 8–12, 25–29, et passim.

300. Dillingham, William B. *An Artist in the Rigging: The Early Work of Herman Melville*. Athens: University of Georgia Press, 1972, pp. 9–30 et passim.

301. ———. *Melville's Short Fiction, 1853–1856*. Athens: The University of Georgia Press, 1977, passim.

302. Eigner, Edwin M. *The Metaphysical Novel in England and America: Dickens, Bulwer, Melville, and Hawthorne*. Berkeley, Los Angeles, and London: University of California Press, 1978, pp. 153–54 et passim.

303. Flibbert, Joseph. *Melville and the Art of Burlesque*. Amsterdam: Rodopi N.V., 1974, pp. 17–33 et passim.

304. Franklin, H. Bruce. "Herman Melville: Artist of the Worker's World," in *Weapons of Criticism: Marxism in America and the Literary Tradition*. Ed. Norman Rudich. Palo Alto, Calif.: Ramparts Press, 1976, pp. 287–309 [288, 292–94, et passim]. Reprinted in revised form in B305.

305. ———. *The Victim as Criminal and Artist*. New York: Oxford University Press, 1978, pp. 34–35, 39–42, et passim. Chapter 2 is a revision of B304.

306. Grejda, Edward S. *The Common Continent of Men: Racial Equality in the Writings of Herman Melville*. Port Washington, N.Y. and London: Kennikat Press, 1974, pp. 13–27 et passim.

307. Gross, Theodore L. "Herman Melville: The Nature of Authority," in *The Heroic Ideal in American Literature*. New York: Free Press, 1971; London: Collier-Macmillan Ltd., 1971, pp. 34–50 [35–36].

308. Hauck, Richard Boyd. "The Descent to Faith: Herman Melville," in *A Cheerful Nihilism: Confidence and "The Absurd" in American Humorous Fiction*. Bloomington and London: Indiana University Press, 1971, pp. 77–132 [79–83 et passim].

309. Henderson, Harry B. "Melville: Rebellion, Tragedy, and

Historical Judgment," in *Versions of the Past*. New York: Oxford University Press, 1974, pp. 127–74 [128–29].

310. Higgins, Brian, comp. "Introduction," in *Herman Melville: An Annotated Bibliography, I: 1846–1930*. Boston: G. K. Hall & Co., 1979, xi–xv [passim].

311. Hubbell, Jay. *Who Are the Major American Writers? A Study of the Changing Literary Canon*. Durham, N.C.: Duke University Press, 1972, passim. Reprints P275.

312. Kenny, Vincent S. *Herman Melville's Clarel: A Spiritual Autobiography*. Hamden, Ct.: Archon Books, 1973, passim.

313. Lebowitz, Alan. *Progress into Silence: A Study of Melville's Heroes*. Bloomington and London: Indiana University Press, 1970, pp. 25–39 et passim.

314. Miller, Edwin Haviland. *Melville*. New York: George Braziller, 1975, pp. 118–32 et passim.

315. Parker, Hershel and Harrison Hayford, eds. *Moby-Dick as Doubloon: Essays and Extracts (1851–1970)*. New York: W. W. Norton & Co., 1970. Reprints B19, P270, B45, B80, P384, P410, and P411. Reprints in part P261, P280, P284, P285, P324, B73, B85, B96, P378, and P423.

316. Parker, Hershel, ed. *Shorter Works of Hawthorne and Melville*. Columbus, Ohio: Charles E. Merrill Pub. Co., 1972, p. 161. Reprints P19.

317. Pavese, Cesare. *American Literature: Essays and Opinions*. Trans. Edwin Fussell. Berkeley, Los Angeles, and London: University of California Press, 1970, passim.

318. Pops, Martin Leonard. *The Melville Archetype*. Kent, Ohio: Kent State University Press, 1970, pp. 26–64 et passim.

319. Pullin, Faith, ed. "Preface" and "Melville's *Typee*: The Failure of Eden," in *New Perspectives on Melville*. Kent, Ohio: Kent State University Press, 1978; Edinburgh: Edinburgh University Press, 1978, pp. vii–xii, 1–28.

320. Rosenberry, Edward H. *Melville*. London and Boston: Routledge & Kegan Paul, 1979, pp. 34–42 et passim.

321. Rountree, Thomas J., ed. *Critics on Melville*. Coral Gables, Fla.: University of Miami Press, 1972. Reprints reviews, scholarly articles, and sections of books that discuss or at least mention *Typee*.

322. Sastri, P. S. *Herman Melville*. Bombay and New Delhi: Tata McGraw-Hill Pub. Co. Ltd., 1972, pp. 10–12 et passim.

323. Scorza, Thomas J. *In the Time Before Steamships: Billy Budd, the Limits of Politics, and Modernity*. De Kalb: Northern Illinois University Press, 1979, pp. 10–11, 29–31, 66–68 et passim.

324. Sealts, Merton M., Jr., comp. *The Early Lives of Melville: Nineteenth-Century Biographical Sketches and Their Authors*. Madison: University of Wisconsin Press, 1974. Reprints several biographical

sketches which either discuss or briefly mention *Typee*.

325. Seelye, John. *Melville: The Ironic Diagram*. Evanston, Ill.: Northwestern University Press, 1970, pp. 11–24 et passim.

326. Seltzer, Leon F. *The Vision of Melville and Conrad: A Comparative Study*. Athens: Ohio University Press, 1970, passim.

327. Solomon, Pearl Chesler. *Dickens and Melville in Their Time*. New York: Columbia University Press, 1975, pp. 119–21.

328. Spengemann, William C. *The Adventurous Muse: The Poetics of American Fiction, 1789–1900*. New Haven: Yale University Press, 1977, pp. 178–88 et passim.

329. Wadlington, Warwick. *The Confidence Game in American Literature*. Princeton: Princeton University Press, 1975, pp. 45–46, 56–68, et passim.

330. Zoellner, Robert. *The Salt-Sea Mastodon, A Reading of Moby-Dick*. Berkeley, Los Angeles, and London: University of California Press, 1973, pp. 71, 276, et passim.

1980–81

331. Adler, Joyce Sparer. *War in Melville's Imagination*. New York: Columbia University Press, 1981, pp. 5–12 et passim.

332. Haberstroh, Charles J., Jr. *Melville and Male Identity*. Rutherford, N.J.: Fairleigh Dickinson University Press, 1980, pp. 25–27, 32–41, et passim.

333. Herbert, T. Walter, Jr. *Marquesan Encounters: Melville and the Meaning of Civilization*. Cambridge, Mass.: Harvard University Press, 1980, pp. 13–15, 149–90, et passim.

334. Karcher, Carolyn L. *Shadow Over the Promised Land: Slavery, Race, and Violence in Melville's America*. Baton Rouge and London: Louisiana State University Press, 1980, pp. 3–5, 7–8, et passim.

INDEX